PRESERVATION MICROFILMING

PRESERVATION MICROFILMING

A Guide for Librarians and Archivists

Second Edition

Edited by
Lisa L. Fox

For the
Association of Research Libraries

Edited in 1987 by Nancy E. Gwinn

American Library Association
Chicago and London
1996

Lisa L. Fox is a preservation consultant, based in Atlanta, Georgia, who has worked in library and archives preservation since 1983. She founded the SOLINET Preservation Program in 1985 and was instrumental in developing the model under which regional bibliographic networks have begun offering preservation services. Fox has done pioneering work in the development of state-based preservation programs and served as consultant to several of them. She has taught more than 165 workshops nationwide on preservation issues and, in collaboration with the Commission on Preservation and Access, developed and serves as primary trainer in the Preservation Management Seminar for college libraries. She is editor of *A Core Collection in Preservation* (Chicago: ALA/ALCTS, 1993) and co-editor of *Training for Collections Care and Maintenance: A Suggested Curriculum—Volume V: Library and Archives Collections* (Washington, D.C.: National Institute for Conservation, forthcoming). Fox has served as chair of the ALA/ALCTS Preservation of Library Materials Section and of the SAA Preservation Section.

While extensive effort has gone into ensuring the reliability of information appearing in this book, the publisher makes no warranty, express or implied, on the accuracy or reliability of the information, and does not assume and hereby disclaims any liability to any person for any loss or damage caused by errors or omissions in this publication.

Project editor: Joan A. Grygel
Text designed by Dianne M. Rooney
Composition by Publishing Services in Bodoni and Times Roman using a
    Xyvision/Linotype L330
Printed on 50-pound Arbor, a pH-neutral stock, and bound in Roxite C-Grade cloth
    by Edwards Brothers, Inc.

The paper used in this publication meets the minimum requirements of American National Standard for Information Sciences—Permanence of Paper for Printed Library Materials, ANSI Z39.48-1992. ♾

Library of Congress Cataloging-in-Publication Data
Preservation microfilming : a guide for librarians and archivists /
    edited in 1987 by Nancy E. Gwinn. — 2nd ed. / edited by Lisa L. Fox
    for the Association of Research Libraries.
        p.   cm.
    Includes bibliographical references and index.
    ISBN 0-8389-0653-2
        1. Preservation microfilming—United States.   I. Gwinn, Nancy E.
    II. Fox, Lisa L.   III. Association of Research Libraries.
    Z681.3.M53P73   1996
    025.8′4—dc20   95-4741

Contents

4   Microfilming Standards and Practices   164

6   Calculating and Controlling Local Costs   263

Appendixes

Figures

Preface

*P*reservation Microfilming: A Guide for Librarians and Archivists has been assisting the preservation efforts of librarians and archivists since the guide was prepared for the Association of Research Libraries (ARL) in 1987 by a group of preservation experts. Immediately upon its publication, it was recognized as an excellent preservation resource, and it continues to be cited as one of three core texts in preservation microfilming. At the 1988 Society of American Archivists Annual Meeting, *Preservation Microfilming* was awarded the Waldo Gifford Leland Prize, given to "reward writing of superior excellence and usefulness in the field of archival history, theory or practice."

In early 1993 ALA Publishing reported that the last print run for *Preservation Microfilming* had been depleted. At the 1993 ALA Annual Conference, the Executive Committee of the Preservation of Library Materials Section of the Association for Library Collections & Technical Services (ALCTS) underscored the need for the continued availability of this tool and urged ARL to pursue reissuing this essential publication. In November 1993 the OCLC Online Computer Library Center, Inc., awarded ARL a grant to support revision and enhancement of the manual. Lisa Fox, preservation consultant, took on the task of revising and updating the manual. She brought to this task admirable organizational and research skills, enthusiasm, willingness to put in extraordinary time, and matchless care for details.

The second edition of the manual reflects technical advances and operational improvements over the past eight years, as well as new standards and guidelines that have transformed the field of preservation microfilming. This new edition also reflects the growth and diversity of cooperative preservation microfilming projects. Numerous content and organizational changes were made with this new edition. The manual draws extensively upon the recent documentation prepared by the Research Libraries Group (RLG), and Lisa Fox collaborated closely with Nancy Elkington at RLG to ensure complementarity between this new edition and the two RLG manuals (cited in appendix A). The new edition also includes materials developed by the Northeast Document Conservation Center; Preservation Resources, Inc.; the Southeastern Library Network, Inc. (SOLINET); the Library of Congress; and a host of other organizations too numerous to list here. The acknowledgments section reflects the extent of these contributions. A debt of gratitude also goes to the members of the Project Advisory Committee and the many preservation administrators and experts who assisted in the revision process.

Preservation Microfilming provides an overview of the whole process, outlines the technical requirements of preservation microfilming, and provides guidance on planning for and managing preservation microfilming projects. It can be used to design an ongoing program or to implement a one-time preservation microfilming project.

This edition of the manual provides a well-tested guide for librarians and archivists. It brings together a rich variety of technical information, reference documents, work forms, and budgeting information. It is our hope that this second edition will continue to serve as a vital tool in libraries and archives.

JUTTA REED-SCOTT
Senior Program Officer for Preservation
and Collections Services
March 1995

Acknowledgments

When Jutta Reed-Scott (Senior Program Officer, Association of Research Libraries) first broached the subject of my writing a new edition of *Preservation Microfilming,* I little knew that we would be inextricably bound together by this project over the course of almost two years. Jutta has not only read every word of this manual in its multiple drafts; she has been my best reader and editor, kept a crystal-clear vision of this manual, and provided encouragement in those moments when it began to seem the project would never come to fruition. Through her work on this project, Jutta has taught me a great deal about what humane leadership can be.

OCLC generously awarded the funds that made it possible to produce this new edition of *Preservation Microfilming.* OCLC not only provides an important bibliographic resource for preservation microfilming but is the parent organization of one of the nation's premiere microfilming services. Thus, OCLC's goals and ours were well suited to this partnership.

It was a pleasure to work with the strong Advisory Committee ARL appointed to assist me in the revision. Each agreed to provide information and review drafts of one chapter. The team consisted of

> Meg Bellinger, President, Preservation Resources—chapter 3
>
> Sherry Byrne, Preservation Librarian, University of Chicago—chapter 1
>
> Steve Dalton, Director of Field Services (formerly Director of Reprographic Services), Northeast Document Conservation Center (NEDCC)—chapter 4
>
> Nancy E. Elkington, Assistant Director, Preservation Services, Research Libraries Group—chapter 6
>
> Crystal Graham, Serials Cataloging Section Head and Microforms Cataloging Coordinator, University of California, San Diego—chapter 5
>
> Marcia Watt, Preservation Officer, Emory University—chapter 2

Each of them helped me shape the new chapters, read multiple drafts, and answered questions by every conceivable electronic means. Their knowledge of the ins and outs of preservation microfilming provided not only the technical foundation but also the broad perspectives that have enriched the manual. These colleagues shared their time and insights with a generosity that has characterized the field of preservation microfilming. I am grateful for their assistance, but I alone retain responsibility for errors that may be here.

Thanks also go to Ann Swartzell (University of California, Berkeley) and Peter Scott for providing in-depth review of the manuscript for chapters 3 and 4 (respectively). As authors of those chapters in the 1987 edition, they contributed a great deal to my understanding of those technical subjects and of the changes that have occurred in the intervening years.

I must extend special thanks to Nancy Elkington and Crystal Graham. Nancy helped me define the scope of this revised manual when it was but a gleam in the eye, helped ensure that it would build upon and complement the RLG handbooks, made herself constantly available to answer myriad technical and programmatic questions, and read several of the chapters. Her insights have greatly enriched the book, and her friendship—much as I prevailed upon it over the months of writing—remains an inspiration.

Deep within my PC, perhaps there is a microchip that knows which words in chapter 5 are mine and which are Crystal Graham's. The work was so collaborative that we came to speak of it as "our chapter." Crystal guided me safely through the waters of bibliographic control and saved me from the twin threats of oversimplification and spurious detail.

I benefited tremendously from day-long site visits at three strong filming labs. At the Massachusetts Institute of Technology's Document Services unit, Keith Glavash and Jack Eisan provided a solid tutorial on microfilm production and expanded my understanding of current microfiche production methods. Steve Dalton and Shawne Cressman at NEDCC were most generous in introducing me to the issues of a nonprofit filming service and conveying a sense of the complexities of handling fragile materials. The staff at Preservation Resources—including Meg Bellinger, Lee Dirks, Harriet Winer, and every camera operator I bedeviled with questions throughout a very long day—were clear and patient as they explained their many innovative methods of microfilm production and quality assurance. The work with these organizations contributed much to the discussions in chapter 3 on identifying qualified preservation microfilming service providers.

Many other colleagues were generous in responding to questions and sharing information and documentation. I am happy to express in this public forum my thanks to Wesley Boomgaarden (Ohio State University), Charlotte Brown (University of California, Los Angeles), Margaret Byrnes and Carol Unger (National Library of Medicine), Myron Chase and Robert Harriman (Library of Congress), Christi Craig and Sandra Nyberg (the Southeastern Library Network, Inc. [SOLINET]), Janet Gertz (Columbia University), Charles Harmon (then at the American Library Association headquarters library), Robert Herskovitz (Minnesota Historical Society), Erich Kesse and Bob Harrell (University of Florida), Robert Mottice (Mottice Micrographics, Inc.), Karen Motylewski (NEDCC, now at the University of Texas), Kate Nevins (OCLC, now SOLINET), Sherelyn Ogden (NEDCC), James Reilly (Image Permanence Institute), Wendy Thomas (*Microform Review*), and Eileen Usovicz (CBR Consulting Services, Inc.). Some of their contributions are explicitly recognized in credit lines and footnotes in the manual, but those do not adequately convey the richness of these colleagues' contributions.

Several people responded to our "desiderata" list by providing photographs for the book. While a few were able to send existing images, most went to great pains to set up photographs tailored for this book. Thanks go to the following:

Robin Dale, Columbia University

Steve Dalton, NEDCC

Keith Glavash, Massachusetts Institute of Technology

Robert Herskovitz, Minnesota Historical Society

Ann Olszewski, Cleveland Public Library

Rebecca Ryder, University of Kentucky

Charles Stewart, University of California, Berkeley

the staff of Preservation Resources, Inc.

Several people were instrumental in the production of the book. Walter Henry (Stanford University) used his marvelous technological capabilities to digitize the first edition of *Preservation Microfilming,* so that I had machine-readable text from which to work at the beginning of the project, and allowed me to use the Conservation DistList listserv as a bulletin board for posting queries related to the manual. Jean Baronas (Association for Information and Image Management) helped me understand the workings of AIIM and the American National Standards Institute (ANSI) and reviewed appendix A for accuracy in her very last hours at AIIM.

The staff of ALA Editions exceeded my expectations *and* my hopes. Joan Grygel was the editor of my dreams. Concepts that lay smothering under my sometimes-arcane prose sprang to life through her gifted work, and I was sustained throughout the long process by her encouragement and wisdom. Arthur Plotnik and David M. Epstein made the whole process humane and efficient. Every writer should be so lucky as to work with such a fine editorial and production staff.

Personal thanks are due to those who helped me keep body and soul together during the process. At the top of that list is Lynn Shrewsbury, who provided important "jump starts," reminded me to eat and sleep, shopped for me when chapter deadlines were looming, and took an active interest in the status of the writing throughout the long process. The staff of the Urban Coffee Bungalow provided me with the best working environment a writer can have; most of these pages were edited on their deck, with a never-ending coffee supply at hand.

Finally, I acknowledge a debt of gratitude to Nancy Gwinn, editor of the first edition. My respect for her achievement only grew as I worked to create in this second edition a volume that would approach the clarity and coherence of hers. Her vision helped to shape and systematize the field of preservation microfilming, and that legacy endures here.

Lisa L. Fox

Preface to the First Edition

I t happened again. When I finished my keynote address at the 1986 Preservation Microfilming Institute at the Library of Congress, a staff member from a local university appeared at my elbow during a coffee break. "When will that manual be finished?" she asked. She explained that her institution had received a grant for cataloging a collection and preserving it on microfilm and that she had been asked to plan the project. "We've never done it before," she said, "and I don't know where to start. It's *so* complicated!"

She was the very person the advisors to the Association of Research Libraries (ARL) had in mind when they suggested that preparation of a manual on preservation microfilming should be a top priority. ARL wrote a proposal and obtained funding from The Andrew W. Mellon Foundation. They found a co-sponsor in the Northeast Document Conservation Center (NEDCC) and asked Andrew Raymond, at that time NEDCC's Director of Photoduplication Services, to be the project director, with Jeffrey Heynen, ARL's program officer for preservation, as co-director. Raymond secured additional funding from the National Historical Publications and Records Commission to include information related to microfilming of archives. After much consultation, he chose the people to begin writing the individual chapters. He asked me to be the general editor, and bravely we set our first deadline.

Preparation of this guide over the past two years has been a challenge for all participants. As the chapter drafts arrived, it became clear that each author had much to say about preservation microfilming, and their comments spilled over from their assigned topics into many related subjects. What has emerged is not a book of readings, where each author covers a distinctive topic in a unique style. Rather, information migrated among chapters; it was revised, reshaped, and rewritten; additional material was sought and inserted; and finally the manuscript was reorganized into what we hope is an integrated description of the process of preservation microfilming. The guide now contains contributions from many sources: practitioners, administrators, organizers, coordinators. All are joined to provide you, whether you are new to the subject or an old hand, with instruction and guidance into a fundamental component of the expanding field of preservation.

The principal contributors provided initial chapter drafts, which formed the basic structure of the book. They are:

Introduction
    Pamela W. Darling
        Preservation Consultant

An Overview of Administrative Decisions
    Carolyn Harris
        Preservation Officer
        Columbia University Libraries

Selection of Materials for Microfilming
    Wesley L. Boomgaarden
        Preservation Officer
        Ohio State University Libraries

Production Planning and Preparation of Materials
    Ann Swartzell
        Associate Librarian (Preservation)
        New York State Library

Microfilming Practices and Standards
    Peter Scott
        Head, Microreproduction Laboratory
        Massachusetts Institute of Technology

Preservation Microfilming and Bibliographic Control
    Jeffrey Heynen
        Program Officer
        Association of Research Libraries

Cost Controls
    Patricia A. McClung
        Associate Director for Program Coordination
        Research Libraries Group, Inc.

An Afterword
    Andrew Raymond
        Preservation Consultant

A very special word of thanks goes to these experts. But another must be given to Sherry Byrne, Preservation Officer, University of Chicago Libraries, who contributed information about costs and the process of contracting for preservation microfilming, prepared the sample contract, provided the target examples, and augmented several of the technical chapters under a very tight deadline. A hat also goes off to Helga Borck, Special Projects Librarian, New York Public Library, who put together the bibliographical references and verified footnotes.

The introduction sets the stage for the rest of the manual by providing a historical context and examining the environment in which local microfilming programs operate. The first chapter, An Overview of Administrative Decisions, is an extended abstract of the entire manual and presents a bird's-eye view of all the facets of preservation microfilming. The chapter may also be used as a checklist against which to measure programs in progress.

Each of the remaining chapters explores a phase of preservation microfilming in depth. Selection of Materials for Microfilming discusses how to go about deciding what to film and whether an item can be filmed successfully. It also points out the place of microfilming in a comprehensive preservation program with its variety of options. Production Planning and Preparation of Materials reviews the steps toward organizing the work of moving volumes and documents from an institution's shelves to the camera and back again. Microfilming Practices and Standards explains in detail what is required to ensure the quality and permanence of microform products. It makes plain most technical issues for the nontechnician and guides the reader among the existing body of published standards and specifications. Preservation Microfilming and Bibliographic Control emphasizes the importance of cataloging preservation microforms and of sharing that information—and the need to develop institutional support for this endeavor. In Cost Controls, how to estimate costs and what elements to consider in planning a budget for preservation microfilming are covered. Finally, the Afterword points out the need for further research concerning preservation microfilming and for constant review of methods and procedures.

The appendixes are among the most valuable parts of the manual. Here you will find the exact citations to published standards and specifications and information on how to obtain them, a sample contract for microfilming services to use as a basis for designing your own, a glossary of terms used throughout the manual, and a listing of institutions and organizations with expertise to offer when you need more advice. The Index complements the Contents. Certain topics, such as contracting for services or quality control, reappear throughout the manual, approached from a variety of viewpoints. The Index draws these discussions together so that you will not miss any relevant information.

You can approach this book in many ways: as an overview of the whole process of preservation microfilming, as a detailed—but not exhaustive—guide to each step of the operation, as a reference book to other documents or programs to meet your specific needs, as a fact book, as a checklist, as a place to find sample forms or photos—in short, as a helper to keep right behind your desk. Read it through, then go back as needed for specific facts and referrals. You won't find in detail every procedure that you will require—many of them must mesh with local priorities and conditions—but the critical issues are all covered. We hope the book will end up being well-thumbed.

There is one area where this guide cannot help—the decision as to which of your collections should be filmed. Some institutions are part of regional or national consortia, which are tackling this issue in cooperative ways and within which an institution must fit its own plans. Some collections have national prominence but no local constituency; others are of high value locally but are duplicated many times over. In the end, it is a matter of policy, which each institution must develop based on its unique environment and relationships with others. As long as the investigation into existing programs is thorough and duplication of effort avoided, possible choices are wide-ranging. There is much work to be done.

Preservation microfilming programs depend on an understanding of voluntary micrographics standards, which are developed and maintained in the United States by the American National Standards Institute (ANSI), the Association for

Information and Image Management (AIIM), and other allied organizations. In referring to these standards throughout the manual, we use the organization acronym(s) plus a number (e.g., ANSI/AIIM MS23–1983). The year cited is the most recent revision at the time the manual was written, but the latest edition should always be consulted. Appendix 1 lists all relevant standards with their full titles, current as of this writing. Copies can be obtained from the appropriate organization, the address of which appears in Appendix 4.

Other organizations, especially the Library of Congress, the Research Libraries Group, the National Historical Publications and Records Commission, and the Society of American Archivists, also have issued specifications and guidelines. These too are cited in full in Appendix 1, with appropriate addresses in Appendix 4. The number of citations throughout the book to these standards and specifications emphasizes how important it is for all staff involved in preservation microfilming projects to become thoroughly familiar with them.

NANCY E. GWINN
July 15, 1987

Acknowledgments for the First Edition

In addition to the reviews of chapter drafts by the author team, the guide benefited tremendously from the work of a dedicated group of other reviewers, who read the entire manuscript from beginning to end and who provided numerous worthy suggestions that were incorporated into the draft. These reviewers were:

Myron B. Chace
Head, Special Services Section
Library of Congress Photoduplication Service

Veronica Cunningham
Director, Photoduplication Services
Northeast Document Conservation Center

Heinz Dettling
Technical Director
University Microfilms International

John D. Kendall
Head, Special Collections and Rare Books
University of Massachusetts at Amherst Library

Madeleine Bagwell Perez
Medical Center Archivist
Bowman Gray School of Medicine, Wake Forest University

Tamara Swora
Assistant Preservation Microfilming Officer
Library of Congress

George L. Vogt
Director, Records Program
National Historical Publications and Records Commission

Gay Walker
Head, Preservation Department
Yale University Library

In addition, the draft was circulated to all members of the ARL Committee on Preservation of Research Library Materials. These persons, primarily directors of major research libraries, took their role seriously and organized reviews of the manuscript by appropriate staff within their institutions. The committee members were:

Harold W. Billings
    Director, General Libraries
    University of Texas at Austin

John Laucus
    Director
    Boston University Library

Deanna B. Marcum
    Vice President
    Council on Library Resources, Inc.

Kenneth G. Peterson
    Dean of Library Affairs
    Southern Illinois University Library

John B. Smith
    Director of Libraries and Dean
    State University of New York at Stony Brook

Peter Sparks
    Director, Preservation Office
    Library of Congress

William J. Studer
    Director
    Ohio State University Libraries

David C. Weber, chair
    Director
    Stanford University Libraries

Another vote of thanks goes to Karen Garlick, conservator, and Merrily Smith, National Preservation Program specialist, both at the Library of Congress, who spotted inconsistencies in those sections that describe the conservation options of a comprehensive preservation program and helped us correct our terminology. Eileen Usovicz, Columbia University Libraries, improved our understanding in several technical areas of microform production. All of the persons so far mentioned have helped to make this text as authoritative as possible.

The text is only one portion of the guide, however. Its utility in the end will also rely on the helpfulness of the sample forms, the clarity of the tables, the ease of use of the flow charts and target sequences, the logic of the worksheets, and the relevance of the photographs. Many helped to prepare them. Mary Ann Ferrarese, assistant chief of the Library of Congress Photoduplication Service, organized the majority of the photographs, with additional contributions from

Veronica Cunningham, Northeast Document Conservation Service, and National Underground Storage, Inc. Marilyn Courtot made certain our standards citations were up-to-date and gave permission for us to use several illustrations from standards publications produced by the Association for Information and Image Management. Her counterpart at the Research Libraries Group, Inc., Jennifer Hartzell, extended the same courtesy. CACI, Inc., a graphics design firm located in Fairfax, Virginia, produced the target sequences, which were prepared by Sherry Byrne based on actual targets used for microforms produced by Columbia University Libraries. We hope that all of these friends will accept our gratitude for their contributions that add illumination and luster to the text.

As I began on a personal note, let me now end on one. First, to Nicola Daval, who managed the production of the manuscript and negotiations with the publisher for the Association of Research Libraries, and especially to Margaret McConnell, who keyed and rekeyed and rekeyed again the numerous drafts and revisions, I offer unbounded appreciation. With them, cordiality and a willingness to meet and work with my schedule were always the order of the day. But without the intelligence and dedication brought to the management and oversight of the preparation of this guide by Andrew Raymond and Jeffrey Heynen, it would not have happened. Not only did they offer advice and critique various drafts, but they also wrote portions of the book. Andy selected contributors, managed the budget, and turned an understanding ear to my many attempts to sort out the technical questions and contradictions that inevitably arose. Jeffrey allowed me to absorb his time on numerous evenings and week-ends, providing sound advice and much moral support.

PRESERVATION MICROFILMING was a group effort from start to finish. I am pleased that it had such a happy result.

N.E.G.

Acronyms and Abbreviations

AACR2	*Anglo-American Cataloguing Rules,* second edition
AIIM	Association for Information and Image Management
ALA	American Library Association
ALCTS	Association for Library Collections & Technical Services
ANSI	American National Standards Institute
APMP	Archives Preservation Microfilming Project
ARL	Association of Research Libraries
ASERL	Association of Southeastern Research Libraries
ASPP	Art Serials Preservation Project
ATLA	American Theological Library Association
BIP	*Books in Print*
BOD	*Books on Demand*
CSB	*Cataloging Service Bulletin*
CC:DA	Committee on Cataloging: Description and Access
CCM	*CONSER Cataloging Manual*
CEG	*CONSER Editing Guide*
CIC	Committee on Institutional Cooperation
CLR	Council on Library Resources
CONSER	Cooperative ONline SERials
CoOL	Conservation OnLine
CPMP	Cooperative Preservation Microfilming Project
GCMP	Great Collections Microfilming Project
GMIP	*Guide to Microforms in Print*
GTR	*Guide to Reprints*
ILL	interlibrary loan
IPI	Image Permanence Institute
ISO	International Organization for Standardization
LC	Library of Congress
LCNAF	Library of Congress Name Authority File
LCRI	*Library of Congress Rule Interpretations*

LE	life expectancy
LSCA	Library Services and Construction Act
MAPS	Mid-Atlantic Preservation Service
NAGARA	National Association of Government Archives and Records Administrators
NAPM	National Association of Photographic Manufacturers
NARA	National Archives and Records Administration
NARS	National Archives and Records Service
NEDCC	Northeast Document Conservation Center
NEH	National Endowment for the Humanities
NHPRC	National Historical Publications and Records Commission
NISO	National Information Standards Organization
NLC	National Library of Canada
NLM	National Library of Medicine
NRMM	*National Register of Microform Masters*
NYPL	New York Public Library
OCLC	OCLC Online Computer Library Center, Inc.
PARS	Preservation and Reformatting Section, ALCTS
RFI	request for information
RFP	request for proposal
RLG	The Research Libraries Group, Inc.
RLIN	Research Libraries Information Network
SAA	Society of American Archivists
SIM	*Serials in Microform*
SOLINET	Southeastern Library Network, Inc.
UMI	University Microfilms International, Inc.
USNP	United States Newspaper Program

Introduction

T his is a book about the why's and how's of capturing information on microfilm, information that otherwise may be lost along with the deteriorating paper on which it is recorded. Chances are that if you fit into any of the following categories, this book will help you.

Who Should Read This Book?

Perhaps you are a librarian assigned to "do something" about the crumbling Dewey collection in the old stacks, wondering if microfilming is a plausible "something," and, if so, how you might go about it. Perhaps the Preservation Committee on which you serve has been asked by your institution's director to make a recommendation about joining your consortium's planning for a cooperative microfilming project. Perhaps you have read about the national Brittle Books Program and want to make a contribution to it.

You may be an archivist sure to be buried by one more year of incoming material unless you find a way to miniaturize some of the collection, or a manuscript curator in need of study copies to take the stress off priceless documents that are heavily used. Perhaps you have the go-ahead to write a microfilming grant proposal, or to survey a collection to determine whether it should be filmed.

Maybe you are about to start a new cataloging job that involves working out the bibliographic control procedures for a preservation filming project, or, as selection officer, you have to make preservation decisions about books and serials in your field. Perhaps you are the preservation officer and the time has come to establish a microfilming component in your program.

Or you are a student, hoping for a career in preservation but daunted by the how-complex-it-is tone of the few articles you have seen about microfilming. On the other hand, you may be the faculty member teaching the "Introduction to Preservation" course and trying to determine which are the critical issues to address in your sessions on reformatting.

You may even be the experienced manager of a well-established preservation microfilming program, generally satisfied with the procedures you have developed but interested in comparing them with those in other places and always on the lookout for ways to improve quality and efficiency while controlling costs.

Perhaps you own a microfilming service bureau and want to expand your market to libraries or archives interested in preserving their older collections. Or maybe your company already produces preservation microfilm, but you think you could expand your service array to include preparation, storage, or other operations.

Of course, if you have an interest in preservation microfilming and have read any of the literature in the past five years, you may be among the multitude trying to assess the options of microfilming versus digitization.

This book is not a one-stop, learn-everything encyclopedia on preservation microfilming, but it is a good place to begin, whether you are contemplating a one-time special project or an ongoing program. It includes in-depth considerations of the various procedural and technical aspects—selection, preparation, filming, quality assurance, bibliographic control, storage, and reporting—set in the essential context of administrative planning and the calculating of costs. It can also serve as a sort of manual to the manuals, pointing beyond itself to the various published standards, procedural guidelines, specifications, and instructional handbooks that deal with subsets of the whole. However, this manual is not intended as a substitute or replacement for those other sources of technical information. Instead, it sets out to provide an administrative context, a conceptual, intellectual framework within which specific decisions about the details of individual programs can be made. It contains answers to a number of commonly asked questions. Even more important, it includes many questions that must be addressed to each particular situation if intelligent decisions are to be reached.

There is no such thing as a prepackaged preservation microfilming program— in a book or in any other form. But informed common sense, together with application of appropriate technical resources, can enable any library or archival institution to take advantage of microfilming as a tool for preserving endangered materials.

Why a New Edition?

Recently, I visited a research library with a strong preservation program to study its operations related to preservation microfilming. The library has an ongoing brittle books program and participates in several cooperative microfilming projects. Under the leadership of the preservation librarian, the staff carries out selection of materials, preparation, quality assurance on film produced by filming agents, bibliographic control, and the other work required in a filming program. Although the library now contracts with service bureaus, I learned that the first preservation librarian established an in-house filming lab in the late 1980s based on the information in the first edition of this manual.

The first edition of *Preservation Microfilming: A Guide for Librarians and Archivists*, published in 1987, was the product of many people's work. It built upon and distilled the key elements from national standards for microfilming. Along with the guidelines of the Research Libraries Group (RLG), it has been a major force in shaping preservation microfilming practices in the United States and beyond. The manual has been established in the core literature of the preservation field, appearing in nearly every significant bibliography and even cited in the *Guidelines and Application Instructions* of the National Endowment for the

Humanities (NEH) Division of Preservation and Access as one of the three key resources for project planners.

Like so many others, I read and admired *Preservation Microfilming* upon its appearance. Over the subsequent years, I continued to recommend it in my training and consulting work and occasionally turned to it to borrow language or arguments that would buttress my recommendations.

It was an honor then, in the summer of 1993, to be asked to prepare a second edition of this landmark work. In my initial conversation with Jutta Reed-Scott of the Association of Research Libraries (ARL), it seemed this would require primarily an updating of standards, specifications, and reading lists, along with a few changes in recommendations.

A close rereading of the book, though, revealed that more would be needed. I discovered, to my surprise, that this book had become quite dated. It was not simply that standards and practices have changed, that bibliographic control systems and practices have been upgraded, and so on, but perhaps even more significantly, that the philosophy or "mind set" has changed, become more sophisticated.

That the first edition is now so out of date should be a source of pride to those who worked on it and to the entire community of people engaged in preservation microfilming, for it attests to the great progress we have made in this area. A review of the historical development of microfilming led to this statement in the 1987 edition:

> It was only as the scope and urgency of the problem of paper deterioration began to be recognized in the 1960s and 1970s that the professional community, through its leaders in major libraries, associations, and organizations, began systematically to exploit the tremendous potential of microfilming as a preservation tool.
>
> The key word here is *systematically,* both in the sense of being systematic—logical, consistent, coherent—in planning and carrying out an extended sequence of technical operations, and in the sense of recognizing those operations as elements within an overall institutional system, each one integrated with, dependent upon, and contributing to the whole.
>
> In the past two decades, a small but growing number of libraries and archives have begun to give sustained professional attention to the creation of programs to meet their preservation needs. . . .
>
> It must be said that the growth of microfilming programs and their integration with other approaches to preservation have been a slow, sometimes tortuous process.[1]

What was then just beginning to be a systematic approach to preservation and to the role of microfilming as a preservation strategy is now a mature one.

A major change in the past several years relates to the sheer volume of preservation microfilming activity. Compared with 1987, many more institutions are engaged in filming, more librarians and archivists possess special expertise,

1. Nancy Gwinn, ed., *Preservation Microfilming: A Guide for Librarians and Archivists* (Chicago: ALA, 1987), xxii–xxiii.

there are more models for carrying out preservation microfilming operations, and federal grant funding has increased significantly. Consequently, the collection of preserved titles is much larger now.

The goals of preservation microfilming are increasingly distinct from those of commercial micropublication. In the 1980s there was some hope that commercial micropublishers would come to the rescue of deteriorated library and archival collections. As preservation administrators became more knowledgeable about the technical requirements of microform production and storage, they grew more wary of the permanence of commercially produced microforms. A recent study found that many micropublishers do follow the rigorous standards and guidelines that can ensure the durability of microfilm replacements, but some still do not.[2]

The distinction between commercial micropublication and institutionally based microfilming work relates especially to market factors, for the preservation priorities of libraries and archives seldom match the results of commercial market surveys. Opportunities for mutually beneficial contract arrangements still exist for some very specialized collections. But commercial micropublishers must sell a number of copies of each title to stay in business—often more than can realistically be projected for the bulk of brittle volumes making up research collections today. What has evolved, then, is a de facto division of labor between micropublishers and the library and archival communities, the former attending primarily to major (and particularly current) serials, newspapers, and the more popular monographs.

Other critical developments since the first edition have been in the following areas:

the emergence of a nationwide strategy for the preservation of brittle books

heightened awareness of the preservation problem

widespread impact of automation

an increased level of international programs and coordination

technical advances

improved institutional practices and greater reliance on contracted filming services

the rise of cooperative projects

A discussion of each of these may help set the context for further work.

A Nationwide Strategy for Brittle Books

With its 1986 publication of *Brittle Books,* the Council on Library Resources (CLR) envisioned a national program to ensure the preservation of the most significant research resources of the United States, and the model proposed a rel-

2. For the full report on the study, see Erich Kesse, *Survey of Micropublishers: A Report to the Commission on Preservation and Access* (Washington, D.C.: Commission on Preservation and Access, Oct. 1992), reprinted in *Microform Review* 22 (spring 1993): 65–91.

atively centralized program. What has emerged instead is a coordinated but decentralized effort that has gained widespread acceptance.

The CLR Committee on Preservation reached two conclusions that have fundamentally shaped the national program: that books would receive first priority and that access to what is preserved is as important as the preservation of the information. These conclusions led to reliance on preserving the intellectual content of books through microform, a medium that can be copied easily and inexpensively for borrowing or purchase.[3]

The goal of the Brittle Books Program is to build an accessible national collection of preserved materials. The effort requires the development of a nationwide, collaborative, large-scale filming program to capture the intellectual content of brittle books.[4] ARL, the Commission on Preservation and Access, and other organizations speaking before Congress in support of increased NEH funding laid out a twenty-year plan for preserving on microfilm 3 million titles as the "essential core collection."

Two developments have been instrumental in building the capacity to carry out the national Brittle Books Program. First, the Commission on Preservation and Access was established in 1986 to give focused ongoing attention to the national program.[5] Second, in 1989 the U.S. Congress authorized a significant increase in funding for the NEH Office of Preservation (reorganized in 1991 into the Division of Preservation and Access) to implement the Brittle Books Program. This support has enabled a significant number of institutions to launch preservation microfilming programs.[6]

The predominant role of NEH funding means, of course, that more focused attention has been paid to humanities research collections than to those in areas such as science and technology. Some groups are beginning to address this imbalance. National plans now exist for the preservation of biomedical literature and agricultural literature. (See the discussion of cooperative projects following.) Within the American Library Association's Association for Library Collections & Technical Services (ALA/ALCTS), the Preservation and Reformatting Section (PARS) has created a task force working on issues in science and technology.

Why does the national strategy focus on books? The decision was largely pragmatic. The individuals and organizations involved in shaping the strategy

---

3. Additional analysis of the early CLR directions and the implications of those conclusions today is offered in Sherry Byrne and Barbara Van Deventer, "Preserving the Nation's Intellectual Heritage: A Synthesis," *C&RL News* 53 (May 1992): 313–15.

4. Byrne and Van Deventer, 314.

5. A statement of the Commission's role and directions is provided in a special issue, "Working Paper on the Future," of *The Commission on Preservation and Access Newsletter,* no. 64 (Feb. 1994). For background on the Commission, see Patricia Battin, " 'As Far into the Future as Possible': Choice and Cooperation in the 1990s," in *Advances in Preservation and Access,* vol. 1, eds. Barbra Buckner Higginbotham and Mary E. Jackson (Westport, Conn.: Meckler, 1992), 41–8. The Commission's international program is described in Hans Rütimann, "International Issues and Efforts: The Commission on Preservation and Access' International Project," in *Advances in Preservation and Access,* vol. 1, 107–12.

6. The NEH program is described in George F. Farr Jr., "NEH's Program for the Preservation of Brittle Books," in *Advances in Preservation and Access,* vol. 1, 49–60.

were well aware that there are vast archival, audiovisual, and other collections that are endangered. But brittle books were deemed to be the most "tractable part of the problem."[7] While the nationwide strategy for brittle books is now well articulated and broadly accepted, there is not yet such consensus regarding coordinated strategies for archival materials. The Commission on Preservation and Access sponsored the work of the Task Forces on Archival Selection, charged to articulate selection priorities that could apply to archival materials and on which a nationwide program could be shaped for archival materials analogous to the Brittle Books Program. The task forces were unable to reach agreement on priorities for archival preservation.[8]

The nationwide program focuses on books that are brittle, whose acid content has caused such damage that pages may begin to crumble or break away from their bindings. Microfilming was chosen as, and remains, the preferred reformatting methodology because it alone offers the assurance that a copy once created will remain available for hundreds of years. Thus, the assumption that governs the national program and that shapes this manual is that we will have only one opportunity to get a given title "under the camera." The work must therefore be done as well as possible—to the most exacting technical and bibliographic standards—since the preservation microfilm will become the nation's "archival" copy.

Heightened Awareness

There is now widespread understanding of the brittle paper problem, its causes and solutions. While the first edition of this book labored to demonstrate the extent of brittle books in the nation's libraries, that issue is generally well understood among librarians and archivists. Today, preservation programs no longer are located in a mere handful of research libraries. The 1993–1994 ARL preservation statistics show that 92 of its 119 members now have preservation programs in place, configured as distinct administrative units headed by preservation librarians. In the aggregate, ARL members preserved 127,650 volumes on microfilm that year. Several of the state archival agencies in the United States have full-time preservation officers on staff. Beyond that, a large number of college libraries and a few major public libraries now have developed preservation programs appropriate to their size and collection goals.

The message of preservation has not remained locked within the library and archival communities, though. An important goal of some national organizations, especially the Commission on Preservation and Access, has been to foster public understanding of preservation issues. The Council on Library Resources, The Andrew W. Mellon Foundation, and NEH supported the production of *Slow*

---

7. *Preserving the Intellectual Heritage: A Report of the Bellagio Conference, June 7–10, 1993* (Washington, D.C.: Commission on Preservation and Access, Oct. 1993), 6.

8. See *The Preservation of Archival Materials: A Report of the Task Forces on Archival Selection to the Commission on Preservation and Access* (Washington, D.C.: Commission on Preservation and Access, Apr. 1993).

Fires, a one-hour documentary produced in 1987 and broadcast on PBS television stations, and librarians continue to use it in their outreach efforts. The Commission on Preservation and Access has been especially persuasive in reaching university administrators and scholars, explaining the problem and enlisting their support for appropriate solutions.

The Impact of Automation

Developments in automation and the information environment have radically altered preservation microfilming programs. It is startling to note that the first edition of this manual, published a mere eight years ago, has not a single mention of personal computers. To create targets (titles, guides, and notes included on and within the microform itself), staff members in the filming unit generally used hand lettering; a few of our sophisticated colleagues used mechanical lettering systems. Today, it is almost unthinkable to use anything less than a personal computer and laser printer, and our more sophisticated colleagues link databases, online catalogs, and graphics software to streamline the production of targets and to generate labels, packing lists, and statistical reports.

Significant improvements in bibliographic control practices and system capabilities have been achieved since the original publication of this manual. When the first edition of *Preservation Microfilming* was published, library staff members searched through the extensive volumes of the *National Register of Microform Masters* (an eight-volume union catalog compiled manually from annotated catalog cards submitted to the Library of Congress [LC] and published in book form from 1965 through 1983) and other printed guides to find out if selected titles had been microfilmed. Now we search the OCLC and RLG databases to find not only most of the *NRMM* records, but those from a number of international databases. (See chapter 5.) In a few cases, the staff in one library may search the local online catalog of another library via the Internet to find titles scheduled for filming, to obtain catalog records, and so on. In 1987 "queuing" had just been implemented in RLIN (Research Libraries Information Network, the bibliographic network of RLG) as a way for members to record their intent to film an item. Today, OCLC and RLG offer a variety of methods for queuing, and the two networks exchange records of preservation microforms to simplify searching. Protocols for the Open Systems Interconnection promise searching capabilities that are even more transparent.

Cataloging practices now address the needs of those creating or searching for preservation microforms. A key achievement in this arena was the development of the *ARL Guidelines for Bibliographic Records for Preservation Microform Masters,* which defines the base level and required data elements for preservation microform records.[9] (The *ARL Guidelines* are reproduced in appendix E and discussed in chapter 5.) RLG broke ground in bibliographic control of microform records of archives and manuscripts during its Archives Preservation Microfilm-

---

9. Association of Research Libraries, *Guidelines for Bibliographic Records for Preservation Microform Masters,* prepared by Crystal Graham (Washington, D.C.: ARL, Sept. 1990).

ing Project (APMP) from 1990 to 1994, creating guidelines that build upon those of ARL.

The first edition of this manual called for a nationwide (even worldwide) system that would enable anyone to determine whether a deteriorating item had already been reproduced in accordance with preservation standards. That system—including the technology to support it and the standards and guidelines to govern its use—is now essentially in place, though some further refinements are needed.

International Coordination

This manual retains a focus on U.S. microfilming practices, but preservation—and filming in particular—is increasingly a matter of international coordination. RLG loads the Canadian, British, and European registers of microform masters and exchanges these records with OCLC. Impressed by the achievements of the Commission on Preservation and Access in the United States, members of the European Economic Community are now in the process of establishing an analogous organization that can stimulate coordinated efforts in Europe and relate to organizations in the United States and elsewhere.[10]

Microfilming activity has increased worldwide, not simply within the United States or North America. Under its International Project, the Commission on Preservation and Access has begun to stimulate scholars to address preservation priorities in a more collaborative mode.[11] More than ever before, preservation administrators and bibliographers must take a global view in their selection decisions.

Technical Advances

What could possibly be new in microfilming? Hasn't microfilm been around for ages? What "technical advances" could there possibly be?

Experimental miniaturization of textual information on photographic film began in the middle of the nineteenth century. By the time the 35mm planetary camera was perfected for microfilming use by Recordak in 1935, its possibilities for compact, permanent storage of information contained in bulky and impermanent newspapers were recognized. The Harvard and Yale university libraries, the New York Public Library, and the Library of Congress all began filming newspapers, and then other materials, in the 1930s.

In the next three decades, a few other libraries and archival repositories followed that lead, but during that period most of the developments in microfilming as a technology took place in the commercial sector. Business applications for source document filming (of bank checks, sales records, and parts inventories, for

---

10. See *Preserving the Intellectual Heritage* for details on the conference and a synopsis of preservation activities and needs in represented Western European countries.

11. Basic information on that project is provided in Hans Rütimann, "International Issues and Efforts: The Commission on Preservation and Access' International Project."

example) offered rewards and profits for microfilm service bureaus, as they came to be called. Most libraries became familiar with microforms through the pioneering activities of University Microfilms International (UMI) and the numerous micropublishers who followed its lead.

Technical standards for the several laboratory procedures involved in manufacturing of film, camera work, and film processing were developed, primarily by those in the industry. Working groups within ALA and the Library of Congress identified the particular requirements for handling published and documentary materials in the library or archives setting and prepared guidelines and specifications for filming such materials. The LC specifications and procedures were fundamental in the early effort to tailor micrographics industry standards to library and archival applications.[12]

Since the early 1980s, RLG has been a major force in articulating the requirements of preservation microfilming in libraries and archives, as distinct from the broad standards for source document filming. Since publication of the first *RLG Preservation Manual* in 1983 through the current editions of the *RLG Preservation Microfilming Handbook* and the *RLG Archives Microfilming Manual,* the RLG guidelines have been considered the de facto standards for preservation microfilming. (See chapter 4 for a discussion of standards and guidelines.)

One impetus for the new edition of this manual was the revision in the intervening years of most of the standards and guidelines cited in the first edition. Standards will continue to be revised, and preservation managers must remain well informed of standards development and key research projects.

An important asset to the library and archival community is the Image Permanence Institute (IPI). IPI has conducted research that has contributed to the development of new standards on the stability of photographic enclosures, silver stabilization ("polysulfiding"), the longevity of various film types, and climate control requirements for storage of master negatives.

Surprisingly, in a technology often considered "static," the past few years have seen the introduction of cameras with greatly improved optics. In particular the Hermann & Kraemer camera, developed in Germany and now used in the United States by at least one preservation microfilming agent, records fine detail at levels never before possible. The power of this camera makes it possible to achieve high quality preservation microfilm even of illustrations and photographs that were previously excluded from preservation microfilming programs.

Color microfilm is now available. As noted in chapter 4, Ilfochrome, the most long-lived color film, may have an expected life of hundreds of years. While national standards do not yet warrant it to have the 500-year life expectancy of silver-gelatin film, color film is likely to outlast many original materials, and the cost of color filming may be well justified.

---

12. The following LC specifications shaped early practice: *Specifications for the Microfilming of Newspapers in the Library of Congress* (1972), *Specifications for the Microfilming of Books and Pamphlets in the Library of Congress* (1973), and *Specifications for Microfilming Manuscripts in the Library of Congress* (1980). Procedures in LC's Preservation Microfilming Office were delineated in Tamara Swora and Bohdan Yasinsky, *Processing Manual* (Washington, D.C.: LC, 1981), which served as an important model for many institutions. All are now out of date since new standards and guidelines have been adopted.

Perhaps the most striking technical development is the realistic, affordable availability of scanning and digitization technology. This exciting possibility is discussed in a following section.

Institutional Practices

The introduction to the first edition of this manual observed that institutions then had to develop policies and procedures "from scratch," and it bemoaned the scarcity of established programs and experienced managers. Thanks especially to that edition and to the RLG handbooks, institutions no longer need to reinvent the wheel.

Institutional preservation microfilming programs have matured in the past few years. Preservation administrators have become more conscious of cost factors, developed models for cost analysis, and implemented a number of cost control strategies. Their experience is reflected in chapter 6.

Early publications of the Commission on Preservation and Access referred to the "cottage industry approach" to preservation microfilming and called for a more production-oriented approach to achieve the goals of the twenty-year plan for the Brittle Books Program.

The first and so far the only nonprofit organization established solely to provide preservation microfilming services to libraries and archives is Preservation Resources, established in 1985 as the Mid-Atlantic Preservation Service (MAPS).[13] Many institutions have come to recognize that transporting materials to a central location is often more efficient than enlarging local facilities or creating new in-house filming labs.[14] When it became apparent that substantial funds would continue to be available to support preservation microfilming work, two major micropublishers (Research Publications and University Microfilms) established divisions committed to library and archival filming. Service bureaus like these—along with the Northeast Document Conservation Center (NEDCC), which has maintained a preservation microfilming service since 1979—provide a significant portion of the filming capacity for the Brittle Books Program.

As the national program began to move forward, some preservation administrators recognized they could increase their filming productivity if qualified service bureaus could perform preparation and bibliographic control work, in addition to film production. Preservation Resources was first to add preparation, bibliographic control, and storage to its services, and Research Publications and University Microfilms followed suit.

This edition of *Preservation Microfilming* reverses the assumption of the first edition. Then, only NEDCC was committed to preservation microfilming for a nationwide clientele; now, institutions have many options. Some continue to do

---

13. MAPS was initially funded by private foundations along with support from Columbia, Cornell, and Princeton Universities, the New York Public Library, and the New York State Library. It eventually broadened its service to a national clientele and expanded its service array. Its name was changed to Preservation Resources after it became a part of the OCLC organization in October 1990.

14. *Preserving the Intellectual Heritage,* 13.

As part of inspection, the master negative is inspected over a light box for scratches and other defects. *Cleveland Public Library. Photo by Bill Baltz.*

their filming in-house. Others reserve their in-house filming facilities for special materials and contract out the filming of routine materials. Institutions establishing new preservation microfilming programs generally build those programs on the assumption that film production will be contracted to specialized, preservation-oriented service bureaus such as NEDCC and Preservation Resources. These issues are further analyzed in chapter 1 ("Contracting for Services") and chapter 3 ("Choosing the Filming Agent").

As libraries and archives relinquish control of film production, quality assurance has emerged as a more significant internal function. That is, because the filming is often done off-site and is not within the preservation administrator's direct control, institutions have become more assiduous in checking the film produced by filming agents. Consequently, the discussion of quality assurance operations in this edition represents a significant expansion over its treatment in the first edition.

The Role of Cooperative and Coordinated Projects

Not surprisingly, cooperation among numerous parties has been essential, and a roll call of key participants in this effort will identify organizations that have played crucial parts in almost every aspect of preservation. The Association of Research Libraries initiated and coordinated a series of projects aimed at improving bibliographic control of microforms. Early leadership and support, both moral and financial, were consistently provided by the Council on Library Resources, and the Commission on Preservation and Access has assumed and expanded that role since 1988. Preservation administrators, catalogers, and microform specialists from libraries and service bureaus have worked through appropriate units of the American Library Association to identify needs and problems and hammer out solutions.

The Library of Congress, as the largest noncommercial producer of preservation microfilm and the chief creator and distributor of bibliographic data, guided the development of both laboratory and cataloging standards into the 1980s. LC and the New York Public Library, one of the other major producers of microforms, were leaders in large-scale filming projects for many decades.

The Research Libraries Group provided all-important leadership, especially in the development of specifications and in creating models for coordinated projects that would carry out the goals of the nationwide program. RLG and its members (with early financial assistance from The Andrew W. Mellon Foundation and the Henry Luce Foundation, as well as generous support from the National Endowment for the Humanities) have made significant contributions to the translation of technical standards and bibliographic ideals into working programs on the local level.

Cooperation in preservation microfilming has emerged as an effective way to reach the goals of the Brittle Books Program and to expand the number of institutions engaged in preservation microfilming. Chapter 1 describes the advantages of a cooperative approach and outlines steps in the planning process for one. A few examples will illustrate the range of possibilities.

Coordinated National Programs

The most ambitious coordinated program is the United States Newspaper Program (USNP), established in the early 1980s to locate, catalog, and microfilm newspapers published in the United States since the eighteenth century. The program is funded by NEH, with technical support and project management provided by the Library of Congress.[15] All USNP projects are organized as cooperative statewide efforts, generally with one organization serving as the lead agency.[16] This program is so carefully organized and, at least for now, well funded that no institution should consider microfilming U.S. newspapers outside the context of the USNP.

Coordinated national programs exist for the preservation of agricultural and biomedical literature. The U.S. Agricultural Information Network has proposed a national plan for the preservation of agricultural literature, which relies considerably on microfilming.[17] The program draws heavily on the strong collections of Cornell University and the National Agricultural Library but invites other institutions to undertake complementary projects that will contribute supplementary regional and local materials, as illustrated in figure 1. The National Library of Medicine (NLM) began a massive program in 1986 to microfilm all brittle monographs and serials in the core medical subjects in the NLM collection, and the current emphasis is on serials that are indexed in *Index Medicus.* By the end of fiscal year 1994, 55,000 volumes had been filmed, and copies are sold on request.[18]

In 1984 the American Philological Association pioneered another multi-tiered cooperative approach: scholar-specialists in classical studies assigned priorities to the most important works published between 1850 and 1918 within their subject fields. The works were sought first within the collections of the Columbia University Libraries, and the titles were filmed centrally.[19]

---

15. For a basic overview of the USNP, see Robert Harriman, "The News in Review: The United States Newspaper Program," *Cataloging and Classification Quarterly* 17, nos. 3/4 (1993): 87–103.

16. Each project includes a planning phase followed by work to locate full runs of all newspapers printed in that state, whether held in libraries and archives, other cultural institutions, or private hands. The projects follow a strictly defined work plan and technical guidelines for bibliographic control and microfilming. Funding guidelines for USNP projects are available from the NEH Division of Preservation and Access (see appendix B). Technical guidelines are provided in Walter Cybulski, ed., *United States Newspaper Program Newspaper Preservation Microfilming Manual* (Albany, N.Y.: New York State Library, forthcoming); and Robert Harriman, ed., *U. S. Newspaper Program Planning Guide and Resource Notebook* (Washington, D.C.: Serial Record Division, LC, 1991).

17. Nancy E. Gwinn, "A National Preservation Program for Agricultural Literature" (United States Agricultural Information Network, Beltsville, Md., May 16, 1993, photocopy). Background on the genesis of the program is provided in Dorothy Wright, Samuel Demas, and Walter Cybulski, "Cooperative Preservation of State-Level Publications: Preserving the Literature of New York State Agriculture and Rural Life," *Library Resources & Technical Services* 37 (Oct. 1993): 434–43.

18. Margaret Byrnes, National Library of Medicine, electronic mail correspondence with the author, Feb. 15, 1995.

19. See Carolyn L. Harris and Roger S. Bagnall, "Involving Scholars in Preservation Decisions: The Case of the Classicists," *Journal of Academic Librarianship* 13 (July 1987): 140–6.

FIGURE 1   Distributed Responsibilities in the National Preservation Plan
for Agricultural Literature

MANUSCRIPTS
AND ARCHIVES

Local initiatives

LAND-GRANT
PUBLICATIONS

Assess status,
fill in gaps

CORE HISTORICAL
LITERATURE

(Popular and trade
journals)

University-based,
nationally coordinated

STATE AND
COUNTY
DOCUMENTS

State-based,
nationally
coordinated

**CORE
HISTORICAL
LITERATURE**

**(Scholarly monographs
and serials)**

**Cornell/Mann
Library**

FEDERAL
DOCUMENTS

National
Agricultural
Library

PRE-1862
IMPRINTS

National
Agricultural
Library-led
Project

UNIQUE
COLLECTIONS

(Subject-based,
geography-based,
format-based, etc.)

Local initiatives

NONPRINT
AND AUDIOVISUAL
COLLECTIONS

Local initiatives

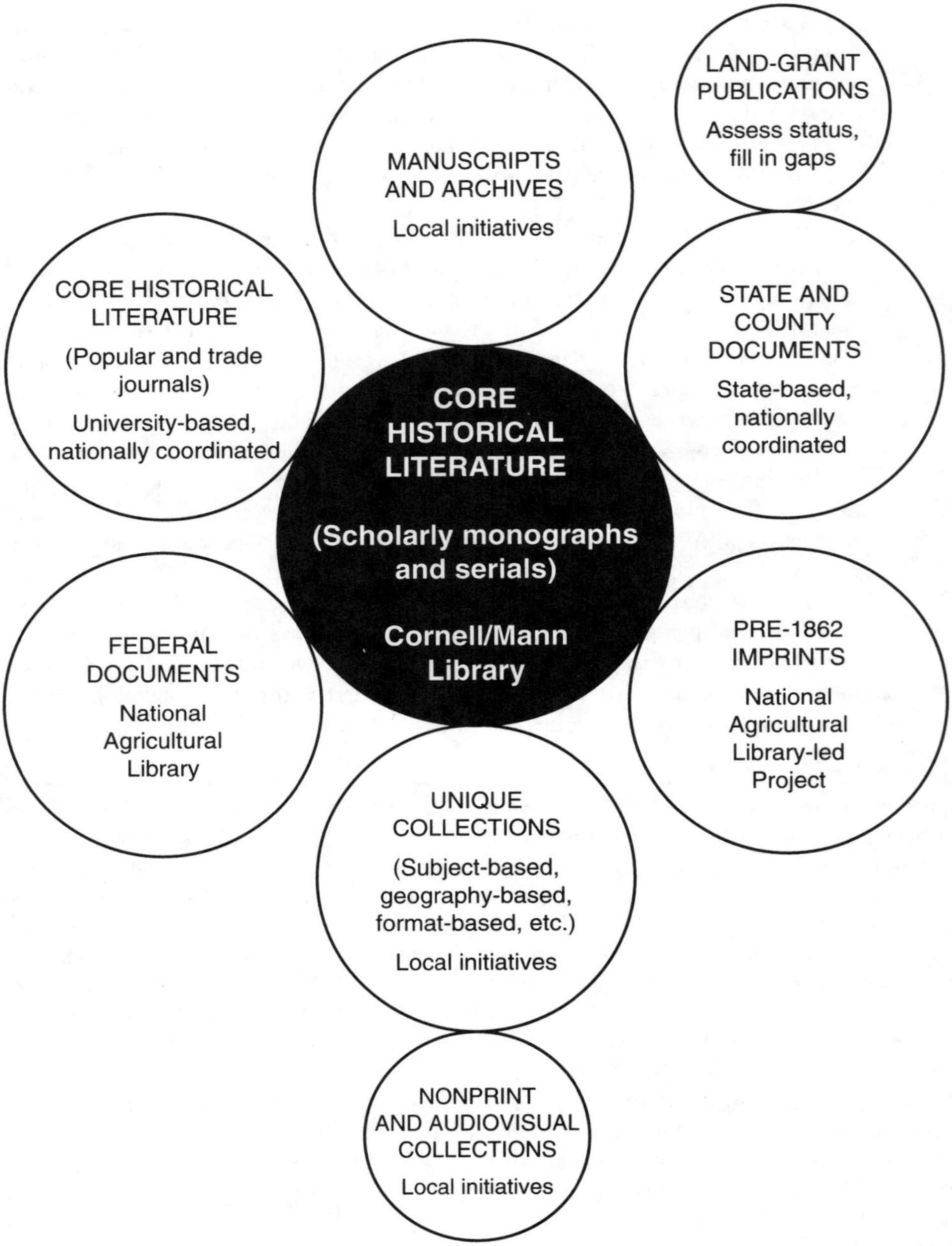

SOURCE: Nancy E. Gwinn, "A National Preservation Program for Agricultural Literature" (United States Agricultural Information Network, Beltsville, Md., May 16, 1993, photocopy), 14.

American Theological Library Association

For almost three decades, the American Theological Library Association (ATLA) Board of Microtext used the facilities of both the University of Chicago Library Photoduplication Department and commercial microfilming services to produce microfilm of deteriorating theological serials identified by ATLA members. Sales of duplicates to other members helped to recover the filming costs. In a dramatic expansion of that effort in 1984, dozens of members pledged substantial annual sums to support the filming of commonly held religious monographs published between 1860 and 1905 to replace the brittle volumes. Early ATLA projects focused on filming materials for which there was high demand. More recently, the project focus has shifted to collections that are more specialized, and market forces have led ATLA increasingly to rely on grant funding.

Research Libraries Group

The cooperative preservation microfilming projects of the Research Libraries Group have emerged as the dominant model in U.S. cooperative projects.[20] Selection strategies and overall project design have varied among the nine distinct efforts managed by RLG over a twelve-year period. For instance, the first RLG Cooperative Preservation Microfilming Project (CPMP I), from 1983 to 1987, used a selection strategy that combined the principle of targeting high-priority areas with the expedience of dividing up the task. Thus, focusing on U.S. publications and Americana that appeared between 1870 and 1920, participants concentrated on subject areas matching their particular collection strengths. Early on, most libraries used their own filming facilities for the production work; currently, most participating institutions subcontract film production to service bureaus.

Early RLG projects provided a way for libraries with established preservation microfilming programs to share the work of filming. As the RLG membership has expanded and more institutions have begun to plan or implement preservation programs, recent RLG cooperative projects have included both microfilming veterans and novices, and the shape of some projects has altered accordingly. For example, for many participants in RLG's Art Serials Preservation Project (ASPP) from 1990 to 1992 and the Archives Preservation Microfilming Project (from 1990 to 1994), these were the first ventures into preservation microfilming. In the ASPP, RLG selected a vendor to provide centralized preparation, targeting, and film production so that institutions could focus on traditional library functions: selection and bibliographic control, in particular. In the archives project, participants worked together to identify, assess, and describe procedures unique to archival collections, thus codifying practice in a wholly new way.

In the course of these projects, RLG has not only created significant models that have helped shape the nationwide effort to preserve endangered scholarly

---

20. For a history of RLG preservation efforts, see Patricia A. McClung, "Consortial Action: RLG's Preservation Program," in *Advances in Preservation and Access,* eds. Higginbotham and Jackson, vol. 1, 61–70. A list of RLG projects and participants in each is provided in Patricia McClung, "RLG Preservation Microfilming Projects: A History," in Nancy E. Elkington, ed., *RLG Preservation Microfilming Handbook* (Mountain View, Calif.: RLG, 1992), 183–5.

resources in the United States,[21] but RLG staff and members have also developed bibliographic tools and systems that support preservation microfilming and have drawn on national micrographics standards to develop the procedures and technical guidelines that define preservation microfilming in libraries and archives.

Committee on Institutional Cooperation

The cooperative preservation projects of the Committee on Institutional Cooperation (CIC), first launched in 1988, closely resemble the RLG model. Like RLG, the CIC membership consists of research libraries, many of which have strong preservation programs in place and deep experience with microfilming.[22] The members coordinate the drafting of project proposals, follow similar approaches in the selection of materials, follow the RLG specifications for filming, and share storage space for master negatives. Whereas RLG projects use the central staff for overall project coordination, grant writing, and management, CIC—lacking designated preservation staff in the headquarters office—has assigned overall project management to one designated project director in a member institution, a position that has rotated among the membership. The project director then serves as liaison to the individual libraries' project managers and with the CIC headquarters, in addition to representing the consortium at sponsors' and other national meetings.

SOLINET

SOLINET (the Southeastern Library Network, Inc.) established a groundbreaking model, beginning with its first Cooperative Preservation Microfilming Project in 1990–1992 in partnership with the Association of Southeastern Research Libraries (ASERL). Whereas research libraries dominate the RLG membership, SOLINET's is more diverse, and the majority of its members do not have systematic preservation programs or preservation microfilming experience. Even within ASERL, fewer than half the institutions have either full-time preservation staff or microfilming experience. In response to the needs of its membership, SOLINET preservation microfilming projects are much more centralized than those of RLG or CIC. SOLINET staff and ASERL members together define the selection criteria for materials to be included in each project. SOLINET selects the service bureaus that will be used for filming and duplication, as well as the storage facility for master negatives. Because the evaluation of service bureaus is centralized, institutions new to filming need not become knowledgeable enough to make individual selections.

Project participants are responsible for the screening and selection of individual titles within the agreed-upon parameters. Selected titles are then sent to SOLINET, where a central staff in the network handles all preparation and bibliographic control work. Prepared materials then are shipped to the service bureau for filming and duplication. Completed films are fully inspected by SOLI-

---

21. McClung, "RLG Preservation Microfilming Projects: A History," 183.

22. The CIC participants are the Universities of Chicago, Illinois, Iowa, Michigan, Minnesota, and Wisconsin; and Indiana, Michigan State, Northwestern, Ohio State, Pennsylvania State, and Purdue Universities. For more information about the CIC projects, contact the office (see appendix B).

NET personnel, and any problems are resolved between SOLINET and the filming agent. Master negatives are shipped directly to an appropriate storage facility,
and printing masters and service copies are returned to the institution along with
the original volumes. Institutions conduct a final inspection for quality assurance.

The RLG and CIC models are quite similar, and both employ largely decentralized strategies because many of their participants have well-established preservation programs and a long history of preservation microfilming—many, in
fact, have helped develop the standards and guidelines that govern national
practice. By contrast, the SOLINET model was conceived as a way to build expertise in selection and preservation management while alleviating the need for
local technical expertise.

If the national preservation program is to grow, more models like SOLI-
NET's are needed. But it is equally clear that the strong programs of RLG and
CIC, drawing upon the research collections and deep experience of their mem-
bers, are likely to remain the backbone of the national effort.

What About Digitization?

"Establishing a preservation microfilming program, with or without . . . cooperative frameworks, represents a major investment in a technology which some
would regard as a temporary stage between the printing press and the computer."
That sentence appeared in the introduction to the first edition of this manual,
which then proceeded to look optimistically to the optical disk pilot project then
under way at the Library of Congress. A 1990 opinion piece in *The Chronicle of
Higher Education* asked, "Why microfilm research library collections when electronic data bases could be used?"[23]

The technology now exists to scan textual and graphic materials and to store
them as images or as text files. They can be maintained on disk or magnetic tape
or in a database. Scanned materials can be output to paper or transmitted in seconds
across the Internet or other communication networks. The accessibility of
scanned materials offers an exciting application of our reformatting systems.

As used here, *digitization* refers to the electronic encoding of scanned documents in digital image form.[24] In the scanning process, documents are captured

---

23. Eldred Smith, *Chronicle of Higher Education,* July 18, 1990, A44; reprinted, with additional
comments from the author, in *Microform Review* 20 (winter 1991): 27–9. An articulate response to
Professor Smith's article was offered by Duane Webster in the *Chronicle,* Aug. 15, 1990, B3–4.

24. This working definition is also offered in Anne R. Kenney and Lynne K. Personius, "The Future
of Digital Preservation," in *Advances in Preservation and Access,* vol. 1, 196. As of this writing, the
following titles provide a good introduction to the concepts of digitization as a reformatting method: Anne
R. Kenney, "Digital to Microfilm Conversion: An Interim Preservation Solution," *Library Resources &
Technical Services* 37 (Oct. 1993): 380–95, and corrections published in *LRTS* 38 (Jan. 1994): 87–95;
Janice Mohlhenrich, ed., *Preservation of Electronic Formats and Electronic Formats for Preservation* (Fort
Atkinson, Kans.: Highsmith, 1993); Donald J. Waters, *From Microfilm to Digital Imagery: On the
Feasibility of a Project to Study the Means, Costs, and Benefits of Converting Large Quantities of
Preserved Library Materials from Microfilm to Digital Images* (Washington, D.C.: Commission on Pres-
ervation and Access, 1991); and Don Willis, *A Hybrid Systems Approach to Preservation of Printed
Materials* (Washington, D.C.: Commission on Preservation and Access, 1992). In recent years the annual

as "electronic pictures." It is possible, in a second phase, to convert the text in these images to alphanumeric form through optical character recognition (OCR) or internal character recognition, but the cost and complexities of doing so are at present outside the scope of most library and archival projects.

The major impediment to the preservation community's acceptance of digitization is the issue of permanence. Preservation microfilming has been based on the commitment to create a permanent or "archival" replacement for deteriorated original materials. Standards exist to guarantee the stability of microfilm for at least 500 years. By contrast, storage media such as magnetic tape and optical disks still have life expectancies in the range of only ten to twenty years.

Admittedly, electronic files can have "virtual" permanence if they are regularly exercised and migrated to new hardware and software platforms. The technical requirements for doing so are relatively straightforward, but much work remains to be done in the area of standards development to ensure both media longevity and compatibility of systems.[25] But will libraries and archives have the programmatic commitment to sustain these operations for the next hundreds of years? Will they do so even when financial constraints force staff cutbacks and reduce operating budgets? Will they do so for reformatted materials that are not heavily used?[26]

In the conceptual logjam between those who resisted digitization because of its evanescence[27] and those who championed its accessibility features, a breakthrough occurred with the recognition that the medium of preservation is not necessarily the medium for access.[28] That is, in this time of rapid technology developments, with many technical, bibliographic, economic, and copyright issues yet to be resolved, the most prudent strategy may be to employ a hybrid systems approach: continue to create and maintain microfilm as the "archival" copy but also provide digital access to those preserved materials.

Two projects that are testing this hybrid systems approach have drawn particular attention. Yale University, with financial support from the Commission on Preservation and Access, launched its Project Open Book in 1990.[29] Micro-

literature reviews in *Library Resources & Technical Services* have tracked key works in digitization, and these may serve as a good synopsis in the future.

25. See Michael Lesk, *Image Formats for Preservation and Access: A Report of the Technology Assessment Advisory Committee to the Commission on Preservation and Access* (Washington, D.C.: Commission on Preservation and Access, 1990); and Peter S. Graham, *Intellectual Preservation: Electronic Preservation of the Third Kind* (Washington, D.C.: Commission on Preservation and Access, Mar. 1994).

26. The Commission on Preservation and Access and RLG have jointly formed a Task Force on Archiving of Digital Information. Reports on its work will be published by the Commission and may bear monitoring.

27. This phrase is drawn from John Swan, "Micropermanence and Electronic Evanescence," *Microform Review* 20 (spring 1991): 80–3.

28. This concept was an important contribution of the Commission on Preservation and Access and its first president, Patricia Battin; see Battin, " 'As Far into the Future as Possible.' "

29. As of this writing, the primary sources of information on this initiative are Donald J. Waters and Shari Weaver, *The Organizational Phase of Project Open Book* (Washington, D.C.: Commission on Preservation and Access, 1992); and Paul Conway and Shari Weaver, *The Setup Phase of Project Open Book* (Washington, D.C.: Commission on Preservation and Access, June 1994), reprinted in *Microform Review* 23 (summer 1994): 107–19.

film created according to preservation guidelines is scanned for digital access. Cornell University, with support from the Commission on Preservation and Access and the Xerox Corporation, is taking the opposite approach: scanning materials first, then outputting the files to film.[30]

More institutions are now beginning to use digitization. RLG has begun a project to digitize photographs, and Preservation Resources and other service bureaus have added digitization to their filming services. The Digital Preservation Consortium was formed in 1994 under the aegis of the Commission on Preservation and Access to enable more institutions to undertake pilot projects to broaden our understanding of the requirements and applications of the technology for preservation purposes. In 1995 the Commission joined with major research institutions to form the National Digital Library Federation, with the goal of implementing a distributed, accessible digital library to consist of holdings already in electronic form as well as collections converted to digital form.[31]

Technical feasibility of digitization has been amply demonstrated. However, much remains to be discovered about adequate indexing and access structures, the mechanics of building and using a large "library" of digitized materials, the impact of this technology on current patterns of publishing and information distribution, operational costs, and the permanence of the medium.[32]

Librarians and archivists must monitor these developments. Each institution must determine when or whether to add a digitization component to its reformatting program. Meanwhile, we are well advised to view preservation microfilm as a "platform for digital access systems."[33]

It is now most prudent to create microfilm with the assumption that it will be digitized. Fortunately, the selection and preparation procedures for reformatting are essentially the same whether the storage medium is microfilm or an electronic format. The library and archival community can continue to expand preservation microfilming activities without fear that the electronic technology, should it prove economically and operationally feasible, will render these efforts obsolete. Indeed, international participants in the Bellagio Conference, assessing the feasibility and priorities of a coordinated Western European preservation initiative, concluded that

> it was important not to delay preserving materials until a particular method has been proved optimal. Instead, the most flexible, dependable

---

30. See Anne R. Kenney and Lynne K. Personius, *A Testbed for Advancing the Role of Digital Technologies for Library Preservation and Access: Final Report by Cornell University to the Commission on Preservation and Access* (Washington, D.C.: Commission on Preservation and Access, 1993).

31. See *The Digital Preservation Consortium: Mission and Goals* (Washington, D.C.: Commission on Preservation and Access, Mar. 1994), and "National Digital Library Federation Agreement Signed," *Commission on Preservation and Access Newsletter,* no. 80 (July 1995), 1.

32. Many important cautionary notes are offered in Paul Conway, "Digitizing," *Library Journal* (Feb. 1, 1994): 42–4.

33. This term was coined in C. Lee Jones, *Preservation Film: Platform for Digital Access Systems* (Washington, D.C.: Commission on Preservation and Access, July 1993), a paper that also includes a solid analysis of key issues in using microfilm for digital access.

and economical methods should be used at once, while experiments and trials of alternatives proceed. . . . The important aspect of the choice of method is to insure the maximum convertibility from the contemporary capture and storage method to the improved techniques expected in the future.[34]

If institutions have in place well-tested and smoothly operating procedures for selecting and preparing materials for conversion, they will be prepared to take advantage of whatever storage medium provides the best result. Further, since the costs associated with document preparation and image capture are incurred at the time of filming, and in light of the high scanning rates claimed by some vendors, the subsequent costs of scanning from film may be quite modest.[35]

The best guarantee for producing film that can be scanned effectively is to follow the highest standards of technical quality. The characteristics of the film itself will determine in large measure the quality of the resulting digital images; they will also directly affect how automatic—and, therefore, how inexpensive—the scanning process is likely to be.[36] The technical and bibliographic specifications outlined in this manual for creating preservation microfilm will generally serve well when those films are scanned. Some special considerations and narrower specifications are required in film that will be digitized, but staff members will need significantly more detail about the technology when planning digitization projects.[37]

As of this writing, microfilming remains the most reliable method of format conversion for paper-based records and is likely to continue as the most economical for storage of less heavily used materials in the foreseeable future. Consequently, preservation microfilming has become firmly established as an essential component of a comprehensive preservation program. It is part of "the system," not just by fiat but through the dedicated efforts of a generation of preservation administrators who have discovered or invented ways to integrate the technical capabilities of the microfilming laboratory with their institutions' procedures for selection, preparation, bibliographic control, storage, and access.

If It's That Complicated, Is It Worth It?

It is often much more difficult and lengthy to describe *how* to do something than it is to do it. Try writing instructions on how to shift gears in a standard transmission car for someone who has never driven, for example; or think about the manual that comes with a washing machine or stereo system.

---

34. *Preserving the Intellectual Heritage,* 8.

35. Anne R. Kenney, "Planning for the Future: Film Digitization," in *RLG Archives Microfilming Manual,* ed. Nancy E. Elkington (Mountain View, Calif.: RLG, 1994), 96.

36. Kenney, "Planning for the Future," 96.

37. Further details on the technical requirements of film to be scanned—so far as we now understand them based on today's technology—are outlined in Kenney, "Planning for the Future."

Widely held serial titles have proven especially amenable to cooperative preservation approaches. Microfilming is often the preferred solution for materials in poor condition. *University of Kentucky Libraries Reprographics Department. Photo by Estil Robinson.*

Learning any new set of skills requires time, patience, and attention, and it is certainly easier to master them if you have a human teacher to demonstrate, guide, and correct. I would not like to ride with someone who learned to drive solely from a book, and I would be uneasy consigning irreplaceable documents to a preservation microfilming operation set up solely on the basis of information in this or any other book. But I use the car manual to show me how to drive my new car, to interpret a dashboard light that goes on, or to connect the cables when my battery goes dead. And I would use this manual in the same way: to set the stage, to introduce major issues, to find references to other sources of information, and to guide me if something goes wrong.

This manual attempts to codify and present the many technical, procedural, and administrative issues that have been found by experience to be essential to the establishment of a successful preservation microfilming program—a program in which staff members must select things intelligently, prepare them physically so they can be copied, produce legible long-lasting film, and make its existence known so that the intended beneficiaries of all that effort, the patrons of libraries and archives now and in generations to come, can actually find and use the material.

Those who conceived of the first edition of this manual hoped that it "would have a significant impact on the quality and efficiency of current filming work and would facilitate the establishment of new filming programs."[38] The first edition did just that. This new edition reflects the technical advances in the intervening years, as well as the programmatic innovations individual institutions and cooperative projects have contributed. That more—much more—filming must be done soon if we are not to lose large portions of our intellectual heritage is certain. It is clear that as the endangered materials documenting that heritage are distributed among libraries and archives throughout the country (indeed, the world), so the efforts to preserve them must be distributed.

No single institutional or government program could begin to handle everything, but individual institutions need not reinvent the wheel. Adapting procedures developed by others is much faster and safer. In the case of published materials, work done in one place need not be duplicated in another. Pooling efforts by sharing filming facilities, dividing responsibility for filming commonly held materials, and collaborating on improvement and refinement of procedures will make the inevitably "too-few" dollars stretch to encompass more of the task.

Getting into this business, then, is not for those who prefer to work in isolation or eschew professional meetings and reading. ARL, the Commission on Preservation and Access, RLG, and preservation groups within ALA, as well as a growing list of consortia, networks, and regional programs, are active in both planning and supporting new preservation microfilming developments and in sharing information with their respective constituencies. Make sure your office is on the appropriate mailing lists, because after you finish reading this book, you will want to know what has happened since it went to press.

---

38. Shirley Echelman, letter to James Morris, Aug. 5, 1983.

An Overview of Administrative Decisions

Many institutions, when they begin to think about preservation microfilming, think first of the filming process itself—whether or where to get a camera, how to film materials, and so on. Camera work is undeniably a central tool in preservation microfilming. But it is only a small part of a complex procedure to transfer the contents of books and documents to film.

Immediately, other questions arise: Which materials are to be filmed first? Have these volumes or documents already been preserved on film? How does one identify the materials on the film? How should they be prepared for filming? Should they be preserved on film or fiche? The librarian or archivist may contact a consultant, who raises questions about standards, specifications, and quality control. What standards should be followed and how? What about access to the film? Should the paper copy be preserved? How do you decide?

You will have to answer all these questions and more if a filming program is to be successful. You begin to realize that preservation microfilming is an administrative challenge that requires broad and careful analysis. This manual is designed to give guidance to the librarian or archivist planning and implementing a preservation microfilming program, whether it is a local initiative or part of a national or regional cooperative project.

Purposes and Definitions

Microforms have many functions within a library or archives. For example, libraries and archives provide microform copies of their most rare and fragile items, thus affording security and preservation by reducing handling of the original item. Microforms produced by libraries, archives, commercial micropublishers, and other organizations provide remote access to collections that cannot or should not be transported because of their rarity, fragility, or bulk. Many research libraries produce microfilm instead of loaning some items to offsite users, and most large archives do this routinely.

Newspapers are excellent candidates for microfilming. Many are brittle and damaged, and they require a great deal of storage space. The U.S. Newspaper Program offers a coordinated approach to the preservation of newspapers. *University of Kentucky Libraries Reprographics Department. Photo by Lewis Warden.*

Microforms have been used extensively as a means of building retrospective collections. Many volumes long out of print are available in microform. Micropublishers are able to bring together large collections of materials located in many repositories. Universal access to unique documents housed in historical and personal archives is now possible through microform. Often, business records are routinely kept only in microform, and many archives house cabinets full of rolls of film or drawers of microfiche that are themselves primary source documents.

Microfilm stores information in up to 90 percent less space than is required for the corresponding paper copy.[1] Thus, microfilming is especially useful for extensive runs of newspapers and other serials whose use does not warrant the shelf space they require and for replacement of the paper copy of modern business or government records.

Microfilming is the process of recording in facsimile on photographic film, reduced so as to require optical assistance to be read, the intellectual content (that is, the written or printed matter and illustrations) of archival and library materials.

1. Pamela W. Darling, "Developing a Preservation Microfilming Program," *Library Journal* 99 (1974): 2803–9.

National standards of the American National Standards Institute (ANSI), Association for Information and Image Management (AIIM), and other bodies govern a wide range of issues—from the nature of the film stock, through the procedures and quality requirements of film production, to requirements for inspection and storage. Micrographics standards are updated regularly. Every year sees revisions to some of the key standards that relate to preservation microfilming, so the staff must keep abreast of these changes. (See chapter 4 regarding the role of standards.)

Preservation microfilming has some unique features and benefits that distinguish it from the many kinds of source document filming defined in the national standards. The primary purpose of preservation microfilming is to provide replacements for materials written or printed on paper of poor quality, most likely that has already become brittle, so that the contents will continue to be available to the scholarly and research community forever. What distinguishes preservation microfilming as a special subset of source document filming is the intention to create a permanent replacement, an archival medium.

But if you consult the standards for a definition of or guidance on what is called "preservation microfilming," you will search in vain. There is no national standard that governs only preservation microfilming. Preservation microfilming results in a product: silver-gelatin microfilm with certain characteristics of technical quality and legibility. National standards specify many of those criteria. But preservation microfilming is also a whole system involving the selection of materials, their preparation and filming, quality assurance by the filmer and repository, bibliographic control, and storage. Specifications for preservation microfilming select from or augment existing standards and supplement them with guidelines that define "best practice." For example, national standards do not specify the number of density readings required when inspecting a reel of film, but preservation microfilming guidelines do; and preservation microfilming programs go well beyond national standards regarding the kinds of targets (sheets of technical and bibliographic information that are filmed along with an item) necessary to facilitate users' access to works on film.

While national standards focus on technical issues, guidelines and specifications for preservation microfilming address all phases of the operation:

selection and identification of materials

preparation of materials for filming

film production, duplication, and quality assurance

bibliographic control

storage

Preservation microfilming guidelines are designed to provide optimal technical and bibliographic quality. They generally adopt or even exceed the strictest ANSI/AIIM standards in technical areas and supplement them in areas, such as bibliographic control, that are unique to library and archival applications.

This manual not only outlines the technical requirements of the film (issues addressed by the wide array of national standards) but also provides guidance on the design and management of the whole system by which the technical standards and guidelines can produce a product that meets preservation goals. The primary sources for written documentation on all aspects of preservation microfilming are the guidelines of RLG.[2]

Almost any item found in a library or archives may be a candidate for preservation microfilming, but generally they are those printed on paper, for example, books, serials, newspapers, scrapbooks, photographs, historical records, and archival records. Some nonpaper materials, such as lantern slides and photographic negatives, are also suitable for microfilm. It is an especially appropriate choice to preserve not only items of little artifactual value but also items with very high artifactual value, where a surrogate can protect the original from damage or theft. Microfilming is a technology that is well understood in archives and libraries, long lasting, and space saving.

Libraries and archives have somewhat different preservation problems. Published materials in libraries are not usually unique but are one of a set of identical, or mostly identical, items that may be found in many other libraries. Archival repositories, on the other hand, hold unique materials, often large, complex collections that have to be internally organized for use and made available to patrons at distant locations. At the same time, many libraries do house archival materials, and some archival repositories own books. The two types of repositories may have differing needs for filming programs, but the basic filming procedures are the same. Materials must be selected, prepared, filmed and processed according to standards, stored, and provided with a means of access.

The Deterioration of Paper

Library and archival repositories house the historical and intellectual record of human progress, both the original sources for scholarship and the production of past scholarly work. The primary purpose of housing these materials is to preserve their contents—the text and illustrations—and to make them available to current and future scholars. For a subset of those materials, their aesthetic and physical features contribute to, may even equal or surpass, the value of their intellectual content. The great majority of that record is either written or printed on paper, which, because it is an organic substance, deteriorates over time. Some papers made before the mid-nineteenth century deteriorate much more slowly than modern paper. Early hand paper-making techniques and the use of alkaline materials contributed to the longevity of paper. The industrial revolution of the nineteenth century provided the machines, and the spread of literacy the impetus, for inexpensive mass-produced paper that, because of its acid content, bears the seed of its own destruction.[3]

---

2. Nancy E. Elkington, ed., *RLG Preservation Microfilming Handbook* (Mountain View, Calif.: RLG, 1992), and Nancy E. Elkington, ed., *RLG Archives Microfilming Manual* (Mountain View, Calif.: RLG, 1994).

3. A more detailed (and quite entertaining) account of these developments and their consequences in library and archival collections is provided in Verner W. Clapp, "The Story of Permanent/Durable Book-Paper, 1115–1970," *Scholarly Publishing,* Part 1, Jan. 1971, 107–24; Part 2, Apr. 1971, 229–45; Part 3, July 1971, 353–67.

Libraries and archives also have a role in the deterioration of paper. Paper deteriorates much more quickly when housed under poor environmental conditions. All too often, libraries and archives have provided environments that are too hot, too dry, too humid, or too changeable. They use lights that emit high ultraviolet radiation levels. The air may be polluted with sulfur dioxide, ozone, and other chemicals, as well as dust and other particulate pollutants. These problems, at least partially correctable for the future, cannot now be rectified for the past.

The bulk of the materials in most libraries and archives was written or printed after 1850. Materials from earlier periods may be well-protected in rare book collections, but the later ones are often accessible in open stacks. Therefore, the number of items with poor-quality paper, combined with poor environmental conditions and storage practices, has made the problem of preserving the historical and intellectual record one of crisis proportions. In some large research libraries surveys have shown that more than one-third of the collections are printed on paper that has become so brittle as to be unusable.[4] The published data on collection condition come primarily from U.S. research libraries. The patterns of these data suggest that the percentages of brittle materials are applicable to other, older collections and that the problem is especially severe in collections that have not been stored in air-conditioned buildings.

In younger collections, brittleness rates may be much lower. For example, in the condition survey conducted at the Wellesley Public Library, because of the relative youth of the collection (86 percent of it published after 1960), an insignificant number of brittle books were found. However, the fact that 46 percent of the collection had acidic paper led the staff to predict that half of the current collection will be brittle within 25 to 40 years.[5]

For the United States alone, such percentages translate into daunting figures. Nearly 80 million books in North American research libraries are threatened with destruction because they are printed on acidic paper.[6] An early study by the Council on Library Resources concluded that 3.3 million volumes in research libraries were brittle and merited microfilming, at a projected cost of $198 million.[7]

This problem has not gone unnoticed, especially among scholarly publishers, thanks to efforts to highlight the issue on the part of ARL; the Commission on

---

4. Two key studies that documented the extent of the problem are Sarah Buchanan and Sandra Coleman, *Deterioration Survey of the Stanford University Libraries Green Library Stack Collection* (Stanford, Calif.: Stanford University Libraries, 1979), and Gay Walker et al., "The Yale Survey: A Large-Scale Study of Book Deterioration in the Yale University Library," *College and Research Libraries* 46 (Mar. 1985): 111–32. See also Richard B. King Jr., *Deterioration of Book Paper* (Berkeley, Calif.: University of California Libraries, Office of Library Plans and Policies, Nov. 1981), and "Survey of Book Condition at the Library of Congress," *National Preservation News* 1 (July 1985): 8–9.

5. Anne L. Reynolds, Nancy C. Schrock, and Joanna Walsh, "Preservation: The Public Library Response," *Library Journal* (Feb. 15, 1989): 130.

6. *Preserving Knowledge: The Case for Alkaline Paper* (Washington, D.C.: ARL, 1988).

7. Robert Hayes, *The Magnitude, Costs and Benefits of the Preservation of Brittle Books* (Washington, D.C.: CLR, 1987), 2.

Preservation and Access; government agencies such as NEH and the National Historical Publications and Records Commission (NHPRC); professional organizations such as ALA, the Society of American Archivists (SAA), and the National Association of Government Archives and Records Administrators (NAGARA); and professional librarians and archivists. A number of paper manufacturers now produce alkaline papers, and there is growing evidence that a large number of American publishers and printers are in compliance with the national standard for permanent paper, first published in 1985.[8] While these efforts may help to mitigate the problem for the future, much of the paper in collections today will deteriorate in less than fifty years. Furthermore, many publishers outside North America and Europe do not use permanent/durable paper.

Microform Replacement versus Other Treatments

As discouraging as are the numbers of brittle and deteriorated materials, nonetheless many libraries and archival repositories are mounting preservation programs that are making great strides toward preserving the intellectual heritage of this country. In making preservation choices, you must keep in mind that although the number of items that might be microfilmed is high, microfilming suddenly moves into more favorable light when compared with the cost and efficacy of other preservation options. Reasonably inexpensive physical treatments do not yet exist to restore brittle paper to its original suppleness and strength. Nor are such treatments likely to appear soon.

Conservators' services are expensive, in line with their skills and training and the time-consuming nature of the work, so professional conservation treatment is generally reserved for especially rare and valuable materials. Full conservation of a badly damaged rare book can cost as much as $3,000 or more, including disbinding, cleaning, washing and deacidification, page repair, rebinding, and construction of a custom-fitted enclosure. Even an alternative treatment, with encapsulation and post binding in lieu of page repairs and rebinding, can be in the range of $2,000. By contrast, the filming of that same volume, one that has many physical features that complicate filming, might be only $150. This, admittedly, is higher than the $100 typical cost for routine filming of general collections, but it is still vastly less expensive than conservation treatment.

Of course, not all volumes are of such value or have such severe damage that they warrant full-scale conservation treatment. In many cases, simpler "collections conservation" procedures can be used to stabilize a volume that is not badly deteriorated. Several library binders and other organizations might provide resewing and rebinding or deacidification, encapsulation, and post binding for prices in the range of $100 to $200.

If it is not necessary to retain a volume in its original form, another option is available. Some repositories create a "preservation photocopy" of items that receive heavy local use. A preservation photocopy is a photocopy made with per-

---

8. *American National Standard for Information Sciences—Permanence of Paper for Printed Publications and Documents in Libraries and Archives,* ANSI Z39.48-1992.

manent/durable paper on a machine that produces a thermoplastic image by heat and pressure fusing through electrostatic charges.[9] The photocopy machine must use an appropriate toner and be adjusted to be sure there is proper fusion of the toner to the paper, or the image will not be permanent. After photocopying, the text block then may be bound by a commercial library binder. It might cost $85 to create a black-and-white preservation photocopy of an average sized 300-page book, and colored materials might be photocopied for up to $3 per page.[10]

In the past decade a great deal of research and development has gone into the search for an effective, affordable mass deacidification process, but none has yet been widely accepted in the library and archival communities.[11] Deacidification will neutralize the acid in paper and stop it from becoming brittle but will not reverse deterioration that has already occurred. Even if mass deacidification were a well-proven and readily available technology, librarians and archivists have come to realize that it would still be too expensive to employ as a wholesale solution. There are not only the direct costs (now estimated in the range of $12 to $15 per volume) but also the indirect costs of selection, record keeping, and institutional effort. Early visions of mass deacidification as the "universal cure" have given way to increasingly cautious assessments and the realization that this treatment—like most others in librarianship and archival practice—will require careful decision making and selective application.[12] The older deacidification technique, appropriate for rare or unique materials with artifactual value, generally requires handling materials a leaf at a time and, thus, is considerably more time consuming and labor intensive than the mass treatments. Therefore, deacidification does not solve the problem of brittle paper, and it has limited cost effectiveness for the treatment of acidic paper that is not yet brittle.

The technology now on the horizon is digitization—scanning text and images for electronic storage, for generation of paper or film replacements, and for transmission across data networks. As discussed in the introduction, this technology offers many advantages for enhancing access to library and archival materials. However, the electronic record cannot yet be considered a preservation medium nor have storage and migration issues been addressed satisfactorily thus far. Meanwhile, the best approach appears to be a "hybrid system" in which the item is

---

9. Guidelines for preservation photocopying are provided in "Guidelines for Preservation Photocopying," *Library Resources & Technical Services* 38 (July 1994): 288–92; programmatic issues are addressed in Gay Walker, "Preserving the Intellectual Content of Deteriorated Library Materials," in *The Preservation Challenge: A Guide to Conserving Library Materials,* by Carolyn Clark Morrow (White Plains, N.Y.: Knowledge Industry, 1983), 103–5. For technical specifications, see Norvell M. M. Jones, *Archival Copies of Thermofax, Verifax, and Other Unstable Records,* Technical Information Paper No. 5 (Washington, D.C.: NARA, 1990).

10. These figures provided to the author by Craig Jensen, BookLab (Austin, Texas), Dec. 21, 1994. As with the cost of other treatments, it is important to keep in mind that these estimates are subject to many variables, including the size of the item, the volume of work being done, and so on.

11. As this book goes to press, new research and testing results are being released by the Library of Congress, and such developments merit continued monitoring.

12. See the discussions by library administrators and preservation librarians in Peter G. Sparks, ed., *A Roundtable on Mass Deacidification: Report on a Meeting Held September 12–13, 1991, in Andover, Massachusetts* (Washington, D.C.: ARL, 1992).

reformatted onto microfilm to provide a permanent or "archival" copy and the digitized version affords improved access.

This is not to say that treatment decisions are to be made on the basis of cost alone or that microfilming is always the best choice. Good preservation management entails a balancing of the condition of the item, its value, the nature and levels of use, and financial issues. For a common twentieth-century newspaper, filming may be chosen because it is both appropriate and the most economical option. A fragile manuscript collection might be treated by a conservator but also filmed to reduce handling of the item; depending on the nature of use, a paper copy of the filmed collection might be generated by preservation photocopying or scanning. A brittle volume with color illustrations that are integral to its use might be filmed, and color photocopies of the illustrations made.

Conservation, preservation photocopying, and deacidification will ensure that many documents and titles will remain available to future readers for a much longer time. These techniques have a great benefit for local users by keeping hard copies on library and archives shelves. Digitization offers greatly expanded access. But the institution that also employs preservation microfilming will be able to provide comparatively inexpensive, usable duplicates to many other institutions and users and, thereby, assist in alleviating the problem that affects institutions worldwide.

Microform Characteristics

Designing a preservation microfilming program requires a basic familiarity with the characteristics of the film medium, its strengths and limitations, so that appropriate decisions can be made. Chapter 4 provides an introduction to the topic and includes details that the preservation manager must understand.

Technical Features

Film stock is categorized according to its expected longevity. The life expectancy (LE) rating measures how many years the film will last when manufactured, processed, and stored in conditions defined by national standards. (See chapter 4.) When libraries or archives reformat their collections for preservation purposes, film with a life expectancy rating of 500 years must be used. Only silver-gelatin film currently offers that degree of longevity, but not all silver-gelatin films do. Therefore, film with an LE-500 rating must be used, and it must be processed and stored according to the standards for LE-500 film.

Silver-gelatin microfilm with a polyester base is the only type appropriate for preservation purposes. It can be more durable than most of the paper on which library materials are printed or written. If manufactured and processed properly, stored under "archival" conditions, and inspected regularly, the preservation master negative has a life expectancy rating of 500 years. If it begins to deteriorate for any reason, which can be caught early through regular inspection, the negative can be duplicated and, therefore, has an unlimited life span. For all practical purposes, once an item has been microfilmed in accordance with ANSI/AIIM standards, RLG guidelines, and specifications outlined in this manual, it can be considered preserved permanently.

The materials of preservation microfilming. *Preservation Resources.*

Panel 1: Acid-free boxes for microfilm reels and microfiche; 35mm roll film on silver-gelatin base, wound on inert plastic reel; button-and-string ties made of permanent materials; lint-free cotton gloves

Panel 2 (clockwise from lower left): Jacketed microfilm and alkaline storage enclosure; 8× loupe used in inspection; alkaline, lignin-free storage box; CD-ROMs for easy access to scanned microfilm; inert plastic reels

Panel 3: (bottom) 105mm microfiche sheet; (center, left to right) 100× stand microscope used for inspecting master negatives; 105mm microfiche film in roll form; 35mm roll film on inert reel in alkaline storage box; (top) 105mm microfiche in individual enclosures stored in alkaline box

Advances have been made in microfilming black-and-white halftone or continuous-tone images, and the results can be excellent. (See chapter 2.) Silver-gelatin film with LE-500 ratings is available for those applications, but the process is slow (exposure times of 17 seconds are not unusual) and expensive. At this point, no color film has an LE rating equivalent to the 500-year benchmark established by black-and-white silver-gelatin film. Color and, to a lesser extent, continuous-tone filming are still considered developmental. Costs and some operational issues have so far limited their application in preservation work.

Either roll film or microfiche may be used successfully for preservation microfilming. The 35-millimeter roll format is most widely accepted in library and archival applications, although there are also national standards for creating permanent 16mm roll film and 105mm microfiche. Chapter 4 describes and analyzes these. Most of the large-scale microfilming projects of the past decade have used 35mm roll film, and those have led to the development of detailed, widely accepted guidelines and specifications for that format.[13] Institutions have a great deal of experience with roll film, and its production is almost completely standardized. Little preservation-oriented guidance is available for production of 16mm film or fiche products.

---

13. The RLG specifications require 35mm silver-gelatin film on polyester base, as do the SOLINET projects. NEH currently requires 35mm stock for microfilming projects.

Preservation microfilming entails production of three generations of film:

Master negative—the film that is in the camera at the time of filming. It is duplicated once to make the printing master, and thereafter kept in "archival" storage as a permanent security copy.

Printing master—a duplicate made directly from the master negative. It, too, should be kept in archival storage. It is used to make all subsequent copies.

Service copy—positive or negative copies subsequently available for research and lending.

Chapter 4 summarizes the production and storage requirements.

User Reactions

No matter which format is chosen, microform is not a perfect replacement medium. It cannot reproduce the intellectual and historical information embedded in the physical characteristics of the volume: the watermark and chain lines, sewing techniques, binding materials, seals or other three-dimensional aspects of the work, or the printing impression.

Microforms are not as flexible and easily used as a book. Given a choice, users will choose hard copy over microform.[14] Patron complaints focus on damaged microforms, difficulties in finding misfiled microforms, quality and number of readers available, restriction of material to use in one location, inadequate reference service, and eye strain. Obviously, most of these complaints are related more to service than to inherent defects in the medium.

Studies confirm that libraries and archives can improve the situation by actions such as the following:

Replace damaged microforms.

Provide appropriate cataloging and indexing.[15]

Extend liberal copying privileges.

Offer well-maintained, readily available displaying and printing equipment.

Provide pleasant reading areas.

As one study concludes, "invariably the indispensable factors for user acceptance are well maintained equipment and knowledgeable, conscientious staff."[16] Educating users about the brittle paper problem will also help.

---

14. This and other observations on user reactions are summarized in Frederick C. Lynden, "Replacement of Hard Copy by Microforms," *Microform Review* 4 (Jan. 1975): 15–24. An excellent overview of use problems is provided in Joan M. Luke, "User Education for Microform Collections in Academic Libraries—A Literature Review," *Microform Review* 18 (winter 1989): 43–6.

15. A powerful argument on that point is made in Elizabeth L. Patterson, "Hidden Treasures: Bibliographic Control of Microforms, a Public Services Perspective," *Microform Review* 19 (spring 1990): 76–9.

16. Mike Gabriel and Mitchell Flesner, "Surprising Responses on the Issue of Convenience of Use: A User Survey of Microforms in One Academic Library," *Microform Review* 19 (spring 1990): 72.

Despite these drawbacks, microform is the most appropriate medium for many of the materials that must be preserved in libraries and archives. It is a long-lived, accepted technology, and its handling, cataloging, and storage are routine in most libraries and larger archives. For brittle paper, it may be the only option, since no technology exists to restore flexibility.

The Role of Microfilming within a Preservation Program

Even with their many positive qualities, microforms are not appropriate for all materials or in all cases. Microfilming is only one option and should be used in the context of a complete preservation program appropriate to the local collection.[17]

A well-balanced preservation program includes prospective and retrospective strategies, as well as administrative functions. Prospective preservation, or preventing the future deterioration of materials as much as possible, includes

environmental controls, including temperature, humidity, light levels, and air quality

shelf preparation for library materials

holdings maintenance for archives

appropriate shelving and storage systems

stack maintenance procedures

collection security

careful handling by staff and users

Binding incoming items that cannot withstand use in their original bindings and, perhaps, deacidification of acidic materials before they become brittle are also prospective strategies.

Despite our best efforts, collections may be damaged through use or because of their inherent instability. Retrospective preservation focuses on the remedial (often physical and/or chemical) treatment of worn or damaged materials. Techniques may include

repair and conservation

binding or rebinding

protective enclosures, including polyester encapsulation

---

17. For a description of a comprehensive library preservation program see Carolyn Clark Morrow, *The Preservation Challenge: A Guide to Conserving Library Materials;* for archival programs, see Mary Lynn Ritzenthaler, *Preserving Archives and Manuscripts* (Chicago: SAA, 1993). A good tool for development of preservation programs in libraries, and not just research libraries, is the *Preservation Planning Program* developed by ARL, including the *ARL Preservation Planning Program Manual* (Washington, D.C.: ARL, 1993) and seven resource guides (covering replacement and reformatting, collections conservation, commercial library binding, collections maintenance, disaster preparedness, staff training and user awareness, and organizational planning).

professional conservation for valuable and rare items

replacement of brittle materials by microfilm or other means[18]

See appendix C for a discussion of preservation treatment options.

Administrative functions such as the following ensure that preservation efforts are well managed and integrated with other relevant functions of the repository. These include

needs assessment

planning and evaluation

financial management and, perhaps, fund raising

advocacy

policy formulation

coordination of units that affect preservation

training and education for staff and users

disaster preparedness

Research and the monitoring of research and technological developments are also crucial, given the scientific and technical bases that affect preservation decisions and strategies.

The problem of brittle paper is a crisis of international proportions, and microfilming is often the best way to deal with it. However, librarians and archivists must exercise judgment about how much program emphasis they should give to microfilming and how much to other preservation strategies. For some institutions that do not have a concerted preservation program, receiving a grant for a microfilming project may provide the focus and enhanced institutional support from which to launch a more comprehensive program. It is important, though, not to become mired in that initial phase and rely on microfilming to meet all treatment needs. There will never be a single, universally effective, cheap solution for preservation and, if a panacea seemed to appear, we probably would eventually discover that it was wrong.[19] Microfilming has a significant role to play in a library or archival preservation program, but the collection will suffer if it is the only strategy that is employed consistently. Chapter 2 explains how to screen materials so that only appropriate ones are selected for filming.

Planning a Preservation Microfilming Program

Perhaps you are reading this manual because you believe you have a significant group of materials that warrant microfilming and your institution is committed to developing a systematic program to handle them. You may need a program that

---

18. Strategies for planning a replacement and reformatting program are outlined in Jennifer Banks, *Options for Replacing and Reformatting Deteriorated Materials* (Washington, D.C.: ARL, 1993).

19. Karen Motylewski and Mary Elizabeth Ruwell, "Preservation and Conservation: Complementary Needs for Libraries and Archives," in *Advances in Preservation and Access,* vol. 1, ed. Barbra Buckner Higginbotham and Mary E. Jackson (Westport, Conn.: Meckler, 1992), 213.

films materials identified by personnel at the circulation desk or in the archives or special collections reading room. You may undertake focused projects in certain areas of the collection. Or perhaps you recognize that an archival collection, serial run, student newspaper, or local history collection should be filmed. Whether you are planning an ongoing program or a special project, two issues are essential to a successful program:

> *Needs Assessment.* Do your collections need microfilming? Which ones? How many materials require attention? Should it be a local effort or done through a cooperative arrangement?

> *Planning.* Who will be responsible for planning and managing the program? How will it be organized? What portions of the work should be done in-house, and what, if any, should be contracted to service providers? What specifications and procedures will you use for the five broad operational areas: selection, preparation, filming and quality assurance, bibliographic control, and storage? What kinds of records and statistics must be maintained? What will it cost, and how will you fund the work?

This manual provides the information needed to design either an ongoing program or a special project. Although the materials in libraries and archival repositories may be different and the size of the project will suggest certain options, the organizational considerations are much the same for all institutions.

Implementing a preservation microfilming program is not a decision to be made lightly. Micrographics is a technical photographic field, and the prefilming and postfilming processes are complex. Your program should be based on the needs and goals of the collection. The decision to implement a program should not be made in isolation, without knowledge of preservation microfilming projects, priorities, and procedures of other libraries and archives.

Planning Strategies

Each institution will have its own mechanisms to coordinate the planning of a program. Particularly if you lack sufficient expertise in microfilming, it might be useful to retain a consultant who can both provide technical guidance and help you work through the programmatic decisions that must be made. Carefully evaluate potential consultants to be sure they are familiar with the special requirements of preservation microfilming in institutions like yours. While the micrographics industry has many consultants who focus on microfilming for records management purposes, only a few people possess expertise in designing programs to produce preservation microfilm. A good consultant will do much not only to improve the efficiency of your planning but also to help build consensus and support within the organization.

If you have some expertise in-house, you may conduct the planning internally.[20] You might find it useful to bring together staff members from across the institution for education and training, to present the issues and problems and

---

20. The *ARL Preservation Planning Program Manual* and Banks's *Options for Replacing and Formatting Deteriorated Materials* outline a sound methodology for this planning.

reach consensus. Program design elements will include establishing criteria and guidelines for all aspects of the filming operation, assigning workflow and developing forms, and writing position descriptions. While the director, preservation officer, or project manager may develop these elements, the wider group must consider the implications for each function. By involving all interested parties in the planning process, you will build an effective institutional commitment to the program. Of course, you may wish to use one or more consultants to augment your in-house resources for portions of the planning.

A much less elaborate planning strategy is appropriate for small or one-time projects. The project manager may study this manual and other key resources and consult with filming agents and others as needed to plan and implement the project.

Staff Involvement

Integrating the elements of a preservation microfilming program into the other functions of the institution is critical to its success.[21] Representatives of all units involved with these functions must participate in the planning process. They must understand the need for preservation microfilming and be prepared to meet the increased demands that will be generated to process and service materials.

The materials generally will be identified first at the collection level, then the staff will make item-level selection decisions. Circulation staff may identify brittle materials as they are returned to the library. Reference archivists may identify them as they are used in the reading room or as part of an inventory or survey. Public services staff may also identify materials in need of treatment. The collection development officers, bibliographers, and curators should be responsible for deciding what is to be filmed. They must both understand the subject of the materials and be able to determine the materials' physical condition with the help of the preservation administrator. Lacking a preservation specialist on staff, they must understand and follow specific criteria and guidelines.

Other staff members may be involved in bibliographic and archival control. Preparation and processing staff may be responsible for indexing archival collections to be filmed. The cataloging staff will provide local and extended (national and international) bibliographic access to the collection.

If you are going to use a reprographic laboratory or photographic services department within your institution, the lab should integrate preservation microfilming into its other functions. The reprographic laboratory may already microfilm items on demand for offsite users, as well as prepare photocopies and photographs. While these operations are functionally similar in many ways to preservation microfilming, there are also profound differences. They range from the technical differences, related to the strictness of the standards and specifications that apply to preservation microfilming, to attitudinal ones such as the different ways of handling fragile materials versus modern business records that may have formed the bulk of the lab's work in the past.

---

21. For a summary of affected areas in library filming programs, see Nancy E. Elkington and Sandra Nyberg, "Operational Impact of Filming Projects on Library Units," in *RLG Preservation Microfilming Handbook,* ed. Elkington, 65–6.

Managing the Preservation Microfilming Program

The administrative principles for a successful preservation microfilming program are as follows:

1. Materials important to scholarship are selected for preservation by staff members with appropriate judgment.
2. Microfilming is found to be the proper preservation technique for those materials.
3. The materials have not already been preserved and made available elsewhere.
4. The materials are properly prepared for filming, properly identified on the film, and as complete as possible.
5. The filming, processing, and duplication meet appropriate standards and specifications.
6. A quality assurance program is in place to verify the film's completeness, legibility, and compliance with standards and specifications for chemical and technical quality.
7. The preservation master negative and printing master are stored with appropriate reels and containers under proper security and environmental conditions.
8. Access to the bibliographic record and physical access to the film itself is provided to the scholarly community and other constituencies.

Organization and management of an ongoing preservation microfilming program present challenges that are typical of matrix management, and one-time initiatives require standard project-management approaches.[22] Success requires coordination of many complex functions.

Before looking at the distinct elements of the program, consider its overall management. A professional staff member (librarian, archivist, or curator) should generally manage the program. However, in some colleges or small repositories paraprofessionals who routinely manage some operations may serve this function for the filming program as well. The staff member should be familiar with preservation techniques, micrographics technology, and library or archival procedures and demonstrate good managerial skills. If you intend to have an ongoing program, a trained preservation administrator should plan and implement it. If that is not possible, or if you envision this as a one-time project or small-scale program, an internal staff member can take on the responsibility. Past success in project management, a willingness to learn, a flexible attitude, and an ability to understand and work with all levels of staff and all functions within the institution are characteristics required of the successful project manager.

Regardless of who is responsible, that staff member will have to manage two functionally distinct elements of the preservation microfilming process: the tech-

---

22. For guidelines on project management, see Joan Knutson and Ira Bitz, *Project Management: How to Plan and Manage Successful Projects* (New York: American Management Association, 1991); J. Davidson Frame, *Managing Projects in Organizations* (San Francisco: Jossey-Bass, 1991); and Paul C. Dinsmore, *Human Factors in Project Management,* rev. ed. (New York: American Management Association, 1990).

nical micrographic elements and the more typical library and archival functions. The latter dominate in the pre- and postfilming phases, involving coordination of functions, materials preparation, and bibliographic control. The former include the camera work, developing and duplicating the film, and quality control. The project manager may be the person who bridges the worlds, and the different languages, of technical micrographics specialists and library and archival staff members.

Any program that includes an in-house microfilming laboratory should hire a technically trained person to supervise it. This person should be familiar with microfilming and photographic techniques and have both mechanical abilities and supervisory skills. Even if the program consists of only one camera and camera operator, the operator should be able to understand photographic processes and make minor repairs to the camera and other equipment. Experienced laboratory managers willing to work for nonprofessional salaries are scarce. A photographer with a solid technical foundation and the ability and willingness to learn might be a good choice if an experienced manager is not available. The laboratory manager should understand and implement the standards and specifications for preservation filming and understand the need for the highest quality product. Personnel from commercial microfilm labs may be available and competent to do the job, but often they will have to be trained in what it takes to film documents according to specifications for permanence. In many cases it may be simpler to train a person who has no experience than to correct the practices or attitudes of someone who has worked in a microfilming bureau that does not follow the standards and practices appropriate for preservation microfilming.[23]

The pre- and postfilming aspects of the process should be coordinated by a librarian or archivist familiar with preservation techniques and issues as well as with bibliographic or archival control. This person should have supervisory skills because much of the routine work can be done by support staff, student assistants, or volunteers. The work of a preservation microfilming program ranges from the routine of collating materials and pushing the camera button to the highly sophisticated coordination of several departmental functions and the development and monitoring of external contracts.

Issues of organizational structure must be addressed when planning an ongoing program. In large research libraries the preservation microfilming activities are often carried out within the preservation department. In this model, cataloging may or may not be performed in the preservation department. If there is to be a central unit for your preservation microfilming program, what functions will be centralized there, and which detailed to other operational units?

It is typical to centralize the following functions within the preservation microfilming unit:

development of contracts and specifications

liaison with filming staff (internal or contracted), storage facilities, and
    other service providers

---

23. Margaret Byrnes, "Issues and Criteria for Comparing In-House and Contracted Microfilming," in *Preservation Microfilming: Planning and Production* (Chicago: ALA/ALCTS, 1989), 33.

An in-house microfilming operation requires space for camera operations, inspection, and various film-handling processes. *Charles Stewart.*

coordination with bibliographers, catalogers, acquisitions staff, and others responsible for functions not handled within the filming unit

retrieval of items from the stacks

replacement searching

preparation

quality assurance

Each institution must determine whether to centralize other functions or establish links between the filming unit and the units responsible for these functions:

updating circulation records and local finding aids

advance cataloging (or "queuing")

bibliographic control

In some cases, for example, catalog librarians have been placed within the preservation microfilming unit to handle bibliographic control activities so that microforms do not compete with current acquisitions for cataloging priority. If a decentralized approach is used, it is important to establish effective linkages and methods for coordinating workflow, as well as clear understanding of expectations and priorities.

Determining Needs and Setting Priorities

Chapter 2 addresses key operational issues in preservation selection. The institutional administrator, usually with key management staff, must address selection at a more global level. If there is to be a microfilming program, what should be its focus?

The needs assessment phase may begin with an analytical statement of the perceived problem. Sometimes it is stimulated by a hunch—informed, of course, by familiarity with the collection and by professional judgment. Staff members who have become educated about preservation issues may become aware that there seem to be many brittle or badly damaged items in the collection for which no replacements are available. In the 1970s and 1980s many libraries had this experience as staff members handled items during recataloging and reclassification projects.

Begin the needs assessment by looking at the collection. Include consideration of

Condition. How many materials are brittle? For how many is preservation microfilming an appropriate treatment? In what areas of the collection are the needs greatest? It is a good idea to "size" the problem. Data from a condition survey can determine the quantity of materials that require microfilming and can pinpoint the segments of the collection in which the need is greatest. In a more detailed survey, you can also ascertain the current availability of replacements for deteriorated items. Survey strategies are discussed in chapter 2.

Importance. Which areas of the collection are of sufficient value (by whatever measure) to warrant preservation?

Use. What is their actual or anticipated use? Many institutions are coming to the conclusion that, all other factors being equal, materials being used today should receive highest priority because use poses the risk of loss and damage to vulnerable materials.

Analyze the needs assessment results in light of the institutional preservation policy (if there is one) or the acquisitions or collection development policies. Preservation microfilming, while it is one of the most cost-effective options available, is sufficiently expensive and arduous that it generally should be reserved for collections that are of great, long-term value.

Based on the needs of the collection, determine the priorities and working principles for your filming program. There are two basic approaches:

Use-driven approach. Materials are identified for filming through use. In a library, this may mean that all items returned from circulation are screened, and brittle ones are routed to the preservation microfilming work stream. In archives, research use may trigger identification of series, record groups, or whole collections for attention.

Systematic subject- or collection-based approach. The needs and value in one subject area may be sufficiently great to merit a focused project to reformat those materials, or you may choose to film a special collection to expand access and provide surrogates for use.

Of course, there is no inherent conflict between these two approaches. In many cases, there is significant overlap between an institution's strongest collections and the ones that receive heavy use.

Other factors require consideration as you work to determine the program focus:

Local priorities. The program can focus on the collections that have greatest value to the institution and its users regardless of their national or international research significance. A student newspaper, the manuscripts of a local but otherwise unheralded author, clipping files, or undergraduate theses might fall into this category.

National priorities. Many library programs are shaped in response to the nationwide Brittle Books Program, which will generally mean a focus on published materials in strong humanities collections. Several scholarly groups have defined their preservation priorities (see chapter 2, footnote 4). If your collections are in subject areas for which some national statement of priorities exists, the filming program might be designed to accommodate those stated needs.

Funding potential. You may choose to focus on the collection areas that have the greatest funding potential. In some cases, that may mean heeding the priorities of the parent institution or local donors. In others, it leads to investigation of governmental granting agencies such as NEH, NHPRC, or state-based programs. Each of these agencies has its own criteria for eligible materials, and those criteria will have to shape institutional selection decisions. This approach offers the obvious advantage that funding may be available. Problems can arise, though, if the staff perceive that institutional effort is being focused on a collection area that is not a high priority for the user constituency.

In a carefully developed collection, there is likely to be a significant convergence among those factors: collections of national stature are built as they receive local priority for acquisitions funding, generally because they support the institutional mission.

This level of global decision making will have a significant impact on the shape of the program and the funding strategies that may be employed. You can then determine the level of program that is appropriate to reach the preservation goals.[24] Some benchmarks have been established for members of the Association of Research Libraries. A study project conducted by ARL defined four levels of program development. Recommended reformatting activity (defined to include both microfilming and preservation photocopying) levels for ARL libraries are summarized in figure 2.

---

24. The Columbia University Libraries cost model, cited in chapter 6, provides one way of determining the level of program that is required to reach specific production goals.

FIGURE 2   ARL Reformatting Program Benchmarks

Level 1: Libraries with no systematic preservation program
Level 2: Those without a preservation department/unit but managed part-time by a professional
librarian
Level 3: Libraries with a formal preservation unit managed by a preservation librarian
Level 4: Mature preservation programs

Program Level	Size of Library Collection (Number of Volumes)			
	Less than 2 million	2–3 million	3–5 million	More than 5 million
1	<50	<100	<500	<1,000
2	50–300	100–500	500–1,000	1,000–3,000
3	300–800	500–1,500	1,000–3,000	3,000–6,000
4	>800	>1,500	>3,000	>6,000

SOURCE: Based on Jan Merrill-Oldham, Carolyn Clark Morrow, and Mark Roosa. *Preservation Program Models: A Study Project and Report.* Washington, D.C.: ARL, 1991.

The National Context

Before launching an ongoing program or a one-time project, you must become informed about preservation microfilming work in other institutions and organizations. For example, the National Library of Medicine's massive filming initiative in health sciences serials will have an impact on local plans, and the same may be true of the national program for the preservation of agricultural literature.

Because so much work has been done through the cooperative programs described in the introduction, you might begin by assessing what filming has been done in major subject areas. Especially if you are developing a grant proposal to film materials within a specific subject area, an analysis of preservation microfilming projects—broad subject areas and collections that have been or are being filmed or in which projects are being planned—is necessary to prevent duplicate work. For example, grant reviewers would look askance at an application that proposed to film theology materials but showed no awareness of the large-scale projects of ATLA, and newspapers should generally be filmed in the context of the U.S. Newspaper Program.

How can planners get more information on these and other projects that will begin in coming years? This is not an easy task; the information is not available in one convenient place. Federal agencies have played a critical role in funding preservation microfilming projects, so their press releases will inform you of collections that have been filmed and suggest areas that have been well covered.[25] Library and micrographics journals carry news items on grants awarded and new

---

25. The National Endowment for the Humanities has developed an electronic information resource; contact NEH at the address in appendix B.

projects, and early announcements of funded projects may be made at conferences such as those of the American Library Association and the Society of American Archivists. Faculty and scholars in a specific subject field may know of projects completed or under way. As in so many other areas, your ability to "connect to the grapevine" will help you learn of projects still in the planning stages.

Suppose that you have only a few volumes that warrant microfilming, or that paper or film replacements are available for most of the deteriorated volumes or documents in your collection, or you discover major preservation projects are already under way in the subject field in which you planned to work. You might work with other institutions to develop a small-scale cooperative project to address common needs. Or your institution could contribute its materials to another project and simply purchase film copies as needed, rather than go to the expense of setting up a local microfilming program.[26]

For example, many libraries have collections of nineteenth-century American language and literature, much of which may be brittle. Because this is a subject that has received a significant amount of attention, an examination would reveal that most of the major titles have been reprinted, are available from commercial micropublishers, or have been filmed by institutions participating in large-scale cooperative preservation microfilming projects such as those of RLG, CIC, or the Southeastern Library Network, Inc. (SOLINET). Filming the same titles covered by these sources is a duplication of effort if good microform copies can be borrowed or purchased.

However, even within such subject areas there is room to film additional titles. This was the experience of the College of William and Mary when the library wished to participate in the first SOLINET cooperative filming project and identified its pre–Civil War materials as the priority for filming. Preliminary searching revealed that 80 percent of the materials had already been filmed, but 400 volumes with local or regional focus were nonetheless identified for filming.[27] The materials thus preserved have added depth and richness to the aggregate resources available nationwide.

It is not uncommon to search and find hit rates as high as 40 percent and still decide to work in the same subject area. In a large collection, that still leaves a great many titles to film, although the costs of searching and identifying titles for the project should be carefully considered.

Cooperative Preservation Microfilming Projects

Once you verify that you need a microfilming program and begin to define the size and focus of your efforts, consider whether involvement in a cooperative microfilming project might help you achieve your goals. Cooperative preserva-

---

26. An explicit goal of the national plan for preserving agricultural literature is for institutions to channel their efforts toward a coordinated plan. See Nancy E. Gwinn, "A National Preservation Program for Agricultural Literature" (United States Agricultural Information Network, Beltsville, Md., May 16, 1993, photocopy).

27. Sandra K. Nyberg (SOLINET), electronic mail correspondence with the author, Dec. 19, 1994.

tion microfilming projects offer many attractive advantages, including the opportunity to increase productivity and share the national and international cost of reformatting brittle materials.

Fortunately for libraries, the majority of brittle materials do not represent unique holdings. A significant overlap among North American collections, coupled with the availability of shared online databases such as OCLC and RLIN, makes it possible for institutions to coordinate their large-scale preservation microfilming efforts to share the responsibility and make the best use of available preservation resources. While it might cost $90 to $100 or more to select, prepare, produce, inspect, and catalog the three microform generations of a typical 250-page book, it could cost only $20 to $30 to produce a service copy for a user or another institution. The cost savings provide a strong incentive to avoid unnecessary duplicative filming efforts.

Archival repositories handle unique materials for the most part, so they do not have the same opportunities to rely on other institutions to film materials that they themselves also own. The cost avoidance enjoyed by cooperating libraries cannot be used as an argument to support the microfilming of unique materials. Nevertheless, RLG's Archives Preservation Microfilming Project suggests there are institutional benefits to pooling efforts in a cooperative project, in addition to the increased access to and protection of the originals that microfilming accomplishes.

With so many materials in need of microfilming, and available expertise in relatively short supply, libraries and archives have relied heavily on cooperative strategies and structures to build local preservation microfilming programs. Cooperative preservation microfilming has steadily extended beyond the ex post facto sharing of bibliographic data to encompass the use of common procedures, specifications, and even facilities for preparation, filming, and, in some cases, a coordinated approach to the selection of items to be filmed.[28]

Participation in cooperative programs requires two levels of planning:

> *Institutional.* Each institution must assess its own needs and requirements and develop many of its own work plans, as outlined in this manual.

> *Consortial.* The cooperative participants must decide how the program will be administered, what specifications will be followed, how it will be funded, and which institutions will film which materials.

Often the last question—what is to be filmed by whom—serves as the stimulus for the cooperative program in the first place. Institutions may decide to cooperate because each has significant holdings in one subject or in different subjects within a geographic area or network.

---

28. See descriptions and analyses of major cooperative projects in the introduction and in Margaret Child, "The Future of Cooperative Preservation Microfilming," *Library Resources & Technical Services* 29 (Jan./Mar. 1985): 94–101; Nancy E. Gwinn, "The Rise and Fall and Rise of Cooperative Projects," *Library Resources & Technical Services* 29 (Jan./Mar. 1985): 80–6; Carolyn Harris, "Cooperative Approaches to Preservation Microfilming," in *Preservation Microfilming: Planning and Production*, 55–65; and Patricia A. McClung, "Consortial Action: RLG's Preservation Program," in *Advances in Preservation and Access,* eds. Higginbotham and Jackson, vol. 1, 61–70.

Institutional Assessment

Over the past decade, regional and national organizations—especially RLG, CIC, and SOLINET—have developed and managed cooperative filming projects to benefit dozens of institutions. Typically, the consortium invites member institutions to nominate themselves as potential participants in a new project. Whether you have received such an invitation or are considering organizing your own project, how will you decide whether to commit your institution to a cooperative filming project?[29]

The following factors would argue for involvement in a cooperative project:

Collection needs. You have materials that warrant and are suitable for filming.

Access. By shaping a cooperative project around titles you need to acquire, you can enhance your local resources. An example of this was the RLG Art Serials Preservation Project (from 1990 to 1994), in which twelve RLG members filmed 100 complete runs of important art journals of which none of the libraries had complete holdings.

Shared expertise. Work plans, procedures, and project specifications are developed collectively, which may mean less institutional time has to be devoted to them. Even if there are no time savings, there may be significant quality improvement because you have access to the expertise of other, sometimes more experienced, preservation project managers.

Funding opportunities. Cooperative projects are attractive to funding agencies.[30] Also, your chances of securing subsequent grants for local projects may be improved after participating successfully in a cooperative project.

Central grant writing and financial management staff. In most cases, the sponsoring organization will assume the bulk of responsibility for preparing the grant proposal, although you should expect to provide collection profiles, local budget data, job descriptions and résumés, and so on. Central money management may be especially attractive if you are in a smaller institution or one that lacks experience in the specialized area of grants accounting.

Cost efficiency. Funding may be used more efficiently in a cooperative project, and participants may receive volume discounts (for filming, storage, etc.) that would not be available to one institution.

Education and training. Some cooperative projects include structured training programs. Others include meetings at which project managers share important information and strategies. At a minimum, your staff will learn a great deal from interacting with the central staff and other participants.

---

29. I am heavily indebted to Carolyn Harris, "Cooperative Approaches to Preservation Microfilming," for the cogent categorization of issues to be addressed at the institutional and consortial levels.

30. Harris, "Cooperative Approaches to Preservation Microfilming," 56.

National strategies and practices. Project specifications may also help develop a national consensus on strategies and recommended practices, as did the early RLG projects.[31]

Cachet. Your institution may reap some intangible benefit by participating in one of the cooperative filming projects that has a strong reputation. Participation may enhance your standing within the local institution as well as among peer institutions and funding agencies.

Some cautionary factors must also be considered. For example, does the institution have the necessary resources to devote to a cooperative project? Will the relationships be mutually beneficial?

Especially if you are planning your first microfilming initiative, you should give strong consideration to doing so through a cooperative project. Cooperative projects can provide the structures and guidance that enable small institutions with little or no preservation expertise to participate. This has been especially true of the SOLINET projects that—in contrast to those of CIC and RLG—have involved many nonresearch institutions. But major libraries and archives, including those with mature preservation programs and extensive filming experience, also benefit from cooperative efforts, as a list of RLG project participants shows.[32]

Planning a Cooperative Project

In many cases, the project participants work together to develop the plans for a cooperative filming effort, but some elements may be prescribed by the sponsoring organization. The key issues to consider in a cooperative project relate to project management, planning and governance, participant responsibility and accountability, technical standards and specifications, selection of materials, and funding and financial management.

Project Management

Is there a central staff to handle project management? Or will one of the participating institutions assume project management responsibilities, as in the CIC projects? The former is possible if the project is conducted under the aegis of an existing network or consortium that has preservation expertise on staff. In other consortia and ad hoc arrangements, one of the participating institutions generally provides project coordination.

---

31. As noted in McClung, "Consortial Action," in *Advances in Preservation and Access,* eds. Higginbotham and Jackson (p. 65), the first RLG Cooperative Preservation Microfilming Project managers "literally and figuratively 'wrote the book' " on preservation microfilming. "The book" was the *RLG Preservation Manual,* 1st ed. (Stanford, Calif.: RLG, 1983), superseded by the second edition in 1986, and significantly expanded in the 1992 *RLG Preservation Microfilming Handbook,* which is now used as a de facto national standard by most libraries engaged in major filming projects.

32. A summary of RLG cooperative projects from 1983 to 1992 (including lists of participants in each) is provided in Patricia McClung, "RLG Preservation Microfilming Projects: A History," in *RLG Preservation Microfilming Handbook,* ed. Elkington, 183–5.

Does the sponsoring or lead organization have the staff, expertise, and other qualifications to coordinate the project? Is there a track record of successful project management?

Planning and Governance

Which elements of the project will be centralized and which decentralized? In the SOLINET projects, selection is decentralized (within project parameters), as is distribution of service copies. Preparation, filming, inspection, storage of master negatives, and bibliographic control are centralized. The RLG projects have generally used a decentralized approach (except for storage of master negatives), but all participants must conform to strict technical specifications. CIC projects are based on the RLG model. The American Philological Association centralized most elements, including funding, selection, and filming, so the key responsibility of participants was to provide materials that had been preselected for filming.

Who will participate? RLG, CIC, and SOLINET typically issue a request for proposals inviting members to participate, and the local institution has the burden of arguing the merits of its collection, qualifications of its staff, and soundness of its overall work plan. If this model is used, explicit written criteria for selecting participants should be developed in advance. Self-selection is another option; representatives of one institution may invite others to participate in a cooperative project. This is especially appropriate for repositories within a locale (for example, three Georgia institutions working together to film Georgiana) or with complementary collections (such as a geographically dispersed group of institutions coordinating the filming of their strong Southeast Asian collections).

Who will own the master negatives and printing masters? Both RLG and SOLINET retain ownership and the concomitant responsibility for storage of master negatives in perpetuity, but participants retain ownership of the printing masters, authority over duplication, and responsibility for fulfilling copy requests.

Participant Responsibility

What must participants do? How will the consortium make sure they do it? What will happen if participants cannot meet their obligations on schedule or at all? Responsibilities need to be outlined for all elements of selection, preparation, filming and quality assurance, bibliographic control, and storage.

Technical Standards and Specifications

What technical standards will be followed? Relevant national standards should be used, but they probably should be augmented by RLG guidelines and others listed in appendix A.

What film format (for example, 35mm roll film or 105mm microfiche) will be used? Will all participants use the same format for the master negative? For printing masters? For service copies?

What uniform project specifications will apply to selection, preparation, film production and inspection, bibliographic control, and storage? In what areas will local variance be allowed?

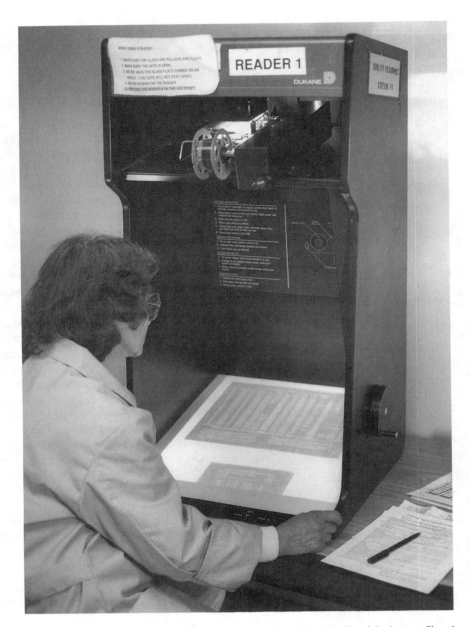

Staff must inspect each frame of film to ensure the bibliographic integrity of the item as filmed and note any irregularities on an inspection form. In addition to the inspection by the filming agent, the institution or its designee must provide a second inspection for quality assurance. *Preservation Resources.*

Selection of Materials

The group must decide what materials will be included in the project. If it is a subject-based project, what subjects will be included? Will only certain formats be included? The scope may be refined by other criteria such as genre, language, and imprint date or place. The interests of the funding source may dictate certain selection criteria. Can you justify your selections based on Conspectus values or other quantitative measures of collection strength?

Funding and Financial Management

The project may be funded by the participants, subscribers who want copies of the film products, a federal funding source such as NEH or NHPRC, a state-based grant program like New York's, some other source, or a combination of these. If the group decides to seek third-party funding, someone must assume responsibility for preparing the grant proposal.

Will some funding be allocated to participants to support local costs (as in the RLG and CIC projects) or used to defray the cost of centralized functions (as in the SOLINET projects)?

What financial records must participants maintain or submit to the managing organization? If participants are to be reimbursed, will this be on a per-unit basis or for specific direct costs such as personnel, supplies, and filming costs? State and federal funding agencies often have extensive regulations affecting project record-keeping functions, and participants must be prepared to adhere to those requirements.

Developing a cooperative project requires planning that is complex. If the group lacks in-depth filming expertise, a consultant may help define the issues, offer alternatives and evaluate the options, and facilitate the whole process. Those who have planned and sponsored cooperative projects may be willing to share white papers and other documentation as well as answer questions. If you are developing a grant proposal, the funding agency may be able to provide guidance, share copies of successful applications, and review draft proposals. Take advantage of these resources to avoid unnecessary mistakes or dead ends.

Contracting for Services

A crucial decision to be made early in the planning process is which operations to do in-house and which to do under contract with an external service provider. The most frequent use of contracts within a preservation microfilming program is for the filming process itself. But depending on the circumstances of the project and the nature of the materials you are filming, service bureaus can be used for any or all of the following:

preparing materials for filming

filming

film processing

film inspection

testing the film for residual chemicals

duplication of film to produce additional generations or copies

bibliographic control

storage of master negatives and/or printing masters

Appendix B lists some of the leading service providers, as well as organizations that can provide referrals to other reputable sources. Some of these are commercial firms, some are nonprofit organizations devoted primarily to preservation, and others are bibliographic networks, associations, and consortia.

There are four basic kinds of service providers:

Specialized companies provide a limited service array such as filming or storage. NEDCC, which offers film production and duplication, and National Underground Storage, Inc., which offers film storage and duplication, are examples of this type.

"Full service" organizations provide preparation, filming and duplication, and bibliographic control. Preservation Resources and others (listed in appendix B) currently provide this wide array of services.

Cooperative nonprofit organizations, such as CIC or SOLINET, provide some centralized services, such as preparation, quality assurance, and bibliographic control, and subcontract others, such as filming, duplication, and storage.

Some institutions or agencies, such as universities or state archives, do some filming and processing for other organizations.

Libraries and archives today rely on the availability of these services and benefit directly from competition among providers.

Access to these services is a tremendous boon to institutions that lack personnel, space, or other resources to do the work in-house. However, in no sense should this be viewed as a simple matter. Regardless of how many functions are contracted out, the library or archives staff bears ultimate responsibility for ensuring the quality of the work. The repository staff must become knowledgeable about standards and specifications, carry out quality assurance operations (or see that they are done by an independent third party), and exercise responsible oversight.

To determine which, if any, contract services are appropriate, the administrator must weigh the relative costs, assess the qualitative factors, and determine what division of labor is reasonable in light of institutional resources and workflow. Institutions with internal filming capabilities still might choose to supplement that activity by contracting some filming. Many research libraries with in-house filming operations now contract for routine filming of brittle materials, and reserve the internal staff for filming particularly valuable items or fragile ones that require especially careful handling.[33]

Weighing In-House and Contract Costs

It is difficult to compare the costs of in-house microfilming operations with those of a contracted filming agent. Most cost studies by universities and other nonprofit repositories (cited in chapter 6) do not include overhead costs, while ser-

33. This approach is well articulated in Margaret Byrnes, "Issues and Criteria for Comparing In-House and Contracted Microfilming," in *Preservation Microfilming: Planning and Production,* 40–1.

vice bureaus must take all overhead costs into account and build in a profit margin when bidding a job. Too often, this leads to "apple and orange" comparisons, with the library or archives comparing only its direct costs with the contractor's prices. Instead, use the worksheet in appendix F to calculate in-house costs for each element, then add indirect costs and administrative overhead. Use the resulting cost estimates for comparison with filming agents' prices.

Data from the RLG Cooperative Preservation Microfilming Project cost study in 1984–1985 illustrate the importance of comparing parallel costs. Of seven institutions in the study, five conducted their filming internally. Per-frame costs for those operations (to produce three generations of film and conduct the technical inspection) ranged from 17¢ to 26¢ per frame. When the institution on the low end (at 17¢ per frame) was able to calculate its costs so as to include such overhead items as utilities and equipment amortization (although the cost of the space was still not included), that figure rose to 28¢ per frame. By comparison, the filming agents used by other libraries in the project were charging 33¢ and 34¢ per frame for the same product. Those figures are too old to be applied directly today, but the difference between them—or, more to the point, the lack of significant difference when using the same basis of calculation—is illustrative.

It is not possible to state categorically that contract filming is either cheaper or more expensive than doing the work in-house. However, it seems safe to suggest that even taking into account the profit margin built into the contractor's prices, the costs of contract and in-house filming can be quite comparable, especially when institutional equipment, management, and overhead costs are included.[34]

Be cautious and somewhat skeptical when you are evaluating contract services. The standards for truly *preservation*-quality microfilming work are high and exacting. While many companies may claim to provide filming, processing, storage, or other services that meet your needs, in fact the community of qualified service providers is quite small. Contact those who are known to be reliable. If others quote prices that are dramatically lower, this may be a signal that the work will not meet the accepted standards for preservation-quality work. If some prices seem too good to be true, they probably are.

The administrator may have to work assiduously with institutional purchasing or procurement personnel, especially in request-for-proposal or competitive-bidding processes, to be sure they understand that selection based solely on low bid is inappropriate. Use the criteria outlined in chapter 3 to evaluate potential contractors, then consider prices as you select among the qualified service providers.

Qualitative Factors

Of course, costs are not the only criteria for comparing effectiveness of in-house and external operations. Several qualitative factors are especially significant in determining whether to contract for filming or do it in-house:[35]

---

34. Byrnes, "Issues and Criteria for Comparing In-House and Contracted Microfilming," in *Preservation Microfilming: Planning and Production,* 39.

35. These factors are drawn from Byrnes, "Issues and Criteria for Comparing In-House and Contracted Microfilming," in *Preservation Microfilming: Planning and Production,* 32–42.

Personnel. A qualified filming agent will probably have staff with expertise equal to or greater than an in-house operation. Contracting for service relieves you of the burden of developing position descriptions and classifications, recruiting, hiring, training, and supervising. In addition to the direct labor costs of employing people with the necessary skills and expertise and of retaining them even when you have no work in the filming queue, consider the less-tangible supervisory costs associated with staffing.

Space. For most institutions the cost of remodeling space to accommodate a filming lab would be quite high. Plumbing capacities may need to be increased, and water filtration and temperature controls are required for processing equipment. The electrical systems may need to be upgraded, including the capacity to control light intensity, direction, and fluctuations. Compliance with health and safety regulations may require further outlays.

Equipment. Basic equipment for filming and processing requires a major capital investment plus ongoing maintenance and supply costs. Even if the institution can afford the initial costs, few seem to be able to purchase upgrades as often as may be necessary. By contrast, some service bureaus have more capital for investment in new equipment and upgrades, and their equipment is likely to be designed for larger scale production that is generally more cost effective.

Film quality. Reputable, preservation-oriented filming agents can produce microfilm that is as good as that from an in-house operation, and they may have equipment with optics and other features that may make superior quality possible. On the other hand, if you are not fully satisfied that the filming agent can match the quality you can achieve in-house, then none of the other advantages can outweigh this disadvantage.

Flexibility. It may be easier to modify procedures and specifications in an in-house facility than with a service bureau, but the contract with the agent can be carefully designed to allow you to make reasonable modifications.

Capacity. In most cases, a service bureau can accommodate more work than an institutional program. In fact, if project deadlines are tight, the filming agent may be able more easily to shift existing employees or hire new workers on a short-term basis. A service bureau may be able to achieve economies of scale that are not possible in a smaller institutional setting.

Management time and administrative problems. In the initial period of working with a new filming agent, significant management time will be required. However, this is probably no greater than would be required in the start-up of an in-house project. But as one preservation manager, after long experience with in-house and contracted filming, observes: "Over the long haul, filming by contract, compared to administering an in-house facility, will require significantly less management time."[36]

---

36. Byrnes, "Issues and Criteria for Comparing In-House and Contracted Microfilming," in *Preservation Microfilming: Planning and Production,* 40.

Given sufficient funds, space, and technical expertise, virtually any organization, regardless of size, can set up an internal laboratory for preservation microfilming. That does not mean it should. In fact, with the organizations that presently specialize in preservation microfilming, few institutions now would establish a new in-house filming lab.

By most measures, contract filming services can compare favorably with in-house ones. However, this is not an "either/or" choice. After weighing all the issues, you may choose to film in-house, through external service providers, or through a combination of the two. You must consider the goals of the program as well as the institution's expertise and other resources. As noted previously, the institution remains responsible for the quality of the film products regardless of which option is chosen.

To Contract for Other Services . . . or Not?

A similar analysis of cost and qualitative factors should inform your assessment of other options you might contract. The chief caveat in this discussion is the issue of the service provider's qualifications. These must be evaluated carefully, and chapter 3 outlines strategies for doing so. Some elements of the program generally should be contracted out, some almost never can be, and most will require a judgment on a case-by-case basis.

Selection

The institution should retain responsibility for selecting materials to be filmed, because selection is based on intellectual content and use considerations as well as physical characteristics of the candidate volumes.[37]

Preparation

It may be appropriate to contract preparation work for library materials, but seldom for archival collections. Preparation of archival collections is likely to require familiarity with the materials and professional judgment that are only available within the repository. Especially if the collection requires significant organization or indexing prior to filming, the work generally must be done in-house.

By contrast, preparation of books, newspapers, and straightforward library materials can often be done effectively and as economically by a service bureau as by library staff. Some of the leading filming agents now provide this service.

The difficulty of estimating preparation time and costs may argue for using contract services. Chapter 6 addresses the wide range of times that preparation may require. Especially if this is your first filming project and, therefore, you lack historical expense data, using a service bureau (which is bound to certain production and cost estimates) may help reduce the risk of grossly underestimating costs.

---

37. There may be exceptions to this recommendation, particularly in the context of cooperative projects. In the American Philological Association projects, titles had been preselected by an advisory board, but that model has scarcely been adopted by others.

Quality Assurance

Only your institution or an organization acting as your agent or representative (such as a third-party contractor, your network or consortium staff, or a neighboring institution) can do the technical and bibliographic inspection to verify that the film products meet your specifications. See chapter 4 for a discussion of quality assurance requirements.

Bibliographic Control

A handful of preservation microfilming bureaus provide bibliographic control services. Using their service may be appropriate if you lack access to OCLC or RLIN and have no cataloging staff trained to do online cataloging as outlined in chapter 5. Contracting for cataloging services can also be the solution when you wish to supplement or expand in-house operations during a short-term project.[38]

Storage

Storage of master negatives should almost always be contracted (see chapter 4). Few repositories have facilities that can meet the stringent standards for archival storage, and offsite storage (preferably in another geographic region) protects master negatives from natural disasters (such as earthquakes, hurricanes, and tornadoes) and from localized floods, plumbing leaks, fires, and so on. Printing masters may be stored in-house, provided the institution has a storage facility with appropriate climate control, security, and fire protection as outlined in chapter 4.

Regardless of the functions performed under contract, the institution is responsible for establishing the specifications that guide the work of contractors, monitoring their performance, and working with them to clarify expectations and resolve problems.

Given that so many elements of a microfilming program *can* be done by contractors, how do you decide when your institution *should* contract out? A few general guidelines may serve as a starting point for your decision making.

> If this is your first preservation microfilming initiative, it is probably wise to contract out as much of the work as can be done effectively by qualified service providers. Then, the staff can focus on the functions that must be done in-house, such as selection and quality assurance. The process will be educational in ways that will equip the staff to assume responsibility for more in-house work in a subsequent phase.

> If most of your needs may be met by a single microfilming project to be accomplished within a finite time period, you should seriously consider contracting for services outside the institution. There is little point in making the necessary and substantial investment in equipment, supplies, and personnel for a one-time, short-term project.

---

38. A task force has been established within the ALA/ALCTS Preservation and Reformatting Section to develop guidelines for vendor cataloging of preservation microforms; if this work comes to fruition, the publication will be available from ALCTS (see appendix B for address).

If you are in a small institution, you may lack the space, staff, or infrastructure to support an in-house operation. By contracting for services, you can focus your resources on the activities you are best able to carry out, especially those related to selection and bibliographic control.

Even if you are in a large institution that has most of the facilities and equipment that are necessary, and even if you are making a long-term commitment to a preservation microfilming program, using outside contractors will increase your output. Some institutions now reserve their in-house labs for filming valuable items that must remain in the institution.

If your microfilming program focuses on materials identified through use (e.g., those screened through circulation), filming generally should be done in-house, for two reasons. First, there generally should be a fast turnaround so that materials can be returned to use quickly. Second, few filming agents are prepared to deal with the volatile ebb and flow of materials generated in a use-based program.

Throughout the United States, libraries are exploring "outsourcing" options. The trend is for institutions to contract as many services as possible, reserving in-house resources for functions that contractors cannot do as well or as efficiently. A similar trend led many libraries to abandon their in-house binderies decades ago. As already noted, though, the use of third-party service providers does not absolve the institution of responsibility for monitoring and ensuring the quality of work performed. Furthermore, the division of labor proposed here is contingent on the use of *qualified* service providers.

Over the past several years, filming service bureaus have turned their attention to the preservation microfilming market. A few nonprofit organizations have devoted themselves to meeting the preservation microfilming needs of libraries and archives. One, in fact, was expressly created to meet the film production needs of a group of research libraries. Preservation microfilming is not a sideline for them, but the whole raison d'être. A few commercial organizations have also aligned themselves with the preservation community, establishing separate units for filming that meets strictest guidelines. All other factors (especially cost and quality) being comparable, it is reasonable for the library and archival communities to support such organizations.[39]

Components of a Preservation Microfilming Program

The major elements of the microfilming program are (1) selection and identification of materials, (2) preparation, (3) film production and quality assurance, (4) access and bibliographic control, and (5) storage. Although each element is distinct, each is interrelated with others. That is, decisions made in each area affect the others.

The following sections serve a twofold purpose: to describe the steps in a preservation microfilming operation and to highlight the administrative decisions

---

39. Even when evaluating service providers that come highly recommended, the institution must heed the cautionary notes outlined in this section and chapter 3.

necessary to plan and implement each step. Detailed descriptions of each component, its prescribed features, and major operational issues are covered in the individual chapters of this manual.

Selection and Identification

The most important aspect of the preservation microfilming program is the selection and identification of the materials to be preserved. No matter how well the process is implemented, if materials that should be preserved are lost or unimportant or inappropriate materials are preserved, nothing has been accomplished. Selection entails difficult decisions. The directions of future scholarship are hard to predict, which makes it almost impossible to consign any item held in our collections to the dust bin.

Selection generally occurs on three levels. First, there is the administrative decision (addressed previously) that establishes the broad organizational priorities in preservation microfilming. The second level is operational: the decision to focus on a particular segment of the collection, often by subject or format (for example, books, newspapers, pamphlets, or manuscripts). The target group can be further refined in terms of imprint date, publishing location, or other criteria. Third, each item within the focus area generally must be screened to make sure it has not already been preserved, that it warrants reformatting, and that it is appropriate for filming. One way to approach the process is to raise a series of questions.

1. *What materials are important for preservation?*

   The archivists, subject specialists, selectors, curators, and other collection development and management staff are the appropriate persons to decide what should be preserved and in what order. These staff members should understand the strengths and importance of various collections, both as collections and in their individual components. Systematic identification and selection for preservation should be integrated into the management of an archival or library collection.

   Local faculty and other scholars may help with selection. A few scholarly groups have identified preservation priorities within their disciplines, and some printed bibliographies may help also.

   As detailed in chapter 2, criteria for selection include current use by scholars and importance to future scholarship. You can identify materials item by item or as a collection. In a collection each item may not by itself be valuable to preserve, but the collection as a whole may represent the breadth of thought or the publishing record of a specific subject or a time period.

2. *Is microfilming the most appropriate technique?*

   The curators and collection development staff should understand all of the preservation options available. It is often the responsibility of the preservation officer or microfilming project manager to make the options clear. Appendix C includes a description of the whole range of preservation options.

Confronted by ranges of worn and damaged materials, the staff must develop a strategy for determining suitable treatments. Condition of the materials, their value, and the use they receive must all be weighed. *University of Kentucky Libraries Reprographics Department. Photo by Lewis Warden.*

3. *Have the materials already been preserved?*

Before you make a decision to microfilm a volume, you must be sure that a suitable replacement for it does not already exist. The volume may have been reprinted in paper copy, published in microform by a micropublisher, or filmed by another library. A reprint (the same or another edition), a pres-ervation photocopy, or a copy of an existing microform is usually preferable to and less expensive than filming.

If the preservation option of choice is microfilming, you must ascertain that the volume is not already available in microform or scheduled for film-ing by another institution. This requires a search of the national bibliographic databases and other online and printed tools. A significant amount of filming and micropublishing has been accomplished, so you must perform this search to prevent duplicate filming. If the exact edition of a title has been filmed or selected for filming by a reputable source, consider it preserved. If the item is important to meet local needs, you can purchase a copy of the microform. Only when no acceptable replacement exists should you consider filming the item. The searching process is described in chapter 2.

4. *What criteria will be used to screen individual items?*

    Many items in library and archives collections will need systematic preser-vation in the coming years. It is appropriate first to preserve those in the most deteriorated condition, those that might crumble with the next use. But eco-nomic factors also come into play here. For example, a manuscript or news-paper might be so badly deteriorated that it requires expensive repairs merely to stabilize it for filming. In such cases you may wish to reconsider your selection decision.

    Chapter 2 outlines screening criteria to apply, including bibliographic completeness, use, considerations related to value, and the cost of filming the item. Each institution must determine how to apply those or other criteria.

5. *How will the procedures to select and identify materials be organized within the institution?*

    The identification and selection processes in a preservation microfilming project are usually absorbed chiefly by existing professional staff. They have the necessary expertise to make informed decisions and must allocate the additional time to do so. They generally will determine the priorities among collections, then review materials on an item-by-item basis. Support staff can assist with identification, condition assessment, and bibliographic searching. Unique collections such as archives or manuscripts may be filmed without searching.

    You will have to design search forms and keep records. Also, consider space requirements: after materials are selected, they must be housed at various points during the work process (while awaiting preparation, filming, or inspection, for example).

6. *Is the material protected under the copyright law or by donor restrictions?*

    Make every effort to observe the copyright law. Determine before filming whether the title is still under copyright. You can film materials in the public domain even if they have been reprinted by another publisher, but film the original, not the reprint. If the materials are still under copyright, attempt to contact the copyright holder if you plan to create more than the one copy allowed for preservation or for scholarly use. This is especially true if you plan to package a set of titles for sale as a collection or if you plan to use digitization in conjunction with filming.

Archival and manuscript materials create special problems due to copyright or donor restrictions. If you cannot obtain the copyright holder's permission to film, or even if you can obtain the permission, it is often best to provide access to the film only onsite or through controlled access that prevents further copying or duplication of the film. For either published or unpublished materials, you should include a copyright statement on the film of books, journals, or documents that are likely to be protected under the law indicating the users' responsibilities for observing the copyright law. See chapter 2 for more details on the copyright issue.

7.   *Will the materials be retained after filming?*

The retention decision is typically made by selectors, generally in consultation with the preservation administrator or project manager, during curatorial review. If the materials have artifactual value, retain them after filming. Otherwise, carefully weigh the access benefits of retaining the originals versus the costs of maintaining both a microform and a hard copy. Even with careful attention, fragile materials may sustain some damage through handling and in filming. If you choose to retain filmed items, you should anticipate that they will require some repair, rebinding, and other treatments after filming.

Preparation of Materials

Many of the decisions made in the selection and identification process affect the preparation of volumes. For example, repair supplies and procedures may differ based on whether materials will be retained or withdrawn after filming.

Preparation of materials is a production-oriented task. The workflow must be carefully coordinated to meet the needs and expectations of the filming lab. The responsibilities of both the preparations staff and the filming staff must be spelled out and understood by each if the process is to proceed smoothly and result in a high-quality film. Chapter 3 describes the process of planning production, the relationships between preparation of materials and the filming process, and the tasks involved in making volumes and documents "camera ready." The major steps and issues in each of the elements of preparation are as follows:

Collation

Collation is the process of examining materials to determine if they are complete and in order.

1.   *Are the materials complete and in order?*

Most materials require page-by-page collation to determine if all sections of the item are present. This is important for archival collections and may be quite time consuming for those materials that are not fully organized.

Collation of books and serials is generally straightforward, unless they are in such poor physical condition that leaves are breaking away from the text block. It may be necessary to remove the binding of a volume and rearrange the pages or to insert special notification in the film to indicate arrangement.

2. *Is this the best copy available?*

To ensure that the best and most complete copy is filmed, you may need to request photocopies of missing pages or borrow another, more complete copy from another institution to film it. Of course, you should secure the permission of the owning institution first. Make every effort to film complete volumes. In some cases no other copy will exist, so the incomplete copy will be the best available. Each institution must establish its own guidelines regarding when it is acceptable to film an incomplete item.

Archival materials are usually unique and, therefore, the only copies. However, the archives may want to complete a microform project by requesting that another archives film a complementary collection, such as the other half of a correspondence.

Physical Preparation

You must prepare the materials in a way that will make possible the highest quality filming. (Preparation activities are covered in chapter 3.) The following are the key administrative issues you need to address.

1. *Will bound volumes be filmed intact or disbound?*

Preservation-oriented filming agents have cameras equipped with book cradles that will support a bound volume to get optimum image quality while minimizing damage to the binding and leaves. In early discussions with the filmer, work to define the limits of the available equipment.

Volumes with tight bindings, little inner margin, or extremely brittle paper may call for disbinding. The institution should decide which methods of disbinding are acceptable and provide instructions to the filmer.

2. *To what extent will archival materials be further organized or finding aids upgraded in conjunction with preparation?*

Especially in collections not under current standards of archival control, it is possible to use the microfilming project as an opportunity for arrangement and description. This decision can have dramatic cost and access implications.

3. *What components of each item should be filmed?*

Decisions are required on such issues as: Should the archival folders also be filmed? Should blank pages be filmed? Should book bindings and endpapers be filmed? While microfilm cannot fully capture bibliographic or artifactual features, it may be useful to capture some design elements in the film copy. To the extent possible, try to standardize practices for the entire project or shipment by shipment.

4. *What guidelines will be established for the physical preparation procedures?*

Preparation can involve a great many other steps, outlined in chapter 3, including removal of fasteners and extraneous items, erasing marginalia, making photocopy surrogates of badly damaged pages, performing minor repairs, flattening pages, and flagging features (e.g., foldouts and overlays) that require special attention by the camera operator. While these can be minimal for routine library materials, they can be extensive for archival materials. Management staff must develop guidelines that will yield a high-quality film within a realistic time frame and cost parameters.

Target Preparation

Targets are sheets of technical and bibliographic information photographed along with an item. Informational targets provide guidance to users. They typically identify the title, contents, and other information about the materials on the film, explain features of the original that may be confusing to a user (for example, pages missing or out of order), and inform the user where materials are located on the film. Technical targets provide technical information needed for production and quality assurance, such as resolution test charts. The process is further discussed in chapter 3.

1. *How will targets be prepared?*

   Target production is most efficient when done with a personal computer, laser printer, and appropriate software. Linkages to the local online system or other databases can allow you to download bibliographic information or finding aids and, thus, speed production and reduce data-entry errors. It is often helpful to enlist the help of the systems office or other automation staff to develop or fine-tune software for these linkages and for production of the targets.

2. *What targets should be prepared?*

   Establish guidelines to ensure that all required targets are produced and that all have been prepared before delivery to the filming agent. A well-targeted collection aids those using the film. Excessive targets, though, can be distracting to the user, slow work during filming, and increase the frame count and, thus, the cost. You must make some judgments about optional targets. For example, in a collection with many missing or damaged pages, it might be more efficient to provide one explanatory target early in the reel than to use targets along with each damaged page.

3. *What targets will be produced in-house and which will the filming agent provide?*

   Most filming agents stock standard targets such as START and END OF REEL/PLEASE REWIND. In your preliminary discussions, identify which targets the filming agent can provide and at what cost. In general, if preparation is being done in-house, most of the targets should also be produced in-house. Also, be sure the filming agent understands where to insert special targets indicating anomalies in the text, changes in reduction ratio, and so on.

Other Preparation Work

After targets are prepared, staff members will determine the contents of each reel and prepare final instructions to the filmer. The following key decisions must be made at this stage.

1. *Who will do the reel programming?*

   Reel programming is the process of determining what materials will be included on each reel. If the other preparation work is done by in-house staff, they generally should do the reel programming. The filmer can do it if you provide clear instructions about where to divide volumes or collections, but expect to pay for this extra service.

2. *What is to be addressed in the written instructions?*

   Preparing final instructions to the filmer can be quite time consuming, especially those for archival collections and for materials with many anomalies. The contract, letter of agreement, or project instructions should cover as many of the general specifications as possible so that the instructions for specific shipments or materials need address only the exceptions.

Preparation of materials for microfilming must be carefully thought out and implemented for each filming project and item. The processes are often routine, but they are critical to the creation of a useful film product. The staff should be well-trained and closely supervised. If the materials are improperly identified, they could be lost for all practical purposes. Inattentive preparation routines could damage fragile volumes; lack of organization will create problems for all subsequent users of the film.

Preparation can be done primarily by students, volunteers, and other support staff, and this helps control the costs. But preparation is generally the most labor-intensive part of the process, so make careful plans to streamline the process and to make it as efficient as possible. Chapters 3 and 6 recommend many strategies for designing efficient workflow and controlling costs.

Film Production

Film production involves not only camera work—the process of recording on film the targets and documents to be preserved—but also film processing, inspection by the filming agent, retakes and splices if needed, duplication, and quality assurance by the repository staff. Preservation microfilming is exacting work and should be performed following the standards necessary to produce the highest quality film possible. Chapter 4 discusses the standards and practices that undergird the production of preservation microfilm. The following issues must be addressed, in addition to the question of which operations to do in-house and which to contract:

1. *How many film generations will be created?*

   You should use a three-generation system in which the master negative is used only once to create the printing master, from which all service copies are produced. But each generation entails production, packaging, and ongoing storage costs. As a cost-saving measure, some institutions make only the preservation master negative and a service copy at the time the film is created, but postpone production of a printing master until they receive a request for a copy of the film. That approach may be justifiable if the material being filmed is unlikely to be in heavy demand, but it requires that you have a fairly accurate estimate of anticipated use. It is less expensive to create the printing master in the initial phase than to do so later, and only the three-generation approach provides the assurance required in preservation applications. Additional guidance is offered in chapter 4.

2. *What film formats and types will be used for the three generations?*

Silver-gelatin film must be used for the master negative and printing master, but diazo or vesicular film may be used for the service copies. National standards exist for the creation of 35mm and 16mm roll film and 105mm microfiche, but 35mm predominates in library and archival preservation programs. You should weigh the factors outlined in chapter 4.

3. *What standards and specifications should be followed?*

National standards produced by ANSI and AIIM provide the basis for preservation microfilming projects, but they do not cover all aspects of a program. They must be adapted to the needs of the specific project, and additional guidelines must be developed. Fortunately, there are model specifications to consider. The RLG specifications have become de facto standards for many libraries and archives; these and others are discussed in chapter 4. Sample contracts can provide a foundation for writing institutional specifications and are cited in chapter 3 (see "Contracting for Filming Services").

4. *How many service copies are required?*

You should make at least one service copy; your estimate of projected use will determine whether additional copies are needed.

5. *Do you expect to create a digital image from the microfilm?*

Microfilm makes an excellent "platform" for digital access systems.[40] If you cannot predict whether you will scan the film, it may be best to establish specifications on the assumption that the film will eventually be digitized because filming practices can simplify or complicate future scanning. For example, lower reductions may be desired for film that is to be scanned, the limitations on "skew" may need to be narrower than allowed in RLG guidelines, and scanning systems may work more efficiently depending on the orientation of pages on the film.

6. *What quality assurance program will you establish to ascertain that film meets your specifications?*

Quality assurance is a critical part of the filming process. As institutions increasingly rely on service bureaus for film production and, thus, cede control of the filming process itself, quality assurance has become the only way to ascertain that the product meets national standards and preservation guidelines.

---

40. See C. Lee Jones, *Preservation Film: Platform for Digital Access Systems* (Washington, D.C.: Commission on Preservation and Access, July 1993).

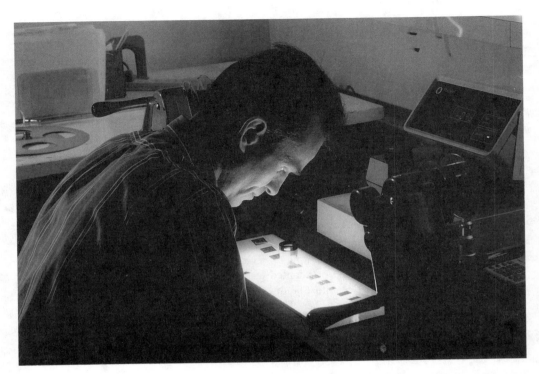

The master negative is inspected over a light box for defects, and a loupe may be used to examine questionable areas. A transmission densitometer (in front of the inspector) is used to measure the density (opacity) of the film at various points throughout the reel. *Northeast Document Conservation Center. Photo by David Joyall.*

Quality assurance involves visual, technical, and bibliographic inspections. The filming agent should perform appropriate technical tests and inspection routines, but the repository must also monitor the filming agent's work by inspecting films as they return. Chapter 4 provides details about the repository's responsibility for quality assurance.

a. *Will you inspect 100 percent of all returned films? Or only a sampling?* Preservation guidelines require the former. If you choose the risky compromise of selective inspection, several precautions (noted in chapter 4) must be taken.

b. *What defects will be grounds for rejecting film?*
   Written guidelines must be established and agreed upon with the filming agent. Errors that affect the longevity of the film must be corrected, but there may be cases when film with minor or cosmetic defects may be accepted.

Access and Bibliographic Control

Access to the information that a title has been preserved and to the film itself is crucial to an effective program. Once you enter records of filmed titles into

OCLC or RLIN, institutions and researchers nationwide will know that a book or set of documents has been filmed and that copies of that film are available through purchase or interlibrary loan (ILL). If scholars cannot determine that the item exists, their work may be impaired. If preservation microfilming programs are not able to identify what has already been preserved, resources will be wasted in duplicate effort. Access has two factors: internal local access and external national and international access. Chapter 5 details the routines required to ensure that microforms, once created, remain accessible.

1. *How will other institutions be informed of your intent to film a title?*

   So much preservation microfilming activity is occurring nationally and internationally that there is a risk that multiple institutions may select the same title for filming. (Of course, that is not a concern when filming unique items.) The most effective mechanism to avoid duplicate microfilming is to record in OCLC or RLIN your intent to film a title. Chapter 5 provides details about this process.

2. *What cataloging standards and procedures will you adopt?*

   Access to the information that an item has been filmed should be accomplished through cataloging the microform on OCLC or RLIN.

   Catalog master negatives according to the *ARL Guidelines for Bibliographic Records for Microform Masters* (also endorsed by ALCTS). These require that records at least meet retrospective conversion standards and include relevant preservation data, and they encourage the provision of at least one subject heading.

   The catalog department or processing unit will have the expertise and tools to provide the proper bibliographic records for the film. Institutional priorities may have to be set also so that the film does not end up in a local arrearage but gets processed routinely with other materials.

3. *How will various automated tools and records be linked?*

   Tremendous efficiencies can be achieved by coordinating or linking national databases, local online catalogs, and stand-alone or shared databases within the institution. There is a great deal of commonality among the data required for and used in condition surveys, replacement searching, target production, cataloging, tracking and inventory control, and statistics and report generation. To the extent you can link the relevant systems, you may save time and reduce data-entry errors.

4. *How will local access be provided?*

   Internal access is a function of local organization. When volumes or documents enter the preservation microfilming stream, they are removed from active use. Local records should be revised to show the status of items in the filming queue, generally through a note in the library catalog record or archival finding aid. Keep records to locate items that may be requested before filming is completed and to insure against loss. You may need to develop a policy regarding retrieval of items from the filming queue, especially if you are filming collections or items that are used regularly.

After filming, a service copy of the microfilm usually will be provided for local use, and the existing bibliographic records either will be updated in or added to the local catalog. Often a record of master negatives that have been produced is kept separately for internal control. In archives, inventory records should be revised to show that film is available, and they may be annotated to reflect that access to originals is restricted now that a microform version is available.

5. *How will additional copies be provided?*

One purpose of preservation microfilming is to provide copies of the items to other institutions and researchers. A mechanism should be established for duplicating film on demand, either in-house or through a service bureau.[41]

Storage

The national micrographics standards and preservation guidelines specify a film product that can have a life expectancy of 500 years. However, to achieve that longevity the film must be not only manufactured and processed appropriately but also kept in accordance with national standards for extended-term storage. Service copies are generally maintained in the working collection of the library or archives, but stringent controls must be provided for the master negative and printing master. These storage costs are ongoing.

1. *Where will the master negatives and printing masters be stored? How will they be housed?*

Few libraries or archives have film vaults that meet the stringent national standards for storage of master negatives and printing masters. Offsite storage in a leased commercial facility that meets standards for extended-term storage is generally the best option. Such facilities generally can provide better environmental control than the library or archives can, and offsite storage protects the masters from disasters that might affect your institution or locale. The quality of reels, film boxes, envelopes, and cabinets is important to ensure the longevity of microforms. The standards for climate control and other storage considerations are outlined in chapter 4.

2. *What program will you establish for ongoing inspection of stored masters?*

The national standards specify that a sampling of master negative films be inspected periodically for signs of deterioration. After reading the standards, you will need to determine the frequency of inspections, develop a sampling strategy, and work with the storage facility to make arrangements for these inspections.

Each of the foregoing elements of the preservation microfilming process is essential to the success of your program. The selection must be informed, the

---

41. Many of the leading preservation storage facilities, such as those listed in appendix B, offer duplication services as an adjunct service. Access to this service might influence your selection of a storage facility for printing masters, particularly if you anticipate high demand for some titles or reels.

Once they pass inspection, master negatives are transferred to storage. Strict preservation specifications govern the composition and design of boxes and labels, and identifying information must be designed to aid in retrieval. *Columbia University Libraries, Preservation Division.*

materials properly prepared and filmed to standards, access provided locally and internationally, and storage conditions designed to ensure long-term preservation of the masters.

Record Keeping and Statistics

Records and statistics are useful to track progress and monitor activity in preservation microfilming programs. However, there is no standardization as to which statistics to keep or in what form. At a minimum, you will need to keep statistics to verify invoices from the filming agent or other service bureaus you are using. If the filming project is supported by grant funds, the funding agency is likely to require both financial and production data, and your system should be designed to generate those as automatically as possible.

Statistics may also help you assess and fine tune your filming operation. For example, if one staff member has markedly higher production rates than others, it might be that she or he has developed unique strategies and that sharing these with other personnel will improve productivity.

At a minimum, statistics should include the number of titles or documents filmed, the number of volumes filmed, and the number of exposures produced either annually or in a specific project. It may also be useful to know the number of feet of duplicate film produced. To monitor and control time, production work may also be counted, such as the number of titles searched, collated, prepared, and cataloged. The cost studies cited in chapter 6 suggest approaches and statistics that may be useful.

The amount of record keeping depends on the complexities and size of the operation. For tracking purposes materials are usually logged into the process, identified while in the filming laboratory or in the hands of a vendor, and logged out after completion.

Other record-keeping devices may include

recommendation, review, and searching forms

circulation records (i.e., titles are charged out to the preservation unit)

a distinct record of completed films

quality control forms

control numbers and contents for reels sent to remote storage

Other forms and instruction sheets will depend on whether filming is performed in-house or outside the institution.

Your plans for future filming or other preservation efforts will refine your decision about what statistics and records to collect. For example, gathering detailed statistics on costs and productivity in one project may greatly simplify budget planning, staffing projections, and productivity estimates for future projects to film similar materials. Similarly, in the selection process you may identify materials that are suitable for filming but not within the parameters of the current project or identify materials that need conservation or other kinds of treatment. You might retain such records for planning future projects or program activities.

Costs and Funding

Preservation microfilming is not cheap. In fact, if you are getting cheap services, they probably do not meet appropriate preservation specifications. The cost merely of filming and processing the three generations of a reel of 35mm film is likely to be in the range of 30¢ per frame (generally with two pages per frame when filming books and one page per frame for archival and oversized materials). Beyond that, there are the institutional costs of personnel, supplies, and overhead related to selection, preparation, quality assurance, and program management; therefore, a total in the range of $90 to $100 per 250-page volume is currently a realistic estimate for routine library materials.

The process is worth the costs, however, when the alternative is the probable loss of a significant portion of our historical heritage. In virtually every step of the process, managerial decisions will affect costs. Specific costs for each step of the process as well as cost control strategies for each facet of the operation are discussed in chapter 6.

When compared with the ongoing costs of keeping unusable materials on a repository's shelves or of space to store research materials, microfilming costs seem in line with others. This is also true when comparing microfilming with other preservation treatments.

Analyze the financial and organizational resources currently available within your institution and determine what should be changed, reallocated, or added. These resources include funding to meet staffing and managerial requirements, to contract for services, to renovate or reconfigure work space, and to procure inspection equipment. Then consider the ongoing maintenance and supply costs. This manual will guide you in generating the information from which to estimate costs. Apart from funding, you must foster a commitment to the program throughout the institution because other departments must be willing to take on the extra functions that result from a microfilming program.

You will need to provide resources to fund the microfilming initiative. Chapter 6 outlines the details about developing a budget. At the program planning stage, you must determine what funding strategy to use. There is often synergy between the funding strategy and the materials selected for filming.

Funding for preservation microfilming may not easily be carved from within an existing institutional budget. But a continuous, effective program requires support with internal operating funds. Some libraries begin by using a portion of the book budget for replacements because microfilming is essentially a reacquisition of an item that is unusable in its current condition. Other institutions may use a formula to earmark a percentage of the materials budget for microfilming (as some also do for cataloging), for there are direct and ongoing expenses for maintaining collection items throughout their life cycles.

Start-up costs or special projects are often funded externally. Federal grants may be available if you plan to film a collection that is a scholarly resource of national significance. Major federal agencies are now well informed of the need to require that projects follow the highest standards, ensure bibliographic access, and avoid duplication of effort. Key federal agencies that support preservation microfilming are NEH and NHPRC, listed in appendix B. (The Department of Education, once a major source of support through the Higher Education Act Title II-C, has played a less significant role in recent years.) In 1985 NEH established a major preservation office, with reformatting on microfilm a high priority for funding, and funding is available both for library and archival materials. In 1989 there was a major increase in the funding level for NEH, with most of that earmarked for preservation microfilming.[42]

A few states now have grant programs for which preservation microfilming projects are eligible. New York has perhaps the oldest and most well funded (see appendix B), but a contact with your state archives or library agency may identify others. In some states, Library Services and Construction Act (LSCA) funds have been used for preservation projects.

Although private donors have not traditionally supported microfilming programs, they are possible resources. A personal or corporate donor may be willing to provide funds to ensure that a certain collection or item is preserved. Foundation support may be available, especially for collections with special appeal.

---

42. The fiscal year 1995 funding level for the NEH Division of Preservation and Access stands at $22.7 million, of which Congress intended that $16.9 million be spent on projects for preservation of and access to library and archives materials (the category that includes filming projects). These levels and the very existence of NEH are, of course, subject to change with the vicissitudes of political life.

Where there is a significant market for the materials to be microfilmed, it may be possible to work with a commercial micropublisher so that no funds need be provided by the institution. Arrangements for micropublication generally require special contracts, which are discussed in chapter 3.

A variation on commercial micropublication is represented by an arrangement in which institutions sell copies to finance or subsidize their filming operations. Using this approach, institutions can become, in a sense, publishers and can accomplish filming projects on a cost-recovery basis.[43] For example, ATLA began an ambitious project in 1984 to film approximately 4,000 titles in one year and to finance this operation from the subscription sale of microfiche copies of all of the titles. As with commercial publication, this approach worked because there was a strong market for the filmed materials.

Assistance in Setting up a Microfilming Program

Preservation microfilming is complex and labor intensive, but it certainly can be accomplished in an archives or library environment. If the subject is new to you or your institution, you may take comfort in knowing that assistance is available in planning and implementing a program. Published information, training programs, site visits, and contacts with colleagues can provide important information.

There is now a substantial body of literature on preservation microfilming. The reading lists at the end of each chapter in this manual constitute a core body of literature, and national standards and specifications are cited in appendix A. *Library Resources & Technical Services* publishes an annual review article summarizing the major publications in preservation, including those about preservation microfilming, and that is a useful way to identify significant works that will help you stay current in the field. It is also helpful to read key micrographics journals to learn about technological developments.

A few training programs are available, many of them from regional preservation programs such as NEDCC.[44] Organizations launching cooperative projects often provide training for project participants, as RLG has sometimes done. You might also encourage your network, professional association, or consortium to contract with qualified instructors to offer workshops or you may hold one for your institution if your staff is large enough to warrant that expense.

Along with ARL and RLG, a major forum for work in preservation microfilming has been ALA's ALCTS, particularly within its Preservation and Reformatting Section (PARS). At least one committee and several discussion groups focus on preservation microfilming, digitization, and other reformatting topics, and relevant institutes and programs are often held at the ALA annual conference. (For information on upcoming ALA meetings, see the address in appendix B.)

---

43. Gwinn, "The Rise and Fall and Rise of Cooperative Projects," 81.

44. Since 1989 and continuing at least through 1996, NEDCC has offered a three-day workshop on planning and managing a microfilming program. For information on the status of that training program, contact NEDCC at the address in appendix B.

Because so many preservation librarians and service bureau staff are involved in the work of ALCTS and PARS, attending these meetings also provides an opportunity for information gathering and discussion with experienced preservation microfilming specialists. Unfortunately, SAA does not now provide comparable resources for archivists engaged in preservation microfilming; that is, there are no structured forums for discussing reformatting issues.

Site visits to other institutions and service bureaus are also useful whether you are just learning about preservation microfilming or fine tuning an existing program. Nonprofit filming agents often have an educational component to their mission, and they may be able to provide tours that are more educational than sales oriented. If you wish to make an educational site visit to an organization such as Preservation Resources, contact the staff in advance to clarify your objectives, explain your needs, develop a plan, and schedule your visit. It is also helpful to visit an institution analogous to your own that has a preservation microfilming program.

Ad hoc advice, documentation, and referrals are available from many sources. The many institutions with filming programs are a rich resource, and many staff members there are willing to share their hard-earned experience. Regional networks with preservation programs, such as the AMIGOS Bibliographic Council, NEDCC, and SOLINET, as well as RLG, CIC, and other organizations engaged in preservation microfilming, are a good source of guidance and referrals. Appendix B lists many of the contacts that will be most fruitful.

Do not overlook assistance available through electronic sources. As of this writing, there is no online forum exclusively devoted to preservation microfilming. However, a wide range of preservation issues are addressed on the Conservation DistList, an online forum (listserv) through which subscribers can raise inquiries, and several institutional policies, specifications, and other documents are available electronically through Conservation OnLine (CoOL), a wide-area information server that provides Internet access to a full-text database of conservation and preservation information.[45]

As noted, consultants may also be used for some purposes in setting up a program. Of course, you will need to evaluate their qualifications as carefully as those of other service providers.

With so many sources of information available, there is no need to "go it alone." Although the work involved in developing a microfilming program is daunting, institutions of all sizes have successfully done it, and you should take advantage of the experience that has been accumulated in this field.

Conclusion

To ensure continued access to the books, journals, pamphlets, and documents in libraries and archives, they must be preserved. Preservation microfilming is often an appropriate technique to afford long-term preservation of their information

---

45. For information on these programs, send an Internet message to consdist-request@lindy. stanford.edu.

content or to reduce the use of and damage to the originals. However, the process is complex, involving much more than the camera work.

All five aspects of the preservation microfilming program must be carefully investigated: selection and identification of appropriate titles, preparation of items for filming, film production and quality assurance, access to and bibliographic control of the completed film, and storage. Preservation microfilming is not accomplished unless all five of these elements are present. The prefilming and postfilming processes are just as important as the filming itself, and they usually are more time consuming and costly.

A decade ago, the Interim Report of the Council on Library Resources' Committee on Preservation and Access strongly recommended that the library community "move in concert" to develop preservation microfilming programs based on local priorities and, ultimately, on national priorities.[46] With leadership especially from ARL and the Commission on Preservation and Access, the scope has broadened to international proportions. Using the principles and guidelines outlined in this manual will ensure that preservation microfilming is performed optimally to preserve materials for users centuries into the future.

Suggested Readings

For readings related to specific components of the preservation microfilming operation, see the relevant chapters in this manual.

Banks, Jennifer. *Options for Replacing and Reformatting Deteriorated Materials.* Washington, D.C.: ARL, 1993.

Child, Margaret. "The Future of Cooperative Preservation Microfilming." *Library Resources & Technical Services* 29 (Jan./Mar. 1985): 94–101.

Gwinn, Nancy E. "The Rise and Fall and Rise of Cooperative Projects." *Library Resources & Technical Services* 29 (Jan./Mar. 1985): 80–6.

Harris, Carolyn. "Cooperative Approaches to Preservation Microfilming." In *Preservation Microfilming: Planning & Production,* 55–65. Chicago: ALA/ALCTS, 1989.

Merrill-Oldham, Jan, Carolyn Clark Morrow, and Mark Roosa. *Preservation Program Models: A Study Project and Report.* Washington, D.C.: ARL, 1991.

Merrill-Oldham, Jan, and Jutta Reed-Scott, eds. *Preservation Planning Program: An Assisted Self-Study Manual for Libraries.* Rev. ed. Washington, D.C.: ARL, 1993.

Morrow, Carolyn Clark. *The Preservation Challenge: A Guide to Conserving Library Materials.* White Plains, N.Y.: Knowledge Industry, 1983.

Preservation of Historical Records. Washington, D.C.: National Academy Press, 1986.

Ritzenthaler, Mary Lynn. *Preserving Archives and Manuscripts.* Chicago: SAA, 1993.

---

46. Council on Library Resources, Committee on Preservation and Access, *Interim Report* (Washington, D.C.: CLR, 1985), 2.

Selection of Materials for Microfilming

I ntellectually, if not in a chronological sense, selection is the first and fundamental activity in preservation microfilming. Archivists and librarians are faced with the fact that books and documents produced since the mid-1800s are likely to become brittle and vulnerable to the point of self-destruction unless something is done to save those texts. Selection involves asking the critical questions: What is to be saved? How?

The literature on preservation selection can be confusing, for "selection" is used in many senses, ranging from very broad strategic activities to the screening of individual items. First, selection refers to the process of setting preservation priorities for the entire collection. In this stage, the staff may consider all the volumes, record groups, or manuscript collections in the repository and reach consensus on which are most crucial to meeting the institutional mission, scholarship, or other goals. This broadest level of preservation selection, addressed in chapter 1, establishes institutional priorities for large classes of holdings.

The second stage of selection typically happens during project planning, perhaps in the development of a grant proposal. You begin to think about particular parts of the collection, by subject, date range, format, and so on, and about the full gamut of preservation actions that are available to deal with them. Which warrant improved environmental control to extend their lives? Which need only proper shelving and storage? Which must be retained in their original format and, therefore, require repair, conservation treatment, or deacidification? Which can be reformatted? And, of course, for which can you obtain the necessary funding and organizational support to implement the appropriate preservation actions? If you are consciously looking for an area on which to focus microfilming activity, you begin to consider the general characteristics of specific segments of the collection in terms of whether they are appropriate candidates. This might lead you away from heavily illustrated subject collections such as art history and design, focusing instead on those where text predominates, or might steer you away from areas where there already has been a great deal of microfilming activity.

In the third stage of selection, sometimes called screening, you assess individual items and their suitability for filming. For example, given the illustrations in a particular volume, is it an appropriate candidate? If a volume in the rare book collection is so fragile and so tightly bound that it is likely to be damaged in the filming process, are the benefits of reduced handling of the original sufficient to outweigh the potential damage?

Preservation microfilming must be but one option out of a full range of possibilities available to the archivist and librarian in a balanced, coordinated program of preservation management. For preservation to be an effective programmatic activity rather than an ad hoc one, there must be a selection process to choose the most appropriate method of preservation for a given item within the context of an institution's stated preservation goals. Since most institutions have limited financial resources to devote to preservation, this selection process often becomes as much a decision of what must be neglected as of which items can be preserved. Certain grant-funded projects may require microfilming as the first choice, but local demands may make it necessary also to retain the original, purchase a hard copy replacement, or create a digital image for enhanced access. In short, selection of items for preservation is a most important and difficult task.

The collections found in libraries and archives are similar in many ways, and preservation managers will encounter comparable problems in determining suitable approaches. Both, for example, acquire, house, service, and preserve large quantities of paper-based materials that are deteriorating at a rapid rate. Both house paper-based materials of varied formats (bound volumes, maps, charts, scrapbooks, pamphlets, manuscripts, etc.). And both would like to retain items of artifactual value in their original format and preserve the intellectual content of other materials through microfilming or other copying methods. But there are also major differences.

Look at how their respective collections are acquired, processed, described, and classified, and you will see that the methods and intent of archival repositories are different from those of libraries. Think, for example, of how researchers gain access to the collections. In libraries, researchers most often use online systems or card catalogs to find single items in the collection, while in archives, finding aids or indexes point to boxes, files, or folders containing groups of documents. Most archival and manuscript collections consist of predominantly flat-paper, single-sheet materials, while the majority of items in the library are bound volumes. The statutory governance of the retention of public records and sometimes other archival materials and the legal implications of controlling access to manuscript collections may differ significantly from policies affecting the use of library collections. Finally, archives are made up of mostly unique items, while library collections consist of publications issued in multiple copies. These differences are significant and suggest that libraries and archives will need to employ quite different curatorial approaches to preservation management in general and to selection for preservation microfilming in particular.[1]

Unfortunately, while there is widespread consensus about selection priorities for library materials, no such consensus has emerged yet in the archival com-

---

1. See Margaret S. Child, "Selection for Microfilming," *American Archivist* 53 (spring 1990): 250–5, for some key distinctions in selection theory and process in libraries and archives.

munity. For books and serials, there is a widespread national focus (and an emerging international one) on materials published since 1850, which are brittle, and which have scholarly significance. These have become so systematized that there are now automated tools that will help evaluate individual items based on condition, risk, and value. As discussed later in this chapter, specific priorities for some scholarly disciplines have been articulated. But, as noted in the introduction, there is no archival approach analogous to the nationwide Brittle Books Program and, thus far, little success in developing one.[2] This chapter outlines criteria that help archives and libraries develop selection guidelines and offers recommendations for managing the selection process.

Responsibility for Screening and Decision Making

Depending on the size and structure of the institution and the expertise of the staff, various librarians or archivists may be responsible for making preservation decisions. Faculty members, scholars, and other users of the collection may also have a role. This process is known as *curatorial review* and is critical to ensure that preservation funds are spent wisely. The sections that follow outline a potential division of duties in institutions with a full complement of staff.

All persons involved in the decision making should be equipped with a clear understanding of the library's collection management and development policy or the archives' accession and appraisal policies. If the institution has a written statement, it is the ideal planning instrument. It should specify the short-, intermediate-, and long-term objectives the institution will follow in selecting and maintaining its collection. To be most useful, the policy should contain information on the following:

- relative strengths of portions of the total collection (especially strong subject collections are top candidates for preservation)
- relative value of current and retrospective collections in different subject areas
- level of use (high-use collections may merit higher priority for preservation activity)
- historical importance or research value of various parts of the collection

The Conspectus (initially developed by RLG and also available through ARL) provides one useful tool for assessing relative collection strengths and current collecting policies.[3] Less-comprehensive assessments are possible through tools such as the North American Title Count Project and the OCLC/AMIGOS Col-

---

2. See *The Preservation of Archival Materials: A Report of the Task Forces on Archival Selection to the Commission on Preservation and Access* (Washington, D.C.: Commission on Preservation and Access, Apr. 1993). A decision model developed out of the task forces' work was subsequently field tested by RLG with disappointing results, and no effort is yet under way to carry it forward.

3. Information about the Conspectus is available in ARL/OMS SPEC Kit 151, *Qualitative Collection Analysis: The Conspectus Methodology,* and from ARL and RLG.

lection Analysis System, both of which yield data on an institution's current holdings and allow comparison with other institutions or groups. The OCLC/AMIGOS system provides for a statistical comparison against peer groups determined by the library.

Preservation decision making becomes one of the most important methods for implementing the collection development or acquisitions policy because the decision to preserve a brittle or deteriorated item constitutes a "reacquisition" of the work. Of course, not all institutions have a formal, written policy. In the absence of such a document, preservation decision makers will need to rely on informal agreements and understandings that guide collection development practices.

Preservation Administrators and Conservators

The preservation administrator oversees the institution's entire preservation program. The preservation officer or, in large programs, another designated staff member in the preservation unit has responsibility for

administering all preservation identification and screening routines

developing a range of preservation options to provide appropriate and suitable treatments for varied types of deteriorated materials

knowing relative costs and benefits of various options

interacting with the selector, bibliographer, subject specialist, or scholar to obtain final preservation decisions for all items

The preservation administrator provides advice on the availability and relative costs of various preservation options, but the bibliographer, subject specialist, or scholar should generally be responsible for the final decision on disposition of individual items.

Conservators provide technical advice to the preservation administrator and subject specialist on the costs and feasibility of conservation treatments for items that have artifactual value. Usually, their main role is to provide the appropriate combination of method and material that will allow the institution to retain items for use in their original format, when that is important. Neither the preservation administrator nor the conservator should make "curatorial" decisions about the importance of items in the collection.

Bibliographers and Selectors

Whether they are called bibliographers, curators, or selectors, it is often the subject specialists within the archives or library who are best qualified to make the final preservation decision for deteriorated items that have been identified as preservation microfilming candidates. Their decisions to film or not to film, to retain or to discard the original after filming, and so on, must be based on their knowledge of the subject, the language, and scholarship in the field; their knowledge of local and national needs; and their sense of current uses and the impact of scholarly trends on future uses of the item. The preservation officers and conservators may bring other factors to the selector's attention. It is the selector's responsibility to answer the question, "What must be preserved in this collection?"

Selecting materials for preservation microfilming calls for involvement of preservation administrators and subject specialists to evaluate the physical condition of the item, its value and nature of use, and the suitability of available options. *University of Kentucky Libraries Reprographics Department. Photo by Lewis Warden.*

Because everything cannot or should not be filmed in a "vacuum cleaner" approach to preservation microfilming, the selector's knowledge of the subject matter will help determine the individual item's relative importance to the collection. The following points will influence the decision:

Strength or national eminence of the collection from which the item comes. One indicator here would be whether the institution has assumed primary collecting responsibilities in certain subjects in order to participate in cooperative projects.

Nature of the current use of the collection or item—its history of use, support of the curriculum, and value to research.

Uniqueness of the item to the area, nation, consortium, or institution and its value as an artifact.

Nature of the discipline or subject area. This is especially important in preserving variant editions of a work. For example, research that emphasizes use of literary materials probably will require that all editions and perhaps even all printings of a work be preserved because a complete documentary record is required for textual analysis. For some works and for some subject areas, the first or the last edition is sufficient.

Permanent research value of the materials' intellectual content. Items that are judged valuable for the study of the history of the subject, that document the existence of new trends and ideas, and that provide a record of increased knowledge in that subject should be preserved.

Place of publication. For example, U.S. libraries might give higher priority to items first published in the United States than to those first published in Europe whose translations were subsequently published in the United States.

Date of publication. Items published during the author's lifetime may be given higher priority for preservation. Also, contemporary events during the publishing history of the work—political events, critics' rebuttals, etc.—influence preservation decisions.

How the item reflects genuine contributions to the local, national, or subject literatures; its historical significance.

The subject specialist should choose from the available options (microfilming, conservation, replacement, etc.) as if these were acquisition decisions in competition with resources for newly acquired materials. Selectors must be as active in making preservation decisions as they are in making acquisition decisions to avoid bottlenecks at the selection stage of the preservation microfilming work stream.

Scholars and Faculty Members

In the past, scholars outside the library or archives were not routinely involved in the selection of materials for preservation microfilming. If your institution lacks subject expertise in certain disciplines on its staff, then faculty members, researchers, or other scholars can be helpful as advisers. They can help determine the intellectual or long-term value of a title to the collection to make sure that preservation dollars are spent wisely.

In the past few years organizations at the national level have worked to engage scholars systematically in selection for preservation. Major initiatives have been fostered by the Commission on Preservation and Access, which has appointed a series of scholarly advisory committees (including some librarians and archivists) to set priorities in the disciplines of art history, modern language and literature, philosophy, and medieval studies.[4] The Commission's successful work in this area has sparked Western European interest in a similar strategy.[5]

There are other models for this broader approach to scholarly involvement. In a project funded by NEH in the early 1980s, for example, a panel assembled by the American Philological Association selected books and journals worthy of preservation in the field of classics.[6] The titles were then sought for filming. With leadership from Cornell University, a major national initiative for the preservation of agricultural literature has been articulated, based on a selection methodology that employed citation analysis and review and ranking by scholars to identify the core literature of the agricultural sciences.[7]

Each of these initiatives has yielded progress in shaping national consensus, reduced the long-standing resistance to microfilm within the academic community, and brought greater understanding of the ways research materials are used. The involvement of scholars at the national or even international level is critical because the kinds of materials being microfilmed are generally ones that are especially important to research and scholarship.

Involving local faculty or scholars in preservation decision making requires careful planning. It is not unlike the involvement of faculty with acquisition or selection decisions, but there are distinct differences. It may be easier to solicit help with a focused project that has a definite beginning and end than with an ongoing program. Harder choices must be made because preservation dollars are even less plentiful than acquisition funds. And it is almost always easier to add something to a collection than to withdraw items from it. If you employ outside consultants in your program, make certain they are fully aware of the preservation options available in your institution and the relative costs.

Local review of miscellaneous titles that are potential candidates for microfilming is only one way in which scholarly expertise can be employed, however.

---

4. Published reports of the committees' work are available as *Scholarly Resources in Art History: Issues in Preservation,* Report of the Seminar, Spring Hill, Wayzata, Minnesota, Sept. 29–Oct. 1, 1988 (Washington, D.C.: Commission on Preservation and Access, 1989); J. Hillis Miller, *Preserving the Literary Heritage: The Final Report of the Scholarly Advisory Committee on Modern Language and Literature of the Commission on Preservation and Access* (Washington, D.C.: Commission on Preservation and Access, 1991); Sophia K. Jordan, ed., *Preserving Libraries for Medieval Studies: Colloquium on Preservation Issues in Medieval Studies, March 25–26, 1990. Sponsored by the Commission on Preservation and Access* (Notre Dame, Ind.: University Libraries, University of Notre Dame, 1991).

5. See *Preserving the Intellectual Heritage: A Report of The Bellagio Conference, June 7–10, 1993* (Washington, D.C.: Commission on Preservation and Access, 1993).

6. Advantages of the involvement of scholars, as well as the pitfalls, are discussed by Roger S. Bagnall in "Who Will Save the Books? The Case of the Classicists," *Humanities* 8 (Jan./Feb. 1987): 21–3; also in *The New Library Scene* 6 (Apr. 1987): 16–18. A more detailed account appears in Carolyn L. Harris and Roger S. Bagnall, "Involving Scholars in Preservation Decisions: The Case of the Classicists," *Journal of Academic Librarianship* 13 (July 1987): 140–6.

7. The proposed national program and background on its development are provided in Nancy E. Gwinn, "A National Preservation Program for Agricultural Literature" (United States Agricultural Information Network, Beltsville, Md., May 16, 1993, photocopy).

Depending on the subject field, you may be able to use published selective bibliographies of literature that will provide the required value judgment. You might also ask local scholars to construct bibliographies of titles important for preservation in a particular field or to review and select from comprehensive bibliographies.

Smaller institutions may find it impossible to organize scholarly input on such a massive scale, but local selection decisions can be informed by these broad-based projects. Extending the decision-making process to include faculty and scholars can have benefits even in a small, local program if it results in a better understanding among library and archives users of the collection's preservation needs.

Methods of Identification

How do you identify appropriate candidates for preservation? You will quickly turn to a systems approach. This part of the program has complex aspects, but its operation can be rather simple and straightforward.

Suitable Categories

Some broad categories of materials are, by their nature, more at risk than others and more amenable to conversion to microform. Experienced institutions have concentrated their attention on

> brittle monographs and pamphlets (usually published after 1850)
>
> newspapers (through the state-based initiatives of the U.S. Newspaper Program)
>
> long serial runs on poor paper
>
> statistical materials
>
> scrapbooks
>
> vertical files (clippings, etc.)
>
> letter books and manuscript materials
>
> ledger books and account books
>
> certain types of atlases or maps, especially those in which color is not critical to the understanding of the images (See the introduction regarding digitization options.)
>
> government reports, foreign and domestic
>
> unstable reproductions such as carbon copies, stencil-mimeograph, Thermo-Fax, and Verifax

The common denominator among these formats is that the majority are produced on paper that is or will become brittle. Some also employ unstable writing or printing media, such as the iron gall inks in many nineteenth-century manuscripts.

The following generally are *not* suitable or appropriate for preservation microfilming:

materials having artifactual, intrinsic, bibliographic, or historical value in their original format, especially if they might be damaged in the filming process

offprints from journals, which are themselves already available in microform

materials that are extremely discolored and have very poor contrast between the text and the background

materials that are being or have been microfilmed by other institutions or micropublishers that make high-quality microform copies available for purchase or loan

If you do not have access to a filming lab that can provide color or continuous-tone microfilming, you may also set aside certain kinds of illustrated materials. For example, in some color illustrations the color contains the information, as in an ethnographic map showing territories occupied by different groups. Such materials probably cannot be filmed successfully in a conventional black-and-white product. (See the "Illustrated Materials" section later in this chapter for a more detailed discussion.)

The screening process will sort out individual items with the previously listed characteristics, but you may also be able to apply broad criteria to whole classes of materials. If you know, for example, that another organization is comprehensively filming Slavic serials, you could exclude that whole category from the identification process unless your holdings complement that project.

Strategies for Identifying Materials

There are two basic strategies by which materials may be identified as candidates for preservation attention. In most institutions, staff members and users routinely come upon items that exhibit damage and deterioration. Identification through these ongoing operations allows for routine attention to local needs. In other cases, perhaps because the staff has become aware that brittle paper is a significant problem or perhaps because of the desire to seek grant funds or participate in a cooperative filming project, the staff may actively seek items that are candidates for preservation microfilming. Each of these identification strategies is discussed in the following sections.

Identification through Ongoing Operations

Depending upon many factors—the size and age of the collection, the magnitude of its deterioration, accessibility of book stacks to users, circulation policies, the capacity of preservation units and their relationship to other units—a workable system for the identification of preservation microfilming candidates will employ one or several routines. Some methods are byproducts of other library or archival functions. For example:

Staff members in the bindery preparation unit may set aside volumes in which the papers lack sufficient strength to benefit from or withstand commercial binding or rebinding.

Circulation, reference, ILL, or photoduplication staff may spot brittle items as they are returned from loan or identified through patron requests or customer orders. These items might be considered high-priority titles because of the clearly indicated level of reader interest. Readers may also bring brittle materials to the attention of repository staff.

Stack maintenance or collection management staff may identify materials requiring preservation attention. Library staff who are trained to be alert for problem materials usually have little difficulty in identifying deteriorated items as they carry out maintenance tasks such as shelving, shelf reading, shifting, or inventory projects. Bibliographers, subject specialists, special collections curators, and individual collection development staff members may identify materials as part of their collection evaluation reviews.

Serials department personnel may select certain titles to film on an ongoing basis in lieu of binding. This should be done with the permission of the publisher, in compliance with the copyright laws, and with assurance that they are not duplicating other libraries' or micropublishers' efforts.

Staff members in acquisition departments may routinely forward incoming new or retrospective monographic materials for preservation microfilming when the paper is of such poor quality that they can accurately predict it will not last as long as needed.

Archives staff members may discover materials while processing incoming collections, carrying out holdings maintenance work, or serving or receiving materials in conjunction with research use.

If the institution employs this identification strategy, the preservation officer would be wise to train staff members to identify materials in the course of their daily work.

Identification as a Focused Activity

While ongoing operations may identify some items that are at risk and warrant preservation attention, a more focused project can bring good results and provide a steadier flow of materials to be filmed. Strategies that have proven useful within this approach include condition surveys, use of bibliographies, focus upon special collections, and coordinated or cooperative projects.

Survey Projects. Item-by-item comprehensive surveys of entire stack areas, or of areas known to have a high degree of deterioration, can be an effective systematic method of identifying materials for screening. This comprehensive, shelf-review approach is similar to an inventory process and will work well if criteria for selection are well defined and if the organizational apparatus is of sufficient size to deal with the quantities of materials gleaned.

Random sampling in certain discrete areas of a collection can also provide information to the preservation officer or collection maintenance officer about the degree of deterioration or the suitability for conversion to microform in that portion of the collection. Explore the possibility of using off-the-shelf software to automate the survey process. Harvard University's Surveyor package (illustrated in figure 3) allows libraries to add or adapt the menus and reports to suit the collection needs, and it has optional sections on illustrative materials and collec-

FIGURE 3   Condition Survey Software

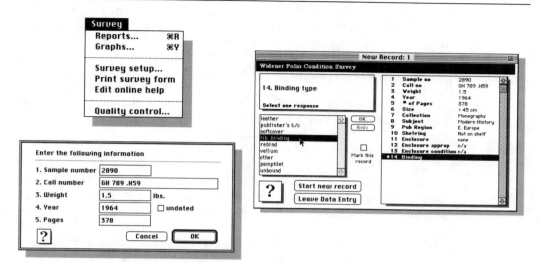

SOURCE: Harvard University Library, Preservation Center.

tion evaluation.[8] This has been a successful way to identify important collection areas that are a high priority for microfilming; elaborate sampling may be unnecessary. If you know a collection largely contains imprints from 1870 to 1930, the age of particularly bad paper, sampling may tell you what you already suspect: considerable brittleness exists, and screening for microfilming candidates will be worthwhile.[9]

Review of collections for imprint date is a third useful method to identify preservation microfilming candidates, especially if the process can make use of automated records and online systems to generate lists of material with particular imprint dates. Another method is simply to review the shelflist and flag records for volumes with certain imprint dates.

Bibliographies. You can also identify candidates for preservation microfilming by using comprehensive subject bibliographies or published catalogs. This process may be especially valuable if the collection is particularly strong. The institution might decide to create a coherent microform collection on a specific subject (e.g., film all the items in a bibliography). On the other hand, it might use the catalog as an indication of the intellectual value of the materials listed and therefore as a selection tool. Commercial micropublishers often use this approach.

Special Collections. An institution may decide that an entire collection is worthy of preservation and that all suitable items in it should be filmed. For example, the archives might select either a collection of all the papers belonging to an individual or all notebooks of an expedition. A library may seek grant funds to enhance a collection that is significant nationally (for example, folklore at Indiana University) and make preservation microfilming a part of the proposal.

Systematic/Cooperative Approaches. Institutions within a consortium, network, or other organization may set up a cooperative program whereby each assumes responsibility for microfilming a different category of items by subject, place of publication, date, or other variables. The parameters could be as

---

8. Surveyor: A Condition Survey Methodology for General Collections, version 1.0 (Cambridge, Mass.: Harvard University Library Preservation Office), is a Macintosh-based software package. Excellent guidance on the design, implementation, and analysis of a condition survey is provided in chapter 6 of *Preservation Planning Program: An Assisted Self-Study Manual for Libraries,* rev. ed. (Washington, D.C.: ARL, 1993), 63–83. Condition surveys previously cited in chapter 1 (especially Gay Walker et al., "The Yale Survey: A Large-Scale Study of Book Deterioration in the Yale University Library," *College and Research Libraries* 46 [Mar. 1985]: 111–32) include guidance on survey design; see also Merrily A. Smith and Karen Garlick, "Surveying Library Collections: A Suggested Approach with Case Study," *Technical Services Quarterly* 5, no. 2 (1987): 3–18.

9. A condition survey need not be as large or exhaustive as the Yale model. The Wellesley Public Library, with a collection of 225,000 volumes, conducted a condition survey by sampling only 703 volumes at a total cost of $9,500 (including consultant services in development, survey, and database design; training of staff and preparation of survey results; presentations to various boards; and staff costs to conduct the survey); see Anne L. Reynolds, Nancy C. Schrock, and Joanna Walsh, "Preservation: The Public Library Response," *Library Journal* (Feb. 15, 1989): 128–32.

broad as reviewing the entire publishing output in a field or could be restricted to types of material (such as monographs) or certain titles (such as long serial runs). Useful models for this approach exist in the projects of ATLA, RLG, CIC, and SOLINET. NHPRC has supported a variety of systematic microfilming projects to gather, select, and film documents from different locations and repositories related to a person, event, or topic of national historic significance.[10] These have included *The Papers of Aaron Burr* (a comprehensive edition of Burr manuscripts from twenty-three states, five foreign countries, and twenty private collections) and *The Papers of Panton Leslie & Co.* (using records from repositories in North and South America and Europe).

Regardless of how individual items are identified as potential candidates for preservation microfilming, they are usually brought together in a central location and batched to expedite an item-by-item review. Then the screening process begins.

The Screening Process

The screening process is a critical stage in the management of a preservation microfilming program. You must assess physical, bibliographical, and intellectual aspects of each item. If you convert a dictionary to roll film, for example, you may make it so difficult to use that its value to the collection is lost. Moving from *aardvark* to *zebra* in the hard copy version takes seconds—on a reel of film it could take several minutes, depending on the size of the original and the speed of the microfilm reader. Consider and carefully examine each filming candidate to judge if it is acceptable for the filming process.

To Retain the Original—or Not?

You must ask yourself a vital question early on in the screening process: "Is it necessary, feasible, or appropriate to retain this item after it has been microfilmed?" The "yes," "no," or "maybe" answer to this question will give you the necessary guidance then to review the menu of preservation and conservation options. Only if you are aware of the full range of preservation options can you make wise decisions about which items are suitable for preservation microfilming. Appendix C outlines the range of choices and the advantages and disadvantages of each. The broad menu of preservation/conservation options recognizes that different situations and problems require a variety of solutions. The institution's overall preservation effort will be stronger if a variety of methods and techniques are available. (See "The Role of Microfilming within a Preservation Program" in chapter 1.) Be wary of indiscriminate or wholesale application of any preservation option in the management of the collection. By following the guidelines for identification, screening, and curatorial responsibility described throughout this chapter, you can determine more easily when preservation microfilming is the best option.

---

10. *Microform Guidelines* (Washington, D.C.: NHPRC, 1986), 1–2.

A satisfactory answer to the question of whether or not to retain the original is critical because the filming process itself can be damaging. Brittle books that have been bound using the oversewing process often cannot be microfilmed without cracking and breaking the pages in the inner margin. Similarly, particularly brittle or fragile volumes in which the sewing structures are also weak may not withstand even the most careful filming. The damage caused by filming ordinary items may be justifiable, but a broad policy to discard *all* volumes that are filmed may not be in the best interests of your institution.

Many items with intrinsic and illustrative value have been microfilmed for the purpose of expanding access while reducing the need for readers to refer to the original rare or valuable item. Also, some institutions provide a microfilm "insurance copy" for certain items in the collection. The decision to film valuable items usually is made only when there will be little or no damage to the original through the filming process; otherwise, suitable conservation treatment may be the better solution.

There are two options for dealing with the damage that may occur during filming. You may decide to leave the volume as it is, but the decision not to remove the binding may affect the film quality, especially if the volume is thick and tightly bound. A second option is to disbind volumes before filming. The most expedient method is to use a cutting machine, known as a guillotine, to separate the text block into single leaves. Alternatives are to remove the covers, divide the text block into segments, or loosen or cut sewing threads. (For a more complete discussion of these techniques, see chapter 3.) If any of these options are selected, the item will have to be resewn, rebound, fitted with a protective enclosure, or otherwise treated after filming; it will not be suitable for reshelving without some treatment.

The decision to "film and retain" versus "film and discard" is often a difficult one. In addition to the balance between artifactual value and potential damage, institutional policies come into play. Can you justify maintaining in "dead storage" materials that are not usable because of their fragile condition? And will the materials thus retained require significant physical treatment (repair, protective enclosure, conservation rebinding, etc.) after filming? There are also costs in bibliographic control and catalog maintenance work associated with the decision to withdraw.

For archives, legal requirements may dictate that hard copies of certain categories of documents be retained. But if that is not the case, participants in the screening process must take great pains to select only those items that are appropriate for preservation microfilming.

The original should be retained if microfilm does not provide a completely acceptable replacement.[11] For example, items with color illustrations might be

11. Before determining what constitutes an "acceptable replacement," it would be instructive to read some of the writings of those who advocate the retention of original documents. See, for example, Barclay Ogden, *On the Preservation of Books and Documents in Original Form* (Washington, D.C.: Commission on Preservation and Access, 1989); and G. Thomas Tanselle, "Reproductions and Scholarship," *Studies in Bibliography* 42 (1989): 25–54.

retained in hard copy, given the current questions about color film and the potential of digitization. (See further discussion of this point under "Illustrated Materials" following.)

Library materials that have been chosen because their paper is brittle should be given strongest consideration for withdrawal. No treatment will restore strength or flexibility to brittle paper (though there are protective strategies including polyester encapsulation and limited access); thus, there is seldom a practical reason to keep a brittle item in the collection.

Screening Criteria

You are now at the stage when many materials have been identified as candidates for preservation. By applying the screening criteria you will determine which items should be microfilmed based on physical factors, cost, and curatorial evaluation. This review may take place as the first step or the last, depending on the material. For example, if the institution has decided to preserve an entire collection, the curators may review it first to determine which items should remain. Generally, however, this review would take place at the final stage, when all information about the item is available. Figure 4 briefly lists the criteria that must be weighed in the screening process.

The balance of this chapter discusses each of the criteria in detail. If you are a new decision maker, you may find the diversity and multiplicity of factors daunting, but many of them will become second nature with practice. A logical progression underpins the screening process. Figure 5 illustrates the major decision points in this progression.

FIGURE 4 Screening Checklist

1. Physical condition, including paper strength/flexibility, condition of binding structure, and legibility
2. Bibliographic completeness
3. Availability of acceptable replacement or duplicate copies in hard copy or microfilm, whichever is more appropriate for the item and the collection
4. Quantity, value, and condition of illustrative or graphic materials that are part of the item
5. Format, frequency, and type of use the item receives or is expected to receive
6. Artifactual, intrinsic, or historical value of the item as an object in its original format
7. Intellectual importance of the material itself, as seen by scholars, custodians, and bibliographers
8. Donor or copyright restrictions
9. Cost of filming
10. Shelf space considerations
11. Likelihood that another institution will film the item

FIGURE 5 Preservation Decision Flow Chart

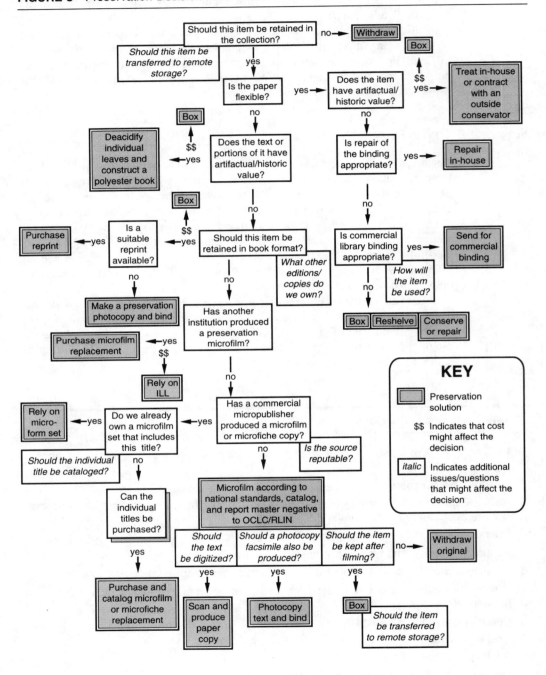

SOURCE: Adapted from *1992 Book and Paper Group Annual*, vol. 11 (Washington, D.C.: American Institute for Conservation of Historic and Artistic Works, 1992), 52.

Physical Condition

The typical rationale for preservation microfilming has been to capture the informational or intellectual content from the text of books and documents with weak and brittle paper. To check for brittleness, test a small corner of the pages with a fold test: if the paper cannot withstand two double corner folds without breaking off, the paper has undergone an irreversible degradation of paper flexibility and is deemed brittle. You may not need to test for brittleness if "haloes" —darkened page edges—are present. This is a trait especially apparent in mechanical wood pulp paper (such as newsprint) and is evidence of particular fragility. The paper may shatter with even delicate handling. Folding a corner is often unnecessary for these items, since the surveyor will see pages broken away from inner margins, jagged broken pages in the volumes, or shards of paper on shelves and floors surrounding these materials. For brittle papers that have reached this stage, preservation microfilming may be the only viable option.

When using physical condition as a criterion, extreme brittleness is not the only factor. The expected rate of deterioration should be considered, and thought

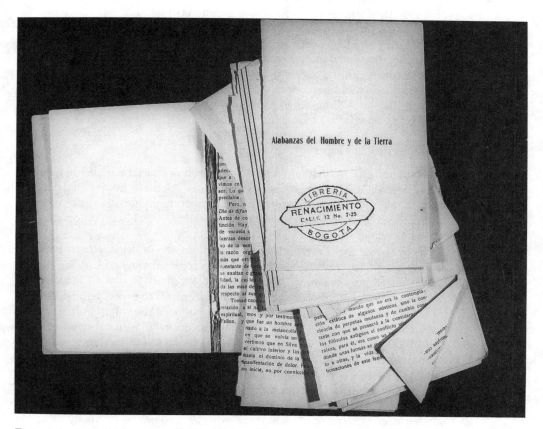

Text may be lost in the inner margin when brittle pages break away from the binding structure. In such cases, missing or badly damaged pages may be replaced through interlibrary loan. If the damage is severe, it may be more efficient to obtain a better copy or reconsider the filming decision. *Library Photographic Service (Conservation Department), University of California, Berkeley. Photo by Charles Stewart.*

should be given to the item's potential problems. This is especially true of books and documents that are on very unstable paper materials, such as newsprint, or those that use unstable copying processes, such as Thermo-Fax. If these materials are selected for preservation before they become extremely deteriorated and discolored, they can be microfilmed less expensively, the film copy will be better, and there is no risk of losing the text because of broken pages. The cost and quality of microfilms made of currently received newspapers versus those made from older, fragile, and darkened retrospective newspaper files is clear evidence. You must consider your priorities for such treatments and the amount of endangered paper in the collection before making the decision to film materials that do not yet require preservation action.

In some situations you also may consider the condition of the binding structure. If a bound volume is so structurally unsound that expensive rebinding or conservation might be required, filming might be the best choice. Some libraries engaged in large-scale, ongoing microfilming programs have elected not to microfilm volumes that are brittle but structurally sound. For example, in planning for its Foundations of Western Civilization project, Columbia University staff identified such volumes for future attention but returned them to the shelf.[12]

When screening for physical condition, always keep in mind the "filmability" of the identified materials. Because of ink bleed-through, extremely poor contrast in discolored or darkened papers, or other features that will cause problems in film legibility, certain copies of published materials should perhaps not be filmed or should be done cooperatively using a "best copy available" approach. Chapter 4 discusses in greater detail the effects of document quality on the filming process.

Bibliographic Completeness

The bibliographic "condition" of the item is part of its overall physical qualities, but it deserves special emphasis. This primarily relates to library materials that exist in multiple copies, because there is an opportunity to fill in missing pages and parts. Both monograph and serial publications should be bibliographically complete before filming.

You should make every effort to replace missing or damaged text in monographs and serial publications by borrowing copies through ILL to fill gaps in holdings and thus obtain a "best," or most complete, copy for filming. Many cooperative microfilming projects include agreements to expedite the fulfillment of ILL requests and to allow extended loan periods. You might also arrange to have another institution, one that also films according to national standards, film the affected portion (particularly if it is lengthy) and splice the film in with yours to make a complete run. This activity is very important in a preservation microfilming program, even though it may increase costs.

At this point, look for obvious page gaps and determine whether you should attempt to fill them or pass the item over. Page-by-page collation during the preparation stage (see chapter 3) will reveal whether a volume is internally complete.

12. Carolyn Harris, Carol Mandel, and Robert Wolven, "A Cost Model for Preservation: The Columbia University Libraries' Approach," *Library Resources & Technical Services* 35 (Jan. 1991): 35.

While bibliographic completeness per se is not often relevant to archives, even repositories that house unique items can improve the completeness of their film products. If the archives wants to film the correspondence of an individual, for example, it might make arrangements with other repositories to borrow and film additional letters or the "letters to" the individual as well as the "letters from."

Availability of Replacements

In library collections, now that you have identified some potential candidates for preservation microfilming, you will need to conduct a bibliographic search that the selector will use to determine whether each item should be retained in the collection and, if so, whether a suitable replacement is available. Well-designed searches will yield information to ascertain

- the importance of this item to the collection as a whole—for example, whether it is only one of several duplicate copies
- its relationship to other relevant editions in the collection, including its relative rarity or scarcity
- the availability of suitable hard copy replacements (reprints or collected works) in the commercial market
- the availability of microform replacements in the institutional or commercial markets
- information that another institution plans to microfilm it (See chapter 5 for an explanation of how institutional commitments to film titles are recorded in OCLC and RLIN.)

This detailed search is a necessary step to provide the selector with enough relevant information to decide about the preservation and disposition of each item. Failure to take these factors into account can seriously damage the collection as a whole and can result in duplicate filming.

A well-designed search form is an invaluable tool in gathering and sharing information on each candidate for preservation. (See figures 6 and 7 for examples of monograph and serial search forms.) Although the amount of information required may vary, the search form can take several physical shapes: on 8½" × 11" paper, 5" × 8" cards, or—increasingly—through the use of a computer database. The search form should accommodate the following information:

- complete bibliographic information (such as a printout of the catalog record or copy of the shelflist card) that provides edition-specific data on the item in hand
- number, call number, publication date, and condition of other copies of that item and/or edition in the collection
- brief information regarding the author: birth and death dates, existence of other titles in the collection by that author
- the existence of any other of the author's works in the special collections department
- if a translation, the existence and condition of the edition in the original language in the collection

FIGURE 6 Search Form for Preservation Replacement: Monographs (side 1)

Bibliographic Information *(Attach printout/photocopy of most complete bibliographic record or fill in form)*

Call Number

Author

Title

Edition

Imprint

Search Record *Place a check mark (✓) in the box to indicate a source has been searched. If a possible replacement is found, attach printout/photocopy of citation. Put a zero (0) in the box to indicate a source was searched but no replacement identified. Leave the box blank to indicate the source was not searched.*

Searcher's Name _____ Date _____

Local Holdings	**Microform**	**Hard Copy**	**Rarity/Scarcity**
□ online catalog	□ OCLC (Rcd #:	□ BIP	□ NUC
□ shelflist/card catalog	_____)	□ BIP Suppl.	
	□ RLIN (Rcd #:	□ GTR	If 5 or fewer,
Last copy? _____	_____)	□ BOD	list locations:
	□ NYPL	□ BIP International	_____
Other editions? _____	□ NUC: Books	□ _____	_____
(Attach printout/photocopy)	□ BOD	□ _____	_____
	□ GMIP	□ _____	_____
Notes:	□ GMIP Suppl.		
	□ _____		_____
	□ _____		
	□ _____		

Curatorial Review and Decision

□ 1. Order microform available: _____ for this edition only _____ for any edition
Fund: _____

□ 2. Order reprint available: _____ for this edition only _____ for any edition
Fund: _____

□ 3. Create microfilm (for those not available as commercial replacement)
Fund: _____

□ 4. Create preservation photocopy (for those not available as commercial replacement)
Fund: _____

□ 5. Do not replace. Instead:
    □ reshelve without treatment   □ provide enclosure and shelve
    □ withdraw from collection   □ repair/rebind and reshelve
    □ transfer to _____

  6. Disposition of original (for items being replaced):
    □ withdraw original   □ retain original and repair/rebind
    □ retain original and reshelve as is   □ retain original and make protective enclosure
    □ transfer to _____   □ _____

  7. Preparation Instructions
    □ complete disbinding o.k.   □ loosen sewing if needed
    □ film front cover only   □ do not film covers
    □ film front endpapers only   □ do not film endpapers
    □ other: _____

Selector's Name _____ Date _____

FIGURE 6 Search Form for Preservation Replacement: Monographs (side 2)

In-process Information: ☐ Create m'film ☐ Buy m'form ☐ Buy reprint ☐ Photocopy MN# _____

☐ Bind ☐ Box ☐ Repair ☐ Reshelve ☐ Withdraw ☐ _____ Referred to: _____

Order Record:

Preservation Office Disposition *Give date completed and initial; indicate with a check mark (✓) when included in statistics.*

	Date Completed	Initials	In Statistics
1. Charged to Preservation	_____	_____	_____
2. Replacement search completed	_____	_____	_____
3. Replacement microform order sent to Acquisitions	_____	_____	_____
4. Replacement hard copy (reprint) order sent to Acquisitions	_____	_____	_____
5. Collation (for "create film" and "create photocopy" items)	_____	_____	_____
☐ title is complete; total pages = _____			
☐ missing page #s: _____			
6. Interlibrary loan			
☐ pages/issues/titles/etc. ordered	_____	_____	_____
☐ items received	_____	_____	_____
7. Microfilming			
☐ sent for filming	_____	_____	_____
☐ received from filming	_____	_____	_____
☐ inspection complete	_____	_____	_____
8. Preservation photocopying			
☐ sent for copying	_____	_____	_____
☐ received from copying	_____	_____	_____
☐ inspection complete	_____	_____	_____
9. Cataloging			
☐ prospective cataloging (record ID# _____)	_____	_____	_____
☐ sent to Cataloging	_____	_____	_____
10. Storage			
☐ master negative sent to storage (MN # _____)	_____	_____	_____
☐ printing master sent to storage	_____	_____	_____
☐ service copy routed	_____	_____	_____
11. Disposition of original			
☐ sent for withdrawal	_____	_____	_____
☐ sent to stacks without treatment	_____	_____	_____
☐ repaired and sent to stacks	_____	_____	_____
☐ rebound and sent to stacks	_____	_____	_____
☐ enclosure made; sent to stacks	_____	_____	_____
☐ _____	_____	_____	_____
12. PROCESS COMPLETED	_____	_____	_____

If in doubt, obtain selector's approval for any option or disposition

---

FIGURE 7 Search Form for Preservation Replacement: Serials (side 1)

Bibliographic Information *(Attach printout/photocopy of most complete bibliographic record or fill in form. Attach holdings record printout.)*

Call Number
Author
Title
Imprint
Previous titles
Subsequent titles

Search Record *Place a check mark (✓) in the box to indicate a source has been searched. If a possible replacement is found, attach printout/photocopy of citation. Put a zero (0) in the box to indicate a source was searched but no replacement identified. Leave the box blank to indicate the source was not searched.*

Searcher's Name _____ Date _____

Local Holdings	**Microform**	**Hard Copy**	**Rarity/Scarcity**
□ online catalog	□ OCLC (Rcd #:	□ GTR	□ NUC
□ shelflist/card catalog	_____)	□ _____	□ ULS
	□ RLIN (Rcd #:	□ _____	
Last copy? _____	_____)	□ _____	If 5 or fewer,
	□ SIM	□ _____	list locations:
Notes:	□ GMIP		NUC ULS
	□ GMIP Suppl.		
	□ Mfm Annual		_____ _____
	□ _____		_____ _____
	□ _____		_____ _____
	□ _____		_____ _____

Curatorial Review and Decision

□ 1. Order microform available: Fund: _____
□ 2. Order reprint available: Fund: _____
□ 3. Create microfilm (for those not available as commercial replacement)
     Fund: _____
□ 4. Create preservation photocopy (for those not available as commercial replacement)
     Fund: _____
□ 5. Do not replace. Instead:
        □ reshelve without treatment   □ provide enclosure and shelve
        □ withdraw from collection   □ repair/rebind and reshelve
        □ transfer to _____
   6. Disposition of original (for items being replaced):
        □ withdraw original   □ retain original and repair/rebind
        □ retain original and reshelve as is □ retain original and make protective enclosure
        □ transfer to _____ □ _____
   7. Preparation Instructions
        □ complete disbinding o.k.   □ loosen sewing if needed
        □ film front cover only   □ film front and back covers
        □ film endpapers   □ _____

Selector's Name _____ Date _____

FIGURE 7 Search Form for Preservation Replacement: Serials (side 2)

In-process Information: ☐ Create m'film ☐ Buy m'form ☐ Buy reprint ☐ Photocopy MN# ____
  ☐ Bind ☐ Box ☐ Repair ☐ Reshelve ☐ Withdraw ☐ _____ Referred to: _____

Order Record:

Preservation Office Disposition *Give date completed and initial; indicate with a check mark (✓) when included in statistics.*

	Date Completed	Initials	In Statistics
1. Charged to Preservation	____	____	____
2. Replacement search completed	____	____	____
3. Replacement microform order sent to Acquisitions	____	____	____
4. Replacement hard copy (reprint) order sent to Acquisitions	____	____	____
5. Retrieval: ☐ NOS	____	____	____
☐ 2nd search	____	____	____
Notes:			
6. Collation (for "create film" and "create photocopy" items)	____	____	____
☐ title is complete; total pages = _____			
☐ missing page #s: _____			
7. Interlibrary loan			
☐ pages/issues/titles/etc. ordered	____	____	____
☐ items received	____	____	____
8. Microfilming			
☐ sent for filming	____	____	____
☐ received from filming	____	____	____
☐ inspection complete	____	____	____
9. Cataloging			
☐ prospective cataloging (record ID# _____)	____	____	____
☐ sent to Cataloging	____	____	____
10. Storage			
☐ master negative sent to storage (MN # _____)	____	____	____
☐ printing master sent to storage	____	____	____
☐ service copy routed	____	____	____
11. Disposition of original			
☐ sent for withdrawal	____	____	____
☐ sent to stacks without treatment	____	____	____
☐ repaired and sent to stacks	____	____	____
☐ rebound and sent to stacks	____	____	____
☐ enclosure made; sent to stacks	____	____	____
☐ _____	____	____	____
12. PROCESS COMPLETED	____	____	____

If in doubt, obtain selector's approval for any option or disposition

if a multivolume set or serial, description of the entire run of holdings in the collection

the relative rarity or scarcity of the item (as defined by the selector) ascertained by a search in the OCLC and RLIN databases and in standard sources such as the *National Union Catalog of Pre–1956 Imprints* or Wilson's *Union List of Serials*

availability, cost, and publisher of hard copy replacement editions listed in in-print sources

the availability of microform copies, with cost and source

space for an indication of bibliographic completeness after collation

space for the selector's decision on treatment and disposition ("film and discard," "film and retain," etc.)

Many libraries also design the form to serve as a control sheet that accompanies the volume through the filming process.

Complete bibliographic and replacement searches can be very time consuming. Estimates for such searches average about twenty minutes per title for full searches but perhaps five to seven minutes for online searches or seven to ten minutes per title for microformat replacement searches. For this reason, you should try to increase search efficiency by outlining a policy regarding preferred replacement formats and the priority and extent of replacement searches. Search forms should be batched in groups of thirty to fifty items. Before searching printed tools, organize the search forms alphabetically by main entry to make the most efficient use of searching time. Exploit the power of automation by using the capabilities of PC-based databases and integrated library systems to streamline as much of the information gathering as possible.[13]

Figure 8 provides information on the most frequently used tools that should be used in a comprehensive replacement search. To facilitate the searching process, search for replacements in the order suggested. Search sources are arranged in a ranking, based on institutional experience, of those that most frequently contain citations for replacements, with the most comprehensive tools first. Be sure to search relevant guides from other countries when the nature of the collection calls for it. After an initial start-up period, it may become clear that some sources most often yield replacements, and the order of searching should be adjusted so that those are consulted first.

It is generally helpful to involve acquisitions and/or cataloging staff in replacement searching, even to have them do it all. The tools cited in figure 8, along with other specialized ones you may need to consult, often are available in the acquisitions department, and experienced staff members will have special understanding of the search strategies, strengths and weaknesses of various databases, catalogs, and bibliographies.

Searching OCLC and RLIN is now generally the best way to determine whether a preservation microfilm has been created or whether another institution

---

13. For some possibilities, see Nancy Elkington, "Preservation and Automation: Bring on the Empty Horses," *Abbey Newsletter* 15 (May 1991): 43–5.

FIGURE 8 Tools for Replacement Searching

For Microform Replacement

Monographs

Online bibliographic databases (OCLC, RLIN, etc.)
New York Public Library Register of Microform Masters: Monographs
National Union Catalog: Books
Books on Demand (BOD)
Guide to Microforms in Print (GMIP) & Supplement
Relevant international guides such as *Association pour la Conversation et la Reproduction Photographique de la Presse: Catalogue de microfilms reproduisant des périodiques*

Serials

Online bibliographic databases
Serials in Microform (SIM)
Guide to Microforms in Print (GMIP) & Supplement
Microform Annual
Others (relevant subject guides, international sources, etc.)

Newspapers

Online bibliographic databases
U.S. Newspaper Program (USNP) *National Union List*
Serials in Microform (SIM)
Guide to Microforms in Print (GMIP) & Supplement
International guides

For Paper Copy Replacement

Monographs

Books in Print (BIP), Supplement, and international editions
Guide to Reprints
Books on Demand (BOD)
Others (subject guides, international sources, etc.)

Serials

Guide to Reprints (GTR)
Others (subject guides, international sources, etc.)

---

has decided to film it. These searches call for special understanding of the bibliographic record structure and of search strategies. Chapter 5 provides guidance.

For certain collections or types of materials, it may be most efficient to allow the selectors to review materials before you undertake the bibliographic search. A good example of the type of material that will not require extensive microform replacement searching would be a heavily used (but brittle) novel or standard historical work available in print or as a reprint. When selectors review these materials before searching, they can easily specify "hard copy search only" or "microform search only" on the search forms.

The search should begin by verifying the item's basic bibliographic information. A copy of the online catalog record, shelflist card, or public catalog card can be attached or copied onto the search form after you ascertain that the record accurately represents the item in hand. This step may include a database search for verification. Gleaning the other necessary bibliographic data to record on the form (information about other copies, the author, translations, rarity/scarcity, etc.) should follow.

Add to this information the existence and availability of hard copy reprints and/or of available microform copies. The order of the search in these sources should follow library policy on preferred replacement format. The type of material (long serial runs versus shorter monographic items, for example) will affect the preference for microform over hard copy replacements.

Institutional policy may also govern the determination of when a "hit" is truly a hit. As acquisition librarians know, finding a title in a catalog or database does not always mean it is an acceptable replacement. There can be concerns about the bibliographic quality of some micropublishers' publications—some may not be seen as producing film that meets preservation criteria—or the single title you need may be one of hundreds in an expensive set. All these must be factored into your definition of a "hit."[14]

It has become accepted in many of the nation's major filming projects to omit a source from the search process if, after an initial period, it becomes obvious that the hit rate in that source is particularly low. It may be acceptable to drop a source after a search of 300 to 500 titles yields a hit rate of less than 5 percent in that source. See chapter 6 for a more precise formula for calculating the break-even point between searching and duplicate filming.

Given the time a complete search takes, it is important to maintain files on previous searching done in this process to avoid expensive duplicate searching and to avoid overlooking an important microform replacement source. Every effort must be taken to locate and purchase existing microforms rather than create duplicates, especially for extensive serial holdings.

Illustrated Materials

Certain types of illustrations can be filmed satisfactorily, but others may not be entirely suitable for reformatting onto microfilm. There are three basic categories of illustrations, each with different suitability characteristics:

- black-and-white line drawings, woodcuts, and other "edge-based" representations
- black-and-white halftone reproductions (especially photographs) and shaded drawings
- color images

For the first category, standard high-contrast microfilm will capture the image quite well, and microfilming is generally an acceptable choice.

Continuous-tone filming will produce good results for the second category, provided appropriate film and very high quality cameras are used. (See the discussion of film media in chapter 4.) In fact, continuous-tone film can be used to

---

14. See Robert DeCandido, "Considerations in Evaluating Searching for Microform Availability," *Microform Review* 19 (summer 1990): 116–18.

produce high-quality prints or negatives of photograph collections. However, there are three practical limits on this technique. First, only cameras with very high quality optics and the capability of producing high resolution levels can produce the desired results. Second, continuous-tone filming is generally more expensive than standard high-contrast filming, largely because of the exposure times required. Finally, it is generally more expensive than standard black-and-white microfilming.

Color illustrations cannot be reproduced satisfactorily on black-and-white film, but some long-lasting color films are now available.[15] At this point, few filming labs can produce high-quality color microfilm, and it is difficult to match the precise colors of the original. The chief drawback, though, is the cost; color microfilm is significantly more expensive than black-and-white.

In some cases, it is difficult to capture pages that have both illustrations and black-and-white text. Some filming agents have dealt successfully with this challenge by filming each page twice—once with settings to capture the illustrations, and a second time with camera settings adjusted to capture the text.

A growing number of institutions now use microfilm as a "platform for digital access," and this may be especially appropriate for illustrated materials.[16] Some options are noted in the introduction.

Depending upon the nature of the textual and illustrative materials under consideration, the screening process may result in decisions to (a) film and discard the item because the film replacement will be acceptable, (b) film and retain the item, (c) film the entire item and retain the illustrations only, or (d) do not film. The basis for any of these decisions will depend on the aesthetic quality and value of the illustrations, how satisfactorily they can be rendered on film and/or migrated to a digital format, their degree of deterioration or the hope for conservation treatment, their physical bulk, whether their relationship to the text is vital, and whether funds are available for continuous-tone or color filming. Illustrations are also a means of determining artifactual value. These might include illustrative processes or examples of considerable artistic merit; engravings; original photographs; high quality photographic reproductions; colored plates; woodcuts, lithographs, etchings, or other prints; or "artists' books."

Formats, Frequency, and Type of Use

Encyclopedias, indexes, music scores, maps, and other materials have been successfully converted to a preservation microformat in several institutions, and numerous bibliographic catalogs receive heavy use in microform. However, you should consider whether microfiche is better suited for use by researchers than is the roll microfilm format.

---

15. While the black-and-white silver-gelatin film used in preservation work has a life expectancy (LE) of 500 years, ANSI standards have not yet established an LE rating for color film. However, tests suggest that Ilfochrome (a silver dye bleach film) may remain stable for hundreds of years if stored in the dark. See further discussion in chapter 4.

16. See especially C. Lee Jones, *Preservation Film: Platform for Digital Access Systems* (Washington, D.C.: Commission on Preservation and Access, July 1993); and *Preserving the Illustrated Text,* Report of the Joint Task Force on Text and Image (Washington, D.C.: Commission on Preservation and Access, 1992).

For some time it was customary to consider preservation microfilming combined with Copyflo production for such items as important, heavily used, and brittle music or reference materials such as dictionaries or encyclopedias.[17] With the advent of the "hybrid systems" approach (discussed in the introduction), these problems may be addressed successfully. The microfilm can serve as the permanent preservation medium, while the needs of users are accommodated by the digitized version available through computer screens or in hard copy output.

In many cases serials are ideal candidates for microfilming. However, filming serials can be more complex than filming monographs. If the holdings are not complete, much time and effort may be spent in locating missing issues or parts. Bibliographic control work requires special knowledge and may be quite complex, especially if no machine-readable cataloging exists. These factors can significantly add to the cost of filming. On the other hand, the space savings can be substantial.

Folded maps from monographic and serial publications may or may not lend themselves to reformatting onto film. Colored maps may be particularly difficult to film due to the slight differences in contrast when using black-and-white film stock, but color filming is an option. Maps printed before certain dates, notably 1850, should be seriously considered for retention in the original format, regardless of size, because of their artifactual value. The size of some maps can make their film reproduction an unsatisfactory option for selectors. Large maps must be filmed in segments (see chapter 3, "Foldouts and Oversize Materials"), making them difficult for researchers to use. A careful consideration of how researchers use such material in oversize or unusual formats must underpin preservation decisions.

Value

Even though most items in a research collection are valued primarily for their intellectual content, certain items may possess intrinsic value as artifacts or objects and should be preserved and retained in their original or near-original forms. Even for these, it may be wise to consider making a microform copy for security reasons or to reduce handling of the original. Various authors have used the terms *intrinsic, artifactual,* and *historic value* to emphasize the special status of the original and the caution with which decisions to microfilm and/or discard should be approached. The terms are often used interchangeably, despite their technical definitions, but their importance in a microfilming program is clear.

> *Intrinsic value:* "historic, bibliographic or artifactual value of an individual item that is dependent on the retention of its original parts,"[18] or "term used to define or describe the qualities of archival materials. Records have intrinsic value or not, depending upon such factors as uniqueness

---

17. Copyflo is a registered trademark of the Xerox Corporation for the equipment and process that creates paper copy from negative microfilm in a continuous roll. The equipment is no longer manufactured or serviced by Xerox, and the service is available from only a few commercial microfilm agents and older library photographic service departments.

18. Carolyn Clark Morrow and Carole Dyal, *Conservation Treatment Procedures: A Manual of Step-by-Step Procedures for the Maintenance and Repair of Library Materials,* 2d ed. (Littleton, Colo.: Libraries Unlimited, 1986), 216.

or value of informational content, age, physical format, artistic or aesthetic qualities, and scarcity. Materials having intrinsic value generally warrant preservation in their original form, while records lacking intrinsic value often can be copied to preserve informational content."[19]

Artifactual value: "the archival term that is applied to permanently valuable records that have qualities and characteristics that make the records in their original form the only archivally acceptable form for preservation. Although all records in their original physical form have qualities and characteristics that would not be preserved in copies, records with intrinsic value have them to such a significant degree that the originals must be saved."[20]

Historic value: "the interest that a book or binding has beyond the information transmitted by its printed words; the integrity of a book in terms of its original production details and accidents of time."[21]

Materials fitting these criteria have qualities—either physical qualities (as physical evidence) or intellectual qualities (as information)—that are totally or significantly lost in their reproductions. It is the physical and informational nature of an item—its age, rarity, historical or technological or bibliographic importance, provenance, close connection with an event, etc.—that should prevent its being discarded, even if it is reproduced in some fashion. The responsibility for determining which items possess intrinsic, historic, or other artifactual value lies in the archives with the curator or archivist and in the library with the selector who has curatorial responsibility for that portion of the collection. Several institutions (among them LC, NARA, and the New York Public Library [NYPL]) routinely microfilm portions of their collections and have outlined guidelines for retention of certain items in original format because of their intrinsic value. Materials having intrinsic or artifactual value will possess one or more of the physical or information qualities or characteristics described in the sections immediately following.

Date of Publication or Creation.
Institutional practice varies in the setting of dates that dictate when an item is to be retained in its original format. Some libraries set 1850 as a cutoff date, others 1801. More often, however, the importance of the date of publication or creation is dependent upon the place and circumstances of publication. Some commonly cited categories of material having artifactual value are incunabula, items printed in England before 1640, any Confederate imprint, imprints with early regional importance (e.g., Chicago imprints before 1871, etc.). Many libraries follow Library of Congress practice in terms of determining when a title should be considered a rare book.[22]

---

19. Mary Lynn Ritzenthaler, *Preserving Archives and Manuscripts* (Chicago: SAA, 1993), 157.

20. U.S. National Archives and Records Service, *Intrinsic Value in Archival Material,* Staff Information Paper 21 (Washington, D.C.: NARS, 1982), 1.

21. Morrow and Dyal, *Conservation Treatment Procedures,* 215.

22. For a list of cutoff dates, see Tamara Swora and Bohdan Yasinsky, *Processing Manual* (Washington, D.C.: LC, Preservation Microfilming Office, 1981), MONO-11. The same list can also be found in *American Imprints Inventory, Manual of Procedures,* 5th ed. (Chicago: Historical Records Survey, 1939), 46.

Certain twentieth-century materials possess as much intrinsic or artifactual value as those of the nineteenth or earlier centuries. Documentary records concerning the radio industry, nuclear power, or computing are examples of items with growing artifactual significance.

Rarity or Scarcity. Rarity or scarcity may be evaluated by searching the *National Union Catalog of Pre-1956 Imprints,* OCLC and RLIN databases, or in a specialized bibliography that verifies rarity, scarcity, or uniqueness. Such items may include those issued in very limited editions, copyright deposit editions, publishers' or reviewers' advance copies of certain works that may differ in content and form from the published edition, or certain published editions of which very few copies exist.

Association Value. Some books may not be valuable in themselves but become so because of their association with persons or events. For example, the book may contain marginalia written by a locally or nationally important person or have valuable ownership marks or book plates. Presentation copies or other inscribed copies are another type, as are some books with manuscript material attached or added.

Items of Aesthetic or Design Value. Books with interesting overall designs are best kept in their original form. These include fine bindings, period bindings, nineteenth- and early twentieth-century cloth-bound volumes with aesthetically interesting cover designs or that document the history of such bindings, and signed or designer bindings.

Unique, Unusual, or Curious Physical Features. Items that possess unique physical features, such as the quality and texture of the paper, imprints, watermarks, decorated endpapers, gilded and gauffered edges, fore-edge paintings, wax seals, inks, or unusual covering materials, generally should be retained.

Evidentiary Value. Items of questionable authenticity, date, authorship, or other characteristics ascertainable primarily by physical examination should be kept in their original form. Books or documents that are suspected of being forgeries or fakes (such as some photographs of UFOs) or documents that show evidence of erasures are examples of questionable items that may have artifactual value.

Legal or Historical Value. Some items must be retained by law or are required to trace the history and policies of an organization. Some examples would include items

> with significance as a record of the establishment or continuing legal basis of an agency or institution. As outlined by the National Archives, these are archival documents with the common characteristic of documenting the shifts in function of the agency or institution at the highest level.

with significance as documentation of policy formulation at the highest executive levels when the policy has significance and broad effect throughout or beyond the agency or institution. Again, as outlined by the National Archives, the characteristics that give policy records intrinsic value are the origin of the records at the highest executive levels, breadth of effect, and importance of subject matter.

that must be retained in original format by legal statute or policy. Depending on the institution or organization, these might include articles of incorporation, constitutions, bylaws, titles, deeds, policies, and so on. Federal and state statutes allow the substitution of microform copies for original documents in many cases.[23]

Exhibition Value.   If items have value for use in exhibits because of their ability to convey the immediacy of the event or to depict a significant issue or quality that only an item in original form can impart, they should be retained. These may include items whose physical form may be the subject for study if they provide meaningful documentation or significant examples of the form. Examples of artifactually valuable items of this type are glass plate negatives, an edition that was the first to be produced by the linotype process, early cloth bindings, early machine-made papers, and early rotogravure pictorial reproductions.

Items with high value under any of these criteria certainly may be good candidates for reformatting to enhance access while reducing wear on the original. However, the staff must weigh these benefits against the potential that the item may sustain some damage in the course of filming.

Intellectual Importance of the Material

Many of the selection criteria deal with physical characteristics. This element in the screening process responds to the intellectual value of the item in the subject or discipline and in the local collection, as seen by scholars, curators, or subject specialists. The knowledge these evaluators should bring to this task is outlined in the preceding section ("Responsibility for Screening and Decision Making") and can be applied at various points in the identification and screening process.

Since the national brittle books crisis began to receive widespread attention and concern in the 1970s, scholars and curators have been vividly aware that preservation selection decisions we make now will have a direct impact on the shape of scholarship and collections in the future. This has often led to great debate about what is most important to save. In a 1991 report the Harvard University Library Task Group on Collection Preservation Priorities rejected the concept of importance as a valid criterion: "Agreement as to what is important would

---

23. William Saffady, *Micrographic Systems,* 3d ed. (Silver Spring, Md.: AIIM, 1990), 6. In addition, ANSI/AIIM MS19-1993, *American National Standard for Information and Image Management—Standard Recommended Practice—Identification of Microforms* (Silver Spring, Md.: AIIM, 1993), specifies targets to use when certification of public records is required. Also see ANSI/AIIM MS48-1990, *American National Standard for Information and Image Management—Recommended Practice for Microfilming Public Records on Silver-Halide Film* (Silver Spring, Md.: AIIM, 1990).

only show that we are well-adjusted, acculturated products of the ideology of our time and place. We have not, however, sought that agreement, for we have instead agreed to reject the criterion of importance."[24] This stance rests also on the belief that if selection criteria such as those outlined here are weighed carefully by qualified scholars, librarians, and archivists, the resulting collections will serve future scholars well.

Donor or Copyright Restrictions

Certain volumes, documents, manuscripts, or papers may not be suitable preservation microfilming candidates if donor restrictions affect either the use of the materials or their withdrawal from the collection. Depending on how the films are to be used, the issue of copyright may also affect selection of items for filming. If you intend to sell copies of the film, then the title to be filmed must either be in the public domain or you should obtain copyright permission. How can you tell?

Under the Copyright Law of the United States of America (Title 17, United States Code), works in the public domain include the following:

publications of the U.S. government[25]

those that bear a notice of waiver of copyright

those published before 1978 without a notice of copyright

those whose copyright has expired because they were published more than 75 years earlier

those whose copyright has expired because they were published between 28 and 76 years ago and copyright was not renewed

While the first four criteria will normally be self-evident from the information in the book, the last one may require considerable research to determine its status, starting with a letter to the publisher and perhaps proceeding to a full-scale search of records in the LC Copyright Office.[26] Copyright issues are even more complex for manuscripts and archives than for published works, and it may be prudent to obtain legal counsel.

The copyright law does allow for preservation of copyrighted works. Section 108(b) states that unpublished works can be "duplicated in facsimile form solely for purposes of preservation and security . . . if [the item] is currently in the collection of the library or archives." Further, Section 108(c) states that published works can be "duplicated in facsimile form solely for the purpose of replacement of a copy . . . that is damaged, deteriorating, lost, or stolen if the library or archives has, after reasonable effort, determined that an unused replacement cannot be obtained at a fair price."

---

24. *Preserving Harvard's Retrospective Collections* (Cambridge, Mass.: Harvard University, 1991), 5.

25. An exception is that works copyrighted by others and published or reprinted by the federal government do not lose their protected status; see Robert L. Oakley, *Copyright and Preservation: A Serious Problem in Need of a Thoughtful Solution* (Washington, D.C.: Commission on Preservation and Access, Sept. 1990), 11–12.

26. The basic file at the Copyright Office is the *Catalog of Copyright Entries,* available from the Government Printing Office and many depository libraries.

Foldouts (rear center) and papers with bleed-through (as in the front left) require extra attention during filming. Scrapbooks and composite items often require multiple exposures to capture the information on each page. With such materials, filming costs as well as labor costs involved in preparation may influence the selection decision. *University of Kentucky Libraries Reprographics Department. Photo by Lewis Warden.*

Copyright concerns are less severe if the items being filmed are esoteric, unlikely to be in heavy demand, and unlikely to have a significant economic impact on the copyright holder. But copyright clearance is crucial for commercial micropublication projects. Copyright issues are even more complex in the context of digitization or scanning projects.[27]

Cost of Filming

The cost of filming an item may be so high, because of either length (a long serial run) or characteristics that require special handling (extreme brittleness, large size, color, etc.), that it would overwhelm the budget. While the item may meet all the criteria for inclusion in a microfilming program, it may have to be set aside until special funding is available.

Shelf Space

Conversely, the institution may decide that filming long runs of serials, theses, or other coherent collections will so significantly ease space constraints that these

---

27. See Oakley, *Copyright and Preservation,* 25.

items should be filmed as a unit even if some individual pieces are less suitable. For example, even if a few issues of a serial title were not acidic or not yet brittle, there would still be advantages in filming the entire run.

Potential for Being Filmed Elsewhere

Microfilming is not a new technology. As early as 1938, the Library of Congress and other institutions began to mount large-scale projects devoted to categories of material. Newspapers received, and continue to receive, great emphasis through the USNP spearheaded by LC and NEH, and no institution should film historic newspapers apart from the state-based initiatives of the USNP. (See the description of this program in the introduction.) Serials have been filmed extensively through commercial micropublication and other ventures. Certain institutions have staked out territories for filming, based on geographic imprints or subjects. For years the Center for Research Libraries filmed African, Southeast Asian, South Asian, and Latin American materials, for example. Certain institutions have long-standing emphases in their microfilming programs, such as Cornell University's focus on Southeast Asian materials. The early efforts (beginning in 1983) of RLG focused on U.S. history. Since the late 1980s, concerted efforts of ASERL and SOLINET have focused on filming southern materials. A large-scale agriculture filming initiative is being launched by Cornell University and the U.S. Agricultural Information Network. The participants in the cooperative filming programs of RLG and CIC have divided responsibilities by broad subject classes, and many different areas have been covered by a decade of concerted filming.

With the vastly increased level of preservation microfilming, spurred by increased federal funds available for this work, the potential for overlap with existing projects is great. You must educate yourself as to what projects are in progress and what the criteria for inclusion are in order to make decisions that complement these efforts. Finding the information, however, is no easy task. There is no centralized source for vetting current or potential projects. Because so many preservation microfilming projects are funded by the NEH Division of Preservation and Access, that office may be a good beginning point. Additional information, especially about projects just in the planning stages, may be available from managers of ongoing cooperative projects and from vendors that specialize in preservation microfilming. You must constantly peruse the library, archival, and information science press and communicate with others to keep abreast of developments.

If it is likely that an item may be microfilmed elsewhere, the decision to put it aside for the time being may be prudent, especially if this is your institution's first filming venture. Alternatively, you may ask another institution specifically to include it. Such ad hoc cooperation is becoming more commonplace, even among established filming programs, as more collections and institutions are engaged in this work. Indeed, it is a featured element of the decentralized, whole-discipline approach advocated in the National Preservation Program for Agricultural Literature.[28]

---

28. Gwinn, *A National Preservation Program for Agricultural Literature.*

Advance Cataloging

The success of the national and international effort to preserve important collections rests not only on selecting appropriate works for preservation but also on avoiding redundant effort. Therefore, once an item has passed the screening process and been selected for microfilming, it is important to record your intent to film the work in one of the national bibliographic databases. This is generally achieved through some form of advance cataloging. Chapter 5 describes and analyzes the options for doing so in OCLC and RLIN. This action ensures that other institutions will discover the record in their bibliographic searches and will save them the time and expense of further searching, evaluation, and filming.

Conclusion

Selection for preservation is essential and often difficult. There exists no easy formula to tell librarians and archivists just what to save and how or what to toss and why. In this process of selection lies the future of the documentary record. It cannot be undertaken lightly.

Although large amounts of textual materials are ensured of a future through preservation microfilming, it is clear that not all library and archival materials are suitable for this or other reformatting techniques. The screening criteria outlined here can be used as a general guide that, combined with common sense and sound judgment, will lead to wise decisions. The only alternative is to let chance and accident make the decisions for us.

Suggested Readings

Atkinson, Ross W. "Selection for Preservation: A Materialistic Approach." *Library Resources & Technical Services* 30 (Oct./Dec. 1986): 341–53.

Bagnall, Roger S., and Carolyn L. Harris. "Involving Scholars in Preservation Decisions: The Case of the Classicists." *Journal of Academic Librarianship* 13 (July 1987): 140–6.

Child, Margaret S. "Further Thoughts on 'Selection for Preservation.'" *Library Resources & Technical Services* 30 (Oct./Dec. 1986): 354–62.

———. "Selection for Microfilming." *American Archivist* 53 (spring 1990): 250–5.

———. "Selection for Preservation." In *Advances in Preservation and Access,* vol. 1, edited by Barbra Buckner Higginbotham and Mary E. Jackson, 147–58. Westport, Conn.: Meckler, 1992.

Cox, Richard J. "Selecting Historical Records for Microfilming: Some Suggested Procedures for Repositories." *Library and Archival Security* 9 (1989): 21–41.

DeCandido, Robert. "Considerations in Evaluating Searching for Microform Availability." *Microform Review* (summer 1990): 116–18.

Gwinn, Nancy E. "A National Preservation Program for Agricultural Literature." United States Agricultural Information Network, Beltsville, Md., May 16, 1993. Photocopy.

Harvard University Library Task Group on Collection Preservation Priorities. *Preserving Harvard's Retrospective Collections.* Cambridge, Mass.: Harvard University, 1991.

Hazen, Dan C. "Collection Development, Collection Management, and Preservation." *Library Resources & Technical Services* 26 (Jan./Mar. 1982): 3–11.

Oakley, Robert L. *Copyright and Preservation: A Serious Problem in Need of a Thoughtful Solution.* Washington, D.C.: Commission on Preservation and Access, Sept. 1990.

Ogden, Barclay. *On the Preservation of Books and Documents in Original Form.* Washington, D.C.: Commission on Preservation and Access, 1989.

U.S. National Archives and Records Service. *Intrinsic Value in Archival Material.* Staff Information Paper 21. Washington, D.C.: NARS, 1982.

Wallach, William K., and Linda M. Matthews. "The Relationship between Archival Appraisal and Selection for Preservation." In *RLG Archives Microfilming Manual,* edited by Nancy E. Elkington, 105–8. Mountain View, Calif.: RLG, 1994.

Production Planning and Preparation of Materials

Once you have completed the selection of volumes, documents, or newspapers to be microfilmed, a new phase of the preservation microfilming program begins. The kind of materials your program will focus on will determine many facets of your production planning. Then the materials must be prepared, sorted, packaged, and delivered to the camera.

Production planning involves many administrative decisions, among which the choice of filming agent is critical. You must think through all the steps of the project from your in-house procedures and workflow through the filming process itself to the ultimate use the film will serve—for example, whether the film will be the end product or used as the base for digitization, what kinds of uses you expect the film to receive, and so on. If you plan to produce microfilm in a hybrid systems approach that will also include scanning, the production planning and preparation issues covered here will still be relevant. Whether you are filming or scanning, preparation of materials is equally labor intensive. But you will need to approach some decisions differently, based on whether you are creating the film or scanning first. (See the introduction for a basic discussion of digitization.)

Preparation of materials for microfilming is a labor-intensive, production-oriented task. Effective planning for this phase requires (1) familiarity with the national standards for preservation microfilming, (2) a thorough understanding of the filming process, (3) good communication with the filming agent, and (4) an analysis of the intended use of the film product. The preparation step is filled with endless details that are equal in importance to the processes of selection and filming. Each decision in the preparation process will have a major impact on the value of the microforms you create, so you need to think through and understand the alternatives before launching your program.

This chapter covers the key issues involved in production planning and in making materials camera-ready. It outlines the steps in selecting a filming agent and rehearses for you the administrative decisions that must be made before you begin the process. The chapter closes with an in-depth discussion of preparation procedures. You may need to integrate into the preparation process some of the routines to handle internal record keeping and statistics, as well as archival arrangement and bibliographic control of the microfilm. See chapter 5 for a discussion of those functions. In addition, be aware of the constant synergy between the production planning and preparation work covered here and the filming processes discussed in chapter 4.

Standards and Guidelines

Before going very far in your planning, and certainly before any discussions with a filming agent, you should be familiar with the various standards, specifications, and guidelines relevant to permanent film (its stability in manufacture, processing, and storage) and microfilming operations. Many of those documents also address the preparation of materials for filming. A list of key standards appears in appendix A, and they are further discussed in chapter 4.

At a minimum you must develop an understanding of the key micrographics standards produced by ANSI and AIIM. But you may also adapt or build on guidelines and specifications produced by such organizations as RLG, which are listed in appendix A. The RLG guidelines merit particular attention because they are generally the most stringent, often going well beyond the requirements of the ANSI and AIIM standards, and because they are tailored to library and archival preservation concerns. It is your responsibility to prepare the technical specifications and filming instructions for the materials you wish to have filmed. But the minimum requirement for any negotiation with a filming agent should be the ANSI/AIIM standards.

Choosing the Filming Agent

A library or archival repository may consider several options for handling the actual filming when planning a microfilm project. Some institutions have an in-house photoduplication laboratory, either within the preservation department or as an independent unit, while others use an outside film laboratory (sometimes known as a service bureau). Chapter 1 addresses key issues to weigh in deciding whether to do the filming or other operations in-house or to contract with a service bureau.

Whatever the organizational relationship between the institution and the filming agent (used here to refer to either in-house camera operations or external contractor), certain responsibilities need to be assigned, and both parties need to have a clear understanding of these duties. In some cases a formal contract delineates these tasks; at other times there may be only informal letters of agreement. In either case, the agreements should be in writing and mutually agreed upon between the institution and the filming agent.

Identifying Filming Agents

Through the mid-1980s, there were few organizations that provided preservation-oriented filming services. Many large libraries and state archives had in-house microfilming operations that accepted institutional projects, and a few would accept contractual work from others. Today there are several commercial and nonprofit filming bureaus that specialize in preservation microfilming. Even if you have an in-house operation, you should investigate contractual services so you can make an informed choice based on costs, services, and other options.[1]

Exercise a healthy degree of skepticism as you evaluate filming agents. While you may have an in-house laboratory, it may or may not have been involved in high-quality preservation filming or have worked with fragile materials. Nor can you assume that an external service bureau has worked with libraries or performed preservation microfilming, even if the bureau uses the word "archival" to describe its service. The definition of *archival* ranges from the photographic-jargon meaning, "temporary storage of actively used information," to legal definitions (such as the requirement for keeping certain records for seven years) to "preservation of information forever." Furthermore, even if a service bureau has worked successfully for another institution, you cannot assume yours will receive the same level of service.

Figure 9 lists the elements you should consider as you evaluate and negotiate with filming agents. Some information will be provided by the filming agent and some by the institution. In many cases, you will need to define your requirements, ascertain the filmer's ability to meet them, and perhaps fine-tune your plans. Some items must be addressed in the early stages of screening prospects, others may arise later in the process, and some may be addressed at multiple points in increasingly greater detail. The checklist reflects points covered in the body of this chapter.

Your first step will be to identify potential filming agents. Look at the library and archival literature for companies that advertise preservation microfilming services. Contact institutions that have carried out microfilming projects. Organizations that sponsor microfilming projects (listed in appendix B) may provide the names of filming agents they have used. In addition, funding agencies such as NEH and NHPRC can provide lists of institutions that have received preservation microfilming grants, and contact with those institutions might yield additional prospects. Some state archives and state records programs may maintain lists of filming agents as well.

You may identify various types of filming agents, including institutions or state agencies (e.g., state archives or records centers) with filming labs, commercial filmers, and nonprofit service bureaus. Some may have significant experience with preservation microfilming projects, some will lack such experience, and others will be in the middle range. Regardless of the type of organization, all potential filmers should be evaluated carefully, according to the guidelines offered in this chapter.

For most collections, the geographic location of the service bureau is irrelevant. Major museums and other cultural organizations regularly ship priceless objects across the continent and abroad. It should be possible to transport your collections safely, provided you get good advice about shipping services and

---

1. Under current NEH guidelines, applicants must obtain at least two price quotations and justify the choice that is made, even if an in-house lab exists.

FIGURE 9 Filming Agent Evaluation Checklist

Filmer's Experience and Capabilities   **Notes**

- ☐ Adherence to standards of ANSI and AIIM, RLG guidelines, and other relevant specifications
- ☐ Extent and type of experience with filming, particularly preservation microfilming
- ☐ Client base
- ☐ Ability and experience handling formats to be filmed
- ☐ Procedures and equipment for handling brittle/fragile materials
- ☐ Type of equipment available in the laboratory (models, age, and numbers of each type)
- ☐ Staff experience, training, turnover rates
- ☐ Capacity—ability to handle projected quantity of documents
- ☐ Services available in addition to film production and duplication:
    - ☐ preparation
    - ☐ bibliographic control
    - ☐ storage
    - ☐ other
- ☐ Environmental conditions in the filming lab and storage areas
- ☐ Security systems and disaster preparedness procedures in place
- ☐ Financial stability

Technical Specifications

- ☐ Type of film and final product (film or fiche; silver, diazo, or vesicular; black-and-white, continuous-tone, or color) to be produced
- ☐ Number and type of film copies required
- ☐ Arrangements for volumes to be disbound:
    by whom (institution or filmer)
    by what methods
- ☐ Types of targets to be supplied and by whom
- ☐ Guidelines for frame counts and reel programming
- ☐ Technical inspection procedures and specifications (for density, resolution, Quality Index, chemical testing) and report format
- ☐ Frame-by-frame bibliographic inspection
- ☐ Policy on correction of errors and splicing
- ☐ Packaging and labeling of completed microforms

Business Arrangements

- ☐ Pricing
- ☐ Schedule, deadlines, and turnaround time
- ☐ Transportation/shipping arrangements
- ☐ Insurance on materials during transit and while in the filming lab
- ☐ Payment terms

follow appropriate guidelines for packaging the materials. Most leading filming bureaus will be able to provide you with appropriate instructions.

If transportation remains a concern, perhaps because of the uniqueness or value of the items, you might hire a private carrier or have staff members deliver materials to the filmer. Inconvenient or costly as these arrangements may be, they are greatly preferable to using a local service bureau whose *only* advantage is its proximity.

Another option is to arrange for on-site filming. Only a few filming agents will do filming in the institution, and there are many operational complexities involved in such an arrangement. This option might be worth pursuing, however, for institutions that cannot operate a filming lab themselves but whose collections are of such value that transportation issues pose a significant risk. More often, on-site filming is done by commercial micropublishers, and only for collections that the publisher has determined have a market. Work with micropublishers requires special negotiations and contract terms addressed in the "Contracting" section of this chapter.

Screening Prospects

Once you have compiled a list of prospective filming agents, contact them to gather basic information about their qualifications.[2] You might first review their standard promotional literature, then schedule an appointment for in-depth discussion by telephone or in person. These preliminary discussions are a good way to determine the level of experience and interest a filming agent may have in your project. The discussions should include the following areas:

Does the agent adhere to ANSI/AIIM standards? You will need to determine whether the bureau does or can conform specifically to those standards required for permanent microfilm. You might also be interested in learning whether the filming agent has experience meeting the specifications of RLG or other key organizations.

Does the company have experience with preservation microfilming as opposed to source document filming? If so, for how many years?

What is the company's client base? Is it accustomed to working with libraries or archives?

With what kinds of formats does it have experience? Depending on the nature of your project, you may be particularly interested in learning whether the filming agent has experience with brittle books, archives and manuscripts, scrapbooks, pamphlets, oversize material, color or continuous-tone materials, or other formats.

Does the service bureau have experience in proper handling of brittle, fragile materials as opposed to the sturdy, modern records that make up the majority of work for most commercial filming vendors?

---

2. Excellent guidance on this and subsequent phases of the screening process is provided in Vickie Lockhart and Ann Swartzell, "Evaluation of Microfilm Vendors," *Microform Review* 19 (summer 1990): 119–23. Also see Sherry Byrne, "Guidelines for Contracting Microfilming Services," *Microform Review* 15 (fall 1986): 253–64, but be aware that many standards and specifications cited there have changed in the intervening years.

What equipment does it have? A written list will help you determine whether it has the equipment for proper filming, processing, and quality assurance.

What film products does it produce (e.g., 35mm roll film, 105mm microfiche, or microfilm jackets)?

Can it produce all three generations of film (the master negative, printing master, and service copy)?

Does it offer services in addition to filming and duplication, such as preparation or storage?

Does it have the capacity required for your project? This is especially significant if the project is large or has a short time frame. What kind of schedule and turnaround time can you expect? The equipment list will give you some sense of capacity. You should also ask about the size of the staff, especially the number of camera operators.

How many years of experience do the staff members have? You might ask for average length of service for camera operators and other categories of personnel.

What data are available to document the stability of the company?

Finally, ask the service bureau to provide you with a list of clients for whom they have worked. You may wish to ask specifically for organizations of your type or those for whom the agent has filmed materials similar to yours.

Contacting References

Contact the references you have been given. If possible, also contact a few clients not given as references. Prepare a standard list of questions for your interviews with these clients, perhaps including the following areas of exploration:[3]

nature of the project for which the institution used the filming bureau (collection size, format of materials, and other features that can help you judge the extent to which the issues are applicable to your concerns)

quality of the film produced, the length of time it took to produce the film, and the nature and extent of inspections performed by the client (to determine whether the institution's quality control procedures were sufficient to detect problems)

how refilming was handled, the extent of corrections necessary, turnaround time, and quality of the corrected film

whether materials were returned in good order and without undue damage or stress from filming

whether the filming agent met agreed-upon deadlines

how clear, prompt, and cooperative the filming agent was in communicating about problems and adjustments

---

3. This list is a revised and expanded version of the one in Nancy E. Elkington, ed., *RLG Archives Microfilming Manual* (Mountain View, Calif.: RLG, 1994), 12.

to what extent the invoices conformed to the institution's expectations based on the agreed prices

overall satisfaction with the filming agent's role in the project

Also seek the clients' perspectives on the information you received from filming agents to see whether their experience verifies it.

A negative reference does not necessarily mean you should eliminate a filming agent from consideration. Even the most respected service bureaus have had some projects that were fraught with problems. If you receive one or two anomalous references, you might contact the agent to get additional information and especially to ask what measures have been taken to limit such problems in the future.

Think twice—or three or four times—before working with a service bureau that lacks preservation microfilming experience. Filming agents performing work for libraries or archives for the first time often do not understand the complexities of preservation microfilming and, therefore, do not realize the time and expense that will be entailed. It may be possible to get a product that meets your specifications, but usually it will require a significant amount of education, support, and communication with the filmer to achieve preservation goals. Some agents may make prices attractive because they want to get into the preservation microfilming market, develop your institution as a continuing client, or obtain useful subsequent references. If you choose to use such a service bureau, perhaps only time and experience will allow the filmer accurately to estimate costs that can be held stable for a reasonable period of time.

Site Visits

Strong communication and mutual understanding are critical to the success of any project. If your institution has an in-house filming laboratory that reports to the preservation administrator, constant communication should already be a routine part of the process of supervision. But if you will be working with a photoduplication laboratory in another department or with an external contractor, meeting with the filming agent is crucial.

Filming agents are a rich source of technical capacity, knowledge, and expertise, but they must be willing to work closely with clients to perform the services required. The better informed the filming agent is about preservation microfilming and the goals and objectives of your institution, the better the agent will be able to respond and to provide quality service. Do not underestimate the judgment necessary to interpret and apply the technical specifications. If, through constant communication, the institution and the filming agent grow to think alike, the foundation for a productive relationship is established.

A site visit is a good opportunity to see if a filming facility lives up to its billing. The visit should be prearranged with the filming agency so that you can have access to staff members who can best answer your questions and provide explanations you need. If other full-time staff members in your institution will be working directly with the filming agent, it may be a good idea for them to participate in this visit. Plan to spend from a half day to a full day for a site visit that will include discussions and an examination of the facilities. In addition to

A site visit to a filming service bureau gives you the best chance to assess a filmer's qualifications, including equipment capabilities and operators' handling practices. *Preservation Resources.*

helping you make your selection, this may be a good time to provide more information about the project you are planning and to discuss some of the information you gleaned from the reference interviews.

During your tour, note whether the facility is clean, orderly, and dust free. Note where materials are received and stored, and how they are handled in unpacking and throughout laboratory processing. If valuable originals are to be filmed, look for a safe or vault to store the documents while they are not being filmed. Note, if you can, whether materials are handled with the care that fragile or precious documents require.

The filming laboratory should have reasonably good temperature and humidity controls. Levels in the vicinity of 70°F and 50% relative humidity are reasonable. These will help avoid the ill effects of static electricity, especially during high-speed duplication of roll film. Static electricity can interfere with the proper functioning of electrical parts of cameras and other equipment, and it can also result in minute sparks, which may register on film in lightning- or tree-shaped forms. Inappropriate climate control can also accelerate the aging of items at the lab. Find out how the laboratory monitors temperature and humidity; you might even request copies of charts or printouts from environmental monitoring equipment.

Observe the equipment in operation. Familiarity with the equipment will help you understand what is required in physical preparation. What kinds of cameras are available? Some reliable cameras are older models, so age is not necessarily a negative indicator, provided appropriate maintenance routines are in place. If you anticipate filming bound volumes, make certain the agent owns and uses a book cradle. Are appropriate film splicers in use? Is there appropriate redundancy in the equipment? If a lab has only one camera, one densitometer, or one splicer, a breakdown could create a significant production problem. Chapter 4 will give you a better understanding of the key issues related to the equipment.

Ask to see how targets are prepared and what stock targets are available. (See the section on targets later in this chapter.) The filmer's options for target production will affect preparation procedures, so you need to understand those options in advance.

Spend some time at the camera work stations. Is there adequate space for materials in process? Are appropriate "memory aids" posted, such as targets (sheets of technical and bibliographic information filmed along with an item), target sequences, exposure or lamp settings, and non-Arabic numbering systems? How are exposures controlled to ensure consistent density? (See chapter 4 for specifics on these technical matters.) Especially look for formats similar to those you plan to film, and see how they are being handled.

Look for work stations to support the technical and bibliographic inspection of the finished film. Does the lab have the proper equipment for quality control? Are handling procedures appropriate to avoid damage to the camera negative during inspection? What kinds of testing are done in-house, and which are verified by third parties? How are errors corrected? The "Quality Assurance" section of chapter 4 provides guidance that will help you in this evaluation.

In the course of your visit, talk not only with the management or marketing staff but also with technicians in the various parts of the operation. Do they seem to understand the intricacies and impact of their work? Do they appreciate the fragility and importance of the materials they are filming? While the attitudes and knowledge of the senior staff and managers are important, much depends on the knowledge and commitment of the technical staff.

If you are planning a small-scale filming project, and if you are planning to use a filming agent with a strong reputation for preservation microfilming, you might not need to make a site visit or submit a sample for filming but may proceed directly to the discussion of prices. However, keep in mind that those steps serve important purposes: they build a strong foundation for communication, help the filming agent and client understand each other's goals and needs, and help establish a firm price estimate. If you omit the site visit and sample, you should find other ways to meet those objectives.

Preparing a Sample for Filming

Once you have narrowed the field of prospective filmers, prepare a sample for each of them to film.[4] The filming sample serves two primary purposes. First, the agent uses it to estimate how long the filming will take and, thus, to develop

---

4. A detailed case study and analysis on preparation and inspection of the film sample is provided in Lockhart and Swartzell.

appropriate pricing and realistic production schedules. Second, the sample allows you to evaluate the quality of the filming. As a side benefit, it may also allow you to identify shortcomings in your plans and filming instructions. Even if you are considering only one filming bureau, the sample will help you and the lab staff develop schedules, refine instructions, and resolve problems before work begins.

What size should your sample be? The accurate answer is, "Enough to give you a clear sense of the filmer's capabilities." But more guidance may be needed, especially if this is your first filming project.

The minimum should be at least 200 frames—approximately 200 pages of archival documents or 400 regular-sized book pages. It is preferable, though, to provide a sample large enough to fill a reel of film. The reel capacity chart (figure 18) in this chapter will help you determine how many pages this would be.

Talk with the filming agent beforehand about the size and nature of the sample you are preparing. Items that might seem equivalent to the novice (e.g., a reel of bound pamphlets and one of brittle monographs) may present vastly different challenges to the filmer. While most service bureaus should be willing to produce a reel of straightforward book or manuscript pages, filming a full reel of scrapbooks could be a massive undertaking. It would be reasonable for filming agents to assess a charge for filming such a large sample.

The final consideration in determining the size of the sample is the time it will take your staff to evaluate each filmer's work. A full frame-by-frame inspection must be carried out on each sample reel. The more prospects you have, the smaller the sample you may wish to have filmed.

Provide a representative sample, one that reflects the variety and range of items in your project. Examples are volumes with very yellowed or discolored paper, bound and unbound materials, volumes that contain variations in paper color and opacity, items with color or illustrations, oversize materials, scrapbooks, bound pamphlet volumes, materials in non-Roman alphabet languages, volumes with numerous foldouts, and so on. Include at least three sample volumes, folders, series, or other physical units. Keep in mind, however, that there may be no such thing as a truly "representative sample" of an archival microfilming project. A single archival project could, for example, include one collection of diaries, one of letterpress volumes, one of scrapbooks, and so on. The filming agents can provide guidance on what mix of materials will best enable them to develop valid time and price estimates. If you are considering more than one service bureau, strive to develop nearly equivalent samples for each one so the results will be comparable.

Before you submit the sample for filming, talk with the filming agent about your technical specifications and procedures. You will need to prepare the items as you plan to do in the course of the project, including written instructions for the sample and flags for the camera operator. (See the "Preparation Procedures" section later in this chapter.) Then ask the potential filmers to film the sample in accordance with your prepared technical specifications and instructions.

Have the filming agents prepare all three generations of film (master negative, printing master, and service copy) according to your specifications. In addition, suggest that the service bureau retain a duplicate service copy. This will facilitate communication; when you have inspected the samples and wish to discuss problems or questions your in-house inspection may reveal, both you and the filming agent can look at the film simultaneously. Otherwise, much time may be lost as you transport reels back and forth between your institution and the lab.

The sample will enable you to evaluate the filming agent's technical quality, judgment, common sense, and ability to follow instructions. It will allow you to find out the agent's strengths, weaknesses, or limitations, and to correct some production problems before the project begins. Upon discussion with the filming agent, it may also turn out that some of your instructions, specifications, or targets were not clear, and this will allow you to make modifications before the project begins. To make these judgments, you must inspect the completed samples using the quality assurance procedures outlined in chapter 4.

If your filming project is small (under 50 reels or so), you may not need to have a sample filmed to get a price quote from the filmer. The sample filming and your review of the sample will streamline work once you initiate the project. If you skip that step, be sure to have the filmer submit the first couple of reels for your review in case some specifications, instructions, or procedures need to be revised.

Reviewing Completed Microfilm Samples

The samples should be returned along with the filmer's quality control report forms. Review the forms and the film thoroughly and promptly for quality and adherence to specifications and instructions.[5] Chapter 4 details the inspection procedures you should use.

Communicate with the service bureau once you have completed your inspection. If you sent samples to several filming agents as part of the selection process, give clear comments and suggestions to the best of them. Ask the agents to refilm and make corrections as necessary until the sample is fully acceptable. This process will allow you to evaluate the agents' policies and procedures for corrections, as well as assess their responsiveness. If there are significant problems, additional samples should be prepared and filmed until you are confident about the quality of the film and its adherence to required standards and specifications.

Prices

After the sample is filmed and any corrections made, agents should supply cost data or price estimates based on the actual materials they have filmed and the specifications you provided. Thus, there are two variables: whether your sample is a valid representation and whether the specifications you provided will be applied with little or no modification in the actual project.

Filming agents will base their prices and schedules on the sample. The per-frame charge will be based on the expectation of the number of frames per hour the lab can film. Once the project begins, if actual production varies far from that estimate, and if that deviation is because your sample was not representative, the filming agent may be entitled either to assess a special handling charge or to renegotiate the price.

---

5. See Lockhart and Swartzell, "Evaluation of Microfilm Vendors," regarding lessons learned in one university's experience of evaluating filming samples.

Prices for filming are usually on a per-frame (per-exposure) basis, with additional charges possible for target preparation, duplication, special handling, certification of the filming (for public records and legal documents), polysulfide treatment, special inspection requirements, special boxing or labeling requirements, or shipping and handling. This price generally covers the preservation master negative. Charges for additional copies (including the printing master and service copies) may be at a flat rate or based on film footage.

Be sure your specifications enumerate all the products and services you will need so that you can obtain prices for all of them. For example, it may be possible to establish an inclusive per-exposure charge that would cover a standard order (e.g., a preservation master, a printing master, and a service copy). If you require a copy-on-demand service or expect the filming agent to provide storage for master negatives or printing masters, supply the relevant specifications and ask the filmer to provide these prices.

Without instructions from the client, some filming agents will provide itemized charges, others will provide a "rolled-up" total based on the anticipated number of exposures, and a few may provide both. Fair comparison of the prices will be easiest if you have the potential filming agents provide a total "rolled-up," per-frame charge, that is, one that takes into account all your specifications, special requirements, copies, and so on and translates that into a total per-frame price.[6]

If you plan to film straightforward materials such as brittle books, the filming agent may be willing to provide an estimate by phone. Before committing to any price, however, a service bureau will typically want to receive your filming specifications and a sample of materials (as recommended here), so it can develop precise estimates of productivity and cost. It would be unwise for you to base any grant proposal budget or work plans on the estimate you might receive unless the filmer has evaluated your sample of materials.

The concept of "ballpark estimates" is largely irrelevant when planning a project to film archival materials because there are many more variables. The price per frame (which generally translates into a document page) may be higher for archival materials than for books due to the degree of difficulty involved in handling a particular format, the number of additional exposures that may be needed to capture text, and the number of targets that may be required. Different archival formats may entail significantly different prices, ranging from sturdy modern records to challenging formats such as scrapbooks and letterpress copies.

Workflow

You should plan your workflow and discuss your expectations with the filming agent before the project begins. Are the materials to be delivered and filmed at one time or in batches over a period of time? What amounts of materials will be sent on what schedule? Is there an end date for project completion, for instance, grant funds that must be used by a certain deadline? What happens if either side does not meet expectations for work? A clear, advance understanding of requirements and concerns is the best policy for successful workflow.

---

6. For further guidance, see Lockhart and Swartzell, "Evaluation of Microfilm Vendors," 121–2.

The rate of preparation of materials must be compatible with the filming rate so that the staff in each stage are used most efficiently and appropriately. Keep in mind the additional time required for the preparations staff to perform quality assurance and other postfilming routines such as assembling materials and documentation, closing out records, forwarding master negatives to storage, and so on.

Contracting for Filming Services

The steps outlined so far in this chapter are equally relevant whether you are using an in-house filming lab or an outside filming agent and whether you plan to develop a formal contract. It may be to your advantage to develop a request for proposals (RFP) or request for information (RFI) and to develop a written agreement, and those require some special considerations.

There are many reasons to develop a good RFP and/or contract. Most obviously, the RFP elicits detailed information and comparable data that allow you to make important evaluations, and the contract ensures a clear mutual understanding of the institution's and filming agent's expectations and commitments. Perhaps equally important, developing these documents requires you to do the advance planning that will help project implementation go as smoothly as possible.

Requests for Proposals

An RFP or RFI should be issued after you have made your initial inquiries and generally identified those filming agents that appear qualified to undertake your project.[7] Much of the information gathering discussed earlier in this chapter (prices, schedules, etc.) can be incorporated into the RFP process. The RFP should include the following major components:

cover letter inviting the agent to submit a bid or cost estimate

overview of the project—its beginning date and duration, funding status (are funds available or contingent on a grant award or special allocation?), the required turnaround time, and other general parameters

detailed description of the collection to be filmed, including the type or format of materials and their condition

the quantity of materials to be filmed—both the number of units (for example, volumes, folders, or titles) and the average number of pages per unit

services you want the filming agent to provide—filming only or others such as preparation services, duplication, bibliographic control, or storage

sample contract, including the institution's project instructions

bid sheet or other form on which the agent provides price quotations

Your purchasing department should be able to assist you in the legal aspects of the RFP process, and this manual along with others cited here should help you

---

7. Sample RFIs and RFPs (for basic or expanded services) are included in Nancy E. Elkington, ed., *RLG Preservation Microfilming Handbook* (Mountain View, Calif.: RLG, 1992), 101–18.

develop the content of the RFP. As noted in chapter 1, the institutional administrator or project manager must work to ensure that proposals are not evaluated merely on the basis of pricing.

Contracts

It is customary to include a draft contract with the RFP or RFI. The contract would then be finalized with the filming agent that is selected. A contract is a legally binding instrument for which you will need legal counsel and clearance from your parent organization.

Most contracts contain three sections, one devoted to general terms and conditions, another to technical specifications, and a third to the budget or cost figures. Both the institution and the filming agent benefit from a clear, written understanding of what is expected. A handshake is not enough.

If a contract is to be let, some discussion may take place as part of a meeting of potential bidders, and some points may also be included in the final contract specifications. Figure 9 lists topics that must be thoroughly explored and understood by all to ensure a satisfactory relationship.

General Terms and Agreements. The general section of the contract sets out in detail the responsibilities of the institution and the filming agent and the conditions and terms under which both agree to work.[8] Common topics are

prices and pricing policies

price escalation frequency and procedures

invoicing procedures

payment terms

compliance with specifications

responsibilities of the institution and agent for pre- and postfilming operations

improvements and innovations—the option to use new methods or materials developed after contract signing

errors and delays—including the amount of time the institution will be allowed for inspection and refilming requests

communication—the designated contact at the institution and filming lab, modes of communication, means by which official and ad hoc agreements will be documented, and the institution's right to make site visits

cancellation of the contract

dispute resolution

---

8. An excellent discussion of contract provisions and issues related to contract development appears in Elkington, *RLG Archives Microfilming Manual,* 16–23, and a sample contract is on 124–32 of that manual. Some of the items in the following list are adapted from that section. A sample contract is also included in Elkington, *RLG Preservation Microfilming Handbook,* 119–29. See also Byrne, "Guidelines for Contracting Microfilming Services."

subcontracting

warranties and liabilities

insurance and security

copyright—institution's warranty that it has the right to make copies and indemnification of the filming agent for any charges of infringement

pickup and delivery arrangements

right of the institution to establish filming specifications in areas such as disbinding, reel programming, and reduction ratio

contract extension terms

Some special certifications and disclosures may also be required. For example, federal grant recipients and all their subcontractors (including filming agents) may be required to provide certifications regarding nondiscrimination statutes, federal debt status, drug-free workplace policies, and lobbying activities. Your institution may have other special requirements. Be sure you are aware of any special provisions with which subcontractors must comply and include them in the contract.

Technical Specifications.   The contract should have detailed specifications for filming, processing, duplication, and inspection of the microfilm. Some filming agents provide a wide variety of other services such as bibliographic searching, preparation, cataloging, storage, and on-demand duplication. If you choose to contract for those additional services, detailed specifications for each of them must be included in the contract. You may need to add local or special instructions for filming or handling, especially if you are microfilming brittle materials to be kept after filming.

While the "general terms and conditions" section may be the most important part of the contract for the fiduciary concerns of your organization, the technical specifications are most critical to the quality of the film product. Specifications and guidelines may be included in the body of the contract, with details provided in an often-voluminous group of appendixes. In either case, the following matters (addressed in chapter 4) might be included in your specifications:[9]

overview description of the filming project

film format and types for camera master, printing master, and duplicates

quality control requirements (bibliographic inspection, density, resolution, Quality Index, chemical tests)

reduction ratios

reel programming

image arrangement and orientation

instructions for types and placement of targets, specifying which the institution will provide and which the filmer will supply

---

9. I am indebted to the sample contracts in Elkington, *RLG Preservation Microfilming Handbook,* 123–9, and to those provided by NEDCC and Preservation Resources.

splicing methods and limits on number of splices

storage containers, reels, ties, and labeling

instructions for the master negative numbering system if the filmer is to supply the numbers

packaging of shipments—boxes and packing materials to be used

instructions for handling errors—how errors and significant defects will be handled, how responsibility for them will be determined, and who will pay the shipping and filming costs in each case

The technical specifications should clearly delineate the filmer's and the client's responsibilities in each area. Throughout the technical specifications, relevant standards and guidelines (such as those of ANSI/AIIM and RLG) should be cited.

A variety of appendixes may be needed, such as summary lists of micrographics standards and specifications to be followed; shipment schedules; sample packing slips, targets, reports, and forms; and a copy of the institution's tax identification certificate. A sample set of targets with instructions for their use will complete the document.

Commercial Micropublication. Contract costs can sometimes be reduced if the contractor is also a commercial micropublisher. Over time, a substantial amount of library and archival material has been filmed as a result of agreements with micropublishers. In this case, the commercial publisher bears the cost of filming materials for publication in return for the right to sell copies of the film. An example is the American Antiquarian Society's association with the Readex Corporation for the Early American Imprints Project. However, the publisher customarily approaches the library or archives rather than the other way around.

The terms of such agreements will vary with the circumstances and particularly with the expected marketability of the product. You should expect to receive at least a service copy in return for making your materials available, and sometimes you can negotiate additional compensation. At a minimum, contracts should require publishers to reimburse any costs the institution sustains in cooperating with the publisher. They should also stipulate that the filming will be done in accordance with appropriate national standards, that bibliographic records for the microforms will be added to OCLC or RLIN, and that the resulting master negatives will be stored in accordance with existing national standards. Contractual terms may specify how preservation of the master negatives will be ensured if the company goes out of business.[10]

---

10. For issues particularly associated with commercial micropublishing, see Subcommittee on Contract Negotiations for Commercial Reproduction of Library and Archival Materials, "Contract Negotiations for the Commercial Microform Publishing of Library and Archival Materials: Guidelines for Librarians and Archivists," *Library Resources & Technical Services* 38 (Jan. 1994): 72–85; and Kenneth E. Carpenter and Jane Carr, "Microform Publishing Contracts," *Microform Review* 19 (spring 1990): 83–100. The latter includes a sample micropublishing contract and detailed commentary on it.

Communication

As the work begins and progresses, the library or archives should try to establish strong lines of communication with the filming agent so that problems, changes, and special instructions can be freely shared. It is in your best interest to provide the filming agent with constructive feedback on a regular and timely basis, based on your own quality assurance program, drawing especially on problems or anomalies you discover in your quality assurance operations. This is your primary means of maintaining control of the project.

The filming agent will need to report the inevitable bibliographic problems, missing paperwork, and other situations. Your contract or written instructions should specify one individual who will serve as the primary contact with the filming agent. Make every effort to ensure that the filmer's questions are answered promptly because delays can be a serious problem in a production-oriented shop.[11]

A good service bureau will also play a vital role in suggesting methods of filming and layout of materials that take into account the way the service bureau operates. The filmer often will be able to suggest alternative ways of meeting your needs while taking into consideration the lab's methods of operation. Any time you ask for something that departs from normal practice, regardless of whether it may seem easier or faster, the costs probably will be higher—and, of course, the risk of error is increased. To take full advantage of these opportunities, you must make sure that your contract is flexible enough to allow revisions and be aware of the price implications.

Administrative Decisions

There are three stages of preparation: physical, editorial, and final preparation. Physical preparation deals with the completeness of the materials and treatments that must be done prior to filming. In editorial preparation, you plan the arrangement of materials on the film and produce informational targets. During final preparation, all work is checked and instructions to the filmer are prepared. Administrative decisions will guide the approach to all aspects of preparation. (Some key decisions are highlighted in chapter 1.) RLG advises participants in its large cooperative projects to anticipate a six-month start-up period, and you may consider a similar lead time.

You need to discuss a number of topics with the filming agent, whether you are using an in-house or outside facility. There are direct connections between preparation work and camera operation, and decisions about and capabilities of each affect the other. For example, decisions regarding disbinding will be based partly on the agent's having appropriate book cradles, and your use of instruc-

---

11. The availability of fax and electronic mail have vastly simplified communication, perhaps especially when the client and service bureau are separated by several time zones; see Lockhart and Swartzell, 123.

tional flags may change as you learn more about how the camera operators work. To the extent you learned about and discussed film production issues while selecting the filming agent, this level of production planning can go more quickly. Even if you are contracting out the preparation work, you should make most of the operational decisions outlined in the balance of this chapter and include those in your written specifications to the contractor.

Procedures Manual

Planning a procedure for preparation of materials means trying to anticipate problems so that once the process begins, it will continue with few interruptions. This allows efficient use of personnel as well as a steady flow of materials to the camera. A detailed procedures manual is almost always a requirement for ongoing programs and long-term or complex projects. The manual can help ensure consistency over time and among various staff members. It can be the basis for initial training and is especially helpful in institutions that experience significant staff turnover. It will help ensure that practices are based on administrative policy and priorities rather than individual preferences or idiosyncrasies.

If yours is a new project—and likely to be long term—plan a start-up phase to include preparation of a clear and thorough procedures manual. Projects with

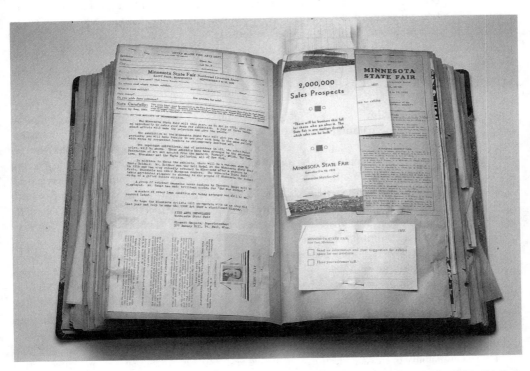

Standard procedures are especially important in a filming effort that includes complex materials. Uniform decisions should govern how to handle overlapping materials and fasteners, for example. *Minnesota Historical Society.*

immediate goals for completion, because of funding or filming schedules, publication deadlines, or other reasons, may demand more administrative supervision for on-the-spot policy decisions, which may eventually generate a procedures manual.

Your internal procedures manual should be closely correlated to the overall project instructions included in your contract or agreement with the filming agent but will go into more detail about your in-house operations. In developing the manual, look for models you can adapt. Consult printed bibliographies, electronic databases accessible through the Internet, and some of the institutions and organizations cited in appendix B.[12]

Staffing Requirements

The actual number of full-time staff needed to prepare materials for a filming project is not a figure to be read from a table. Some institutions filming brittle books have found that it takes one full-time staff member to search, collate, and prepare targets for enough materials to keep one camera running full-time. The type of material will affect the amount of time required; complex materials such as scrapbooks or some archival collections require more staff time than straightforward books or serials. The division of labor may vary, with different units responsible for searching, collating, and targeting. The preparations staff may also be responsible for quality assurance and other postfilming operations, which will add to the work load. The guidelines here should help you determine what procedures to undertake and how to evaluate preparation problems in the materials you have selected for filming.

You must develop an estimate of staffing requirements appropriate to your project. Other institutions that have been engaged in preservation microfilming may provide some guidance, and the cost studies cited in chapter 6 may provide some figures that will aid you in making estimates and controlling costs. It is a good idea to do some "test runs" to get actual time estimates for the collections you have chosen to film. Large or ongoing projects may warrant a more complex analysis of staffing requirements. An excellent cost model developed by Columbia University Libraries is applicable to other institutions.[13] The labor of preparation is too often overlooked in program development, but skimping on it will seriously compromise the microforms produced.

Many preservation microfilming managers have developed tools to assist in calculating staffing needs and schedules, and you should develop contacts to identify these. Institutions and organizations in appendix B may provide some guidance. Some electronic sources such as the Conservation DistList and its

---

12. One good model is the *SOLINET Preservation Microfilm Service: Procedures Manual* (Atlanta: SOLINET, 1991 or most recent), available from SOLINET. The University of Michigan's Library Preservation Division is also willing to share copies of its *Microfilming Preparation Manual*. Others may be available through CoOL.

13. See Carolyn Harris, Carol Mandel, and Robert Wolven, "A Cost Model for Preservation: The Columbia University Libraries' Approach," *Library Resources & Technical Services* 35 (Jan. 1991): 33–54.

CoOL database contain relevant information and may provide a forum for raising your questions.

Some of the decisions and subsequent actions in preparation of materials will involve a variety of units in the institution.[14] Once materials are identified for filming, they are collected and assembled (public service/paging activity). They are screened during curatorial review, then queued or cataloged (cataloging function). Missing items are borrowed (ILL activity). The status of items in a project should be noted to patrons (circulation/reference activity), and finding aids or other guides provided (archival function). Repair, disbinding, or other physical treatment may be required (conservation function) before or after filming.

It should be clear that one central coordinating office or position (sometimes called the preparation manager) should be designated to push and pull materials through the necessary channels. This becomes even more important when dealing with an outside filming facility, which will need a single point of contact for questions or problems that arise. A small organization may have one person doing it all; in larger organizations a full-time position may be needed just to coordinate the flow of materials, with different specialists handling each distinct activity. A greater degree of specialization of tasks may allow you to handle a large number of materials efficiently, but it also emphasizes the manager's role in project supervision. You can also increase capacity by contracting with a service bureau to do some or all preparation work, as discussed in chapter 1.

Expected Use of Microform

The expected use of a microform should be considered in advance, for that will affect preparation procedures as well as selection decisions and filming specifications. For example, will the film be used frequently to generate paper copy, either through reader-printer equipment or in conjunction with scanning? If so, this may affect the way the pages are oriented on the film and should be discussed with the filming agent for consideration in the technical setup of the film. If you are using a hybrid systems approach, combining the use of microfilm and scanning, the preparation decisions and procedures will be further complicated. (See the introduction.)

Is the filming project based on an existing bibliography, or are you preparing a guide or other finding aid for it? If your users will normally use these tools first, you may need to consider including the bibliography's citation numbers on the film or a location key from the film to the guide, so that users can easily locate specific items.

Will your end product be roll microfilm or microfiche? The advantages and disadvantages of each are detailed in the "Film Formats" section of chapter 4.

Disposition of Originals

The previous chapter pointed out that decisions about the disposition of the originals must be made as part of the selection and screening routine. This deci-

---

14. A useful summary of the operational impact of filming projects on library units appears in Elkington, *RLG Preservation Microfilming Handbook*, 65–6.

sion has a substantial impact on preparation procedures. Before any collection or item can be prepared for the camera, the staff must know whether it will be retained after filming. This decision especially affects the repair and disbinding that may be part of physical preparation.

The extent and types of repairs you provide will be based primarily on the disposition decision. If the item is to be discarded after filming, you may make less costly and simpler repairs, ones that do not conform to conservation standards. If original documents are to be retained, you must use appropriate conservation procedures in flattening them, but if the items are to be discarded, you might use less time-consuming measures (such as misting documents with water and ironing them).

When disbinding is required, the disposition decision will govern which disbinding methods are acceptable. Possible methods are outlined in the "Tight or Fragile Bindings" section of this chapter.

Disbinding can be done in-house or by the filming agent. Consider whether you have enough staff with appropriate skills and appropriate equipment and supplies to do the work efficiently. Also consider whether the volumes may be transported more safely in a bound or disbound condition. For hand disbinding of valuable volumes, assess whether the institution or the filming agent has the greater expertise.

If you elect to have the filming agent disbind, provide clear instructions for each volume, shipment, or project (whichever level is appropriate) that specify whether disbinding is permissible and, if so, which methods may be used. In the past, many clients have required that the filmer contact the institution for case-by-case decisions. This practice creates serious problems for production; the volume must be pulled from the work stream and set aside until the client receives the message, consults with appropriate selectors, reaches a decision, and conveys instructions back to the filmer. Make and communicate your decisions in advance to improve project efficiency.

Bibliographic and Archival Control

An administrative decision must be made regarding the extent to which the staff will upgrade bibliographic records and archival finding aids during the preparation phase. (Bibliographic control cost implications are noted in chapter 6.) Especially with archival collections, there may be a strong temptation to upgrade the existing bibliographic record or finding aid to produce one that is more detailed. A collection may have undergone cursory processing at an earlier date, and the curatorial staff may wish now to provide full archival arrangement and description. Such actions will have great benefits to users but may have a significant negative impact on the preparation time.[15] You may conclude either that this time is well spent or that it is important but is so costly and time-consuming that you must reconsider your earlier decision to film the collection at all.

---

15. In the RLG APMP cost study, the extent of archival control work included in the preparation phase was a major factor in costs. Preparation time for two linear feet of archival material ranged from 15 minutes to 232 hours, and the extent of arrangement or reprocessing work was a major factor in the longer times; see Elkington, *RLG Archives Microfilming Manual*, 26–8, 174–6.

Record Keeping and Statistics

Once materials are charged out to preparation, you must have a mechanism in place to track the many items flowing through the whole processing stream (through preparation stages, filming, and postprocessing to cataloging and storage). What goes in at one end must come out the other. The larger the flow of materials, the more important, but also the more time-consuming, record keeping becomes.

If a unique microform shelf or location number (such as the master negative number) can be assigned early in the process, this may suffice for tracking purposes. The simplest method may be to assign a control number for each title and to track the workflow by maintaining a logbook or using a bar code and scanner to track items moving through the work stream. As preparation begins, the title is logged in. The logbook or database can be expanded to include the date materials are sent to the filmer and when they are returned. Combined with packing slips you maintain for each shipment, this may be the best way to tell if something has gone astray. If an external service bureau is used, information about the quantity and contents of shipments can be used to verify invoices. Once filming is complete, the title is logged out when the film and originals are routed to other units.

Some information associated with each title or collection needs to be maintained in one place throughout processing. This is an in-process record or file that can be linked to the material through the title control number. It might consist of a bibliographic record and worksheet or decision form for recording search information, the decisions to retain or withdraw, and a borrowing history. Files for serials and manuscript collections will often include collation information used for preparation of targets, instructions for filming, or information for cataloging.

The degree to which a system needs expansion depends on the size of the project or workflow and whether filming is performed in-house or outside. Much of this work can be done by using the capabilities of an integrated library system and database management software on a personal computer.[16] The computer program structure and your technical expertise will determine how you can best use and adapt them to automate the record keeping, tracking, and generating of statistics. Using a single database or linked ones will help you reduce manual entry or re-keying of information, save time, and reduce the risk of errors. The system should be designed so you can update it at various points, perhaps using a bar code reader to track items through the process, then using it to print out various documents (such as targets, labels, and reports) and generate statistics.

Plan to collect statistics to measure how much work is accomplished by the unit over time and to measure individual as well as unit production levels and performance. Decide what you need and how it will be used before you determine what data to collect. In the preparation unit you want to know how many titles, volumes, or items have been processed. A breakdown by staff member and

---

16. See sample applications in Patricia Brennan and Jutta Reed-Scott, comps., *Automating Preservation Management in ARL Libraries,* SPEC Kit 198 (Washington, D.C.: ARL Office of Management Services, 1993).

type of material (such as books, serials, newspapers, or manuscript collections) may be useful. Clearly, a title count would be an inappropriate measure for comparing the production level of a staff member working on serials with that of one processing monographs. Later, you will need to know how many items were filmed, the number of exposures, and the number of feet or reels duplicated, and need to have a breakdown by staff member and by project. Besides giving you administrative control, this information will be helpful when you begin to plan staffing and develop budgets for microfilming other collections.

Some records warrant long-term retention. These include

selector review and search forms (Especially if yours is a use-based filming program, an item once considered but rejected for filming may later enter the queue again.)

quality control reports (These are useful in the event that problems are discovered during use or in subsequent inspection of stored film, and some of the technical information will be especially important for future scanning of the film.)

log of film location or storage numbers

Chapter 1 provides further discussion of record-keeping requirements.

Preparation Procedures

With the administrative decisions made, and assuming you have a firm grasp of the film production issues outlined in chapter 4, preparation work can now begin. In a large institution, the work might pass at this stage from the preservation administrator to the preparation manager. In a smaller institution, the administrator simply puts on a different hat.

The goal of preparation is twofold: to deliver complete, camera-ready materials to the filming agent so the camera operator can simply "turn and shoot" the individual pages with a minimum of questions or problems and to create a product that researchers can use easily.

When preparing books, the novice should learn the series of tasks or steps in each stage before moving on to the next. After tasks are mastered, it is best to process several titles at a time to gain efficiency. By contrast, each stage in the preparation of an archival or manuscript collection should be approached individually, concentrating on one theme or task in each complete pass-through of the materials. Serials fall somewhere in between, but they are generally complex enough to be processed one title at a time. With experience, staff members will come to think simultaneously about editorial preparation and physical preparation and what instructions need to be prepared for the film.

Physical Preparation

In the initial review, materials are examined for physical condition. Pages that are uniform in size and contrast, are in good condition, and lie flat on the camera bed can be filmed most efficiently. But many other factors can affect the quality of the film and may require special handling: filming of tightly bound volumes, treatment of folded material, minor repairs, unusual items in archival collections, and so on. The paper may have yellowed and darkened, become brittle, or have been folded or curled. Items that have deteriorated due to acidic paper, dirt, poor storage conditions, or mishandling are likely to require the most attention.

Even if they are produced on high-quality paper, older materials may have suffered as a result of earlier attempts at repair or restoration. Manuscripts from different periods will reflect greater variations in the paper, types of inks, or writing instruments used and, hence, may present greater problems in exposure control. Printed materials are generally more uniform in size and contrast and may be easier to film than archival or manuscript materials. Given careful preparation and filming, however, it should be possible to reproduce the significant record detail in most collections. You must combine a knowledge of the filming process, the value of the materials, and the time and money available to select from the many options in physical preparation that will affect both the final film quality and the cost.

Collation

The key purposes of collation are to make sure that the most-complete version possible is filmed and to identify physical conditions that will require targeting, special attention by the camera operator, or other actions. Collation of library materials requires going through each volume once, examining each page. Archival collections often require a two-phase approach, as discussed in the next section.

You should make every effort to assemble the complete title prior to filming, possibly using the resources of other library collections to fill in gaps in individual volumes or serial publications. Since you are preserving materials once (and we hope for all time), you should set up procedures through ILL or other local borrowing networks to accomplish this. While some people may feel that incomplete serials or other volumes are not worthy of filming, an exception may be made if the materials are the most-complete or best copies available.

For published material, high-quality photocopies should be acquired to replace missing or damaged pages identified during collation, or the preparation staff can borrow volumes and photocopy needed pages themselves.[17] The copies should be cut to size and inserted in their correct places within the volume. If the number of inserted pages is so large it might create stress that would damage the binding structure, place them in a separate envelope and insert a flag in the volume directing the camera operator to those pages.

If entire volumes are missing, they should be borrowed and filmed in correct sequence. Of course, this means such volumes will need to be moved to a side track while you await the borrowed volumes or pages. The resulting delays could be significant enough to wreak havoc with your filming schedule, especially if you are borrowing serial volumes or issues from multiple institutions. That pos-

---

17. See instructions in *Guidelines for Preservation Photocopying of Replacement Pages* (Chicago: ALA/ALCTS, 1990) and "Guidelines for Preservation Photocopying," *Library Resources & Technical Services* 38 (July 1994): 288–92.

Collation requires a careful examination of the item to be sure it is complete. A printout of the catalog record travels with the volume during preparation. Irregularities are noted so missing pages can be replaced, and the notes will be used for the LIST OF IRREGULARITIES target. *Cleveland Public Library. Photo by Bill Baltz.*

sibility needs to be accommodated in the selection decision as well as in your production planning and scheduling.

During collation, be alert to problems such as these:

errors or irregularities in pagination

missing pages

damaged pages where text is lost

pages with extensive underlining or highlighting (especially when it obscures text)

illustrations that will require intentional second or multiple exposures

blank pages that should be (or should not be) filmed

Make notes about these, which will be used in preparation of targets and in preparing instructions to the filmer.

Collation may present some special challenges if you have chosen to film materials that use non-Roman alphabets or that have non-Arabic pagination. Your staff will have to deal with preparation of those that proceed from right to left (such as in Hebrew and some Asian collections) and may need to learn to interpret numerals other than Roman and Arabic. Also, you will need to provide clear instructions to the filming agent for sequencing such pages. For example, if the collection includes non-Arabic pagination, you should provide a table the camera operator and inspection staff can use to translate page numbers to the vernacular.

Arrangement of Archival Collections

Many of the steps and issues in physical preparation of library collections are equally applicable to archival collections. Procedures for dealing with repairs, disbinding, and so on are not inherently different for archival versus library materials per se so much as they differ based on the physical condition of each item and on whether it has intrinsic value.

Whereas the arrangement of library materials is generally dealt with by straightforward collation, the question of archival arrangement is much more complex. It is important not to confuse archival processing, done as part of arrangement and description, with the arrangement done in the early stage of physical preparation. While there is overlap between the tasks done in these two functions, they are best kept separate.[18] Note, too, that most funding agencies recognize archival processing as a step distinct from filming preparation.

While it may be relatively easy for a researcher to make sense of an unprocessed folder, there would be significant difficulties in dealing with the same collection on film. The physical arrangement must be reviewed with an eye to the needs of the user, and this may require some reorganization. For example, while it is common to attach an envelope to the back of a letter in the folder, it should appear *before* the letter on the film. Whereas users of a photograph collection typically see the image first, then turn it over to see identifying information, the description on the back should appear prior to the image in the filmed collection. Also, it is customary to film file folder labels as helpful guideposts.

Where it is possible, without compromising the bibliographic or archival integrity of a collection, group the materials by size. A wide range of sizes in a collection may require frequent changes in reduction ratios, which will increase filming time and, therefore, increase filming costs. For some record series, especially those in which oversize items are the exception, it may be practical to move oversize items to an end position using an OVERSIZE ITEMS FILMED AT END OF (FOLDER, REEL, etc.) target.

In most archival collections, you will encounter duplicates and items that should not be filmed. During preparation, you should either remove those or flag them so the camera operator will not film them.

When preparing archival collections, first you must determine the sequence of documents. Then you can begin physical preparation of the individual items, noting the physical problems of manuscript and archives materials in the first pass through the materials. Necessary repairs are made in the second pass.

---

18. See Madeleine Perez, Andrew Raymond, and Ann Swartzell, "The Selection and Preparation of Archives and Manuscripts for Microreproduction," *Library Resources & Technical Services* 27 (Oct./Dec. 1983): 357–65.

Tight or Fragile Bindings

A review of bound volumes in library or archival collections will determine whether they can be filmed intact. The decision also has administrative and curatorial implications, discussed in chapters 1 and 2. This review usually involves assessing the flexibility of the paper and the tightness of the binding to identify those that will not survive the filming process and those that cannot be filmed successfully without disbinding.

As pages are turned, check to see whether brittle paper cracks along the stiff ridge created by the cover's hinge. This typically occurs in the first and last few pages and is particularly prevalent in oversewn volumes. In some cases, the stress of opening volumes 180 degrees can break sewing or loosen the text block from its case. If the selector has indicated that the volume will be retained after filming and cannot be disbound, sort out the materials that will not make it through the filming process and have them reviewed before any further processing takes place. With this kind of information on the condition of the material, a curator who had originally decided to retain the volume may wish to reconsider and withdraw it instead. If filming proceeds and materials will need repair, set up a routine to flag volumes for treatment at the end of the process, before they are returned to the shelf. As noted in the "Minor Repairs" section to follow, there may be cases where repairs should precede filming. Another alternative for such materials, if they cannot be filmed, is to locate another copy more suitable for filming.

Also determine whether the binding will interfere with successful filming. On a flat surface, open the volume 180 degrees to see if pages lie flat. If the inner margin is too narrow and the binding is tight, a gutter shadow may appear in the film. If text falls in this gutter, it will be out of focus and obscured in shadow. (Gutter shadow also poses a significant problem for currently available scanners.) A volume can generally be filmed intact if at least ¼-inch of the inner margin remains parallel to the surface of the page when the volume is opened at various places. Another rule of thumb is to open the volume flat and lay a pencil in the inner margin; if the pencil does not obscure any text, the volume can probably be filmed without disbinding.[19]

There are several options for filming tightly bound volumes. Some volumes with only marginally tight bindings can be filmed successfully by using a book cradle, which supports the binding and flattens pages beneath a glass plate. If you anticipate problems, alert the curator before filming and, if necessary, note the volume's prefilming condition in case questions arise during postfilming inspection.

If the volume is too tightly bound for the book cradle option and it must be filmed, it must be disbound. A range of techniques is available:

> The sewing can be loosened or some threads cut enough to let the volume be filmed successfully.

> Covers may be removed from the text block if it appears the boards or case (rather than the sewing structure) are causing the tightness.

---

19. These tips and other practical guidelines are provided in Kenney, "Preparation of Materials," 26–38.

Some volumes require disbinding due to the brittleness of the paper or the inflexibility of the binding. The condition of the item and the retention decision are key factors in determining whether it requires a conservator's attention or can be disbound mechanically (using a guillotine like the one at right after the cover is removed by hand). *Left: Minnesota Historical Society. Right: Preservation Resources.*

The volume can be divided into multipage sections thin enough to allow successful filming. This strategy will generally improve openability and simplify camera operations for two-up filming.

The volume can be entirely disbound and the sewing removed by hand. If this method is used on a volume that is to be retained because of its artifactual value, the disbinding should generally be done by a book conservator, who will be familiar with historic sewing structures and binding techniques. If possible the disbinding should be done by the same lab or conservator who will subsequently do the rebinding. Furthermore, disbinding inevitably affects artifactual value; so if the volume is being retained for its artifactual value, there may be no disbinding method that is acceptable. The cost and curatorial implications of this approach may call for reconsideration of the decision to film such a volume.

The spine can be sliced off using a machine appropriately known as a guillotine. If materials are to be disbound this way, be sure to alert the filming agent to pages that must be separated by hand, such as folded materials, plates or charts sewn through the fold, or text with floating inner margins.

It must be stressed that all these techniques render the volume unsuitable for further use without treatment after filming. Even "loosening the sewing," as gentle as it sounds, will require remedial attention after filming. Disbound volumes must be resewn, recased, or boxed (that is, placed in a protective enclosure such as a phase box or clamshell box) in-house, at a commercial library bindery, or by a conservator, depending on the condition and value of the item and the availability of services.

Because guillotining is the fastest method, some libraries and filming labs have routinely used that option on all volumes destined for withdrawal. However, some filmers find it easier and faster to film bound materials than single sheets and, therefore, may prefer one of the "minimal" disbinding techniques even on items that will be discarded after filming. For example, to retain the signatures, some filmers will disbind a volume by hand rather than guillotine it, especially if the specifications call for filming two pages per frame.

You must also determine whether the disbinding is to be done in-house or by the filming agent, determine which disbinding methods are acceptable, and communicate your guidelines. Make the decisions in conjunction with the selector, filming agent, and the staff that will carry out postfilming treatments on disbound items. The choices will generally have cost implications as well.

Removal of Fasteners

Remove clips, staples, or other fasteners to allow materials to lie flat and to facilitate efficient "turn and shoot" operation at the camera. Some filming agents will remove fasteners, but there are two benefits to having the preparations staff do this work. First, if you deliver the materials to the filmer without such fasteners, the camera operator can work more quickly. Second, the institution may be equipped to do the work more carefully. This may be especially important for deteriorated fasteners, such as rusted paper clips, that are physically attached to documents and require particularly careful removal.

In library collections removal of fasteners is generally a relatively straightforward process because fasteners are usually extraneous. However, it is a more complex matter for archival materials, where paper clips and other fasteners assist in the ordering of collections. In those cases, you may remove fasteners and insert alkaline paper sheets to serve as markers between one document or group of documents and the next. Be sure to plan for significant postfilming time if these collections are to be retained because all targets and other insertions will need to be removed and original order restored.

Minor Repairs

Administrative policy and selectors' decisions regarding disposition of originals will guide your repair procedures. If items are to be discarded after filming, repairs should be kept to the minimum required for the production of good film.

It is unusual for paper or binding repairs to be undertaken on ordinary library books or serials before filming unless the damage is such that it will affect the quality of the film. Examples of necessary physical treatments include separating pages that are stuck together, repairing pages so badly torn that they may not make it to the camera in one piece, and removing dirt, mold, discolored tape, and other defects that obscure the text. Newspaper pages that are stuck together may be steamed apart, interleaved with a nonadhesive material such as silicone paper, and left to dry for a few hours.

Japanese paper and heat-set mends are expensive conservation procedures that may be warranted for pages in books or documents with artifactual value that will be retained.[20] Ordinary pressure-sensitive tape (the "invisible" or matte type) is suitable to mend torn pages in materials to be discarded. If pages are crumbling or page tears are extensive, the leaves may be placed in polyester sleeves to hold them in place during transport and filming.[21]

You must decide when to perform repairs on items that are to be retained. Because of expense and delays in processing, always keep prefilming repairs to an absolute minimum; instead, route items to the conservation staff after filming is complete. On the other hand, if you determine that an item needs additional strength or consolidation to reduce damage during filming, complete that work beforehand. The time required for these procedures, as well as the condition of the original materials, must be considered. In some cases, extensive repair needs may lead you to reconsider a filming decision or to develop a compromise strategy.

Foldouts and Oversize Materials

Oversize items and foldout sheets in bound volumes may be handled several ways. The sheets may be placed under glass and filmed in one exposure (using a higher reduction ratio than for other pages in the volume, which should be indicated in a target) or may be filmed in overlapping sections, moving from left to right and from top to bottom, with at least a one-inch overlap between adjacent sections, as shown in figure 10.[22] Both these strategies work best if the item is removed from the volume. Excellent guidelines for dealing with foldouts and oversize materials are included in the microfilm preparation contract developed by NLM.[23]

Sectionalized filming adds to the frame count for the job, may be very difficult for the user to interpret, and could be impractical for later reproductions from the film. On the other hand, the higher reduction ratio used for single-frame filming of oversize materials may not record necessary details. A better solution is to use the single frame, full view (using a higher reduction ratio as necessary) for the user's orientation, followed by sectionalized filming (at the reduction ratio used for the rest of the work) for closer study. In some cases, you may decide the item should also be retained in its original form, and a target may be placed on the film to direct researchers to it.

20. Issues related to conservation mending are addressed in Mary Lynn Ritzenthaler, *Preserving Archives and Manuscripts* (Chicago: SAA, 1993), 148–9.

21. See Ritzenthaler, *Preserving Archives and Manuscripts,* 189–93, for instructions on polyester encapsulation.

22. *Practice for Operational Procedures/Inspection and Quality Control of First-Generation, Silver Microfilm of Documents,* ANSI/AIIM MS23-1991 (Silver Spring, Md.: AIIM, 1991), sec. 4.8.1, p. 21. For sectionalized filming of newspapers, see *American National Standard for Information and Image Management—Recommended Practice for Microfilming Printed Newspapers on 35mm Roll Microfilm,* ANSI/AIIM MS111-1994 (Silver Spring, Md.: AIIM, 1994), sec. 5, p. 4.

23. Available on CoOL. Send an e-mail message to condist-request@lindy.stanford.edu.

FIGURE 10   Sectionalized Filming

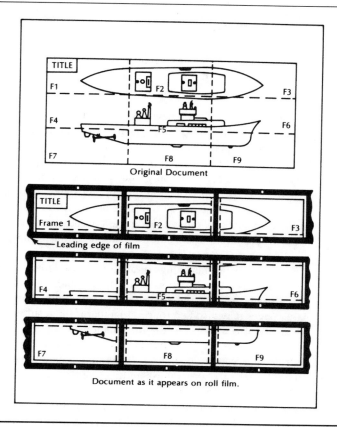

Original Document

Document as it appears on roll film.

SOURCE: *Practice for Operational Procedures/Inspection and Quality Control of First-Generation, Silver Microfilm of Documents*, ANSI/AIIM MS23-1991 (Silver Spring, Md.: AIIM, 1991), 23.

Flattening

Curled or folded single sheets can be pressed in a weighted folder or flattened using an ordinary iron if they are to be discarded later. The heat of an iron will cause accelerated aging and perhaps other kinds of deterioration in the document, so this strategy should never be employed on items that are to be retained. However, it is an appropriate and commonly used practice for flattening newspapers and other items that will be discarded after filming.

For items that will be retained after filming, use procedures that are more conservative. Stubborn creases and wrinkles can be removed by lightly spraying unbound pages with distilled water to humidify them, then stacking them neatly between sheets of blotter paper in a large press for twenty-four hours.[24] Humid-

---

24. See instructions in Ritzenthaler, 184–9.

ification might be skipped in a project that is short on time, but camera time may increase and special handling charges may be incurred for work on materials in poor condition.

If individual items are only slightly curled and are to be filmed under glass, the weight of the glass may be sufficient to flatten them. This topic should be discussed with the filming agent during production planning.

Scrapbooks and Clippings

Preparing scrapbooks or newspaper clippings for filming presents a real challenge in terms of film product quality and filming costs.

Clippings, notes, and other small miscellany of assorted sizes can be grouped together in the preparation phase for the camera operator's ease in handling, or they may be filmed with only one item per frame. The single-frame option is easier for the person arranging the clippings and will expedite subsequent reference to individual items on the film, but it will not make the most efficient use of the film stock. A more economical approach is to trim the clippings of extraneous information, being sure to retain notations or dates that may be useful for identification. Then group the individual items on carrier sheets, using either "quick-and-dirty" fastenings or archival procedures (whichever is appropriate to the final disposition decision) to facilitate handling by the camera operator. This will also ensure editorial control of the groupings. Large clippings or full newspaper pages may also be grouped together if the resulting rearrangement does not adversely affect access to the information.

Scrapbooks are probably the most challenging format for the preparations staff and the camera operator.[25] They may contain overlapping newspaper clippings, layers of photographs, multicolored items such as tickets or brochures, various writing media (pencil, light and dark pens or printing inks, etc.) that require intentional multiple exposures, and multipaged pamphlets, not all of which may have to be filmed. The goal of preparation should be to facilitate camera operation as much as possible, while taking into account the way researchers will use the film. As with other materials, before work begins certain administrative decisions must be made on what is and is not to be filmed, and the preparations staff may need to do some mending, loosen stuck items, and relax folds. Notes made during the physical preparation stage will be cumulated for later targeting and general instructions to the filmer.

Letterpress Volumes

Letterpress volumes present some unique problems. The translucent paper used in most letterpress copies is so thin that ink shows through. This makes it difficult to get a good image on film. You may interleave the pages, but that is time-consuming and can create enough stress to damage the bindings. Disbinding may simplify filming but will typically require that you spend time and money to

---

25. Useful guidelines for dealing with scrapbooks and other overlapping materials are provided in Erich J. Kesse, "Strategies for Microfilming Scrapbooks and Layered Objects," in *RLG Archives Microfilming Manual*, 133–5.

rebind the item or place it in a protective enclosure after filming. You may opt to have the filmer do the interleaving, which will avoid prolonged stress on the binding structure, but that step will slow production and increase costs.

Editorial Preparation

The second phase of preparation addresses editorial concerns. Having attended to the physical preparation of the materials, you now focus more specifically on how they will be laid out on film, especially on how that layout will affect future use.

Editorial preparation, also called bibliographic preparation, includes three key activities: further arrangement of the materials, preparation and insertion of targets and other informational or instructional materials, and determination of what will appear on each reel of film (called "reel programming").

Library Materials

Monographs and pamphlets generally require few editorial decisions, so editorial preparation is usually straightforward. Generally, all they require is the production and insertion of targets to provide a good layout.

Serials may consist of volumes, parts, supplements, indexes, and so on; therefore, they are usually more complex. The arrangement should be checked and volumes assembled in correct order. In some cases, other arrangements, which might be attributed to such factors as the library's binding policies, may be acceptable as long as they are logical and consistent. Variant arrangements that might be confusing to the user should be noted on the LIST OF IRREGULARITIES target (see figure 11) or with the FILMED AS BOUND target. Indexes may be filmed preceding the text of the serial or series to which they relate. Then prepare the GUIDE TO CONTENTS target based on information from the final arrangement of volumes and the notes collected during collation.

Archival Collections

There are some special issues in editorial preparation for archival records and manuscripts. How much time and difficulty are involved will, of course, vary according to the materials. The novice preparer should follow these steps separately, but as experience grows, they can be combined in whatever way is convenient. Some may be covered in general instructions to the filming agent; others will require production of specific targets or instruction sheets at the point they occur.

1. Flag blank pages so they will not be filmed. If documents are paginated, explain the deletion of blank pages on the corresponding target or, if the problem recurs, in the LIST OF IRREGULARITIES target.

2. Remove duplicates or flag them so that they will not be filmed. Also remove three-dimensional items such as handkerchiefs, buttons, or dried flowers, and other extraneous items. Include an explanatory note about your decisions in the introduction or guide, if produced, or on the FOLDER target.

FIGURE 11 List of Irregularities Target

LIST OF IRREGULARITIES

CALL
NO: _____

MAIN
ENTRY: _____
_____
_____

List volume and pages affected. If the irregularity is extensive, use the term "throughout" rather than listing specific pages. If filming more than 10 pages of borrowed text, include the name of the lending institution.

☐ Missing: Volume(s) _____
Issue(s) _____
Page(s) _____

☐ Illegible and/or damaged page(s): _____

☐ Date of publication incorrect: _____

☐ Page(s), issue(s), or volume(s) misnumbered: _____

☐ Bound out of sequence: _____

☐ Page(s), etc. filmed from other copies: _____

Name of lending institution: _____

☐ Filmed from photocopied pages

☐ Intentional duplicate exposures: _____

☐ Other: _____

SOURCE: Adapted from Debra McKern and Sherry Byrne, *ALA Target Packet for Use in Preservation Microfilming* (Chicago: ALA, 1991), 46.

3. Arrange endorsements appearing on the backs of wills, deeds, letters, or contracts to be filmed before the text of the document.

4. Place an enclosure immediately after the letter to which it corresponds or after the pages of a book between which it was found. Envelopes, if filmed, should precede their contents.

5. Position indexes immediately preceding the text or document series to which they relate, or use a flag to alert the filmer. Otherwise, the index is apt to appear on the film at the end of the text, making the film difficult to use. An index that is an integral part of the item to be filmed, such as in ordinary monographs, is filmed in place.

6. Arrange folder labels, if they are to be filmed, before the contents of the folder. If the information is both sufficiently complete and legible—rarely the case— the label can be used in lieu of a folder target, but RLG specifications require that a large (30-point) type size should be used for the FOLDER target.

After the initial arrangement is complete, check everything again to make sure all items are accounted for and in the proper sequence. If the sequence of pages or items is not clear and easy for the camera operator to follow, pencil in a page number or other identifying sequence enclosed in brackets in the upper right-hand corner of the page being filmed. For manuscripts and other unpublished materials especially, you may have to follow this practice throughout the collection. Alert the camera operator to pages with holes or other missing sections by slipping a sheet of paper behind such pages.

Targets

Targets are separate sheets of paper or board containing technical or bibliographic information that are filmed along with the publication or document, thus becoming part of the film itself. They are used to identify or add information about the materials on the film, to record details about the filming process and allow technical evaluation of the filming, to explain anomalies in the materials being filmed, and to serve as pointers or notes to the user.

A series of targets accompanies each title or collection. Target production is guided first by ANSI/AIIM standards.[26] For guidance specific to library and archival materials, see the detailed descriptions of targets and illustrations of target series in the RLG handbooks and *ALA Target Packet*.[27]

Indicative of the growing international coordination in microfilming, some international graphic symbol targets have also been adopted, and a few examples of these are incorporated in the *ALA Target Packet*.[28] Their use is not yet mandated for preservation microfilming.

Target Production. Target preparation is usually the responsibility of the institution, although an increasing number of filming agents offer targeting services. To guard against errors or misunderstandings, you should provide the filming agent with clear instructions about the use of targets, including copies of those to be used and their sequence. Review the targets to be supplied by the filming agent, and reach an agreement about those to be supplied by the institution. The filming agent will generally supply technical targets and often can

---

26. See especially ANSI/AIIM MS23-1991, sec. 4.6, pp. 12–21. Supplementary guidance is provided in *American National Standard for Eye-Legible Information on Microfilm Leaders and Trailers and on Containers of Processed Microfilm on Open Reels,* ANSI/NISO Z39.62-1993 (Bethesda, Md.: NISO, 1993).

27. Elkington, *RLG Archives Microfilming Manual,* 137–67; and Elkington, *RLG Preservation Microfilming Handbook,* 26–35, 143–53; Debra McKern and Sherry Byrne, *ALA Target Packet for Use in Preservation Microfilming* (Chicago: ALA, 1991).

28. An AIIM subcommittee is currently working to develop a standard for use of graphic symbols in library and archival microfilm, but as of this writing, the work appears far from completion.

The most efficient way to produce targets is to use a personal computer and laser printer with the ability to produce very large fonts such as the 60-point type used on this eye-legible title target. You can gain further efficiency by linking target production software to OCLC or RLIN, your local catalog, and database management software. *Columbia University Libraries, Preservation Division.*

provide standard targets (START, END OF REEL, etc.), but will assess an extra charge to produce customized targets.

Some targets must be eye-legible; that is, they can be read from the film without the use of a film reader or other optical device. Letters on eye-legible targets must produce images on films that are at least 2mm (0.08 inch) high.[29] Consequently, the letters must be large enough to allow for reduction. In practice, a 60-point type, which measures ⅝ inch (16mm) when printed, will generally qualify as eye-legible when filming at reduction ratios of from 8:1 to 14:1.[30]

The simplest way to produce targets is to use a laser printer with a personal computer. You can achieve further efficiency by developing an interface with an online database (OCLC or RLIN), your local online catalog, and perhaps a local database software package, as noted in chapter 1. You must determine how to configure and use these links to best advantage. Some targets will use a combination of laser printer and handwriting. For example, the LIST OF IRREGULARITIES

29. ANSI/AIIM MS23-1991, 12.

30. ANSI/NISO Z39.62-1993, sec. 4.1. p. 2; also Elkington, *RLG Preservation Microfilming Handbook,* 28.

target (illustrated in figure 11) may be a computer-generated form with hand-written notes.

If your institution does not have these computer capabilities, you may use the camera-ready standard targets in the *ALA Target Packet*. Custom targets may be made informally, using a typewriter (if they need not be eye-legible) or a wide-tipped felt marker. Targets prepared by hand must be neat and clear. More-polished versions can be constructed with lettering systems available from art supply stores. Manual target production is so time-consuming and cumbersome, however, that it may be worthwhile to investigate what your filming agent would charge for this service. For a large project, the volume of work might justify the purchase of a personal computer and laser printer.

The following discussion provides an overview of the targets required for filming books, serials, and archival collections. It describes the range of required targets as well as optional targets that may be used at your discretion. When preparing targets, try to find a balance between the minimum number of required targets and the necessary extras that will help people use the film. You can err on the side of too many targets just as easily as too few. Remember that unnecessary targets can be time-consuming to prepare and distracting to the user. They also add to your frame count and, thus, to your filming cost because charges are typically on a per-frame basis. Appendix D provides detailed guidance on the purposes, content, and sequence of targets for monographs, serials, and archival collections.

Informational Targets. Two types of targets are generally used in preservation microfilming: informational and technical. Informational targets provide bibliographic data about the material filmed, technical data about the filming process, and explanatory notes for the user. Some standard targets are required at the beginning and end of every reel and at the beginning and end of each title or collection—for example, START or END OF REEL/PLEASE REWIND, the MASTER NEGATIVE NUMBER target, BIBLIOGRAPHIC RECORD target, and so on. Others are required if necessary. For example, the LIST OF IRREGULARITIES is required if there are anomalies in the text, and the VOLUME target is required when filming multivolume titles. Some targets, such as PAGES MISNUMBERED or DAMAGED PAGES, are optional but may be used within the text. These provide additional information and explanations or indicate variations from what a user would expect to see on the film. They precede the material or are inserted in their appropriate place among the pages.

Bibliographic information should include an eye-legible title and imprint (on the eye-legible title target); a copy of the catalog record (BIBLIOGRAPHIC RECORD target); list of missing pages, volumes, and other parts (LIST OF IRREGULARITIES); title or collection guides (GUIDE TO CONTENTS target); and perhaps longer notes such as series notations and references to separate indexes, finding aids, or supplementary bibliographic and descriptive data. The cataloging staff should be involved in creating the bibliographic targets. (Chapter 5 notes the key relationships between bibliographic control and the content of targets.) The introductory bibliographic targets form the preliminary sequence for each title or collection and are filmed at the beginning of each title or preceding the first page of the material described. The filming agent also supplies technical data on the reduction ratio, image orientation, film size, and name and location of filmer, either as a separate target or written in on the BIBLIOGRAPHIC RECORD target supplied by the institution. (See figure 12.) This, too, becomes part of the film.

Additional informational targets, some eye-legible and some in large (30-point) or regular type, are used on an as-needed basis and may be required throughout. In library collections, particularly with multivolume sets of serials, informational targets are used to identify each bibliographic or physical unit (such as volumes, issues, or parts) and include volume numbers and/or dates. In archival collections, informational targets are used to identify each organizational unit (record series, file folders, etc.) and include its number and a title or short description of the contents.

Other informational targets used on an as-needed basis often indicate problems or irregularities on a page, within a volume, or throughout a serial or collection. The most typical use is to indicate that material is missing. The page numbers of missing pages should appear in the LIST OF IRREGULARITIES target. Gaps in serials are included in the GUIDE TO CONTENTS (see figure 13) or on the LIST OF IRREGULARITIES targets for a specific volume or other unit. Information missing from manuscript collections, or folders not filmed, should also be indicated in the preliminary sequence. Gaps within the text may also be marked with an eye-legible target, for example, PAGE(S) MISSING, in the appropriate place within the text. This notifies both the reader and staff member performing film inspection that the omission is not a filming error and allows space for splicing in the missing pages if they should be located later. The same procedure can indicate damaged pages where the meaning of the text is obscured and when other physical conditions of the original will affect its legibility on film. Examples include the DAMAGED PAGE(S) or TIGHT BINDING targets.

Targets also may be placed within the text to indicate sequences of irregular pagination, extensive changes in a series title, unusual variations in the arrangement of a serial file or manuscript collection, or other problems that would mislead readers. When titles fill more than one reel, it is a good idea to repeat some targets (especially the eye-legible title, BIBLIOGRAPHIC RECORD target, and GUIDE TO CONTENTS target) at the end of a reel for purposes of quick identification. This is especially true of serials and some archival collections.

Informational targets within the text may also add notations from sources outside those at hand; an example of this is "J.S. refers to John Smith, brother of the letter's author." In view of the cost implications, administrative decisions should govern the extent to which such information will be added.

The camera operator may add some other targets during filming. Such targets might be added to indicate a change in reduction ratio or to flag a frame as an INTENTIONAL SECOND EXPOSURE, for example.

Technical Targets. Two targets belong to this category. For many years one has been called *the* technical target. The second is the uniform density target. The technical target (sometimes called the "test card" by filming staff) contains the resolution test charts (specific combinations of numerals and lines of varying widths and lengths) defined by ANSI/AIIM MS51-1990 (ISO 3334-1989) and their use is mandated by ANSI standards.[31] (See figure 14.) During inspection,

---

31. ANSI/AIIM MS23-1991, sec. 4.6.4.1, p. 13.

FIGURE 12 Bibliographic Record Target

BIBLIOGRAPHIC RECORD TARGET

Pitts Theology Library
Emory University

RLG Great Collections Microfilming Project
Phase IV

Master Negative Number: _____*(filmer or institution supplies)*_____

(bibliographic record photocopied here)

Technical Microfilm Data

Microfilmed by
University Microfilms International
Ann Arbor, Mich.

On behalf of
Pitts Theology Library, Emory University
Atlanta, Ga.

Film size: 35mm microfilm
Reduction ratio: ___:1___
Image placement: IA   IIA   IB   IIB
Date filming began: *(filmer supplies)*
Camera operator: *(filmer supplies)*

SOURCE: Marcia Watt, Preservation Officer, Emory University.

FIGURE 13 Guide to Contents Target: Serial

LIBRARY OF CONGRESS Preservation Microfilming Office Guide to Contents	Shelf Number Microfilm (o) 85/9215 MicRR
Author Belgium. Institut national de statistique.	Call Number HF203.A17
Title Bulletin mensuel du commerce avec les pays étrangers.	Page 1 of 3
Inclusive Volumes	Inclusive Years 1901–1940

CONTENTS

Reel	Date	Reel	Date
1	Jan. 1901–June 1901	25	May 1924–Oct. 1924
2	July 1901–Dec. 1901	26	Nov. 1924–Feb. 1925
3	Jan. 1902–Apr. 1903	27	Mar. 1925–Apr. 1925
4	May 1903–Dec. 1903	28	May 1925–June 1925
5	Jan. 1904–Aug. 1904	29	July 1925–Aug. 1925
6	Sept. 1904–Apr. 1905	30	Sept. 1925–Oct. 1925
7	May 1905–Dec. 1905	31	Nov. 1925–Dec. 1925
8	Jan. 1906–Dec. 1906	32	Jan. 1926–Feb. 1926
9	Jan. 1907–Aug. 1907	33	Mar. 1926–Apr. 1926
10	Sept. 1907–Apr. 1908	34	May 1926–June 1926
11	May 1908–Dec. 1908	35	July 1926–Aug. 1926
12	Jan. 1909–Aug. 1909	36	Sept. 1926–Oct. 1926
13	Sept. 1909–Apr. 1910	37	Nov. 1926–Dec. 1926
14	May 1910–Dec. 1910	38	Jan. 1927–Mar. 1927
15	Jan. 1911–Aug. 1911	39	Apr. 1927–June 1927
16	Sept. 1911–Apr. 1912	40	July 1927–Sept. 1927
17	May 1912–Dec. 1912	41	Oct. 1927–Dec. 1927
18	Jan. 1913–July 1913	42	Jan. 1928–Mar. 1928
19	Aug. 1913–Feb. 1914	43	Apr. 1928–June 1928
20	Mar. 1914–Apr. 1914	44	July 1928–Sept. 1928
	[1919]	45	Oct. 1928–Dec. 1928
	Jan. 1920	46	Jan. 1929–Mar. 1929
	1919 & 1920 [1st 5 months]	47	Apr. 1929–June 1929
21	1919 & 1920 [1st 11 months]	48	July 1929–Sept. 1929
	1919 & 1920 Annees	49	Oct. 1929–Dec. 1929
22	1921 & 1922 [1st 3 months]	50	Jan.1930–Mar.1930
	1922 [various months]	51	Apr. 1930–June 1930
	Jan. 1923–Feb. 1923	52	July 1930–Sept. 1930
23	Mar. 1923–Sept. 1923	53	Oct. 1930–Dec. 1930
24	Oct. 1923–Apr. 1924	54	Jan. 1931–Feb. 1931

WANTING

July 1902–Dec. 1902
Jan. 1906–Apr. 1906
May 1914
[1919]
[1921]

NOTES: Publication suspended June 1914–Jan. 1919.

ISSUES LISTED AS MISSING WHEN ORIGINALLY FILMED. IF LOCATED AT A LATER DATE MAY BE INCLUDED AT THE END OF THE APPROPRIATE REEL.

SOURCE: Tamara Swora, Assistant Preservation Microfilming Officer, Library of Congress.

FIGURE 14 Technical Target

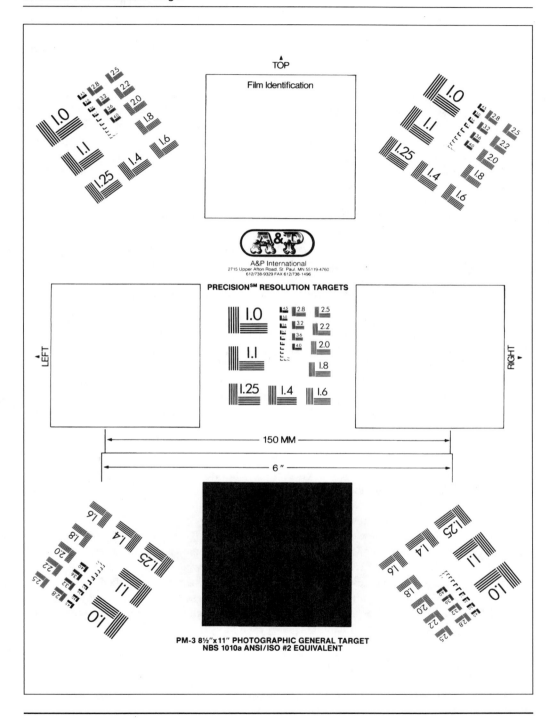

SOURCE: Paul Montgomery, A&P International, St. Paul, Minn.

staff members use the filmed version of the technical target to test the reduction ratio that was used and the filming system's resolving power (its ability to record fine detail). (Chapter 4, "Quality Assurance," explains how such tests are conducted.) The filming agent normally supplies this target. It is filmed at the end of the preliminary sequence of targets and again at the end of the reel, as detailed in appendix D. There should be *no* splices between the technical target and text at the beginning of the target sequence.

In addition to the resolution test charts, the technical target may include other test elements used in production and quality control. It may also include a ruler or other measuring device, text in various font sizes, white or black patches used for measuring density, a gray scale (in continuous-tone filming), and space on which the camera operator can record details about the filming procedure (reduction ratio, image orientation, etc.). Filming labs can construct their own or purchase ones like figure 14 from micrographics suppliers.

A uniform density target is also filmed at least twice on each reel, as specified in appendix D. It is used by inspection staff to verify that the camera provides uniform illumination across the copy surface. These targets are sheets of paper or card stock, and the ANSI/AIIM standard specifies their size, reflectance, and composition.[32] The filming agent usually provides this target.

The filming agent will leave "flash spaces," or blank frames, between targets and the first page of text, between volumes filmed sequentially, and between the last page of text and the final target.

Target Sequence. The target sequence, or series, for each publication or set of manuscripts includes both standard and customized targets, some of which are eye-legible and some in regular fonts, as detailed in appendix D. The target sequence must agree in every detail with the final collation of material being filmed. It must account for all items or pages, missing pages, mutilations that affect the text, or other irregularities in the source document. Although there are many similarities, target sequences differ somewhat, depending on the format of the material being filmed.

Preservation guidelines clearly define the target sequence required for 35mm film products. As noted in chapter 4 ("Film Formats"), there are some complexities in adapting the recommended target series for use in a microfiche product.

The best illustration of a target series is the sequence itself. Samples are provided in figures 15, 16, and 17.

Monographs. Since most monographs are self-contained and can fit on a single reel of film, a target sequence for monographs is generally straightforward. Figure 15 graphically illustrates the target sequence for a monograph, and a narrative description of the sequence appears in appendix D.

Serials. Because serials often are lengthy enough to require more than one microfilm reel or microfiche, they require a slightly different target series. Each title requires identification, as does each physical unit (reel or fiche). The library

---

32. See *American National Standard for Information and Image Management—35 mm Planetary Cameras (top light)—Procedures for Determining Illumination Uniformity of Microfilming Engineering Drawings,* ANSI/AIIM MS26-1990 (Silver Spring, Md.: AIIM, 1990); and Elkington, *RLG Preservation Microfilming Handbook,* 36–7.

FIGURE 15 Target Sequence for Monograph

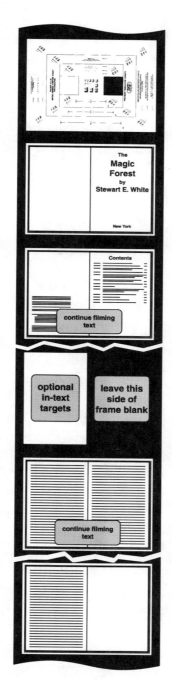

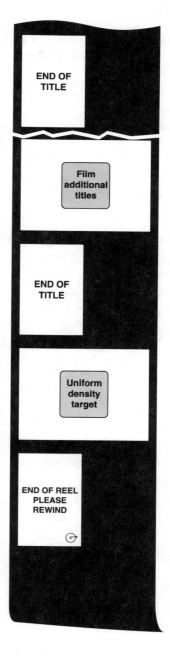

FIGURE 16 Target Sequence for Serial

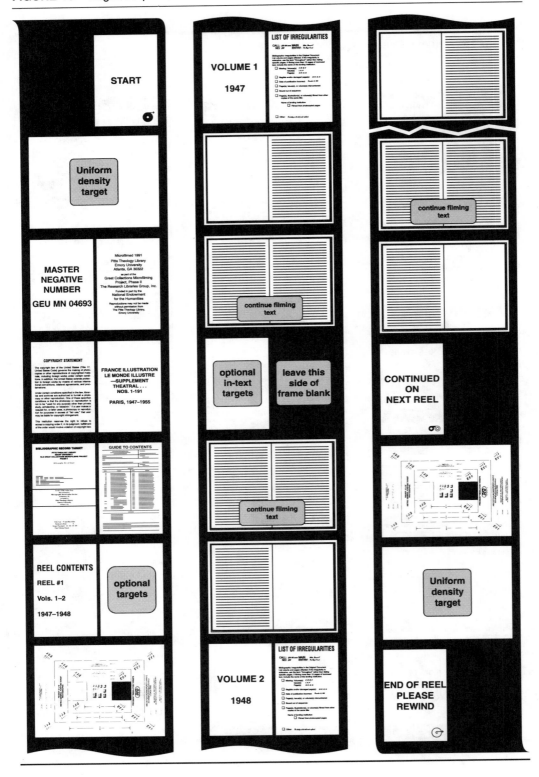

community has developed consensus-based guidelines for the target sequence of serials on microfilm reels (reflected in the *RLG Preservation Microfilming Handbook*), but no such guidance exists for fiche, where some of the target information may appear on the eye-legible header. The GUIDE TO CONTENTS target alerts the reader to the actual contents of a serial (see figure 13). It should list the volumes, issues, or other parts being filmed; the missing volumes, issues, pages, or mutilated pages (on which text is obscured) that cannot be corrected prior to filming; and the contents of each reel. Figure 16 provides a sample target series for a serial, and further description appears in Appendix D.

Archival collections. For the most part, the guidelines for target preparation and the target sequences that have been described can be adapted for archival and manuscript collections, with appropriate substitutions. For example, it is often useful to film the finding aid, inventory, register, or folder listing for the collection. (See chapter 5 for a discussion of the desirability of preparing guides.) This may include an introduction to the collection with information concerning provenance or scope as well as a brief biographical sketch, much of which may also be included in the online catalog record. The use of an automatic frame counter during filming makes it possible to correlate the numbers appearing along the top or side of each frame with the starting points of specific record series or containers. If a frame counter is used to provide a numbering system, its use should be explained in the finding aid. Figure 17 illustrates a target series for a manuscript collection. Appendix D further explains the sequence.

Instructional Flags

Instructional sheets or "flags" (sometimes imprecisely called "targets") are not filmed. They tell the camera operator how to film a specific item that requires handling not covered either in overall project instructions or in the reel or title instructions (the latter are discussed under "Final Preparation"), or they note that an item is to be handled as an exception to those other instructions. For example, if a collection of German-language materials included one item in Hebrew or some other language that reads from right to left, you might place a flag before the item, alerting the operator to film it correctly.

Instructional flags should be on one color of paper (other than white), which is used consistently throughout and will stand out from the other materials in the collection. They may be handwritten legibly, but most institutions use laser printers to generate them and keep a supply on hand to speed processing.

The preparations staff should insert these instructional flags where appropriate within the volume or stack of documents. Typical flags are: "film front endsheets only," "do not film reverse side," "unfold clippings before filming," "following pages bound out of order—film in correct sequence," and "film 'borrowed from . . .' target here." The camera operator removes the sheets, follows the instructions about filming, then replaces them. Since all of this takes time, try to keep instruction sheets to a minimum.

Frame Counts

After you complete all other preparation work, calculate the number of camera exposures required for the material. A single exposure equals one frame of film,

FIGURE 17 Target Sequence for Manuscript Collection, Reel 1

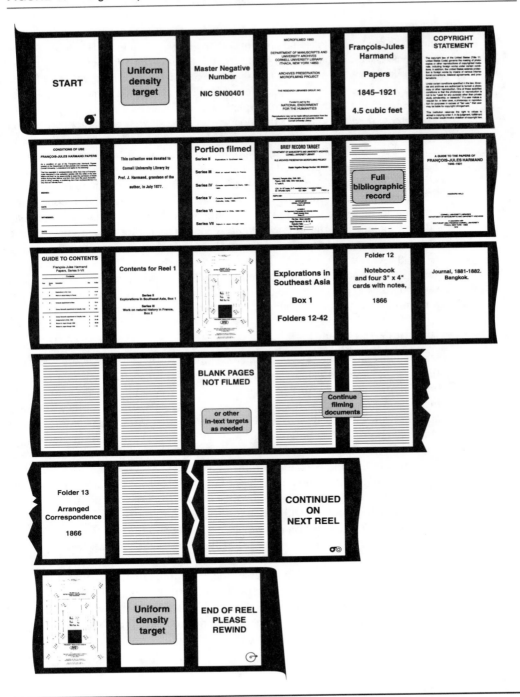

The preparation area should include a well-stocked supply of standard forms and often-used materials. Preprinted instructional flags, for example, should be kept on hand for insertion when needed. *Columbia University Libraries, Preservation Division.*

but some pages may require multiple exposures. The frame count will determine how much can fit on each reel as well as the cost of filming. Later, when the material is returned, you will compare this frame count with that reported by the filming agent to get a preliminary indication of whether any materials may have been skipped.

Bound volumes are generally filmed two pages per frame ("two-up"), so a 250-page book will result in slightly more than 125 frames, depending on how the book is paginated, plus the targets that are added. Special features also may add to the frame count. Since an enclosure (extraneous material not part of the book) is filmed immediately following the page on which it is found, each enclosure will add an additional frame or more, depending on the number of exposures required for each one. Maps or other illustrations that are attached to and overlap the text are first filmed in place, then folded back or out to reveal the text beneath. This, too, will add frames to the count. Any folded material that must be filmed in segments (as illustrated in figure 10) requires careful calculation. Intentional second exposures, often needed to capture the information on pages that include both text and illustrations, will also add to the frame count.

Single sheets of manuscript or archival material with writing on one side will require a single frame of microfilm each or two frames per sheet if there is writing on both sides. Letters and documents with overwriting (writing that runs in several directions) or writing with different colored inks and papers may well require intentional multiple exposures to produce a legible microfilm copy. The frame count for clippings will depend on whether you group them together on sheets or film each one separately. Scrapbooks may include multipaged items and may require intentional multiple exposures, which will elevate the frame count.

The total number of reels required for a collection will be calculated on the basis of the frame count, the bibliographic criteria for determining reel breaks, the size of the materials, and the reduction ratio at which the items are filmed. The "Computing the Filming Cost" section in chapter 6 provides further instructions on frame counts.

Reel Programming

Reel programming is the process of determining the contents of each reel prior to filming. It ensures that reel breaks occur at a logical bibliographic or chronological break, such as the end of a title, serial volume, or archival folder or the end of a year of correspondence.[33]

Reel programming should be done before materials are delivered to the camera. When reel breaks are determined in advance, you can prepare the necessary targets listing the contents of each reel, the number of reels for the set, and the contents of each reel. Appendix D describes the reel contents target, required for monographs and serials, and the GUIDE TO CONTENTS target, required for serials and archival collections.

The first decision to be made—and made before project initiation—is whether the institution or the filming agent will do the reel programming. In gen-

---

33. Reel programming is one area in which the distinction between national standards and preservation microfilming guidelines is operative. It does not affect the stability of the film and is not required by the ANSI/AIIM standards. However, RLG guidelines require it, as do those of most other major library organizations, because it ensures logical breaks between bibliographic units and improves the organization of the film. Strictly speaking, the camera operator can simply fill reels to maximum capacity by breaking the text at the end of the reel whenever it might come, even in the middle of a single issue of a journal. However, this approach will create many problems for users.

eral, the staff that handles collation and targeting should do the reel programming. If the institution does all the other preparation work (perhaps with the exception of creating some of the standard targets), then it is most logical for the institution's staff to calculate reel breaks. On the other hand, if the institution contracts for preparation services, the contractor will do the reel programming.

There are several benefits to doing your own reel programming. First, the institutional staff is best able to determine the logical break points in a collection, especially in archival collections, where logical divisions are not always self-evident. Second, most service bureaus will assess an extra charge to do the work, unless they are also doing the other preparation work. Third, filming begins more quickly and can usually be done in a shorter amount of time if reel programming has been done. It is typical for the filming agent to distribute a large collection to several different cameras. If the collection has already been reel-broken, the filming agent can immediately disperse it to different cameras and, thus, begin work on it sooner. Otherwise, the agent has to complete all the reel programming before any filming can begin.

As with the other preparation activities, your staff will need some time to understand and practice the techniques for reel programming. But with the many guidelines that exist now, reel programming is not particularly daunting.

If you elect to have the filming agent do the reel programming, provide guidelines about where reel breaks are or are not acceptable (whichever you can more clearly and consistently describe). This could include instructions such as "Do not break a reel within the contents of a box/folder/volume" or "Keep each year's issues on a single reel."

Whether reel programming is to be handled in-house or by the filming agent, you must develop guidelines for it and include those guidelines in your procedures manual. If the filmer will do the reel programming, guidelines should be in the contract or letter of agreement as well.

There are many sources of information on reel programming. The RLG microfilming manuals provide instructions, including tables for calculating reel capacity.[34] Since those manuals were published, Kodak has adopted a 40-meter roll in place of the 100- and 125-foot reels that were standard. To assist you in reel programming for such film, figure 18 provides a new guide for calculating reel capacity. The capacity of a reel depends on the size of the materials you are filming and the reduction ratio being used.

Figure 18 can be used to determine the maximum number of exposures that will fit on a standard 40-meter reel of 35mm film. In the left column, find the appropriate line for the materials you are filming; use their height if filming in the A (cine) position or their width if filming in the B (comic) position. Those positions are illustrated in figure 23. Across the top of the chart, find the column for the reduction ratio you are using. The cell where the two intersect shows the approximate number of exposures that can be included on the reel. The filming agent can also provide guidance on reel programming as you begin drafting your

---

34. See Elkington, *RLG Preservation Microfilming Handbook,* 132–8; and Elkington, *RLG Archives Microfilming Manual,* 32–6. Especially note the step-by-step instructions for reel programming in the *RLG Preservation Microfilming Handbook,* 132–5.

FIGURE 18 Reel Capacity

Maximum Exposures: 40 Meter Reels

Reduction Ratio

Height (A) Width (B) (inches)	8	9	10	11	12	13	14	15	16	17	18	19	20	21
6	1,423	1,542	1,682	1,850	2,056	2,176	2,313	2,467	2,643	2,643	2,846	2,846	3,083	3,083
7	1,276	1,423	1,542	1,682	1,850	1,947	2,056	2,176	2,313	2,467	2,643	2,643	2,846	2,846
8	1,121	1,276	1,370	1,542	1,609	1,762	1,850	1,947	2,056	2,176	2,313	2,467	2,467	2,643
9	1,028	1,156	1,276	1,370	1,480	1,609	1,682	1,850	1,947	2,056	2,176	2,176	2,313	2,467
10	949	1,057	1,156	1,276	1,370	1,480	1,609	1,682	1,762	1,850	1,947	2,056	2,176	2,313
11	881	974	1,088	1,194	1,276	1,370	1,480	1,542	1,682	1,762	1,850	1,947	2,056	2,056
12		902	1,000	1,088	1,194	1,276	1,370	1,480	1,542	1,609	1,682	1,762	1,850	1,947
13		860	949	1,028	1,121	1,194	1,276	1,370	1,423	1,542	1,609	1,682	1,762	1,850
14			881	974	1,057	1,121	1,194	1,276	1,370	1,423	1,542	1,609	1,682	1,762
15			841	902	1,000	1,057	1,156	1,233	1,276	1,370	1,423	1,480	1,609	1,682
16				860	925	1,000	1,088	1,156	1,233	1,276	1,370	1,423	1,480	1,542
17					881	949	1,028	1,088	1,156	1,233	1,276	1,370	1,423	1,480
18					841	902	974	1,028	1,121	1,156	1,233	1,276	1,370	1,423
19						860	925	1,000	1,057	1,121	1,194	1,233	1,276	1,370
20							881	949	1,000	1,057	1,121	1,194	1,233	1,276
21							860	902	974	1,028	1,088	1,121	1,194	1,233
22								881	925	974	1,028	1,088	1,156	1,194
23								841	902	949	1,000	1,057	1,088	1,156
24									860	902	974	1,000	1,057	1,121

SOURCE: Preservation Resources, Bethlehem, Pa.

procedures and can later comment on refinements that are needed once reel-broken materials are delivered to the camera.

Titles less than one roll in length should not be split between reels, nor should reels include microfilm of more than one month or more than one year unless all months or all years contained on the reel are included in their entirety. When filming serials, do not combine multiple titles on a reel; upon consultation with the cataloging staff, you may make exceptions for some title changes. Acceptable and unacceptable types of bibliographic units for newspaper and serial runs are shown in figure 19.

When shorter publications, such as monographs or pamphlets, do not have enough pages to fill a standard reel of microfilm, you must choose between two approaches. Both will affect service copies of the film.

First, you may fill reels to capacity by putting several titles on one reel. This affords the most efficient use of storage space. A decimal system is often used for bibliographic identification of individual titles on a reel; that is, number 468.3 is the third title on reel 468. (See the discussion of master negative numbers in appendix D.) This method presents limitations for duplicating film copies of individual titles. In most cases, it is necessary to copy the whole reel of film and not the individual titles, and that may increase the cost to be passed on to customers.

In the second approach, you may allow only one title per reel or allow a large space (four feet) between titles. This is the more practical option if your institution plans to supply film copies of individual titles on demand. Filming only one title per reel is probably inadvisable because it wastes much of the film stock and increases your costs for storage of master negatives. The alternative is to fill the camera negative but to provide service copies separated on individual reels.

FIGURE 19   Reel Breaks for Serials

Acceptable
- a. January 1–10   January 11–20   January 21–31
- b. January 1–15   January 16–31
- c. January 1–31
- d. January 1–February 28
- e. January 1–March 31
- f. January 1–June 30
- g. January 1–December 31
- h. January 1, 1990–December 31, 1991

Unacceptable
- a. January 1–January 17   January 18–February 9
     February 10–February 26   February 27–March 15
- b. January 1, 1990–January 5, 1991
- c. January 6, 1991–December 25, 1992 (unless these are *exact* dates on beginning and ending issues)

SOURCE: Adapted from *Specifications for the Microfilming of Newspapers in the Library of Congress* (Washington, D.C.: Library of Congress, 1972), 1.

That will require that the filmer either leave extra space between titles so you can cut them apart or insert START and END targets between titles, but it will waste film and increase costs. If you choose this option, you must do so before you begin your preparation and provide clear instructions to the filmer.

If you anticipate little copying activity, fill reels and provide bibliographic access for individual titles to allow for easy retrieval and use. For single monographs and records series, use common logic to balance the editorial sense with technical efficiency.

Final Preparation

The final steps in preparation are to check the materials and the work done in physical and editorial preparation, write instructions to the filming agent, and package and transport the materials to the filming lab. Are all materials and accompanying targets in the correct place? Are all operating instructions and problems included in the instructions to the filmer? The final review is especially critical for complicated serials and manuscript collections for which preparation and filming decisions may have been made over a long time by different staff members.

The filming agent will let you know what kinds of instructions are needed to ensure smooth work on the project. There are generally three levels or types of instructions: general or project instructions; instructions for a specific collection, shipment, reel, or title; and flags for the camera operator. Instructional flags are created during physical and editorial preparation, and they generally relate to individual items. The distinction between project instructions and reel or collection instructions is subtle, and it generally depends on the scope and nature of your filming and the preferences of the filming agent.

General instructions, typically provided at the beginning of a project or contract year, were addressed as part of contracting for filming services. They outline routine operating procedures that apply to the majority of materials. Instructions to accompany materials with special requirements or problems are then prepared as the need arises. You can provide thorough general instructions at the outset to minimize the need for special instructions.

General instructions, as distinct from technical specifications, usually deal with handling procedures, editorial decisions, and directions that reflect local options and that do not change from one title or reel to another. Instructions can be broad, covering procedures for handling many categories of materials or formats (monographs, serials, and manuscripts), or specific, applying to individual items. They will tell the filming agent how to assign reel numbers and determine reel breaks, how much space to leave between multiple titles filmed on a single reel or between serial volumes or file folders, how to handle intentional multiple exposures for graphic materials, and so on. Instructions might specify that a frame counter should be used for manuscript and other unpaginated materials.

Another large category of instructions includes filming procedures for special materials that occur on a regular basis. Guidelines for filming folded materials, overlays, blank pages, loose items or enclosures, folded news clippings, and file folders that precede manuscript materials are a few examples.

One final but important instruction covers what the camera operator should do when problems are encountered at the camera—for example, how to target pages when their physical condition affects legibility. Establish clear procedures for handling such situations so that filming schedules are not held up. Be sure the institutional contact provides prompt responses to the filming agent's questions.

If your filming project is large or diverse, you may also need to generate instructions for individual shipments, reels of serials, monographic titles, or archival collections, particularly if they contain materials that must be handled in ways that depart from the general project instructions. Specific instructions might also be unique to a reel or serial volume. For example, if one anomalous shipment or reel in your project includes materials with a large number of foldouts or photographs that require intentional second exposures, your reel instructions would cover how to handle them. To the extent that the instructions are thorough and applicable to the entire reel or title, you minimize the need for instructional flags, reserving them for items that are exceptions to these instructions.

The reel or title instructions are compiled during final preparation. However, you will probably begin accumulating them during the course of physical and editorial preparation. For example, if your project instructions specify that covers not be filmed, but you encounter a series of books whose covers *should* be filmed, you should include that instruction for the reel so that the preparations staff will need to flag only the exceptions for the camera operator. Then instructions to the filmer are compiled during final preparation and included with the shipment.

It can be exceedingly difficult to capture all the nuances of a project on paper (in the contract, general project instructions, flags, etc.). Therefore, it is often a good idea to submit a relatively small batch of materials, enough for two to three reels, to the filmer as your first shipment. That will allow prompt inspection that will identify any areas for which your instructions may have been unclear so you can fine-tune them and clarify any misunderstandings.

Postfilming Activities

Preparations staff may be responsible for many postfilming operations. Staff members will need to "un-prep" the collection. Removing targets and flags that were inserted for filming is a basic step in reversing camera readiness. You can instruct the filmer to remove them before returning the materials, but most institutions find it helpful to have targets and flags in place during inspection to help staff members interpret the camera operator's work. If collections were significantly rearranged for filming and originals will be retained, an administrative decision must be made regarding which unit of the library or archives should restore the original arrangement.

A variety of other postfilming work may be done by the preparations staff or other units. You will conduct quality assurance inspections, identify errors or corrections to be filmed, and ensure these are resolved appropriately. The staff must assemble originals, microforms, and accompanying documentation, then process or forward them to other units, especially those involved with bibliographic or archival control. Some materials may be routed for treatments that were identified during physical preparation. Master negatives must be forwarded to the storage facility. Records must be closed out and various reports generated. These postfilming steps are detailed in chapter 4. Remember that nearly everything that was done in preparation will need to be undone as part of the postfilming routine.

Conclusion

This chapter has attempted to alert you to the many possibilities, limitations, and implications of particular options, so that each microfilm project will result in useful products. During the initial planning of a project, preparation of materials for filming is the step most likely to be overlooked or compromised—even when its importance is recognized—due to other pressing demands in a project's implementation. Preparation requires that you carefully consider the materials to be filmed and their intended use and that you have in-depth knowledge of microfilm production processes. To meet the dual goals of facilitating efficient camera operation and ensuring a user-friendly product, preparation concerns must work synergistically with the technical issues of microfilm production discussed in chapter 4.

Suggested Readings

Several national standards and specifications also address preparation procedures. See appendix A.

Brennan, Patricia, and Jutta Reed-Scott. *Automating Preservation Management in ARL Libraries.* SPEC Kit 198. Washington, D.C.: ARL Office of Management Services, 1993.

Byrnes, Margaret. "Issues and Criteria for Comparing In-House and Contracted Microfilming." In *Preservation Microfilming: Planning and Production,* 32–42. Chicago: ALA/ALCTS, 1989.

Carpenter, Kenneth E., and Jane Carr. "Microform Publishing Contracts." *Microform Review* 19 (spring 1990): 83–100.

Elkington, Nancy E., ed. *RLG Archives Microfilming Manual.* Mountain View, Calif.: RLG, 1994:
> Kenney, Anne R. "Preparation of Materials," 26–38.
> LaFantasie, Maxine. "Choosing a Vendor and Contracting Out," 11–25.

Elkington, Nancy E., ed. *RLG Preservation Microfilming Handbook.* Mountain View, Calif.: RLG, 1992:
> Arnott, Julie. "Request for Proposal for Basic Preservation Microfilming Services," 104–9.
> Craig, Christina L. "Reel Programming," 132–8.
> Lilley, Barbara. "Sample Microfilming Contract," 119–29.
> Nyberg, Sandra. "Sample RFI for Expanded Preservation Microfilming Services," 101–3.
> Walker, R. Gay. "Request for Proposal for Expanded Preservation Microfilming Services," 110–18.

Lockhart, Vickie, and Ann Swartzell. "Evaluation of Microfilm Vendors." *Microform Review* 19 (summer 1990): 119–23.

McKern, Debra, and Sherry Byrne. *ALA Target Packet for Use in Preservation Microfilming.* Chicago: ALA, 1991.

Subcommittee on Contract Negotiations for Commercial Reproduction of Library and Archival Materials. "Contract Negotiations for the Commercial Microform Publishing of Library and Archival Materials: Guidelines for Librarians and Archivists." *Library Resources & Technical Services* 38 (Jan. 1994): 72–85.

CHAPTER 4

Microfilming Standards and Practices

For most librarians and archivists, the most challenging aspect of setting up a preservation microfilming program may be learning enough about the filming process itself to evaluate and work effectively with in-house and external filming agents. Fortunately, of all aspects of the process, this is the one for which there is the most help for novice managers. In addition to the accepted national and industry standards, which an institution can adapt for its own filming specifications, there are numerous books and articles written on all aspects of the process. In fact, the problem may be that there is so much material, a great deal of it extraordinarily technical in nature, that it can be overwhelming at first. Yet it is important that you learn enough about the filming process to make wise decisions, evaluate the products you receive, and assist the filmer with some problem solving. Visits to preservation-oriented microfilming service providers will greatly improve your understanding of film production issues.

This chapter is designed for the librarian or archivist unacquainted with the technical aspects of microphotography. It explains the nature of micrographics standards, how they are developed, and the most important features of them, so that the manager can understand their importance in this complex field. It provides enough information to enable you to understand the basic terminology and processes and includes a step-by-step discussion of film production from receipt of documents in the filming lab to delivery and inspection at the institution. Because selection and preparation of materials (covered in chapters 2 and 3) are so closely related to the filming process, this chapter will also help you plan your activities in those areas. However, this chapter does not provide the information you would need to set up a filming facility. To do that, you would need to develop a greater mastery of microphotography and the technical standards.

The previous chapter emphasized the importance of good communication between the preservation staff and the filming agent, and that point must be underscored here. Many filming agents maintain that projects generally go more smoothly if the client has developed a reasonable familiarity with the process of producing preservation microfilm. A visit to one or more filming agencies may help you to develop the necessary level of understanding. High-quality filming practices and adherence to standards will ensure the stability of microforms for the next five hundred years or more.

Overview of National Standards

Microforms have been subject to more standards and to more analysis of their stability and image quality than any other recording medium in history. Today's microform standards serve to protect the consumer, to educate the user, and to guide the manufacturers of microfilm materials and those engaged in research and testing.

Microform standards cover such topics as equipment, the legibility and stability of microforms, the arrangement of images on microfiche and roll film, storage conditions and enclosures, and packaging and labeling. Staff members responsible for microfilming programs must be familiar with the basis of the standards and their scope and provisions.

How Standards Are Created

The micrographics industry benefited from early standards written under the auspices of the National Bureau of Standards to promote the production of durable and long-lived films for the motion picture industry. Today, U.S. standards, guidelines, specifications, or recommended practices are produced by many different organizations, primarily under the auspices of ANSI, which is a federation of trade associations, technical societies, professional organizations, consumer groups, and private companies.[1] (See figure 20.) Other groups develop standards that are forwarded for ANSI adoption, including such industry associations as AIIM and the National Association of Photographic Manufacturers (NAPM). Specifications are also developed by the U.S. government (in the form of federal and military specifications), state governments, and library organizations such as ALA, RLG, and the Library of Congress. Although U.S. standards are not under the jurisdiction of the U.S. government, many foreign standards are written under government auspices.

The committees that devise standards may be lodged administratively in different organizations. For many years, for example, the responsibility for developing permanence standards, including the necessary test methods to qualify raw stock and processed microfilm, has lodged with the ANSI-accredited Committee for Physical Properties and Permanence of Imaging Media, IT9, whose secretariat is NAPM. The responsibility to develop standards for formatting of microforms, micrographics equipment, and quality control procedures now rests with AIIM, an ANSI-approved standards-developing organization that currently has more than forty-five micrographics standards, all of which have also been approved as American National Standards under ANSI.[2]

---

1. William Saffady, *Micrographic Systems,* 3d ed. (Silver Spring, Md.: AIIM, 1990), 19.

2. Some AIIM standards are labeled as "standards" and some as "recommended practices." Both are standards, but recommended practices are written to be more explanatory or tutorial.

FIGURE 20 Standards Development Organizations

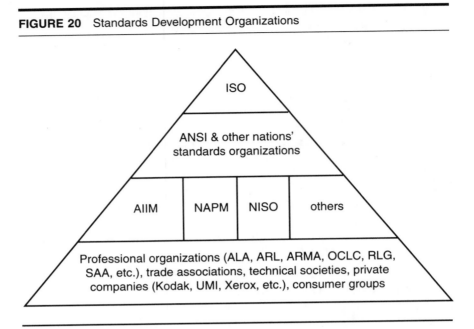

Most ANSI-accredited standards committees have subcommittees, task forces, or ad hoc committees where the actual work of debating the issues and writing the standards is performed. While the process varies slightly from one committee to another, all agree to operate under formal ANSI procedures. Normally, this means the basic draft is sent out for ballot to the subcommittee members and subsequently, after resolution of any negative votes, to the parent committee where it is balloted again. Negative votes must be addressed before the standard is forwarded to the ANSI Board of Standards Review. Prior to issuance as an American National Standard under ANSI, there must be consensus on its adoption, with *consensus* defined as "substantial agreement."

ANSI rules state that all standards committees must have a balanced mix of users and producers to ensure that the standards blend the expertise and economic interests of the manufacturers with the preferences and best interests of the consumers. Thus, microform committees comprise film producers; equipment producers; service agencies; and industrial, commercial, and nonprofit users. Committee members are volunteers.

The creation of standards often involves considerable technical research and experimentation, which must be conducted in well-equipped laboratories. These services are normally contributed free by the manufacturers of materials and equipment.[3]

---

3. A major new resource in the past few years has been IPI (see appendix B), a nonprofit research laboratory chiefly devoted to research in the longevity of imaging media for library and archival applications.

ANSI is the U.S. representative to the International Organization for Standardization (ISO). Under the auspices of ISO, national standards delegations work to establish international standards, many of them based on individual countries' standards. ISO requires 75 percent approval by the member bodies voting for a standard to be adopted. It is ANSI practice, whenever possible, to adopt international standards when they will replace comparable U.S. ones to avoid dual and potentially incompatible standards. In such cases, a standard often bears two numbers, as does *Specifications for Safety Film,* which is designated as ANSI IT9.6-1991 and ANSI/ISO 543-1990.

Standards are written, at least all those ultimately approved by ANSI, according to strict semantic and legalistic rules. The words *shall* and *should* are used with respect to stated requirements, which means that if the standard is incorporated into a contractual agreement, the "shall" items have mandatory adherence, while the "should" items remain optional. Standards in the United States do not have automatic legal authority, but they may be incorporated into legal, contractual arrangements so as to be enforceable.

How soon after the introduction of new processes, materials, and applications should a relevant standard be written? Practical experience is normally required before a standard can be attempted, lest the standard have a restrictive effect on innovation. On the other hand, if standards specifications come too late, arbitrary variations may create undesirable system incompatibilities. Therefore, white papers and technical reports concerning new materials are sometimes produced prior to a standard to prevent arbitrary excursions into multiple formats. As an example, in the early days of microfiche applications in the United States, producers used 3″ × 5″, 5″ × 8″, and 6″ × 8″ fiche before the 105mm × 148mm fiche became a standard. Today, a similar situation exists with color microfilm, where there exist few definitive standards.

New materials and new processes create continuing challenges in standards development. Optical disks and scanning and digitization technologies fall into this area. Considerable work is needed before the stability of these processes and materials is ascertained and specifications are written. Some of the new materials are known to be quite unstable, and their use is justified only with a general understanding that they will not be permanent. Until objective research is conducted, however, claims for image stability for new materials should not be accepted.

It generally takes many years to complete a standard. At today's hectic technological pace there is a danger that the introduction of new imaging materials and technologies and the current slow process of researching their stability will be out of phase. Valuable new materials with the promise of great stability may be developed, but the current mechanism of writing standards is too slow to cope with this situation. Increased funding of technical investigations to analyze the properties of new materials would expedite the process. However, the ultimate evaluation of the test findings would still have to be conducted by volunteer committees composed of the blend of manufacturers and users characteristic of the current ANSI and AIIM committees.

The primary microform standards today not only contain the specifications for stable microforms but also a host of comments incorporated into the forewords and appendixes that, while not officially part of the standards, are of great value in educating the user of microforms. Studied in its entirety, the standards literature describes good practice and offers clear explanations of the reasons for recommended and mandated procedures. Appendix A cites the key standards related to preservation microfilming of library and archival materials.

For new project managers, one of the most useful standards to read is *American National Standard for Information and Image Management—Practice for Operational Procedures/Inspection and Quality Control of First-Generation, Silver Microfilm of Documents* (ANSI/AIIM MS23-1991), which recapitulates and offers commentary on many of the fundamental standards related to preparation, filming, processing, inspection, testing, and storage.[4] It includes discussions of some practices used in source document filming (for example, the use of high-speed, rotary cameras) that are not appropriate for preservation microfilming. The preservation administrator will benefit from a study of the entire standard to extract those portions relevant to preservation microfilming, skipping occasional pages and paragraphs clearly intended for microfilming of business records.

Standards Revision

Over the years microfilm standards have been revised many times, and all of them continue to be reviewed by the designated subcommittees. There is relatively little risk of a national standard's becoming seriously out of date because ANSI protocols require that standards be reviewed every five years and be revised, reaffirmed, or withdrawn on the basis of that review. Certain standards change even more frequently. Product changes, new techniques, and unexpected events, such as the appearance of microscopic blemishes on film in the 1960s, have made it necessary to question and review constantly the recommendations and specifications in the standards.

As this manual goes to print, several issues are receiving much attention in the preservation community. Organizations are investigating the permanence of color microfilm, limits on density ranges, and the interplay between microfilming and digitization. Standards for these and other emerging issues will develop and continue to be improved in the light of ongoing research.

Standards versus Guidelines and Specifications

Keep in mind that microform standards have not been written solely for the preservation needs of the library and archives communities. They also encompass the needs of businesses, corporations, or other organizations concerned with retention of documents on microform for only a few years. The purposes and longevity requirements of these groups sometimes differ from those of libraries and archives, so a stricter interpretation of the standards may be required for your applications. That is, there is a wide range of practices that may be acceptable within the broad scope of "source document microfilming," but the subset that is "preservation microfilming" requires greater stability and legibility.

Based on those more stringent needs, many library and archival organizations have developed specifications that draw upon national standards but may

---

4. A committee has been appointed to revise ANSI/AIIM MS23-1991, but the time frame for the revision and balloting cannot yet be projected.

require tighter controls, narrower tolerances, and so on. The guidelines of RLG are considered most strict and conservative. For example, while ANSI standards allow use of tape and rubber cement for splices, RLG goes further, requiring ultrasonic but not heat-weld splices. Similarly, the national standards require only the most perfunctory targets for titles, but library and archival organizations typically require and use ones designed to support better bibliographic control and access.

Permanence of Microforms

The rationale for preservation microfilming is to create a permanent, reformatted copy of the source documents. Three elements determine the permanence of a microform: the composition of the film stock, the quality of the film processing, and the conditions under which the film is stored. National standards define the requirements in all three areas. *American National Standard for Imaging Media (Film)—Silver-Gelatin Type—Specifications for Stability* (ANSI/NAPM IT9.1-1992) defines the criteria for physical stability of the film stock and elements of processing that will render the image chemically stable. Storage requirements are chiefly outlined in *American National Standard for Imaging Media—Photographic Processed Films, Plates, and Papers—Filing Enclosures and Storage Containers* (ANSI IT9.2-1991) and *American National Standard for Imaging Media—Processed Safety Photographic Films—Storage* (ANSI/NAPM IT9.11-1993).

These standards are the most important of those pertaining to permanence of microfilm. At first glance, they may appear dauntingly technical if you are just establishing a microfilming program. The forewords and appendixes of the standards are written with you in mind, however, and they elaborate in lay language on some aspects of film permanence.

Film can be classified according to several different criteria. First, films are categorized according to their life expectancy. In addition, films are classified according to their base type (polyester or acetate), emulsion (silver-gelatin, silver dye bleach, diazo, and vesicular), positive or negative polarity, generation, and format (35mm, 16mm, or 105mm roll film, or 105mm fiche sheets). These criteria are explained in the next sections of this chapter.

Life Expectancy

Preservation literature prior to 1992 often discussed the need to use "archival" film, which was the commonly accepted term until the 1992 revision of ANSI/NAPM IT9.1.[5] The "archival" designation was dropped because of the many different, and sometimes conflicting, meanings it had in different fields:

> The term "archival" has been interpreted to have many meanings, ranging from "the preservation of information forever" to the photographic-jargon meaning, i.e., "temporary storage of actively used information."

---

5. There was a brief period, from 1989 to 1992, when the standards began to move away from the term "archival" and use "permanent," "long-term," and "medium-term" designations for film longevity.

It is, therefore, recommended that the term *archival* not be used in standards for stability of recording materials and systems.[6]

Since 1992, the terms *archival film* and *archival storage* have not been used in micrographics standards.

There remains a standard definition of *archival medium* as "a recording material that can be expected to retain information forever so that such information can be retrieved without significant loss when properly stored."[7] The definition goes on to explain, however, that this quality of infinite endurance, while theoretically desirable, is technically impossible.

The current approach is to categorize film longevity in terms of its life expectancy (LE), defined as "the length of time that information is predicted to be retrievable in a system under extended-term storage conditions."[8] In practice, films are generally rated in one of three categories: LE-10, LE-100, or LE-500.[9]

When a film manufacturer rates a film as LE-500 (or when that rating is validated by an independent testing laboratory according to tests specified in the standards), that rating is predicated on the film's also being processed and stored in accordance with the applicable national standards. That is, to realize its 500-year potential, the film must be chemically processed according to the requirements of ANSI/NAPM IT9.1-1992 and stored in conformity with ANSI/NAPM IT9.11-1993. Only then can it be considered a preservation copy.

The only films that so far have an LE-500 rating are certain silver-gelatin films, so only these are appropriate for use as preservation masters. Be aware, though, that not all silver films have LE-500 ratings; for example, no color film has an ANSI-assigned life expectancy that long. The LE-500 rating must be specified in contracts, purchasing specifications, and other documents.

Films rated LE-100 or even LE-10 may be appropriate for use as service copies. Diazo and vesicular films (discussed in following sections) may have ratings as high as LE-100.

Film Stock

The composition of the film stock is a key issue in determining the permanence of a microform. Film consists of a base and emulsion.[10] The base is the plas-

---

6. *American National Standard for Imaging Media—Photographic Films, Papers, and Plates—Glossary of Terms Pertaining to Stability,* ANSI/NAPM IT9.13-1992 (New York: ANSI, 1992), 1.

7. ANSI/NAPM IT9.13-1992, sec. 2.2, p. 2.

8. ANSI/NAPM IT9.13-1992, sec. 2.21, p. 3. *Extended-term storage conditions* are defined in IT9.13 as those "suitable for the preservation of recorded information having permanent value."

9. It has been reported that the IT9 committee took a conservative approach in establishing LE ratings for silver-gelatin film, opting to risk under- rather than overestimating film longevity potential, so films may exceed their LE ratings *provided they are kept in extended-term storage conditions* required in ANSI/NAPM IT9.11-1993. See *Micrographic Film Technology,* 4th ed. (Silver Spring, Md.: AIIM, 1992), 40.

10. Two sources are particularly useful for further exploring the technical aspects of film composition. For a solid general introduction, see Saffady, *Micrographic Systems.* Technical, in-depth coverage is provided in *Micrographic Film Technology.*

tic support, and the emulsion is the light-sensitive coating in which the image forms.

Two types of base have long been used: polyester and acetate.[11] Both are also classified as safety films, meaning that unlike cellulose nitrate, they are not flammable.[12]

Only certain polyester-base films qualify as LE-500; in contrast, films on acetate base are not rated above LE-100. Since polyester-base films are also virtually tear proof both during processing and in subsequent use, they are the recommended choice. The RLG guidelines and most preservation microfilming managers now require the use of film with a polyester base.

Most manufacturers of microfilm offer a variety of films intended for different micrographic applications. Film used for preservation should be the sharpest available, that is, capable of achieving the highest possible resolutions. (An exception is made in continuous-tone filming, where high contrast is not desirable.) Virtually all microfilms offered by major film manufacturers (Kodak, Agfa, Fuji) qualify under permanence standards for raw stock, but not all manufacturers produce equally sharp film or film that is equally abrasion resistant. Filming agents should make intermittent comparison tests to determine the sharpest and most durable films.

It is unwise to economize in the choice of film for preservation projects because the cost of materials represents only a tiny fraction of the cost of producing a preservation microfilm. The film stock is the first and primary element in producing a long-lived microform, so the highest quality film must be used.

Choice of Film Types

Three types of film are used in microfilming: silver, diazo, and vesicular. It is important to understand their characteristics in order to select among them and plan for appropriate storage.

Silver-Gelatin Film

Silver-gelatin film is the oldest of the currently used materials. Silver is known to be a stable metal, and the image on silver film is metallic silver. The gelatin in which the silver is suspended has been observed for many years in photographic film and other applications, some of which date back about two centuries. Silver-gelatin films have received more attention—more testing to establish their permanence—than any others. The conclusion is that these films will remain stable for 500 years if processed according to ANSI/NAPM IT9.1-1992 and housed in the extended-term storage conditions outlined in ANSI/NAPM IT9.11-

---

11. The ANSI standards refer to these by their technical names: "poly(ethylene terephthalate)," more commonly known as polyester, and "cellulose-ester," which includes cellulose acetate, cellulose acetate propionate, or cellulose acetate butyrate. See ANSI/NAPM IT9.1-1992, ii.

12. Specifications for safety film are provided in *American National Standard for Photography—Photographic Films—Specifications for Safety Film,* ANSI IT9.6-1991 (New York: ANSI, 1992).

172 ■ *Microfilming Standards and Practices*

1993. Only silver-gelatin films are appropriate for the master negative and the printing master.

Silver-gelatin film includes a protective layer, emulsion, substratum, antihalation layer, and base. Figure 21 shows a cross section of silver-gelatin film. The *protective layer* is a clear coating designed to reduce scratching, staining, or other physical damage. The *emulsion* is a light-sensitive coating that captures the image. It consists of microscopic silver-halide crystals suspended in gelatin. The *substratum* is a clear adhesive that binds the emulsion to the base. The *antihalation* layer is a backing that may reduce static and improve image quality. The *base* is the film support. When light strikes the emulsion, it converts the microscopic silver-halide crystals to metallic silver. At that point, a latent (invisible) image is formed. After the film is processed, the emulsion will contain metallic silver grains where light was received and the original silver-halide crystals in areas not exposed to light.

Silver-gelatin is the only film appropriate for the camera negative, but it does not always provide the most-durable or permanent service copies. It has these primary weaknesses in use:

The gelatin layer scratches easily, especially when used in readers that are not maintained carefully.

It is subject to fungus (mold and mildew), which can attack the organic gelatin and destroy the image by depriving the silver particles of their support. If reasonably low temperature and humidity conditions prevail, fungal growth does not usually occur.

It can develop redox blemishes (microscopic red/orange spots and rings).

FIGURE 21 Cross Section of Silver-Gelatin Film

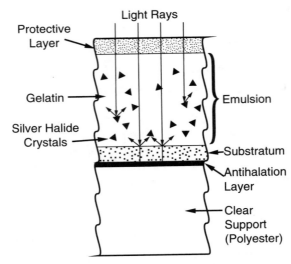

SOURCE: *Micrographic Film Technology*, 4th ed. (Silver Spring, Md.: AIIM, 1992), 34.

It is subject to image destruction if too many residual chemicals remain after processing.

It is sensitive to water and humidity damage to a greater extent than other film materials.

Continuous-Tone Film

Two special types of silver film have recently gained wider interest in the preservation microfilming community: continuous-tone film and color film. Continuous-tone film, used to film photographic prints, etchings and engravings, and other nontextual material, is a silver-gelatin film that can have an LE-500 rating.

In conventional black-and-white filming, a high-contrast film yields the best image for printed documents. However, this high contrast is a drawback when filming photographs and other continuous-tone materials. A lower-contrast film is preferable for those applications. The use of continuous-tone film for preservation purposes is still at a relatively early stage of development, with considerable experimentation under way.

Color Film

Color film used in preservation programs is typically a silver dye bleach film, and the completed film has a dye image. At the current state of research and development, those dyes are susceptible to fading and color change, and no color film yet has a proven life expectancy of 500 years.[13] To achieve their greatest possible longevity, color camera masters must be kept in the dark and in extremely low temperature, low humidity storage conditions.[14]

An obstacle to the acceptance of color microfilm as a preservation medium is the lack of standards governing image stability. ANSI/NAPM IT9.1-1992 provides definitive measures for the visual density and chemical stability that yield a stable image for black-and-white film, but there are no equivalent specifications for color images. The national standard for color film defines ways to measure the stability of color film, but it does not define limits on what degree of stability is acceptable.[15]

Although color film cannot be considered permanent, it does have appropriate uses. For example, one writer advocates that color film provides an effective surrogate for heavily used color original documents:

---

13. As of this writing, Ilfochrome (a silver dye bleach film formerly marketed as Cibachrome) is the only color microfilm that appears stable enough to warrant use in preservation projects. Tests conducted by IPI suggest the dyes, emulsion, and polyester base used in Ilfochrome are stable enough to last many centuries in appropriate storage conditions. See "Research on the Use of Color Microfilm," *Microform Review* 21 (fall 1992): 142–4.

14. See *American National Standard for Imaging Media—Stability of Color Photographic Images—Methods for Measuring,* ANSI IT9.9-1990 (New York: ANSI, 1991) and ANSI/NAPM IT9.11-1993. *Association for Information and Image Management Technical Report—Color Microforms,* AIIM TR9-1989 (Silver Spring, Md.: AIIM, 1989) also provides useful guidance. However, no standard offers definitive guidance for color film that will remain stable for 500 years, as the standards for black-and-white silver-gelatin microfilm do.

15. ANSI IT9.9-1990, iii.

If your originals are going to be retained, by all means substitute a color microform as a user's copy. Improvements in film permanence, in reader optics, and in storage capabilities are all moving forward. Even if only twenty-five years are gained before the color microform fades, that nevertheless gives an important and life-extending respit [*sic*] for fragile color materials.[16]

It is clear that color film is needed to capture a wide range of materials that warrant reformatting. For the time being, however, the lack of objective standards is a barrier to the wider acceptance of color film for preservation work.

Diazo Film

Diazo film is never used for the camera negative, but it is intended to be used for service copies. *American National Standard for Imaging Media (Film)—Ammonia-Processed Diazo Films—Specifications for Stability* (ANSI IT9.5-1992) defines the requirements for diazo film. It must be polyester based and can have a life expectancy rating of 10 or 100 years in extended-term storage conditions.

Diazo film has an emulsion of diazonium salts. When exposed to ultraviolet light transmitted through a camera negative, the salts are dispersed in areas of the diazo film that correspond to the light areas in the master. Ammonia fumes are generally used to develop the latent image, as the ammonia combines with the diazonium salts to produce deeply colored (often blue or near-black) azo dyes. Diazo film is sign-maintaining; that is, dark areas on the master will be dark on the diazo copy.[17]

Because of the possible fading of the dyes and staining of the clear portions of the film, diazo films are limited to an LE-100 rating. Within that time limit they should show little change if kept in extended-term storage conditions.

For use copies, diazo film has some characteristics that may pose problems. First, like silver-gelatin, it is subject to fungal attack when temperature and humidity are not carefully controlled. Second, it may suffer significant damage upon exposure to light for more than three hours in microform readers.[18] Despite these concerns, the relative economy of diazo film compared with silver film leads many institutions to use it for service copies.

Vesicular Film

Vesicular film is not used as a camera film but is intended for service copies. *American National Standard for Photography—Processed Vesicular Photo-*

---

16. Peter McDonald, "Color Microform: New Possibilities." *Microform Review* 17 (Aug. 1988): 149. Significant testing and product development have been done since publication of that article, but the author's analysis of the longevity of color film in balance against the vulnerability of some color documents is worth consideration.

17. For further detail on the chemistry of diazo film, see *Micrographic Film Technology,* 23–30, and Saffady, *Micrographic Systems,* 79–80.

18. *American National Standard for Imaging Media (Film)—Ammonia-Processed Diazo Films—Specifications for Stability,* ANSI IT9.5-1992 (New York: ANSI, 1992), 14.

graphic Film—Specifications for Stability (ANSI IT9.12-1991, ANSI/ISO 9718-1991) defines the stability requirements of vesicular film. All vesicular film is polyester based, and it can have an LE-10 or LE-100 rating in extended-term storage conditions.

Vesicular film, like diazo, uses diazonium salts as the light-sensitive element suspended in a polymer. To expose it, ultraviolet light is transmitted through the master film, and nitrogen gas is formed and trapped in the polymer where the light strikes. Heat is then applied to soften the polymer, and the nitrogen expands to form tiny bubbles (called "vesicles") in exposed areas. When the film cools, the vesicles become stable and rigid. In use, the vesicles scatter light to create the visible image. Vesicular film is generally sign-reversing, so if the master film is negative-appearing, the vesicular copy will be positive-appearing.[19]

Vesicular film is an exceptionally tough and durable material under use conditions. In many instances, it will withstand adverse environmental conditions in libraries and archives better than silver film. Unlike silver, vesicular film is not vulnerable to fungal growth and does not develop redox blemishes. The polymers used in vesicular film are usually hard enough to provide excellent scratch resistance.

Two potential drawbacks apply to vesicular film. Bubble collapse due to pressure is possible, and continuous elevated temperatures can deform the bubbles.

Film Stock Assessment

In conclusion, only silver-gelatin film on polyester has been rated LE-500 and is appropriate for preservation masters. Diazo and vesicular films can only be considered for production of service copies.

It is important to remember, too, that only silver-gelatin film manufactured, processed, and stored according to the ANSI standards has the capability of lasting 500 years. Preservation administrators will find it constantly tempting to seek ways to stretch their limited budgets when negotiating with filming agents. Adherence to national standards, however, is not an area for compromise in a project designed to produce permanent microfilm replacements.

Many institutions continue to use silver-gelatin film for all three generations because of its stability and high image quality. The desire for a more durable use copy and for cost savings leads others to make service copies on one of the non-silver films. That option is acceptable because service copies do not have to be "archival." Indeed, by virtue of the uncontrolled storage conditions in a working collection, they *cannot* be "archival."

Film Formats

Besides deciding what type of film to use for each generation, you must determine the film format to use—roll film or sheet format. Roll film comes in three sizes: 35mm, 16mm, and 105mm. Sheet film can be microfiche made from precut

---

19. For further detail on the chemistry and technical properties of vesicular film, see *Micrographic Film Technology*, 43–50.

sheets or 105mm rolls or microfilm jackets.[20] Each is described and analyzed in this section.

As has been noted elsewhere in this manual, preservation microfilming is a highly specialized programmatic activity that relies on the national technical standards as its foundation but includes more rigorous technical and bibliographic requirements. This distinction—between the technical requirements for "permanent" film and the additional specifications that are generally accepted as "best practice" for library and archival preservation purposes—is critical in evaluating film and fiche formats.

Standards exist for permanent film regardless of its size—35mm or 16mm roll film or 105mm microfiche. That is, the size of the film does not affect its stability or life expectancy. The choice of format, however, has a great deal to do with legibility, editorial decisions, use, and cost.

35mm and 16mm Roll Film

Preservation microfilming traditionally has been based on the use of 35mm roll film for reasons relating especially to image quality and legibility. The primary standards governing roll film are *American National Standard for Information and Image Management—Specifications for 16mm and 35mm Roll Microfilm* (ANSI/AIIM MS14-1988) and *American National Standard Dimensions for Reels Used for 16mm and 35mm Microfilm* (ANSI/AIIM MS34-1990).

The width of 35mm roll film allows great flexibility in filming library and archival materials. Most can be filmed at low reduction ratios, typically 8:1 to 14:1. (See the discussion of reduction later in this chapter.) It also allows considerable flexibility in image positioning (detailed later in this chapter) to save space and increase storage capacity.

The 16mm film is only half as wide as 35mm and requires higher reductions, usually in the range of 24:1. It may be used for materials that are legal size (11½" × 14") or smaller.

Roll film is the least expensive microform to create in terms of both equipment and labor.[21] The cost differential between a 16mm and a 35mm master film lies merely in the cost of the raw stock and this, overall, is not meaningful. However, if you plan to create many duplicate service copies in addition to the preservation master negative, then you might consider 16mm because the total savings is substantial.

Microfiche

If you choose microfiche for your project, then the reduction ratios and spacing of images should follow the national standard: *American National Standard for Information and Image Management—Microfiche* (ANSI/AIIM MS5-1992), and

---

20. The technical micrographics literature often distinguishes these generally as "non-unitized" microforms (reels) or "unitized" microforms (microfiche sheets, microfilm jackets, and aperture cards). See, for example, Saffady, *Micrographic Systems,* 35. Aperture cards are scarcely used in preservation microfilming and are not addressed in this chapter.

21. Saffady, *Micrographic Systems,* 27.

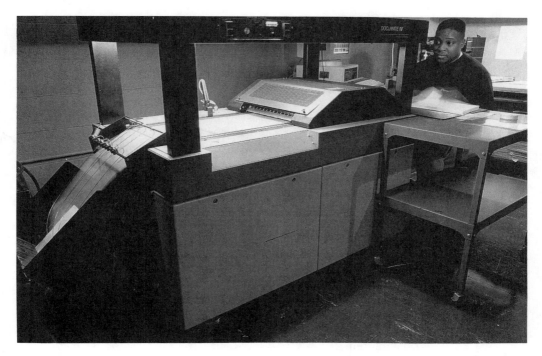

A step-and-repeat camera, such as this Documate IV, is one of the few that can produce microfiche that meets ANSI standards. Once the operator places the sheet in the feeding mechanism, the filming is highly auto-mated. *Massachusetts Institute of Technology. Photo by L. Barry Hetherington.*

the 24× reduction format would normally be chosen. There are a number of ways to create microfiche. The required method for preservation microfilming programs is to film directly onto a roll of 105mm microfilm using a step-and-repeat camera (discussed in the "Camera Equipment" section of this chapter), then cut the film into sheets of individual microfiche that measure 105mm × 148mm (approximately 4″ × 6″). Archives and records management programs, more often than libraries, create 16mm film in a planetary camera (see the "Camera Equipment" section of this chapter) and insert strips of the film into microfilm jackets.

105mm Roll Film. Filming onto 105mm rolls is the only acceptable method for creating fiche for preservation purposes. A step-and-repeat camera should be used.[22] This camera automatically adjusts to position images properly on the fiche. After filming and processing, the roll is cut into individual sheets from which copies can be made.[23]

---

22. For more information on the features and operation of step-and-repeat cameras, see Saffady, *Micrographic Systems,* 65.

23. To retain the master negative in its roll form for storage purposes, it is possible to make a duplicate negative for cut-down to individual sheets. The standards for extended-term storage conditions (ANSI/NAPM IT9.11-1993) and enclosures (ANSI IT9.2-1991) include specifications for storage of fiche.

Microfilm Jackets. The second way to create microfiche, using microfilm jackets, requires more explanation. Microfilm jackets are plastic, transparent carriers that contain grooved channels to hold strips of 35mm or 16mm film. The jackets, with film inserted, are then used as masters to make duplicates on single sheets of film. However, the resulting duplicates are often inferior to copies made directly from film.

To meet the standard for microfiche (ANSI/AIIM MS5-1992), the frames on the film inserts must line up in a grid pattern that meets certain requirements for image distribution, and this is usually difficult to achieve with jacketed film. The sheet film copies can meet the standard in external dimensions, but neither the internal distribution of images in rows and columns nor the placement of the heading is likely to conform, except in extraordinary circumstances. Further, the film inserts may slip or slide in storage over the long term. The use of microfilm jackets will generally result in a product that does not meet the ANSI/AIIM standards.

The primary use of microfilm jackets is in records management programs that require a microform that allows addition of documents to previously filmed files.[24] There is general consensus that microfilm jackets do not belong in a preservation microfilming program.

Other Methods. Filming agents may mention other ways to create microfiche from roll film. For example, *strip-up* involves taping strips of film together to create a fiche, or the film may be attached to a sheet of plastic by molecular adhesion. Neither of these is appropriate for preservation microfilming. The first method, like any that uses adhesives, may harm film in the long run. In the second, air bubbles and lint tend to get trapped between the film and the plastic sheet. Neither meets the permanence standards that are your guide.

Decision Factors

Either roll film (16mm or 35mm) or 105mm microfiche may be used successfully for preservation microfilming. How is an institution to choose among these formats? Special attention should be given to the following elements in decision making:

> the availability of appropriate national standards and preservation-oriented guidelines
>
> reduction ratio and image quality
>
> factors associated with the service and end use of the product
>
> cost considerations

The following discussion analyzes the options according to those factors.

Standards and Guidelines. Many institutions opt for 35mm roll film in their preservation microfilming programs because of the greater number of standards and specifications for all phases of its life cycle and because of the disad-

---

24. Saffady, *Micrographic Systems,* 39.

vantages of the higher reduction ratios required for fiche and 16mm roll film.[25] For example, current guidelines of NEH allow only 35mm film; microfiche production is not eligible for funding. Similarly, the RLG preservation microfilming specifications are based on the 35mm format. Furthermore, there is more preservation-oriented technical guidance on the use of 35mm roll film than on any other format. Finally, the availability of models like the RLG guidelines simplifies project design and contract development, especially for the new project manager.

Reduction Ratio and Legibility.   Microfiche and 16mm film generally use a reduction ratio twice as high as 35mm for materials of the same size. A book that might be filmed at a reduction of 10× on 35mm would probably be filmed at 24× on 105mm fiche. Compared to 16mm roll film and microfiche, 35mm film is capable of producing larger images, images at lower reduction ratios than the other two formats, and this is an important quality consideration. Among many preservation microfilming specialists there is a strong belief that "bigger is better" when it comes to image size, and 35mm is the best choice according to that criterion.

The capabilities of the camera largely determine whether higher reduction will reduce legibility. Filming guidelines generally require resolving power of 120 line pairs per millimeter. (See "Resolution" later in this chapter.) Modern step-and-repeat cameras with advanced optics, such as the Documate IV (manufactured by Terminal Data Corporation, now sold and serviced by Banctec), are capable of producing film with very high resolution, in the range of 192 line pairs. This exceeds the older Kodak MRD2 planetary cameras and is comparable to the advanced planetary cameras such as the Herrmann & Kraemer. (Both are discussed in the "Camera Equipment" section.)

Talk with the filming agent about the cameras used and their capabilities. Also discuss your reduction ratio specifications. There is still a great variety of ratios employed by different filming agents, too often based on economic factors rather than on the optimum in image quality.

Use.   Aside from production considerations, the end use of the microform can influence the choice of format. Microfiche provides easier access to brief information such as indexes, reference books, pamphlets, and monographs that will be heavily used; whereas serials, manuscripts, multivolume works, and low-use items are best suited for roll film. Consultation with your institution's reference staff and microform specialists regarding microformats and associated bibliographic tools in local use may be the key to a wise decision on the most appropriate format.[26]

---

25. See Myron B. Chace, "Preservation Microfiche: A Matter of Standards," *Library Resources & Technical Services* 35 (1991): 186–90, for related arguments regarding the use of 35mm film rather than fiche for preservation work.

26. See Roger S. Bagnall and Carolyn L. Harris, "Involving Scholars in Preservation Decisions: The Case of the Classicists," *Journal of Academic Librarianship* 13 (July 1987): 140–6, for further discussion of the comparative advantages of microfiche and film.

Fiche is often perceived as more "user friendly." The eye-legible titles on microfiche allow for quick retrieval of individual works. Microfiche readers are easier to operate and usually less expensive than roll film readers and reader/printers. Microfiche is less subject to wear and tear than roll film.

Cost.   Most institutions find that microfiche is more complicated than roll film to produce and, thus, more expensive initially, but it is less expensive than roll film to duplicate. Cost comparisons must take into account staff time for editorial and layout work and quality assurance, filming charges, and duplication costs.

Per-frame filming charges may be the same for 105mm fiche and 35mm film. However, the creation of the fiche may be more expensive because of the additional labor cost to plan and lay it out.

Duplication requires careful cost analysis. Frame for frame, fiche duplication is slower and more expensive than 35mm roll duplication. Cut-down of fiche is time-consuming, and if the 105mm film is stored in roll form, the filming agent will generally assess labor charges for locating the title or section that is to be duplicated. However, it is less expensive to duplicate a single title (excluding serials) in fiche format than to copy a 35mm roll. One filming agent provided cost estimates for duplicating a single 250-page monograph, and the charge for duplicating the reel was almost six times the cost of the fiche copy. Why is this so? Because it is necessary to copy the entire roll of 35mm film, which includes some five titles, whereas the fiche copy only requires about three sheets. Careful analysis will be required to determine whether the duplication-cost savings offset the added production expense. In addition, you need to anticipate the extent and kinds of copies you will need. In general, if you anticipate many orders for single titles, duplication costs will be lower if they are on fiche.

There are two further decisions to make before you can complete your technical specifications. They are polarity and number of generations.

Film Polarity

Polarity refers to "the change or retention of the light to dark relationship of an image."[27] For example, duplicating a first-generation negative to a second-generation positive indicates a polarity change, while a first-generation negative to a second-generation negative indicates the polarity is retained.

Films may be described as sign-maintaining or sign-reversing, depending on whether the film maintains or reverses the polarity of the image. Thus, if a silver-gelatin master negative is copied onto a direct-duplicating silver film (which is sign-maintaining), this second generation is also a negative. A third silver generation can then be created using a silver-gelatin print film (which is sign-reversing) that will reverse the polarity to create a positive-appearing copy.

Silver films may be sign-maintaining or sign-reversing, depending on the type of film used. Diazo films are sign-maintaining, whereas vesicular films are

27. *Association for Information and Image Management Technical Report—Glossary of Imaging Technology,* AIIM TR2-1992, 55.

generally sign-reversing. These attributes become important when selecting film types for duplication.

Generations

Using a silver-gelatin film with an LE-500 rating for the camera negative is the basic requirement in producing a preservation microform. A preservation microfilming program should generate at least two, but preferably three, film copies. The three-generation system consists of the following:

> the silver-gelatin film actually used in the camera, called the "camera negative" or "first-generation film." A camera negative that conforms to strict specifications regarding film stock, processing, and storage may properly be called a "master negative." The camera negative should be used only once, to generate the printing master, and thereafter be kept in extended-term storage conditions as a permanent security copy.

> a printing master on silver-gelatin film, also called the "duplicate negative," "printing negative," or "second-generation film." It generally has negative polarity, but it can be positive. All subsequent copies are made from the printing master.

> the service copy or use copy, designed for use by the repository's clientele or for interlibrary lending, as the third generation. Unlike the other two generations, both of which are generally negative polarity, this one is most often a positive copy, although some institutions opt for a negative service copy.

Few of the ANSI/AIIM standards address the possibility or benefits of the three-generation system. Instead, they distinguish only between the "storage copy" (i.e., camera negative) and "use" or "distribution copies." However, the three-generation system is required in the RLG guidelines and in the national standard for microform copies of public records with permanent value.[28]

Creation of the printing master is critical if there will be requests for additional film copies. Some preservation microfilming projects target research materials that are likely to receive low use. In those cases, some managers may opt to create only the service copy from the camera negative, producing a printing master only if and when there is a request for another copy. If you anticipate that lending requests will necessitate your making copies, then it is essential to produce a printing master at the outset.

The distinction between the master negative and printing master versus service copies is critical. Different guidelines apply to their inspection and storage. For example, master negatives must be stored under the most-stringent conditions in ANSI/NAPM IT9.11-1993, whereas less-rigorous temperature, humidity, and other conditions may be acceptable for storage of printing masters. Longevity requirements also differ; LE-500 film must be used for master negatives, whereas film with an LE-10 rating may be appropriate for service copies.

---

28. *American National Standard for Information and Image Management—Recommended Practice for Microfilming Public Records on Silver-Halide Film,* ANSI/AIIM MS48-1990, sec. 7.1, p. 4.

The Film Production Process

In addition to meticulous adherence to national standards, professional guidelines, and institutional specifications, the success of a preservation microfilming program depends on successful communication between the filming staff and those in the library or archives. Library or archival staff members and filming agents should meet periodically to examine projects and services, explore new services, discuss problems, and make sure that services are provided and needs met in the most economical and efficient way possible. Evaluate the contract, services, and budget once a year. If necessary, make changes when the contracts are renewed and bids are negotiated.

The filming process begins when the filming agent (whether an in-house laboratory or an external service bureau) receives prepared materials from the client and ends when the completed films, accompanying paperwork, and original documents are returned. As explained in the following subsections, the production steps include

preproduction work

camera operation

film processing

quality control inspection of master negative

film correction

duplication

quality control inspection of duplicates

returning microforms and documents to the repository

Preproduction Work

If you have prepared your materials well, preproduction work will go quickly in the filming lab. The filming agent's first task is to read carefully your general instructions and check the items to be sure that they are arranged in reasonable order, are in physical condition to be filmed, and include all needed bibliographic and technical targets (discussed in chapter 3). Since the material may contain both informational targets to be filmed and instructional flags intended to convey messages to the camera operator, the agent must take care that the latter are not inadvertently incorporated into the film.

Chapter 3 explains the options for dealing with volumes whose bindings are too tight to allow full text capture. The filming agent may loosen or disbind materials, if you have authorized this, and will follow your instructions regarding which methods are and are not acceptable.

As noted in chapter 3, the filmer may supply certain informational targets that explain the camera operator's observations or procedures. Typical targets of this type are: PRECEDING PAGE ILLEGIBLE or INTENTIONAL SECOND EXPOSURE. The filming staff will also determine reel breaks if you have not done so; however, these details should have been worked out with the filming agent before the start of the project.

Camera Equipment

There are two basic types of cameras for microfilming: planetary and rotary. The step-and-repeat camera, used to produce 105mm microfiche, is essentially a planetary camera engineered to position image frames in standard rows and columns on microfiche and is often equipped with an automatic document feeder.[29] Notwithstanding the view sometimes expressed that microfilming is a static technology, there have been many innovations in recent years, involving the use of automated procedures, improved optics, and better controls over light levels. This does not mean that newer is better, though; the Kodak MRD camera introduced about 60 years ago remains the workhorse for many filming labs.

Cameras and camera peripherals should be well-maintained mechanically, but they should also be uncluttered by extraneous materials, such as personal effects, taped notes, pictures, unwieldy stacks of original materials to be filmed, film supplies, and so forth. This applies to the area immediately surrounding the camera also. Dirty, cluttered facilities with storage materials and supplies stacked under and around equipment are not likely to yield good film or fiche. Cameras should be separated by dividers to prevent light reflections from interfering with the illumination provided by the camera equipment itself. They must be located in areas that are not prone to vibrations from mechanical equipment, traffic, or other sources.

Camera Operators

Trained camera operators are not easy to find. Most come to the job without any prior experience, and the microfilming laboratory takes on the responsibility for their training. Consequently, the quality of the work depends heavily on the strength of the laboratory training program and the knowledge and skills of the laboratory supervisor. It takes at least two months to train a camera operator to the point of being comfortable at the camera, but the operator will need a great deal of supervision and assistance with problem solving for several more months. With time, the operator will develop the judgment and skill to handle the wide range of materials and problems that come into the lab.

If you are evaluating a service bureau, a primary criterion is whether the operators are experienced in preservation microfilming for libraries and archives. Following are some additional criteria you may use to assess the capabilities of the camera operators.

> *Longevity on the job.* Beware of a firm that has high rates of turnover or has recently increased its staff size significantly. While a rapid expansion of staff is not inherently a cause for concern, be sure the organization has high standards for hiring and training, lest quality suffer.

> *Productivity.* If the production levels are too high, this may indicate that operators are not handling materials carefully enough. On the other hand, very low rates could pose problems in meeting your schedule. Obvi-

---

29. See Saffady, *Micrographic Systems,* 38–69, for explanations of the operation of microfilming cameras.

Camera operators need systematic training and ongoing supervision as they develop the judgment and technical skills that are needed for successful preservation microfilm production. *University of Kentucky Libraries Reprographics Department. Photo by Lewis Warden.*

ously, rates will differ greatly depending on whether the materials are straightforward books or challenging materials such as scrapbooks and crumbling newspapers. It will take some conversation with the filming agent and with experienced preservation managers for you to get a sense of the rate (typically in frames per hour) that is "just right" for the kind of materials you are filming.

Consistency. Are the quality control procedures such that the operators can provide uniformly high quality work? Are project communications in the lab adequate to be sure that the camera operators can handle customized job specifications?

Number of filming hours per day. Many reputable filming labs limit camera operators to less than six hours per day at the camera and periodically assign them to other tasks to provide variety that can help operators maintain their alertness and attention to detail.

Cross training in quality control and duplication. Understanding of these additional processes will generally improve the operator's filming work.

Experience with similar materials. Look for operators who have worked with materials like yours and who have exercised care in dealing with fragile materials.

Reduction Ratio

The technician or technical supervisor will determine the proper settings on the camera so that the reduction ratio is optimal for the material, or you may specify the reduction ratio during preparation. The reduction ratio expresses the relationship between the size of the original document and the corresponding size of the microform image. It refers to the number of times the original is reduced on film, a linear measurement. For example, a 14:1 reduction ratio means that any line on a microfilm image is $\frac{1}{14}$ the size of the corresponding line on the original. The typical reduction for microfiche is 24×, which refers to an image 24 times smaller than the original. The actual image area, however, is reduced exponentially. Figure 22 illustrates these two concepts.

FIGURE 22   Reduction Ratio

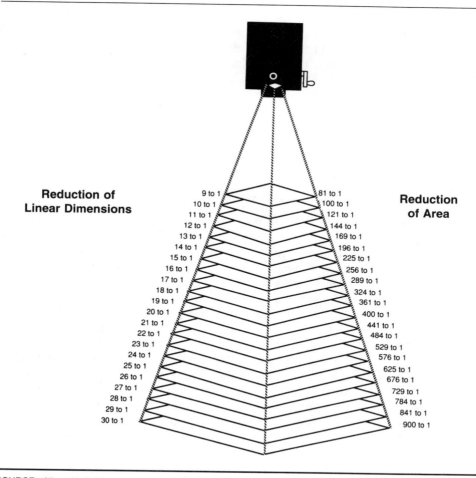

Selection of a reduction ratio depends on the size of the documents or volumes to be filmed and the type of microform to be produced. The ANSI/AIIM standards do not specify upper or lower limits on reduction. The guidelines for RLG cooperative microfilming projects state that the reduction ratio should be such as to approximately fill the image area across the width of the film as seen on the camera's projected image area, but not go lower than 8:1 or higher than 14:1.[30] The RLG guidelines reiterate common practices, such as that all edges of the document shall be visible in the image. Avoid reduction ratio changes within the same title; chapter 3 suggests ways to arrange materials to avoid or minimize reduction changes. However, especially with some archival collections, reduction changes may be unavoidable, and such changes should be identified by target.

If roll film is your choice, and assuming you do not specify the reduction ratio, the camera operator will select the lowest reduction ratio that will accommodate the manuscripts, documents, or volume pages on hand. If the sizes of the pages in a given collection vary substantially, it would increase the cost of the project unduly if the reduction ratio were changed for each manuscript. Instead, the camera operator will choose a compromise reduction ratio that accommodates the majority of the documents. For example, if the bulk of the material consists of $8\frac{1}{2}'' \times 11''$ pages and there are only a few oversize pages, then the reduction ratio should be set for the $8\frac{1}{2}'' \times 11''$ pages and changed whenever the larger pages require it. If, however, a substantial mix of sizes is present, then the entire film, for the sake of reasonable economy, should be filmed at the reduction ratio that accommodates the larger documents. The Quality Index computation (discussed later in this chapter) should be used to make certain that the reduction ratio chosen is compatible with the Quality Index required in your project specifications.

Image Orientation and Arrangement

There are two ways to orient images on film: for textual material, the lines of print either run lengthwise on the film or at a right angle to the film edge. The A position has long been known as the "cine" mode because images appear on the microfilm as frames appear on motion picture film. The lines of print or writing are perpendicular to the film edge. The A position is termed the "vertical" or "portrait" position in recently issued standards. The B position is often called the "comic" mode, because it resembles the layout of frames in a comic book. It is now referred to as the "horizontal" or "landscape" orientation. In the B position, lines of print are parallel to the long edge of the film.

ANSI/AIIM standards allow several options for image arrangement, but preservation microfilming almost always uses the simplex format. In simplex filming, a single frame occupies the width of the film. If one page appears in that frame, it may be referred to as "one-up" filming. "Two-up" filming records two pages per frame. These concepts are illustrated in figure 23. In the figure, positions IA and IB are single-page exposures, also called "one-up" filming; positions

---

30. Nancy E. Elkington, ed., *RLG Preservation Microfilming Handbook* (Mountain View, Calif.: RLG, 1992), 40.

FIGURE 23   Microfilm Image Placement

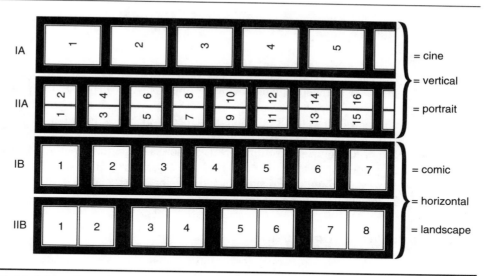

SOURCE: Adapted from Nancy E. Elkington, ed., *RLG Preservation Microfilming Handbook* (Mountain View, Calif.: RLG, 1992), 133.

IIA and IIB are double-page exposures termed "two-up." Positions IA and IIA, with text perpendicular to the long axis of the film, may be described as cine, vertical, or portrait orientation. Positions IB and IIB, with text parallel to the long axis of the film, are also known as comic, horizontal, or landscape orientation.

Preferred orientations, as well as the standard dimensions for 16mm and 35mm roll film, are covered in ANSI/AIIM MS14-1988, *American National Standard for Information and Image Management—Specifications for 16mm and 35mm Roll Microfilm.* The standard also prescribes the limits of the images on the film lest they intrude on the film edges, where they would be subject to abrasion in roll film readers.

Your written instructions should specify the institution's preferred orientation. The capabilities of your microfilm readers may dictate a preference for one orientation over the other. Many project managers also find that the A position is the more cost-effective approach for bound materials, allowing more frames to be included on a roll than is possible in the B position. If you plan to scan the microfilm, scanner capabilities may lead to a choice of one orientation over another.[31]

Image arrangement sometimes relates to your disbinding decision. Two-up filming is generally most cost effective for bound materials, but single leaves are typically filmed one-up to avoid the time-consuming process of correctly and

31. Some commercially available scanners scan one-half the width of 35mm film, then the other, to get the highest image resolution; with those, best efficiencies are obtained with two-up filming in the cine mode because the scanner can capture one entire page image on each pass.

squarely positioning two loose leaves side by side. Therefore, if a volume has been disbound but signatures are retained, it might be filmed two-up; one-up filming will generally be faster if the volume has been reduced to single sheets.

Skew

Documents should be placed on the copyboard or camera bed so they will appear in proper, parallel alignment with the film edge. Any departure from this square placement is called "skew." While ANSI/AIIM MS23-1991 does not limit the amount of skew, the RLG guidelines specify that skew must not exceed 10 percent (9 degrees) from parallel with the length of the film.[32] As institutions have begun to digitize microfilmed texts, it now appears that even a 3-degree skew may pose significant problems for today's scanners.[33] If you plan to scan your film, you should investigate this and perhaps use stricter specifications than are in the current RLG guidelines.

Glass Plates and Book Cradles

To get a good film of the material, the operator will work to have the pages on a single plane so that all sections of the pages are the same distance from the camera lens. Loose-leaf documents can be filmed on a camera bed without cover glass if they lie perfectly flat. If the pages curl or are significantly wrinkled, the operator will use glass covers. The glass should be plate glass, since window glass frequently has impurities that may impair the quality of the film image. In the case of bound materials, glass-topped book boxes or cradles, which will present a flat single or double page to the camera, are required. The filming lab should have cradles that allow gentle support for the binding and that will not damage book covers during filming.

Frame Counters

An internal numbering system will facilitate access within and reference to images on the film. For most library materials, the volume's own page numbers will provide this point of reference. For manuscripts and archival collections, preparations staff may wish to add numbering sequences that correlate filmed materials with external finding aids or published bibliographies, for example.

---

32. Nancy E. Elkington, ed., *RLG Archives Microfilming Manual* (Mountain View, Calif.: RLG, 1994), 115; and Elkington, *RLG Preservation Microfilming Handbook*, 42.

33. Reporting on a research project, a September 22, 1994, memorandum from Preservation Resources states: "A 3 degree skew is hardly noticeable when the image is viewed on a microfilm reader, but becomes quite evident in an image file. Post-scan image editing can include skew correction, but involves additional cost as the rotation algorithms involved are very math intensive and time consuming. . . . The advent of digital imaging is requiring us all to re-examine heretofore accepted guidelines." There are also some scanners that can de-skew automatically by attempting to find straight lines of text, then aligning the pages perpendicular to them; this approach is of no use, however, when scanning illustrative material. (Feb. 2, 1995, electronic mail correspondence between Preservation Resources staff and the author.)

A book cradle may facilitate filming of a tightly bound volume on a planetary camera. The space down the center of the cradle supports the spine, and the left and right sides can be adjusted for height to avoid excess pressure on the binding structure. The pages are pressed down by the glass cover on the cradle. *University of Kentucky Libraries Reprographics Department. Photo by Lewis Warden.*

It is also possible for the camera operator to use an automatic frame counter, a numbering device located within the camera's field of view. Keep in mind, however, that some frame counters allow little flexibility if corrections require later retakes. That is, because they can only number sequentially, retakes spliced into the reel would have out-of-sequence frame numbers. Some frame counters now on the market are infinitely adjustable. Your filming agent may have one of these.

Image Legibility

The creation of legible images on microfilm remains an art rather than a pure science. Various standards recommend ways to produce sharp, legible images, but they are not totally scientific and depend in part on the camera operator's judgment. Cameras must be monitored daily for sharpness over the entire image area. The best standard to consult with respect to image quality is *Practice for Operational Procedures/Inspection and Quality Control of First-Generation, Silver Microfilm of Documents* (ANSI/AIIM MS23-1991). The standard provides two guidelines for the creation of legible images. One concerns background density, and the other is called the Quality Index. While there are other technical aspects to the filming process that affect image quality, you must understand these two in order to communicate successfully with the filming agent.

Background Density

Background density is the degree of blackness of the part of the negative film image that corresponds to the page background. ANSI/AIIM standards address many different density measures: visual, diffuse, spectral, and others. Different film types require the application of different density standards, and different density types relate to different features of the film. Preservation microfilming requires particular attention to background density as a measure of the legibility of the image.

Density depends on photographic exposure and processing. Exposure is a measure of the light that strikes the emulsion to create the image; it is a product of the intensity of the light and the duration of exposure. Control of exposure has normally been exercised in microfilm cameras by a change in light intensity, but some newer cameras instead allow for altering the shutter speed or lens stop as in normal photography. Controlling exposure is the primary factor in ensuring that background density meets specifications.

A document with high contrast—black, heavy lines and a clear white background—can be recorded on microfilm with minimum difficulty by aiming for a high background density that still leaves the line images clear on the film. With originals of this type there is a great exposure latitude, and moderate over- or underexposure will still produce a legible and reproducible image.

The nature of the source documents typically filmed in preservation programs poses challenges for exposure and density control. There are problems in microfilming pages of low contrast, as well as those containing fine lines, and the problem increases with higher reduction ratios.

In a document that has lines that are fine, gray rather than black, or faded to a light brown, the slightest overexposure of the original will tend to produce a negative film image with "filled-in" lines: the background of the negative film is black but the lines are not clearly distinguishable. Lines that are quite thin, even if printed with dark black ink, will appear on the film as if they had been gray in the original document. The greatest challenge to a camera operator is a document that contains lines that are both fine and light in color. To choose the correct exposure, a microfilm camera operator must judge the entire character of the page or pages in each frame as well as the reduction ratios employed. Good quality in a camera negative means the creation of images of maximum background density commensurate with the retention of completely clear lines of text.

Density is measured after the film is processed by using a densitometer. Density is expressed numerically, usually in ranges (e.g., 1.00 to 1.30). ANSI/AIIM MS23-1991 and the RLG specifications classify documents according to contrast and type of writing, and recommend ranges of background density most compatible with the microfilming of each group (see figure 24).

The density recommendations in various standards are based on the premise that a heavily lettered, "contrasty" original should be given maximum exposure, while all documents with fine lines or less-black lines require a compromise exposure resulting in a lower background density but retaining the clear, open character of the lines. This exposure principle cannot be taken to an extreme because substantial underexposure will result in too light a background and the widening of heavy, bold lines of text, which will also lead to reduced legibility.

FIGURE 24 Background Density

Background density for the master negative should be based on the characteristics of the original materials.

High contrast   1.00–1.30

High quality, high-contrast printed materials and black typing; fine-line originals, black opaque pencil writing; documents with small, high-contrast printing

Medium contrast   0.90–1.10

Pencil and ink drawings; faded printing; very small printing; bold text on moderately darkened paper or on lightly colored paper

Low contrast   0.80–1.00

Low-contrast manuscripts and drawings; graph paper with pale, fine colored lines; letters typed with a worn ribbon; poorly printed faint documents, especially those on moderately to badly darkened paper; faint text on tissue, onionskin, or light-colored paper; text on dark-colored paper

Very low contrast   0.75–0.85

Documents with exceptionally poor contrast between printing/writing and paper

---

SOURCES: *Practice for Operational Procedures/Inspection and Quality Control of First-Generation, Silver Microfilm of Documents*, ANSI/AIIM MS23-1991 (Silver Spring, Md.: AIIM, 1991), sec. 5.1.4, pp. 26–7; *RLG Preservation Microfilming Handbook* (Mountain View, Calif.: RLG, 1992), 39.

Other factors, such as color or glossiness of the document, also affect proper exposure.

Exposure control is the most difficult task for the camera operator. In conventional planetary cameras, the operator controls the voltage of the camera lamps to yield what should be a proper exposure (and, thus, an appropriate density). However, this has often depended on the operator's ability to distinguish among very fine gradations of paper color and ink colors.[34]

Proper camera exposure is especially challenging when filming manuscripts. If poor judgment is used in the choice of exposure, then the adoption of a high Quality Index (explained in a following section), the use of well-maintained cameras, the most careful handling of the film in subsequent processing, and careful checking will not produce a good film. Either inferior training or inadequate experience of a camera operator frequently causes the production of substandard film images. How exposure is controlled constitutes a primary difference between the filming of business records and the filming of library materials or archival documents. Customarily, commercial filmers of records use either automatic exposure control or a single, preset exposure. However, as pointed out, complex original materials such as manuscripts require that the exposure be changed frequently in response to the various background colors, fineness of lines, or fading that may be present.

Complex materials cannot be filmed optimally using a fully automatic exposure control. Automatic exposure controls tend to produce images with similar background densities but different degrees of grayness of the text. These films have filled-in lines, which are not easily duplicated or reenlarged with good legibility. Such quality lapses have surely contributed to the resistance to microforms.

Good exposure control also includes frequently rechecking the illumination emitted by the camera lamps and adjusting them so that the film image of a white page shows even density from edge to edge (as subsequently measured on the uniform density target). This requires *uneven* illumination of the copyboard, the platform, or other device that holds the material to be filmed because some of the light reflected from the edges of the copy is lost (for optical reasons) before it reaches the film. Variations in light intensity are achieved by altering the voltage to the lamps with the aid of a rheostat. In less critical, commercial operations, voltage settings are used for exposure control. However, altering the voltage setting does not necessarily result in the desired intensity change. Preservation microfilming should be based on exposure meter readings of the actual light emitted by the lamps, not on the presumed change in light intensity resulting from voltage changes.

ANSI/AIIM MS23-1991 and the RLG specifications group documents into categories based on the contrast between the text and paper in the originals. MS23 allows density ranges from 1.30 to 1.50 for high-contrast originals to as

---

34. For filming labs that use the Hermann & Kraemer camera, there is a patented system designed to produce preservation film with very narrow density ranges. ExpoSure™, developed by Preservation Resources, couples the high resolution inherent in the Hermann & Kraemer cameras with extraordinarily narrow density ranges (often less than 0.05 density point) on a film reel. See C. Lee Jones, *Preservation Film: Platform for Digital Access Systems* (Washington, D.C.: Commission on Preservation and Access, July 1993), 3.

low as 0.70 to 0.85 for the lowest-contrast documents.[35] The RLG specifications for density readings differ from ANSI/AIIM MS23 especially because RLG's are tailored to the older, deteriorated documents that preservation microfilming programs generally encounter. Figure 24 presents recommendations synthesized from the RLG specifications and the deliberations of the AIIM committee working to revise MS23.

RLG further specifies that density readings may not vary more than 0.20 within a title or reel.[36] Any variations required (as may be the case with very faint or badly faded text) must be explained to the client in writing on the filming agent's inspection-report form.

The permissible density ranges in figure 24 may appear quite narrow. However, the density scale is logarithmic, so every 0.30 change in density points represents a doubling of visual opacity.[37] Therefore, in film with a density of 1.30, the background *appears* twice as dark as that with a 1.00 density.

While preservation guidelines allow a range of 0.20 density point within a reel, narrower ranges may be required if you plan to scan the film. The narrower the range of densities on a film reel, the fewer adjustments will be required during scanning.[38] You may help maintain a narrow density range in your reel programming work by grouping documents with similar contrast on the same reel.

It is not easy for a camera operator to determine exactly which category a given document falls into, which is where judgment enters. In the case of manuscript material, the problem is particularly acute because any page may have a range of different problems, from background stains to extremely faded lines, and each leaf may be on a different color or tone of paper. If manuscripts predominate in your filming project, the filming agent may need to construct a more detailed exposure guide specific to your collection.

When a page exhibits a range of problems, as is often the case with scrapbooks, it may not be possible to film it legibly in a single exposure. In such cases, the camera operator may take two or more exposures to render each segment legible, also filming an INTENTIONAL SECOND EXPOSURE target between the frames.

Resolution

Resolution is a measure of the ability of the entire photographic system to record fine detail.[39] *System,* as it is used here, covers the camera, lens, film, illumination system, book cradle, camera room, and film processor—in short, every component that might affect the definition of the image. Because resolution is a test of the entire system's performance, preservation microfilming agents regularly per-

---

35. This issue is reportedly being reconsidered by the committee revising ANSI/AIIM MS23-1991, and the revised standard may reduce the permissible ranges according to a Dec. 15, 1994, telephone conversation between Robert Mottice (Mottice Micrographics, Inc.) and the author.

36. Elkington, *RLG Preservation Microfilming Handbook,* 39.

37. *Micrographic Film Technology,* 8.

38. Jones, *Preservation Film,* 3. Also see Anne R. Kenney, "Planning for the Future: Film Digitization," in Elkington, *RLG Archives Microfilming Manual,* 98.

39. ANSI/AIIM MS23-1991, 45.

FIGURE 25   Resolution Test Chart

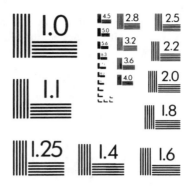

SOURCE: Paul Montgomery, A&P International, St. Paul, Minn.

form resolution tests on each camera to identify and remedy any potential problems. Master film from each camera should be read daily, and a focus test from an independent lab should be done each week.

The camera operator will film a resolution chart on each reel, normally the ISO Resolution Test Chart No. 2 (as specified by *American National Standard for Microcopying—ISO Test Chart No. 2—Description and Use in Photographic Documentary Reproduction,* ANSI/AIIM MS51-1991 (ANSI/ISO 3334-1989) and reproduced in figure 25), as a part of the technical target. ANSI/AIIM MS23-1991 defines the exact placement and spacing of the five test charts on the technical target. The chart contains many patterns of fine lines, each pattern containing finer and more closely spaced lines than the previous one and associated with a numerical value. By recording these patterns on film and viewing the resultant film image under a microscope, an inspector can determine which bundle of lines is still distinguishable on the film as a group of distinct lines rather than as a gray mass. The number associated with the smallest of these "recognizable" patterns, multiplied by the reduction ratio that was used to record it, represents the resolving power of the system in lines per millimeter and is a measure of the quality of the system. If the resolution of one part of the film frame is lower than the other parts, then the entire frame shall be rated according to the lower resolution reading.

Contractual microfilming agreements frequently specify that the completed film must resolve a minimum number of lines, typically a minimum resolution of 120 to 150 line pairs per millimeter in the camera negative. An alternative, and one more suitable for printed materials, is to stipulate a required Quality Index rating (discussed in the following section) that takes into account not only resolution but also the reduction ratio and size of text in the original. Higher resolution may be desirable if you plan to scan the film into a digital format.[40]

---

40. Jones, *Preservation Film,* 2.

Quality Index

The resolution patterns provide the means to evaluate the system's inherent ability to record fine lines; it does not take into consideration the effect that the point size of the text has on the legibility of the microfilm. A concept called the Quality Index (QI) takes all these factors into account; it can only be used with films containing images of printed text.[41]

The Quality Index uses the resolution chart, described in the previous section, but adds to it a measurement of the type size (based on the height, in millimeters, of the lowercase letter "e") in the original document. This measurement is then multiplied by the smallest resolution pattern that is resolved on the film, and the resultant number is used as the Quality Index. This does not involve as complex a mathematical computation as it sounds. The relationships have been plotted on a graph contained in ANSI/AIIM MS23-1991; all the filming agent has to do is measure the "e" and follow the directions for reading the graph. The standard states that a QI of 5.0 is considered acceptable and that a QI of 8.0 is excellent (the figure required in the RLG specifications).[42] Values below 5.0 are increasingly poor as the number decreases, and those below 3.0 are unacceptable.

The Quality Index can only be used for certain printed documents because its calculation is based on there being a standard-sized "e" in the text. Therefore, it cannot apply to non-Roman alphabets, manuscript materials, or illustrations.

Critics of the Quality Index method observe that it considers only resolution and type size. It does not take into account the other qualitative aspects of a document, such as its contrast or legibility. However, if the Quality Index is linked with the guidelines for background density in the tables previously described, the best possible results can be obtained.

Latent-Image Fade

Competent filming agents will take an extra step between filming and processing. The latent image (the invisible image that only becomes visible when the film is developed) on the film loses density slightly between exposure and processing. If a camera operator needed an entire day to expose a roll of film, and if the film were processed directly after the last image was exposed, then the first images on the film would have been subject to eight hours of latent-image fade, but the last images to only a few minutes. This causes an undesired, albeit small, density difference between the frames at the beginning and those at the end of the film. Since latent-image fade becomes, for all practical purposes, insignificant after approximately eight hours, there is little difference between images exposed eight hours ago and those exposed any time before that. Consequently, the filming agent should give film a minimum rest period of eight hours between exposure and processing. An overnight delay is desirable.

---

41. See ANSI/AIIM MS23-1991, 46–9, for a detailed discussion of the Quality Index.

42. Elkington, *RLG Preservation Microfilming Handbook,* 41. See also National Historical Publications and Records Commission, *Microform Guidelines* (Washington, D.C.: NHPRC, 1986), 5, which states: "An index of at least 5 (preferably 8) is required at the level of the specific number of generations used in the system."

Processing the Film

Between the camera operation and the processing tank lies the splicing area. In a micrographics operation using a large processor, the single-reel films used in the camera commonly are spliced temporarily into longer rolls, normally up to 1,000 feet long, before they are processed.

The splicing area must be dust free and devoid of stray light. Too dry an atmosphere in the splicing room and fast winding of the films is frequently the cause of static marks on film. Therefore, it is important to maintain appropriate humidification in the area. Unless care is exercised, scratches can also be introduced into the film at this point. If the filming agent uses a small, tabletop processor, the splicing operation to create 1,000-foot reels is not necessary because the tabletop units accept films only in single-reel lengths.

The splicing that is done before rolls are processed is entirely separate from the archival splice used on the camera negative to correct filming errors. Almost any temporary splicing method may be used. At the end of processing, the splices are cut off, and the rolls are returned to their original lengths for quality control and inspection procedures.

Processors

The microfilm is developed in a processor that runs the film through a series of steps. Typically these are (1) development, (2) an acid stop bath, (3) a fixing bath (using thiosulfate), (4) a water bath, and (5) drying. Figure 26 shows the basic processing steps, but processors may be configured in various ways. The process-

FIGURE 26 Steps in Conventional Microfilm Processing

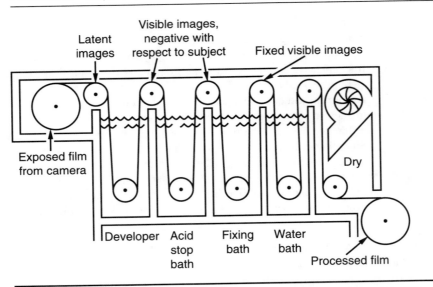

SOURCE: Adapted from William Saffady, *Micrographic Systems*, 3d ed. (Silver Spring, Md.: AIIM, 1990), 72.

ing is controlled by the appropriate mixture of chemicals, the processing and drying temperatures, the rate at which film moves through the processor, and in a good processor, the adjustment of the amount of film immersed in any one tank. This is done by raising or lowering the banks of rollers that carry the film.[43]

It is preferable to have a processing cycle that involves two separate fixing baths. It is also useful to add a solution of potassium iodide to the fixing bath that will prevent or retard the formation of microscopic blemishes that might otherwise develop on the film in storage. If you choose to include polysulfide treatment in your processing, it may be added to one of the tanks of a large processor or applied in a separate run in a tabletop model. Many processors provide two or even three water baths to ensure thorough washing. The filming agent may have a deep-tank processor or a small tabletop model.

Achieving consistently good quality in a processor depends first upon scrupulous, routine maintenance, including cleaning of the equipment and of the areas around it. Proper maintenance of a processor includes frequently cleaning or replacing the film transport components to prevent film scratching. The chemicals must be replenished continuously and changed intermittently, and the tanks must be kept free from deposits. No corrosion or rust should appear on the metal surfaces. The chemical solutions must be tested periodically, at least daily, to ensure that each chemical fulfills its proper function. Water coming into the processor should be filtered, and the filters should be examined frequently and changed when necessary.

A benefit of the deep-tank processor is that it allows very precise control of the processing and drying temperatures and of the rate at which film moves through the tanks. If the processor is well made and these variables are carefully monitored, they afford a high level of control, which can even improve densities from the camera negative to the printing master. A typical preservation microfilming lab may process film at 75°F to 85°F; speed is varied (usually within the range of 50 to 100 feet per minute), depending on the number of tanks and the density required. By contrast, labs not oriented toward preservation specifications may process film at significantly higher temperature and faster speed. The processor may have a wetting agent at the end of the wet cycle to avoid getting water spots on the film; an air squeegee may be used instead to avoid adding chemicals to the film. The drying box should have adequate film capacity so that the film dries gradually.

Tabletop processors use higher temperatures, typically 90°F to 110°F, to make up for their lack of tank capacity. The process involves short immersions in hot solutions for development, fixing, and washing, followed by high-temperature drying. The tabletop processor does not allow operators to vary development times. While it can process film to meet all the fixing and washing requirements in the national standards, there are some objections to the use of these small processors. At the higher processing temperatures, the contrast of the film cannot be as readily controlled, and clear areas of the film may be less transparent than in deep-tank processing. Many preservation projects benefit from the

---

43. See *Micrographic Film Technology,* 36ff, for a technical discussion of the processes and equipment involved in processing silver film.

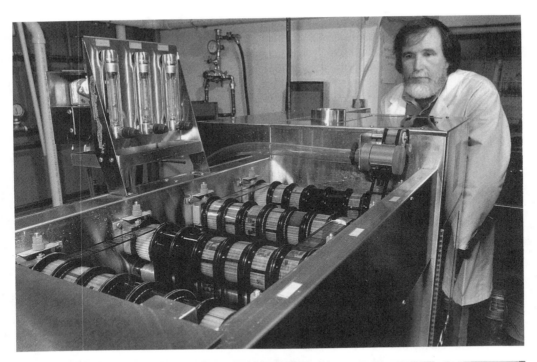

On the top is a deep-tank film processor, which can hold approximately 1,000 feet of film at a time. Note the multiple tanks through which the film passes. On the bottom is a tabletop film processor with automatic fixer and developer replenisher on the countertop at left. *Top: Massachusetts Institute of Technology. Photo by L. Barry Hetherington. Bottom: University of Kentucky Libraries Reprographics Department. Photo by Estil Robinson.*

ability to vary the contrast in the film, which is more easily done in a deep-tank processor than in a tabletop model.

Polysulfide Treatment

Earlier sections of this chapter report that silver-gelatin film has a life expectancy of 500 years, provided it is manufactured, processed, and stored according to national standards. While good controls over manufacturing and processing are generally possible, it can be difficult to guarantee that storage conditions consistently will meet the rigorous storage standards throughout the 500-year life of the master negative.

Over the years there has been much discussion and concern over the appearance of redox blemishes (reddish or orange-colored spots or rings) on microfilm. While microscopic blemishes occur quite frequently, the number of incidents in which they impair or destroy legibility are statistically very small. Research conducted by the Image Permanence Institute has determined that this deterioration of the silver is a combined result of exposure to high temperature, high humidity, and atmospheric pollutants. Particularly damaging are peroxides, sulfur dioxide, ozone, and nitrogen dioxide that may exist in air pollution or be released by storage enclosures that do not meet the requirements of ANSI IT9.2-1991, the national standard for storage enclosures. Even if film is processed according to the strictest preservation guidelines, subsequent peroxide attack and oxidation of the silver can cause redox blemishes, image fading, and silver "mirroring" effect.

Film labs can provide chemical treatments that convert the silver to a form that better resists attack. The options are

using sulfur compounds to convert the silver to silver sulfide (a process known as "polysulfide treatment" or "polysulfiding")

using selenium compounds to convert the silver to silver selenide

coating the silver with gold to form an alloy

Each process creates a slight change in the color of the film. Gold substitution creates a blue tone, and the sulfur and selenium processes result in a brown or sepia tone. Polysulfiding is the option of choice in most library and archives filming projects. Two brands currently available are IPI SilverLock™ and Kodak Brown Toner, the former being more widely used.[44]

Polysulfide treatment can be provided as part of the original film processing or as a postprocessing treatment. For new film, it may be applied in-line in deep-tank processors, or in a second processing run in tabletop models. It is also possible to apply the treatment to microfilm (including polyester and acetate films) up to those thirty to forty years old, provided that no deterioration has begun.[45]

A national standard defines the tests that can determine if silver conversion has been achieved. *American National Standard for Imaging Media (Photog-*

44. For good, nontechnical descriptions of the polysulfide treatment, see: Image Permanence Institute, "Polysulfide Treatment of Microfilm Using IPI SilverLock™," in *RLG Preservation Microfilming Handbook,* ed. Elkington, 186–94; and James M. Reilly, "The Case for Image Stabilizing Treatment of Microfilm," in *RLG Archives Microfilming Manual,* ed. Elkington, 168–70.

45. James Reilly (Director, IPI), telephone conversation with the author, Dec. 15, 1994.

raphy)—The Effectiveness of Chemical Conversion of Silver Images against Oxidation—Methods for Measuring, ANSI/NAPM IT9.15-1993, outlines two tests. The hydrogen peroxide test verifies that the film is rendered safe from damage by peroxides, and the dichromate bleach test measures whether the silver has been converted into a form that is less easily oxidized. Treated film must pass both tests to be considered stable after polysulfiding.

ANSI/NAPM IT9.15-1993 only outlines the test procedures for measuring the validity of chemical conversion treatments. No national standard requires the use of such treatments. However, its use is "strongly recommended" in the RLG guidelines.

Who should use polysulfiding? Any institution that is not 100 percent certain that its master negative will be totally protected *for the next 500 years* from the storage conditions that can result in silver deterioration. Thus, there must be complete confidence that temperature, humidity, and air pollutants will conform to the storage standard (ANSI/NAPM IT9.11-1993), that all storage products will conform to ANSI IT9.2-1991, and that both of these standards will continue to be met throughout the expected five-century life of the master negatives.

Filming Agent Inspection and Corrections

Once the master negative has been processed, the filming agent inspects it in ways detailed in the "Quality Assurance" section of this chapter. Following this, any errors or defects should be remedied, perhaps by refilming some materials and splicing corrections into the camera negative, until the film product meets your specifications. Then the printing master and service copy are produced, and the filming agent gives them the full inspection outlined under "Quality Assurance."

Splicing

When the filming agent discovers errors or problems in the master negative, some sections may need to be refilmed and the retakes spliced into the master negative. Every splice weakens film, making it more vulnerable to breakage or tearing in a duplicator, processor, or other equipment. Key decisions must be made regarding how those splices are to be made, how many splices to allow per reel, and where they may be located. ANSI/AIIM MS23-1991 and *American National Standard for Information and Image Management—Splices for Imaged Microfilm—Dimensions and Operational Constraints* (ANSI/AIIM MS18-1992) provide the national standards that apply to splices.

Splicing is a subject on which the ANSI/AIIM standards are not very helpful, for they do not restrict the types of splices that are permissible. Resistance splicers, which use heat to weld the film, have been popular in the past. ANSI/AIIM MS18-1992 recommends, but does not require, that ultrasonic splicers be used for splicing polyester films. Certainly this view led RLG to specify the use of ultrasonic splicers for its project participants. And no less certainly, that decision has caused most preservation microfilming agents to adopt the ultrasonic welding method. On one point there is little dispute: Microfilm that is intended for long-term archival storage should not be spliced with tapes, rubber cement, glues, or any other adhesives.

The client and filming agent should establish the number of splices allowed in the master negative. ANSI/AIIM MS18-1992 and ANSI/AIIM MS23-1991 recommend a maximum of six splices per 100-foot film roll, which has been accepted by most major library and archival projects. The RLG guidelines are the most specific on this topic: they permit only six splices on the standard reel of film (master negative only) and none at all on the printing masters or service copies.[46]

The RLG guidelines note that larger sections may be refilmed (known as retakes) and spliced in to cover an area with many mistakes. It is not a good policy to depend on splicing to correct mistakes in preparation, such as having pages out of sequence, and the filmer should not depend on splicing to correct poor preparation or filming practices. Corrections are possible but expensive and not to be encouraged. Careful and thorough work in preparation and subsequent camera operations are the keys to minimizing the need for corrections.

The location of splices is also important, and the ANSI standards are not strict enough for preservation purposes. RLG specifies that splices not be located between the technical target and the first ten frames of text and that refilming include at least two full frames before and after the frames being corrected. The RLG specifications outline two ways of meeting the guidelines.[47]

Returning Microforms to the Repository

After all film generations have been produced and have passed inspection, the filming agent returns the film. The reels or microfiche should be accompanied by inspection report forms and other records required by the repository. You should request that the original documents be returned at the same time as the microfilm in case questions occur during film inspection.

If original documents are transported from the institution, specify that transportation be carried out in closed vehicles. Pickups and deliveries should be made indoors, to avoid exposing the documents or film to outdoor elements, and at agreed-upon locations.

For better control, all items and targets packed by the institution in one shipment should be returned with completed film at the same time. However, to reduce the risk of costly damage or loss during shipment, master negatives should never be returned in the same box with their printing masters or service copies. In fact, some filming agents ship the master negatives on a different day than the original materials and duplicate film, just in case the transport vehicle should be involved in an accident.

Another option is available to reduce the risk of loss or damage to the master negative. Once you have established a positive relationship with the filming lab and can rely on its quality control program, it may be appropriate to have the filming agent ship master negatives directly to your storage facility after you complete the inspection of printing masters and service copies. Otherwise, the master negative is shipped to the repository and then to the storage facility, doubling the risk.

---

46. Elkington, *RLG Preservation Microfilming Handbook,* 41.

47. For details on this issue, see Nancy E. Elkington, "Splicing: Art or Science," in *RLG Archives Microfilming Manual,* 119–23.

Quality Assurance

The opening comments to RLG's "Recommended Program of Microform Inspection" soberly admonish: "Microfilm inspections are serious tasks, given the investment being made in the product and the ultimate goal of a master negative that will last at least half a millennium."[48] Put another way: quality assurance is the sine qua non of preservation microfilming.[49] To qualify as a preservation format the film must be manufactured, processed, and stored according to preservation standards. But without a rigorous, systematic program of inspection by the filming agent and repository, there is no guarantee that the film will last into the next decade, much less half a millennium.

Quality control requirements are established by the institution. The base level is defined by ANSI/AIIM standards: *American National Standard for Information and Image Management—Practice for Operational Procedures/Inspection and Quality Control of First-Generation, Silver Microfilm of Documents* (ANSI/AIIM MS23-1991) defines the requirements of master negatives, and duplicates are judged according to *American National Standard for Information and Image Management—Recommended Practice for Operational Procedures/Inspection and Quality Control of Duplicate Microforms of Documents and from COM* (ANSI/AIIM MS43-1988). The RLG guidelines, which are more stringent and prescriptive than the national standards in some areas, provide an excellent model for institutional specifications.

Of course, costs are associated with the quality control requirements. To the extent that you require the filming agent to conduct tests and inspections that exceed customary practice, costs will increase. However, you must specify and carry out inspections that will ensure that the film product meets the appropriate criteria for longevity, image quality, and so on.

Responsibility for quality assurance is shared between the institution and the filming agent. Some inspections and tests (such as the methylene blue test, described later) are performed only by the filming agent before returning the film, with results being reported to the institution. Others are conducted by the filming agent and again by the repository; and some are conducted by the repository only. The extent of the filming agent's inspections will be guided largely by the agreement or contract specifications. Your responsibility for quality assurance is not abated if you are using an in-house filming lab. Regardless of what organization or unit does the filming, it is your responsibility to make sure that double-checks are conducted to ensure the quality of the film products.

The initial stages of a filming project will probably constitute a process of learning and getting acquainted as the institution and the filming agent work to resolve misunderstandings, agree on protocols, and develop a smooth routine for inspection and correction.

When you begin a new project or begin work with a new filming agent, you should request that the filming agent return the first two to three reels as soon as

---

48. Elkington, *RLG Preservation Microfilming Handbook,* 160–1.

49. Nancy E. Elkington (Assistant Director, Preservation Services, RLG), telephone conversation with the author, May 16, 1994.

they are complete, rather than waiting for the entire shipment to be finished. Then conduct your quality inspections on those reels promptly. This will give you an early chance to catch any instructions that have been misunderstood, identify any discrepancies between your expectations and the product you received, and work with the filming agent to resolve such problems. This step is critical because it is nearly impossible to capture all the nuances of microfilming specifications and instructions on paper.

Quality assurance has three major categories: general, technical, and bibliographic inspection. All three generations of film must be inspected. Note, however, that you should be particularly careful with the master negative, the "archival" copy, and never put it on a microfilm reader for inspection. The rest of this section outlines the inspection protocols.

Figures 27 and 28 show sample quality control report forms you and the filming agent might use. An explanation of the errors listed, with illustrations of actual pieces of film that contain them, can be found in ANSI/AIIM MS23-1991.

General Inspection

General inspection carried out by the project staff and the filming agent should ensure that the film, packaging, and labeling meet your specifications, that necessary forms have been completed, and that the original materials are not missing or damaged. This inspection requires no specialized equipment.

To begin the inspection process, review the filmer's quality control reports (illustrated in figure 27). Data should be complete and within the required ranges. Results of chemical tests for residual thiosulfate and polysulfide treatment (if applied) should also accompany the films.

Verify that the film meets your specifications—that it is polyester, that all three generations are in the required formats and polarities, and that the leader and trailer (unexposed film at the beginning and end of a reel) are adequate but not excessive. The processed film should be delivered wound with the START target at the outer end. Reels, boxes, and fasteners should meet the specifications in ANSI IT9.2-1991, detailed later in this chapter.

Finally, examine the materials that were filmed. Any use is likely to result in some wear, especially for fragile, brittle items that usually are the focus of preservation microfilming efforts. If materials seem to be unreasonably damaged, talk with the filming agent about handling procedures.

Technical Inspection

Technical inspection involves several elements: Verify that chemical processing tests fall within acceptable limits. Run the tests for density, resolution, and the Quality Index. Identify any scratches, improper splices, and other defects.

Methylene Blue Test

After the film has been processed, the filming agent or an independent lab tests the film for the presence of excessive residual thiosulfate. When microfilm is developed, the silver halide crystals that were exposed to light are converted into

FIGURE 27   Filming Agent Quality Control Report

FILMING AGENT QUALITY CONTROL REPORT
(insert name of institution)

_____ Preservation Microfilming Project

Filming Agent: _____

Master Negative Number _____   Reel _____ of _____

Author _____   Pub. Date _____

Title _____   Volumes _____

1. Filming
Operator (initials) _____ Camera: _____ Filming date (mo./day) _____
Quality Index "e" size (mm) _____ [Pg#:_____] Reduction ratio _____
Image orientation _____ Required changes in orientation or reduction? _____
_____
_____

2. Initial Quality Control
Processor (init.) _____ Inspector (init.) _____ Processing date _____
Density readings 1. _____ 2. _____ 3. _____ (4. _____ 5. _____) Average _____
Resolution pattern required _____ Poorest resolution pattern read _____

3. Filming Errors *(give page numbers)*
Overexposed images _____ Density _____
Underexposed images _____ Density _____
Focus defects _____ Poor contrast _____
Obstruction in frame *(list cause)* _____
Streaks _____ Fogging _____
Other _____

4. Physical Defects *(give page numbers)*
Fingerprints _____
Scratches _____
Water spots _____
Dust/dirt/etc. _____
Other/comments _____

5. Actions to Correct Defects
Refilming of whole title?_____ Refilming of pages *(list)* _____
Splices needed? (number) _____ Number of exposures refilmed _____
Other action/comments _____

6. Approval for Variance from Project Specifications
Variant density (check) _____ Other? _____
Variance approval of project manager (init.) _____ Date _____

7. Certification of Report
Filming agent (init.) _____ Date _____
Project manager (init.) _____ Date _____

If printed on verso of Library Quality Control Report (recommended), no need to fill out author/title information more than once.

SOURCE: Adapted from Nancy E. Elkington, ed., *RLG Preservation Microfilming Handbook* (Mountain View, Calif.: RLG, 1992), 179.

FIGURE 28 Library Quality Control Report

LIBRARY QUALITY CONTROL REPORT
(insert name of institution)

_____ Preservation Microfilming Project

Filming Agent: _____

Master Negative Number _____ Reel _____ of _____

Author _____ Pub. Date _____

Title _____ Volumes _____

Targets/Sequence (Monographs)*	Present?	In proper order?
START Target (eye)		
Uniform Density Target		
Master Negative Number (eye)		
Project ID Target		
Copyright Target		
Title Target (eye)		
Bibliographic Record Target		
List of Irregularities		
[Optional Targets] (eye)		
Technical Target		
Volume Target (eye)		
[In-text Targets] (eye)		
Continuation Target (eye)		
-OR- End of Title Target (eye)		
Uniform Density Target		
End of Reel Target (eye)		

1. **Description of Defects** (missing, illegible, out of sequence, skewed) _____

2. **Conformation Errors**
   Pages missing? *(list)* _____
   Other page defects _____
   Sequence problems _____
   Leader, trailer, spacing errors _____
   Other format defects (reduction, orientation, framing) _____

3. **Actions to Correct Defects**
   Refilming of whole title? _____ Refilming of pages *(list)* _____
   Splices needed? (number) _____ Number of exposures refilmed _____
   Other action/Comments _____

4. **Corrections Made & Approved** Project Manager (init.) _____ Date _____
5. **Certification of Report** Project Manager (init.) _____ Date _____

*Adjust targets and sequence to reflect desired practice for each project or type of materials filmed. This sequence is accurate for monographs. Filming Agent Quality Control Report should be printed on verso.

SOURCE: Adapted from Nancy E. Elkington, ed., *RLG Preservation Microfilming Handbook* (Mountain View, Calif.: RLG, 1992), 178.

metallic silver. The fixer contains thiosulfate (often misnamed "hypo"), which dissolves the unexposed silver complexes. Without fixation, the images on the film would lack permanence.[50] However, if excessive levels of residual thiosulfate remain in the film after it is processed, the image may stain and fade as it ages. The processor's water bath should have been set to wash the film adequately, but the film must be tested to make sure that it is within standards.

ANSI IT9.1-1992 discusses these problems in some detail and sets the standards for image stability as well as for stability of the base and emulsion in silver-gelatin film. It requires the use of a test for measuring residual thiosulfate, and *American National Standard for Photography—Determination of Residual Thiosulfate and Other Related Chemicals in Processed Photographic Materials—Methods Using Iodine-Amylose, Methylene Blue and Silver Sulfide* (ANSI/NAPM IT9.17–1993, also ANSI/ISO 417-1993) specifies how to conduct those tests. At a minimum, the lab should conduct the test whenever any change in film, chemicals, or processing is made; most institutions require daily methylene blue tests. The test must be performed within two weeks after the film is processed (earlier if possible), as specified in ANSI/ISO 417-1993, ANSI/NAPM IT9.17-1993, and ANSI/AIIM MS23-1991.

ANSI/NAPM IT9.1-1992 (the standard for stability in first-generation silver-gelatin film) specifies an upper limit of 0.014g/m^2 on residual thiosulfate in film with an LE-500 rating.[51] No lower limit is specified. The fact that there is an upper limit does not mean that 0 is a desirable goal. There are some indications that overwashing may be undesirable. It is best, then, to do conscientious washing within the limits of the standard and to keep the film under good storage conditions.

If the filming agent performs daily testing in-house, samples should also be sent to an independent laboratory periodically for third-party confirmation. Daily testing by an independent lab could be prohibitively expensive over the life of a large project, so you may need to make a determination on that point if you use a filming agent that cannot do in-house testing.

ANSI/NAPM IT9.17-1993 (ANSI/ISO 417-1993) also allows the silver densitometric test for measuring residual thiosulfate. Unlike the methylene blue test, it can be performed reliably at any time. However, the silver densitometric test is not as precise in measuring residual thiosulfate at the low levels required in preservation microfilming.

Polysulfide Test

If you choose to have your silver film treated with IPI SilverLock or some other polysulfide treatment, the filming agent should also conduct the tests specified in ANSI/NAPM IT9.15-1993. As with the methylene blue tests, these tests can be performed in a small in-house lab, but they should be sent for independent verification on a regular basis. Test results should be recorded on the filming agent's quality report, and you should ascertain that they fall within acceptable ranges.

---

50. The levels of residual silver compounds should be tested to ensure adequate fixing. See ANSI/NAPM IT9.1-1992, sec. 6.5, p. 4, and Annex B, p. 12.

51. ANSI/NAPM IT9.1-1992, sec. 6.4, p. 4. The level of residual thiosulfate is one factor that distinguishes LE-500 from LE-100 film, as higher levels are permitted in the latter—which is unsuitable for preservation purposes.

Density

Use a transmission densitometer to check densities on all three generations of the film. It must be designed and calibrated to conform to ANSI standards for the specific type of density being measured or erroneous results will be obtained. (See the discussion of density earlier in this chapter.)

ANSI/AIIM MS23-1991 states that "the number of density measurements depends on the nature of the documents being filmed and on the tolerance desired or as required by contract or specification."[52] The RLG specifications spell this out, requiring no less than eight readings on each roll of first-generation film, or three per title (two per title for works under fifty pages) if more than one title appears on a roll, whichever is stricter.

There are no guidelines to govern exactly on what part of the film to take density readings. ANSI/AIIM MS23-1991 requires only that they be taken on "representative frames," so it is possible for a lax filmer to find areas with acceptable density readings. To get an accurate measure, you must check densities in a background area of the frame, that is, one that does not have text or image. As a practical matter, because preservation microfilming often deals with brittle materials that are yellowed around the outside edges, it may be best not to take densities in the outer margins.

The filming agent will record density readings on the quality control report, but checking densities must also be part of the institutional quality assurance program.[53] Your eight readings and those of the filming agent will seldom if ever agree exactly because you will probably take readings on different frames, but the averages should be very close. If they are not close, perhaps one of the machines is not being calibrated correctly, or you may be using different procedures for where and how to take readings on the film. As you begin your inspection program, it may take some time to correlate your procedures with those of the filming agent.

Resolution

The filming agent will examine the resolution test charts on the technical target under a microscope to determine the resolution as discussed earlier in this chapter. The guidelines in ANSI/AIIM MS23-1991 call for a microscope with up to 120× power when inspecting film from systems with resolving power of 120 line pairs.[54] Many people find binocular microscopes less tiring to use than monocular models. Closely examine the structure of the microscope to be sure it will not scratch the master negative when a staff member positions the film. Some labs

---

52. ANSI/AIIM MS23-1991, sec. 8.3.5.2, p. 45.

53. Excellent instructions for machine calibration and correct ways to take density readings are provided in the "Recommended Program of Microfilm Inspection," in Elkington, *RLG Preservation Microfilming Handbook,* 169–71.

54. ANSI/AIIM MS23-1991 recommends that the microscope used for measuring resolution have ⅓ to 1 times the expected resolving power when the microform is examined (e.g., for viewing images produced by a system with resolving power of 120 line pairs per millimeter the magnification shall be between 40× and 120×). As a practical matter, microscopes tend to jump from 100× to 200×, so 100× will suffice. However, given the number of newer cameras that can produce resolutions near 200 line pairs, the added expense of purchasing a 200× microscope may be warranted.

use a stand microscope rather than the traditional scientific type because the former is less likely to damage the film.

Quality Index

Once you have determined the resolution, you can determine whether the film meets the desired Quality Index. Figure 29 shows the line patterns to be resolved in a master negative to achieve a Quality Index rating of high quality in the third-generation service copy. First, measure the size of the lower case "e" in the text. Then follow the grid line to determine the line pattern that must be resolved in the poorest of the resolution test charts. You and the filming agent should determine the Quality Index for the three generations of film. This is the ultimate test of the film's legibility. Good instructions are provided in ANSI/AIIM MS23-1991 and the *RLG Preservation Microfilming Handbook.*

Splices

If there are splices, they should be only in the master negative. Check all generations to be sure this is the case. Also, be sure that the number, type, and

FIGURE 29   Line Pattern to Be Resolved in a Master Negative

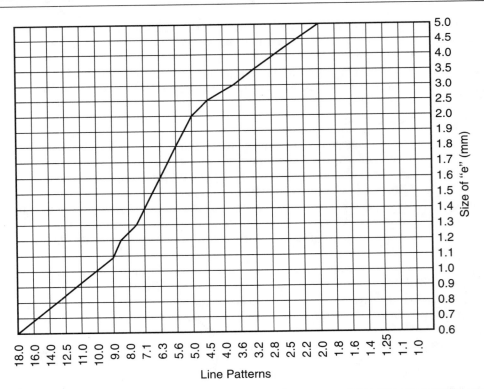

Line Patterns

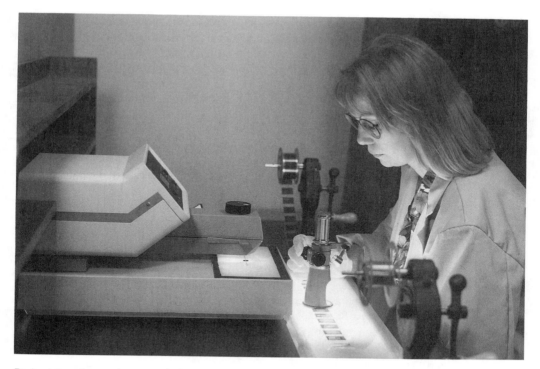

During inspection a microscope helps detect scratches and other flaws. Note the transmission densitometer at left. The film is on supply and take-up reels attached to rewinds. *Preservation Resources.*

locations of splices meet your specifications. Splicing guidelines were previously outlined.

It is relatively simple to detect ultrasonic splices on the master negative because they create a visible and tangible bump on the film. In the duplicates (the printing master and service copies), the splices in the master film are, in effect, "photographed," so they are less easy to spot.

Scratches and Other Defects

The filming agent and the institution must inspect the film visually to determine whether it has scratches or other defects. Inspectors examine the film over a light box to detect the presence of scratches, blemishes, fingerprints, water spots, puckering or peeling of the emulsion from the base, skew, improper frame spacing, and other faults. ANSI/AIIM MS23-1991 includes a detailed description and illustrations of these faults. This inspection must be conducted on all generations of the film.

Bibliographic Inspection

Bibliographic checking requires frame-by-frame inspection in a microfilm reader to ensure that all targets are correct and that they and the text have been filmed in proper sequence and in their entirety. In preservation microfilming projects, it is customary to require that the filming agent provide this bibliographic inspection, but it must also be done by the institution's staff. This quality control step may be performed by the same staff members who prepared the materials.

The inspector should never put the preservation master negative or printing master on a microfilm reader because reading equipment can be a primary cause of scratching. Examine only the service copy on a reader. In very rare cases, there may seem to be a problem that can only be explained by looking at the first-generation film. In such cases, inspect the master negative over a light box with rewinds, viewing the film through a loupe. All staff members who handle film should use lint-free gloves or surgical gloves. During inspection, wind the film on a reel in the standard manner illustrated in ANSI/AIIM MS23-1991 and in ANSI/AIIM MS14-1988.

From a practical standpoint, it must be acknowledged that some institutions and reputable filming agents do inspect master negatives on a microfilm reader because this is faster and easier than light-box inspection. If you do so, and accept the great risk of damage, several precautions should be taken. First, use a microfilm reader with glass flats (the two pieces of optical glass that hold film flat for viewing) that separate when the film is in motion so that no film is dragged against the glass. Second, keep the rollers touching the film emulsion meticulously clean and smooth, so they do not contain embedded particles that would cause scratching. Third, advance and rewind the film very slowly. Finally, clean and maintain reading equipment scrupulously.

Every frame should be examined to be sure that the documents and targets are complete and filmed in the correct order. Verify that all targets were prepared correctly, taking special note of the bibliographic targets that must correlate with the catalog record. If a service bureau prepared the collection and custom-produced some targets, proofreading them and checking their contents may take some extra attention. If you prepared the targets in-house, that step should have been done before filming. As you go through the reel, verify that targets appear in the proper locations and sequence.

Your frame-by-frame inspection must also ascertain that the volumes or documents were filmed in their entirety. In paginated materials (such as books, serials, and pamphlets) and those with frame numbering, the inspector simply goes through the reel or microfiche, viewing each frame to see that all pages have been filmed and placed in the correct order. For some manuscript materials, however, this step may require comparing each frame with the original document and noting its order in the collection—a tedious process. The inspection should also assess the image quality to make sure that every frame is legible, clear, and sharp.

The filmer should have noted in a target any irregularities in the original or changes necessary for technical quality of the film. Occasionally, the same page may be filmed twice for no apparent reason. For example, intentional second or multiple exposures, which may look like accidents to a new quality control inspector, should have targets identifying them as intentional. If you encounter accidental duplicates only rarely, you may wish to establish a local policy to ignore them. If they are recurrent, speak with the filming agent about the camera operators' quality control procedures.

Errors and Corrections

A good filming agent will catch most defects in the initial inspection of the master negative before it is duplicated and returned to you. The filming lab keeps records of the results of the inspection and reports this information to the repository.

Assuming you find some defects or questionable features, you must exercise your judgment regarding whether to accept or reject the microfilm. Errors that relate to the permanence of the film product always must be corrected, but you may occasionally accept errors that do not affect its life expectancy or chemical stability. RLG's "Guide to Defects on First Generation Camera Negatives" provides a useful distinction between defects that are largely cosmetic and those that require remedial action.[55] Be sure to complete the inspection of the entire reel before returning it for corrections.

In the development and implementation of standards and procedures, common sense and good judgment also must be part of the formula. Microfilming is not always an exact science, and the successful use of standards for a quality product requires that they be interpreted and applied by knowledgeable people. For example, there may be instances in which a frame falls within the density "requirements" but, nevertheless, should have been shot at a different exposure to improve legibility. And sometimes a camera operator will shoot the same chart or illustration at three different exposures to be sure to get a legible frame. If two of those three images do not pass the density test, that would not provide sufficient cause to splice them out or refilm the images.

The filmer should correct the lab's filming errors (omitted pages, obscured text) at no charge, following your specifications for splices and retakes. This is ordinarily done by refilming the necessary pages and splicing the new film into the master negative, then providing a new printing master and service copies. Of course, if an error is due to a lapse in your preparation procedures or an oversight in your instructions, this additional work will be at your expense.

Managing the Quality Assurance Program

Depending on the schedule you establish with the filmer, completed materials may flow from the filming agent at a slow-but-steady rate, or they may be returned from a filming agent in large shipments less frequently. A few repositories want to send the entire collection and not receive it until the filming is completed. From the comments about the role of ongoing quality assurance, it should be clear that such a plan is unwise. You need to inspect film materials as they are completed so you can address problems as soon as possible.

Although the filming agent contracts to perform 100 percent quality control inspection on all completed film, this does not alter your responsibility for a second check to ensure quality. Errors can happen. In one case, for example, an experienced filming agent accidentally used on each reel of an entire shipment a target that specified the wrong institution as the owner of the film. The institu-

---

55. See Elkington, *RLG Preservation Microfilming Handbook,* 157–9.

tion's film inspectors caught the error. Quality control is an ongoing responsibility; if you do not point out problems to the filming agent, they are unlikely to be corrected. The inspection process is the only way to guarantee that the film product meets the requirements for longevity, bibliographic completeness, and overall quality. In some ways, quality assurance is the "acid test" of the institution's commitment to preservation microfilming.

Figure 30 lists the basic equipment you need to equip an inspection station. If you cannot perform density and resolution checks locally, you can send samples to a reliable laboratory with technical expertise or arrange for assistance from another institution with in-house filming facilities. A list of chemical testing laboratories is available from AIIM (see Appendix B for the address). The bibliographic inspection function is best retained in-house, and it requires a high-quality microfilm reader.

The inspection staff must be well trained in microform quality assurance. As should be clear, quality control—especially the frame-by-frame bibliographic inspection—requires an ability to stay keenly attentive to detail. It is a good idea to limit the amount of time any one individual spends on bibliographic inspection; a limit of one reel per sitting is a good rule of thumb.

Do you really have to do 100 percent inspection on every completed film? Yes, you should. At the beginning of the contract or project, when the filming agent is new to the project, it is essential that you inspect 100 percent of the completed film to make sure contract specifications are met. After the initial "breaking-in" period with the filming lab, and after you are confident that the ground rules have been firmly established and the work continues to be routine, consistent, and of high quality, you can reduce the rigorous quality assurance performed by local staff to a level as low as 10 percent of the completed microfilm. Frames with bibliographic targets and catalog records should continue to be checked for each title, however. You should institute higher levels of quality control whenever new activities are undertaken, different types of materials are filmed, personnel is changed at the filming agency, or the quality of work warrants it. The quality of the work performed and the completed microfilm are only as good as the inspection measures you and the filmer take. Of course, labor costs are higher when you conduct 100 percent inspection. Good quality control procedures will ensure that the institution's high expectations are met, and only full inspection can provide that assurance.

Postfilming Activities at the Institution

Assembling materials for postfilming handling involves matching the original materials with their microform counterparts and relevant in-process records. All materials should be complete and represented on the microform. Borrowed volumes are sorted and prepared for return. Materials may be separated for different processing procedures, depending on whether they are to be retained or withdrawn. Serials and manuscript collections might be held aside and processed when the full bibliographic unit is completed and gathered in one place. This is also the final opportunity to annotate title guides and finding aids with reel information and frame numbers that may have been omitted or unavailable before filming.

FIGURE 30   Inspection Station Checklist

Notes

☐ Work bench, with adequate space to move microscope and densitometer into position or out of the way

☐ Film rewinds, at least 3 feet apart, mounted on level work surface

☐ Light box built into the work surface between the rewinds, consisting of:
  ☐ Fluorescent light
  ☐ Translucent glass or plastic diffuser, at least 152mm × 254mm

☐ Black velvet swatch, generally located just to the rear of the light box, over which fine detail on film (e.g., scratches) may be more visible

☐ Jeweler's eye loupe, 8× to 15×, with a scale of 1 division equal to 0.1mm

☐ Microscope with magnification between 100× and 200×

☐ Calibrated step tablet (certified) for calibrating densitometer

☐ Transmission densitometer designed to measure visual-diffuse density, with a reading aperture of at least 1mm, adjusted to read a calibrated step tablet to an accuracy of ±0.02 density units over a range of 0 to 2.0, and with a repeatability of ±0.01 density unit.

☐ Microfilm reader that allows manual advance and rewind of the film with glass platens in the open position

☐ Small tungsten lamp, preferably with "swing-away" function, for inspecting film surface

☐ Inspection report forms

☐ Clean, white, lint-free gloves, usually cotton, but nylon and surgical gloves are acceptable

☐ Spare take-up reels

NOTE: This checklist does not include laboratory equipment required for residual thiosulfate and polysulfide tests.

SOURCE: Adapted from ANSI/AIIM MS23-1991, 32, 36; and Nancy Elkington, ed., *RLG Preservation Microfilming Handbook* (Mountain View, Calif.: RLG, 1992), 161.

To ensure prompt and efficient handling, the microforms must carry sufficient information and instructions to allow library or archives staff members to incorporate them easily into the normal work routine. Determine in advance what cataloging information is required and, therefore, what data should travel with the materials. For example, catalogers need to know the final disposition of the original materials, whether newspapers or other serials holdings have been completed by using borrowed issues, and how to describe the various generations of microforms. See chapter 5 for details concerning cataloging microforms.

Once quality assurance is complete and you know that all three generations of the film meet your requirements, you will need to reverse "camera readiness." That is, you must do the reverse of most of the steps you took during preparation: remove all the flags and inserted materials; replace the paper clips or other fasteners that were removed; return items to their folders, boxes, or other containers; and so on. This can be especially time-consuming for archival collections. As noted in chapter 3, you may instruct the filming agent to remove targets and flags before returning materials, but that option can complicate your bibliographic inspection.

Microforms must be boxed and labeled. The filming agent may do the boxing and labeling, or you may provide information that will enable in-house personnel to do it. If the institution has a policy of keeping only one title per reel, staff members may need to divide the reels containing several titles and place each title on a separate reel, as addressed in the "Reel Programming" section of chapter 3. Of course, this will require that the institution have a splicer available to attach blank leader and trailer stock. The division and splicing should be done on the service copy, not the master negative or printing master.

Records can then be logged out, master negatives and printing masters sent to storage, and service copies forwarded to the cataloging staff for updating in bibliographic access tools. The original materials are either withdrawn, returned to the shelf, sent to storage, or routed for physical treatment, depending on decisions made in the selection and preparation phases.

Storage of Microforms

The production of stable film involves film manufacturing, processing, and storage. All the good work done in the first two areas to produce film that will last 500 years will be meaningless if microfilm is not stored according to national standards.

The key standards governing microfilm storage are *American National Standard for Imaging Media—Processed Safety Photographic Films—Storage* (ANSI/NAPM IT9.11-1993) and *American National Standard for Imaging Media—Photographic Processed Films, Plates, and Papers—Filing Enclosures and Storage Containers* (ANSI IT9.2-1991). The preservation manager must be familiar with both to evaluate storage facilities and purchase storage enclosures.

The national standards distinguish two levels of storage: extended term (called "archival" in the past) and medium term. Specifications for extended-term storage apply to film that must be retained permanently, so these conditions are essential for storage of master negatives and printing masters. "Medium-term" storage can be provided for films where the information must be kept for a minimum of 10 years. Both ANSI/NAPM IT9.11-1993 and ANSI IT9.2-1991 address only the requirements for "storage copies," not those in working collections. Similarly, this chapter deals only with extended-term storage specifications for master negatives and printing masters. The storage conditions, along with the film manufacture and processing criteria, determine whether a film can be classi-

National standards outline strict requirements for the storage of master negatives and printing masters. In most cases, a leased facility provides tighter control than institutional storage areas can maintain, and some storage facilities provide on-site duplication as part of their service package. *Preservation Resources.*

fied as a preservation master when creating the 007 fields in the catalog record. (See chapter 5 for the requirement that must be met to code a first-generation film as a master negative.)

The ANSI storage standards provide a wealth of information that will answer most preservation administrators' questions. They contain many references to other standards on air conditioning and fire prevention that come into play, especially if you contemplate constructing or remodeling a room. The curator of a preservation microform collection must be concerned with the following aspects of storage:

storage vaults or rooms

environmental conditions: humidity, temperature, and the chemical nature of the atmosphere in the room

protection from fire, water, and other disasters

storage housing, such as drawers, shelves, and cabinets

enclosures for microforms, such as boxes, envelopes, and fasteners

inspection of stored film

The following sections summarize good practices to observe in storing roll film and fiche.

Storage Vaults or Rooms

Proper storage practices are important for all film copies, but few libraries or archives have a storage vault that fully meets the strict national standards for extended-term storage. While some institutions make compromises for printing masters kept locally, preservation master negatives must be stored in the best conditions, and this typically means leasing off-site storage space in a commercial facility that meets national standards. Master negatives should never be moved from that location unless the printing master is destroyed (or was never created) and a master negative is needed to produce a copy. Some storage companies may also be able to produce microform copies, thereby avoiding the need ever to remove master negatives from the extended-term storage environment.

ANSI/NAPM IT9.11-1993 gives a clear description of what is required for storage of preservation microforms. Most institutions lease space in one of the storage facilities that focuses on storage of permanent records, at least for their master negatives. Some of the major facilities are listed in appendix B. In choosing a storage facility for master negatives, proximity to your institution is irrelevant. In fact, if you are located in an area of the country that is prone to regional disasters such as earthquakes or hurricanes, it is decidedly better to store your film at a distance.

An alternative to leasing your own vault is to buy into a shared storage contract through a nonprofit organization such as Preservation Resources, RLG, or some other library or archival consortium. This provides the obvious advantage of having the facility already screened, and it usually results in lower unit costs for institutions that do not need an entire storage vault for their own materials.

If you are seeking to lease space, site visits may be necessary, especially if you are considering a facility that is not known for permanent film and record storage. Contact experienced preservation managers for recommendations, check references, prepare a checklist of questions and reminders to use in the phone interview or site visit, and exercise a healthy degree of skepticism.

Good housekeeping is essential. If the premises are air-conditioned, the room or vault must be designed so that condensation will not occur on walls and ceilings. Storage rooms should be located above ground level. The facility should be constructed to avoid potential damage by floods, leaks, and sprinkler systems. Be sure to inquire if there have been any problems such as those, and find out whether the company has an adequate disaster plan in place.

The facility should have tight security procedures, and storage rooms must be dedicated to the function of archival storage. No other activities, such as clerical work or repair of film readers, should be undertaken within the confines of the room.

Temperature and Humidity Control

Optimum conditions of temperature and relative humidity are specified in ANSI/NAPM IT9.11-1993. Life expectancy of film is increased by lowering storage temperature, storage humidity, or both. A lower storage temperature can compensate for a higher humidity level to provide the same life expectancy. Therefore, the standard allows several combinations for extended-term storage, shown in figure 31. For silver-gelatin, vesicular, and diazo film, the humidity set point must be within the range of 20–30% in a 70°F vault, but it may be 20–50% in a 50°F vault. Similar combinations are acceptable for color film.

In no case should the relative humidity exceed 50 percent for black-and-white silver-gelatin film or color film. Cycling of relative humidity shall be no greater than ±5 percent over a 24-hour period. If you choose a low-humidity storage environment, be careful to recondition films prior to use because low-humidity storage can extract moisture from gelatin emulsions, producing brittleness or curl.

FIGURE 31 Temperature and Relative Humidity Requirements for Storage

Sensitive Layer	Medium-Term Storage		Extended-Term Storage	
	Maximum Temperature (°F)	Relative Humidity Range*	Maximum Temperature (°F)	Relative Humidity Range*
Silver-gelatin, vesicular, and diazo	77°	20–50%	70°	20–30%
			59°	20–40%
			50°	20–50%
Color	77°	20–50%	36°	20–30%
			27°	20–40%
			14°	20–50%

*The moisture content of the film to be stored shall not be greater than film in moisture equilibrium with these relative humidities.

SOURCE: *American National Standard for Imaging Media—Processed Safety Photographic Films—Storage,* ANSI/NAPM IT9.11-1993, 5.

Black-and-white silver-gelatin film should be stored at a temperature not above 70°F.[56] The fugitive nature of color dyes dictates that color film be stored at temperatures no higher than 36°F.

Air conditioning is normally required for archival storage, and it must provide even air circulation throughout the storage area. Temperature and humidity should be monitored continuously with a recording device such as a hygrothermograph or the more recently introduced electronic dataloggers. Numerous publications by the American Society of Heating, Refrigeration, and Air Conditioning Engineers explain aspects of air conditioning, and those are listed in the ANSI storage standard (ANSI/NAPM IT9.11-1993). Any qualified storage facility should be prepared to provide you with actual data that show its compliance with the temperature and humidity requirements in the ANSI standard.

With very few exceptions, it is almost certain that your own repository cannot achieve and sustain temperature and humidity levels required for storage of the master negative. If the printing master must last longer than ten years, it too must be stored in compliance with the requirements for extended-term storage, and these are equally beyond the capability of most institutional air conditioning systems.

How serious is a "slight" departure from the recommended storage environment? This is difficult to answer because many combinations of variables are possible. Departure by 2°F from a maximum allowable temperature will probably have little effect by itself. However, an increase in temperature and a simultaneous increase in the relative humidity, even if relatively slight, could be fatal to film within a matter of weeks due to fungus activity. Therefore, it is not safe to depart from the recommended practices.

Air Purity

Purity of the air is important for storage of master negatives. Dust is one enemy, and the vault should be equipped with mechanical filters to remove these particles.[57]

Gases contained in the air are also harmful. Sulfur dioxide, hydrogen sulfide, peroxides, nitrogen oxides, ammonia, ozone, and certain acid fumes can cause deterioration of film. The storage facility must be equipped with appropriate filtering systems to remove these gaseous pollutants.

Paint fumes are likely to include oxidizing contaminants that are thought to contribute to the formation of microscopic blemishes on microfilm. Film shall not be stored in a room for three months after painting, nor in any cabinet or other housing that has been painted within three months.

---

56. The benefits of low-temperature storage have been investigated by IPI, and one study shows that the reactions of vinegar syndrome in acetate film (discussed in the "Cellulose Acetate" section of this chapter) will take about 17 times longer at 30°F than at 70°F. See James M. Reilly, *IPI Storage Guide for Acetate Film* (Rochester, N.Y.: IPI, 1993), 16. The publication details the problems with and recommended storage conditions for acetate-base films and explains on page 21 how to distinguish polyester from acetate or nitrate.

57. ANSI/NAPM IT9.11-1993, sec. 7.3, specifies a preference for a dry-media type of mechanical filter with an arrestance rating of at least 85 percent.

Because of the great risk posed by airborne pollutants, the standard notes that extended-term storage vaults should be located as far as possible from an urban or industrial area, where contaminants are most likely to be present in harmful concentrations. Admittedly, an urban facility can be equipped with gas-filtration systems that meet the national standard. However, all it takes is a single malfunction of that complex system to allow pollutants to enter and undo decades of careful air-quality control.

Light

Film should be kept under dark conditions. Keep film in closed containers or housing units. Lights should remain off except when someone is in the storage area.

Fire Protection

Storage rooms should conform to the National Fire Protection Association's recommendations for fire-resistive file rooms, specified in ANSI/NFPA 232-1991, *Protection of Records*. There are ANSI standards (listed in the storage standard) for construction that combines air conditioning with fire detection. For small quantities of film there are fire-protective enclosures on the market intended to keep internal temperatures below 150°F in case of fire, and the storage standard defines the necessary qualities for them. There are unresolved questions regarding fire-protective chemicals incorporated into paper cartons for the storage of film or fiche and their potential effect on the stability of preservation microforms.

After discussing fire protection at some length, the ANSI storage standard (ANSI/NAPM IT9.11-1993) concludes that the best fire protection is a duplicate copy of the film placed in another storage area. At a minimum, you should be sure the storage facility has a means of early and automatic fire detection and signaling.[58] In addition, it is a good idea to store master negatives and printing masters in different facilities.

Storage Housing

Storage housing includes drawers, shelves, cabinets, and racks. Closed housing is preferable, either chests of drawers or shelves or racks within a cabinet with outside doors. If the film is already enclosed in sealed containers, then open shelves are acceptable.

Microform housing should be made of a noncombustible material and be noncorrodible, as defined in ANSI IT9.2-1991. Anodized aluminum or steel with baked-on, nonplasticized lacquer may be suitable. Wood, pressed board, particle board, and other natural products are not allowed under the standard. They are not only combustible but may emit vapors that cause film to deteriorate.

---

58. An excellent guide to fire protection for library and archival materials is Michael Trinkley, *Can You Stand the Heat? A Fire Safety Primer for Libraries, Archives and Museums* (Atlanta: SOLINET, 1993).

Some finishes emit peroxides and contaminants that damage film. Freshly painted housings shall not be used for three months.

The storage housing should be constructed in such a manner as to allow air-conditioned air free access to the films, unless previously conditioned, sealed containers are used.

Segregation of Film Types

ANSI/NAPM IT9.11-1993, the storage standard, requires segregation of certain types of films. Those that can release acidic fumes (such as some vesicular films) or that release damaging gases (such as decomposing nitrate-base film) must be kept in separate storage rooms. Films that show signs of active chemical degradation not only should be in separate storage rooms, but also in rooms with separate air-handling systems. Films of different generic types—such as silver-gelatin, diazo, and vesicular—shall never be on the same rolls or in the same enclosures, and it is generally recommended that they be in separate housing units.

Cellulose Nitrate

Cellulose nitrate film has not been manufactured since about 1951, but older films (primarily motion picture films) on this nonsafety base are occasionally encountered. As these films deteriorate, they give off highly acidic fumes. Under certain high-temperature conditions, there have even been a few cases of spontaneous combustion of reels of motion picture film on nitrate. Under no circumstances may nitrate films be stored with polyester-base film. They may not even be stored in an adjoining vault if the two areas share the same air-handling system. Nitrate-base films should be completely isolated.

How do you tell if older film is nitrate or not? ANSI IT9.6-1991 (ANSI/ISO 543-1990), *American National Standard for Photography—Photographic Films—Specifications for Safety Film,* outlines three practical field tests.

> *Visual inspection.* If the film carries the word "safety" or a capital *S* in the border, it is usually a safety base, not a nitrate-base film. It is possible for safety identification markings to be obliterated or for markings to be transferred from a safety to a nonsafety film in duplication, so this is not a definitive test. If those symbols are missing, and the border does not say "nitrate," then the film is suspect.

> *The flame test.* If you cut a small (approximately 16mm × 35mm) piece of a nitrate-base film and light it with a match, the film will flare and produce a strong acrid odor. By contrast, safety film burns slowly. The test should be done in a well-ventilated area and on a fireproof surface. The person doing the test should never inhale the fumes that result because they can be quite hazardous. To make best use of this test, a small film sample that is known to have a safety base should also be ignited for the purpose of comparison.

> *The float test.* If you drop a small (6mm) square of dry film into a small bottle or test tube containing a solution of trichloroethylene, the film will either sink (nitrate), float to the top (acetate), or float at mid-level

(polyester). The test must be conducted in a well-ventilated area with protective breathing apparatus because trichloroethylene vapor should not be inhaled. If you are unfamiliar with the safety requirements, contact your local OSHA office for guidance.

Both the float test and the flame test present some challenges for the layperson. You will find a clearly illustrated explanation of these tests and the methodology for carrying them out in *Archives and Manuscripts: Administration of Photographic Collections.*[59]

Cellulose Acetate

Film on cellulose acetate base, widely used in microfilming from the 1930s into the 1980s, is vulnerable to "vinegar syndrome." The breakdown of the acetate may be signaled by a vinegar odor, embrittlement of the base, shrinkage that causes the base to buckle away from the emulsion to create "channeling," and the appearance of crystalline deposits or liquid-filled bubbles on the emulsion.[60] It is usually possible to distinguish cellulose acetate from polyester-base film by visual inspection.[61]

Other Safety Films

Standards recommend that diazo, vesicular, and silver-gelatin film be stored separately. The standard for vesicular film (ANSI IT9.12-1991, ANSI/ISO 9718-1991) notes that some commercial vesicular films have released hydrogen chloride during storage. While this did not have an adverse effect on the stability of the film itself, it had a corrosive effect on the enclosure materials. This risk argues for the segregation of vesicular films.

Reels and Containers

The national standard for storage containers is ANSI IT9.2-1991, *American National Standard for Imaging Media—Photographic Processed Films, Plates, and Papers—Filing Enclosures and Storage Containers.* The storage standard, ANSI/NAPM IT9.11-1993, supplements its provisions. Both apply to storage copies (master negatives and printing masters), not service copies.

Average-size rolls generally may be stored on edge, as long as the flanges of the reel extend beyond the film. Microfilm rolls longer than 150 meters should be stored flat, not on edge. If they are stored on edge, the weight on the bottom of the roll will be excessive.

Fiche should never be stacked because the lower sheets can be damaged by pressure. Fiche stored upright should not be packed so tightly as to cause pressure.

---

59. Although the tests are described in ANSI IT9.6-1991, practical instructions are also available in Mary Lynn Ritzenthaler, Gerald J. Munoff, and Margery S. Long, *Archives and Manuscripts: Administration of Photographic Collections* (Chicago: SAA, 1984), 116–19.

60. Reilly, *IPI Storage Guide for Acetate Film,* 12.

61. See Reilly, *IPI Storage Guide to Acetate Film,* 21.

It is preferable to store film in closed containers to protect the film against dirt or physical damage. In the case of films containing dyes, for example, diazo or color films, the films must be protected against light also, using an opaque container or opaque housing.

Reels and containers should be of a chemically inert, noncorroding material that does not give off reactive fumes. In practice, plastics are typically used for microfilm reels and paper products for microfilm boxes and microfiche envelopes.

Paper Storage Products

Based on the work that has been done to define standards for permanent and durable paper storage products, most large-scale filming programs use paper-board containers. They should be made of acid- and lignin-free buffered paper and meet the detailed composition requirements contained in ANSI IT9.2-1991, and they should "pass" the photographic activity test outlined in ANSI/NAPM IT9.16-1994.

Paper envelopes can be used to store microfiche, provided that they also conform to the paper requirements of ANSI IT9.2-1991. The standard also specifies the adhesives that may be used for the seams of microfiche envelopes. Envelopes should not be constructed in such a way that a seam rests across the image area of the microfiche. In fact, the storage standard recommends that microfiche not be stored in envelopes that use any adhesives in their construction, but it is difficult to find such envelopes. Glassine envelopes shall not be used.

Plastic Reels and Containers

Plastics are typically used for microfilm reels and may be used as containers, but you must exercise great care in purchasing plastic products. The photographic activity test (ANSI/NAPM IT9.16-1994) provides a definitive measure of the stability of paper-based products, but it does not apply to plastics. Plastics that are not chemically inert or that give off reactive fumes, notably those containing peroxides, are not acceptable. The consumer generally cannot tell what plastics have been used in the manufacture of a commercially acquired container or film reel. If the material is unidentified, ask the supplier to provide the necessary information.

ANSI committees have criticized certain plastics on the basis of their chemical composition and suggested that they not be used until the manufacturer can show positively that no harmful side effects will ensue. This means that certain plastics may be perfectly safe in conjunction with film, but until the manufacturer is able to *prove* the material innocuous, the material will not be approved.

When plastics are used for storage of microforms, it is considered acceptable to use uncoated polyester materials, since these materials are actually used for the film base. Polyethylene and polypropylene are also acceptable.

Metal Reels and Containers

Metals must be noncorrodible. Stainless steel is a suitable material for reels and containers, although it may be too expensive in most applications. Anodized aluminum is also acceptable. Metal reels and containers must be free from sharp edges that could damage film.

Sealed Containers

At times you may want to protect the film in sealed, airtight containers. Closed containers that are completely sealed against the atmosphere provide a defense against moisture, dust, and gaseous pollutants. However, you must be sure that the atmosphere captured within the container is of the proper humidity and was not subject to atmospheric pollution before the container was sealed. This is very difficult to do. To illustrate: following processing, a film may contain a certain amount of residual moisture. If, after processing, the film is placed immediately into a stainless steel or aluminum container and sealed, the atmosphere within the container will be considerably more humid than is healthy for a film because the controlled air of the storage room cannot penetrate the closed container to dissipate the excessive humidity. The complex requirements for airtight storage are outlined in ANSI/NAPM IT9.11-1993.

Adhesives for Enclosures and Containers

ANSI IT9.2-1991 specifies the requirements for adhesives used in the fabrication of envelopes, boxes, and other containers. Only adhesives that pass the photographic activity test (ANSI/NAPM IT9.16-1994) shall be used. Pressure-sensitive adhesives are unacceptable, as are rubber-based products such as rubber cement.

Inks

Printing inks have been known to cause microscopic blemishes in silver film.[62] There should be no printed matter on the inside of a microform enclosure. Inks used in labels must pass the photographic activity test (ANSI/NAPM IT9.16-1994), and other specifications are outlined in ANSI IT9.2-1991.

Fasteners

Paper bands should be used to secure rolls of film, provided that the paper conforms to the specifications contained in ANSI IT9.2-1991. Rubber bands are not acceptable. Even those that might be chemically adequate can crimp and physically distort film. No adhesive-coated tape should ever be used directly on the film.

Inspection of Stored Film

An important aspect of film storage is regular film inspection. No matter how carefully the film was manufactured and processed, and no matter how carefully the storage facility was constructed or the storage enclosures chosen, there is a possibility that something may go awry.

American National Standard for Information and Image Management— Recommended Practice for Inspection of Stored Silver-Gelatin Microforms for Evidence of Deterioration, ANSI/AIIM MS45-1990, provides the current recommendations for inspection of silver-gelatin film. The standard for microfilming

---

62. ANSI IT9.2-1991, sec. 3.6, p. 4.

public records (*American National Standard for Information and Image Management—Recommended Practice for Microfilming Public Records on Silver-Halide Film*, ANSI/AIIM MS48-1990) is quite specific in establishing inspection requirements for permanent records in accordance with ANSI/AIIM MS45-1990. If you are leasing space in a commercial facility, make sure the lease provides for periodic inspection and allows your institution to go in and perform its own inspection.

Figures 32 and 33 provide forms you may adapt for your inspections. It is good practice to inspect samples of stored film on a systematic basis so that film in each drawer or cabinet is examined at least every two years. There should also be a small amount of overlap to track changes in previously inspected samples.

If there are fewer than one hundred microforms, all one hundred should be inspected. For larger collections, ANSI/AIIM MS45-1990 recommends a sampling technique. The sample size should be 0.1 percent of the whole collection, and the standard suggests ways to get a sample that is representative of the film types, ages, and so on.

The inspection should be done in a clean room, and it should be done near the storage area to avoid the risk of damaging microforms in transit. The inspection area should have about the same temperature and humidity conditions as the storage area. Some archival storage facilities include inspection stations that clients can use.

Inspectors should look for mold or fungus, redox blemishes, film curl or discoloration, and excessive brittleness. Other problems might be separation of the emulsion from the base or evidence of adhesion (films sticking together). Collections that may contain nitrate or acetate film should receive especially scrupulous inspection so that any deterioration can be identified and the films copied before they are beyond salvage.[63]

As part of the inspection, reread the resolution test, and remeasure film density because density changes are a key indicator of image instability. To spot any changes, you must retain the quality report forms from your original inspection, showing the original density readings.

Inspectors should also be on the alert for signs of rust, corrosion, or other deterioration of the cans, boxes, or reels used to store the film. Damaged ones should be replaced, and the cause of the deterioration should be identified.

The biennial inspection report should specify the quantity of microfilm in the storage room as well as how many and which films were inspected. The condition of the microfilm is the focus of the inspection, and the report should state the corrective action required if necessary.

If you spot a problem, launch a more extensive inspection to locate all deteriorating film. Any deteriorated films should be copied onto new silver-gelatin film.

If anything happens to alter storage conditions, such as the temporary breakdown of the air-conditioning system, you must immediately spot check the

---

63. If the staff fully exploits the bibliographic control capabilities of the MARC record, noting what film base was used (as recommended in the "MARC Field 007" section of chapter 5), and uses the 583 field (see chapter 5) to note special treatments, then microforms "at risk" can be more easily identified in the future.

FIGURE 32   Survey of Stored Microforms: Data Collection

I. Film Identification		
1. Name of organization _____		
2. Record series _____		
3. Film identification: Roll or ID no. _____		
Location _____		
4. Name of Inspector _____ Date of Inspection _____		

II. Description of Microform, Storage and Use		

5. Film format
  □ Roll
  □ Jacket
  □ Microfiche
	6. Film carrier type
	
	  _____
	  Manufacturer
	  _____
		7. Processed by
		  □ In-house
		  □ Vendor
		  □ Unknown

8. Year Produced
 	
  _____
	9. Film Type
	  □ CN □ DN □ DP
		10. Film Base
		  □ Acetate □ Unknown
		  □ Polyester

11. Film size
  □ 16mm   □ Thick
  □ 35mm   □ Thin
  □ 105mm
  □ Other
	12. Name of film manufacturer
	
	  _____
		13. Film generation
		  □ Camera master
		  □ Printing master
		  □ Use copy

14. Film container
  □ Cardboard box
  □ Plastic box
  □ Metal can
  □ Paper envelope
  □ Other _____
	15. Reel type
	  □ Plastic
	  □ Metal
		16. Environmental conditions
		  Temp. _____
		  R.H. _____
		  Impurities _____

17. Type of leader (*more than one may be checked*)
  □ Fogged
  □ Clear
  □ Both
  □ Spliced
	18. Type of trailer (*more than one may be checked*)
	  □ Fogged
	  □ Clear
	  □ Both
	  □ Spliced
		19. Density _____
		  Resolution _____
		  First reading? □ Y □ N
		  Compared to previous readings,
		  this reading is □ Same
		       □ Lower

20. Type of splice
  □ Ultrasonic   □ Glue
  □ Heat   □ Other
  □ Tape
	Number of Splices
	  □ None □ 11 or more
	  □ 1–5
	  □ 6–10
		21. Type of restraint used to
		  confine film
		  □ Paper and string
		  □ None
		  □ Rubber band
		  □ Other _____

III. Inspection Data/Deterioration Identified		

22. Type/deterioration
  □ Mold/fungus
  □ Excessive brittleness
  □ Discoloration
  □ Scratches
	□ Water spots/streaks
	□ Dirt
	□ Evidence of adhesion
	□ Poor film splices
	□ Separation of emulsion
		□ Chemical stains
		□ Unusual odors
		□ Torn or nicked film
		□ Redox blemishes
		□ Other

23. Location
 	
  _____
	24. Severity
	
	  _____	

25. Remarks: _____		
26. Overall Condition of Film □ Excellent □ Acceptable □ Fair □ Poor □ Bad		

SOURCE: Adapted from *American National Standard for Information and Image Management—Recommended Practice for Inspection of Stored Silver-Gelatin Microforms for Evidence of Deterioration*, ANSI/AIIM MS45-1990, 18.

FIGURE 33 Survey of Stored Microforms: Data Analysis

1. Name of lot _____
2. Inspection dates _____
3. Name(s) of inspectors _____   _____

4. Number of units in lot _____
5. Number of samples inspected _____
6. Percentage of rolls in sample affected by deterioration _____
7. Types of deterioration detected _____
_____
_____
_____
_____
_____

8. Severity of deterioration _____
_____
_____
_____

9. Remedial action recommended _____
_____
_____
_____
_____
_____

SOURCE: Adapted from *American National Standard for Information and Image Management—Recommended Practice for Inspection of Stored Silver-Gelatin Microforms for Evidence of Deterioration,* ANSI/AIIM MS45-1990, 19.

microforms. If there is any indication of possible damage, take corrective action on the entire vault immediately, particularly if you suspect that fungus damage may be a threat.

Conclusion

Preservation microfilming standards and practices are exacting, and with good reason. Even if paper copies of the filmed materials continue to be available for some time, the commitment to microfilm is a commitment to keep it forever accessible. It is a charge that must be taken seriously because it is doubtful that the funding will ever be sufficient to allow the same volume or collection to be filmed twice.

Even with all its detail, this chapter can be considered only an introduction to the standards and specifications required in a high-quality preservation microfilming program. Further reading and dialogue with people experienced in preservation filming will help you develop the specifications and procedures that will best meet your needs.

Suggested Readings

National standards and specifications of standards organizations such as ANSI and AIIM as well as RLG also include microfilm production guidelines. See Appendix A for those.

Micrographic Film Technology. 4th ed. Silver Spring, Md.: AIIM, 1992.

Reilly, James M. *IPI Storage Guide for Acetate Film.* Rochester, N.Y.: IPI, 1993.

Saffady, William. *Micrographic Systems.* 3d ed. Silver Spring, Md.: AIIM, 1990.

Usovicz, Eileen, and Nancy E. Elkington. "Recommended Program of Microfilm Inspection." In *RLG Preservation Microfilming Handbook,* edited by Nancy E. Elkington, 160–76. Mountain View, Calif.: RLG, 1992.

Preservation Microfilming and Bibliographic Control

To this point, you have read of the rigorous intellectual work and stringent technical requirements involved in producing a preservation microfilm. You have moved through all the steps from identifying and screening items that are candidates for filming to the preparation and production of film. What remains, you might ask, beyond giving guidelines on determining costs? Not a lot, if the only goal of preservation microfilming were to ensure the continued availability of collections for local use. But the goal of preservation microfilming is to ensure widespread and enduring access to the materials, and this requires that the existence of the microform be recorded in a way that is sufficiently descriptive and accessible.

The provision of appropriate bibliographic control is a critical element in a responsible preservation program. The online catalog record for the master negative is essentially "the official record for the nation's permanent copy."[1] Scholars and other users must be able to locate the resource when it is needed and to determine that it is precisely the item they require. Preservation project staff at other institutions must be alerted that you have already filmed (or have decided to film) a title they are screening. Other repositories throughout the world must be able to identify your microform copy as an exact replacement for their deteriorated hard copy.

Ignore this subject at your peril, for there is much to be lost. A single monograph filmed for want of information on an existing film wastes the money spent to create and catalog it. A newspaper or periodical run filmed in duplication of another institution's work could waste thousands of dollars. And the likelihood of duplication is often extremely high. For example, in two projects to film late

---

1. Crystal Graham, "Microform Reproductions and Multiple Versions: U.S. Cataloging Policy and Proposed Changes," in *Serials Cataloging II: Modern Perspectives and International Developments*, eds. Jim E. Cole and Jim Williams (Binghamton, N.Y.: Haworth, 1992), 218. Also published as *Serials Librarian* 22 (1992), nos. 1/2.

nineteenth-century American literature and social sciences, more than 50 percent of the titles slated for filming were found already to have been filmed.[2] The risk of duplicate filming becomes ever higher as more and more institutions undertake this work.

Mechanisms for Bibliographic Control

Using cataloging to establish full bibliographic control over microform versions of books and serials has been a long-sought but elusive goal. The writings of its advocates are insistent, persuasive, and sometimes eloquent. They are also surprisingly extensive, beginning in 1940 with Fussler's "Microfilm and Libraries" and Tauber's "Cataloging and Classifying Microfilm."[3] William J. Myrick summarized matters as they stood in 1978:

> The need for bibliographic control of microforms is generally recognized. Obviously, the technology for establishing such control exists. Just as obviously, efforts so far towards achieving this end have been uncoordinated, poorly supported, and generally unsuccessful. Nevertheless, even the most jaded expect that eventually such efforts will be successful. The question is when. Keyes Metcalf first proposed establishing a national register of microform masters in 1936, a proposal which took 29 years to come into being. If it takes that long for current plans to materialize, microforms won't be brought into the national bibliographic network until sometime early in the next century. It's a long wait, one that shouldn't be necessary.[4]

Fortunately, things have changed. Efforts are now much better coordinated, and libraries are closing in on the goal of a national bibliographic network, although in a form different from the one Myrick envisioned. Instead of creating one enormous shared database, libraries contribute to a "logical" collection of shared cataloging systems connected by exchanges of records via magnetic tapes and by the kind of electronic links supported by the Z39.50 standard.[5]

Keyes Metcalf and many others spoke out for creation of a national bibliography of microfilms. As a result, the Library of Congress in 1965 began publication of the printed *National Register of Microform Masters,* or *NRMM* as it is

---

2. The projects were components of the first RLG Cooperative Preservation Microfilming Project, conducted from 1983 to 1987. This information was supplied by project participants.

3. Herman H. Fussler, "Microfilm and Libraries," in *The Acquisition and Cataloging of Books,* ed. William M. Randall (Chicago, Ill.: University of Chicago Press, 1940), 331–54; and Maurice F. Tauber, "Cataloging and Classifying Microfilm," *Journal of Documentary Reproduction* 3 (Mar. 1940): 10–25.

4. William J. Myrick, "Access to Microforms: A Survey of Failed Efforts," *Library Journal* 103 (Nov. 15, 1978): 2304.

5. *Information Retrieval Application Service Definition and Protocol Specification for Open Systems Interconnection,* ANSI/NISO Z39.50-1992 (Bethesda, Md.: NISO, 1994), provides a protocol that allows users to search and retrieve bibliographic data from different computers without requiring they know the search syntax applied by those systems.

familiarly known.[6] *NRMM* was, in its time, the best tool that could be produced. However, as chapter 2 makes abundantly clear, searching printed bibliographies is tedious, time-consuming, and expensive. With the advent of online cataloging and the growth of the bibliographic networks, it has become possible—and highly desirable—to work toward full online search capability.

The ARL Microform Project was a major stimulus for progress in bibliographic control of microforms. Under this cooperative project, libraries cataloged individual titles in virtually all of the most widely held, commercially published microform sets, made agreements to share these records, and developed mechanisms for providing efficient access to them.[7] With early stimulus from the ARL Microform Project, the Library of Congress, OCLC, and RLG have contributed substantially to this work by creating standards for recording bibliographic data about microforms, encouraging libraries to observe these standards, exchanging bibliographic records for microforms, and enhancing systems to support online searching and cataloging.

The ARL Microform Project built increased awareness and professional consensus that led to two other key projects that have helped build a national database of microform masters. First, in 1981 with funds from NEH, RLG members began to convert to machine-readable form the records for their stocks of master negatives and enter them into RLIN (the bibliographic network of RLG). Second, with funds from NEH and The Andrew W. Mellon Foundation, ARL and the Library of Congress embarked in 1986 on a joint project to convert to machine-readable form the monographic records appearing in the numerous volumes of the *NRMM*. *NRMM* records for monographs in all Western languages are now accessible on OCLC and RLIN. In 1994 a cooperative program to convert master microform records for serials was undertaken by ARL, LC, New York Public Library, and Harvard University.[8]

In the drive toward full online access, a major boon was the agreement between OCLC and RLG to exchange bibliographic records for preservation master microforms so that members of each network have access to the records of preserved titles in the other. Those who catalog preservation microforms on either OCLC or RLIN and fill in the coded information about the film generation (in MARC field 007, discussed later in this chapter) can now be assured that the records they create will be made available in both systems. There remain some limitations in the record exchange, and cataloging personnel must follow specific guidelines provided in the "Methods for Creating Microform Records" section of this chapter.

International records are also included in the record-exchange program. In 1994 RLG loaded the *European Register of Microform Masters* into RLIN. Regular RLIN tapeloading of the British Library's *National Register of Micro-*

6. *National Register of Microform Masters,* comp. and ed. the Catalog Publication Division, LC (Washington, D.C.: LC, 1965–1983).

7. See Shirley Leung, "Bibliographic Control of Microform Sets: Some Recent Accomplishments and Concerns," *Microform Review* 18 (spring 1989): 71–6.

8. Winston Tabb, "Collections Services Update" (Paper presented at the ALA Annual Conference, Miami, Fla., June 13, 1994).

form Masters and the *Canadian Register of Microform Masters* (beginning in 1995) enhances the international scope of the preservation record exchange with OCLC. Especially through initiatives of the Commission on Preservation and Access, there is every prospect that online access to international microform records will continue to improve.

ARL again took the leadership in bibliographic control of microforms when it published its *Guidelines for Bibliographic Records for Preservation Microform Masters* (hereafter cited as *ARL Guidelines*) in 1990.[9] These guidelines increased cataloging productivity by allowing the application of retrospective conversion standards instead of requiring that records meet the standards for new cataloging. At the same time, the *ARL Guidelines* ensured inclusion of essential preservation data by defining "the base level below which a preservation microform master record should not go."[10] The *ARL Guidelines* were endorsed in 1992 by the Association for Library Collections & Technical Services of the American Library Association and now serve as the de facto standard for bibliographic control of preservation microform masters of books and serials.[11] The *ARL Guidelines* are reproduced in appendix E.

Major progress on archival control was achieved by RLG through its Archives Preservation Microfilming Project (APMP) from 1990 to 1994, the first major cooperative filming project that focused on archival and manuscript materials. In the course of the APMP, RLG members developed a set of guidelines for bibliographic control, building upon the *ARL Guidelines* and Hensen's *Archives, Personal Papers, and Manuscripts: A Cataloging Manual for Archival Repositories, Historical Societies, and Manuscript Libraries*. The *RLG Archives Microfilming Manual* defines for archival materials the minimum requirements for preservation elements in the online catalog record, much as the *ARL Guidelines* do for books and serials.[12]

To be shared among libraries—which is, of course, a necessity—machine-readable catalog records must be produced in MARC (MAchine-Readable Cataloging) format, a communications format with standard fields of data. This format allows data to be exchanged among organizations with different computer systems. OCLC, RLIN, and local systems use a variety of methods to create the catalog records for preservation microforms. In all cases, the end product should conform to the *ARL Guidelines*.

---

9. Association of Research Libraries, *Guidelines for Bibliographic Records for Preservation Microform Masters,* prepared by Crystal Graham (Washington, D.C.: ARL, Sept. 1990). Reproduced in appendix E of this manual.

10. *ARL Guidelines,* 2–3.

11. ALCTS Task Force on Bibliographic Control of Microform Master Negatives, "Final Report and Recommendations (Jan. 2, 1992)," adopted by ALCTS as Board Document 92.23 and published in the *ALCTS Newsletter* 3, no. 8 (1992): 102–4. The *ARL Guidelines* also serve as the basis for the cataloging requirements of the Canadian Cooperative Preservation Project; see Canadian Cooperative Preservation Project, *Guidelines for Preservation Microfilming in Canadian Libraries* (Ottawa: National Library of Canada, 1993), especially the "Procedures for Bibliographic Control" section, 22–30.

12. These guidelines are spelled out in Diane E. Kaplan and Nancy F. Lyon, "Bibliographic and Archival Control," in *RLG Archives Microfilming Manual,* edited by Nancy E. Elkington (Mountain View, Calif.: RLG, 1994), 39–50.

The Rationale for Microform Cataloging

Although standards and bibliographic systems are now vastly improved and largely adequate for the recording of microform masters, institutional practices—whether from a shortage of resources or commitment—do not always take full advantage of the capabilities for enhanced control and access. The temptation to defer microform cataloging or to do it minimally may be strong. Yielding to that temptation, however, would be a grave mistake—one that poses unnecessary obstacles to scholarship and thwarts efforts to coordinate national and international preservation work.[13]

Improvement in institutional practice was evident in an unpublished May 1992 ARL survey, "Cataloging Preservation Microform Masters." Survey responses suggested that most research libraries are providing cataloging records for master negatives of books and serials, but less so for archival materials and manuscripts.[14]

A strong economic case exists for making information about preservation masters available in a national database such as OCLC or RLIN. If properly produced, stored, and made available for copies, only one preservation master negative of an item need ever be produced. Consequently, organizations such as ALA, ARL, the Commission on Preservation and Access, NEH, and RLG have advocated the necessity for access both to bibliographic information about the existence of master negatives and, whenever possible (that is, if there are no copyright restrictions), to copies from the master negatives.

Cataloging microforms goes a long way toward preventing costly and wasteful duplication of effort, but this is not its only benefit. First and foremost, it expands users' access to the materials that have been preserved. When archival records are filmed, the cataloging often provides vastly expanded access for scholars who otherwise might not have known the materials existed. Cataloging microfilmed books and serials frequently results in the creation of new machine-readable records that afterward can be adapted by other libraries as they engage in retrospective conversion of their card catalogs. Also, it results in records that can be used by collection development and interlibrary loan librarians seeking copies of items that are needed but not available in their libraries.

These facts are well recognized by organizations that provide support for preservation microfilming projects. The current application guidelines of the NEH Division of Preservation and Access are explicit:

> For projects involving preservation microfilming, . . . records for the preserved items must be entered into one of the national bibliographic utilities that participates in the routine exchange of master negative records. . . . For microfilming projects, the application should confirm that

---

13. Powerful arguments for the importance of microform cataloging are offered in Elizabeth L. Patterson, "Hidden Treasures: Bibliographic Control of Microforms, a Public Services Perspective," *Microform Review* 19 (spring 1990): 76–9.

14. Crystal Graham (Serials Cataloging Section Head and Microforms Cataloging Coordinator, University of California, San Diego), electronic mail correspondence with the author, Jan. 11, 1995.

all service copies of microfilms created with NEH funds will be circulated to users on interlibrary loan, and that copies of microfilmed materials will also be available, as copyright permits, for purchase at cost by other institutions or individuals.[15]

NEH explicitly requires that the catalog records conform to the *ARL Guidelines.* The NHPRC guidelines also urge that microforms be cataloged in an appropriate machine-readable format for inclusion in one of the national databases.[16]

A successful preservation program requires the commitment of senior administrators and significant coordination with staff members in other departments. Having built a commitment to cataloging microforms, you should also develop plans to eliminate or avoid microform cataloging backlogs. To find the additional resources required, the preservation manager and cataloging staff must work together to make this a high priority within the institution. Obtaining this spirit of mutual support requires patience, persistence, and an ability repeatedly to put forward the same message in varied form until it is at last accepted.

Coordinating Filming and Cataloging

Cataloging microforms, like other cataloging, is a technical matter best left to experts: the professional catalogers and others in cataloging units. It is a matter on which preservation administrators give advice on options, but not one on which they should attempt to become experts. Preservation staff can be trained to perform cataloging tasks, and they can and should learn what is required in general terms. But given the complexity of cataloging practices and the frequency with which the formats, rules, and rule interpretations change, they should not attempt independently to master the details of this difficult subject.

This chapter focuses on the major decision points and concerns in which the preservation manager is typically involved, but it also provides technical guidance for staff members who catalog the microforms created in preservation programs. For those who do replacement searching, the chapter will help interpret the screen displays in OCLC and RLIN, and the "Searching" section of this chapter notes some special concerns.

Preservation administrators should approach cataloging administrators as partners in preservation microfilming programs. To schedule their work, catalogers need to know what will be filmed: what projects are being implemented, planned, or even just generally discussed. More than that, whenever possible, they should participate in the development of planning documents, budgets, schedules, and proposals. The scope of the project may have significant cataloging ramifications. For example, if you plan to film foreign-language materials, you must be sure there is staff with language skills to do that bibliographic control work. The expertise of cataloging staff is as essential in planning successful projects as in carrying them out.

---

15. *Guidelines and Application Instructions* (Washington, D.C.: NEH Division of Preservation and Access, n.d.), 10–11.

16. *Microform Guidelines* (Washington, D.C.: NHPRC, 1986), 10.

Searching and cataloging require basic printed materials in addition to online resources. Whether the work is done in the preservation unit or elsewhere will depend largely on local considerations related to work-flow. *Columbia University Libraries, Preservation Division.*

The goals of preservation and access are so intertwined that preservation staff dare not be ignorant of the bibliographic control strategies that will bring their filming work to fruition. Conversely, catalogers must rely upon preservation staff to provide guidance on several data elements that go into the bibliographic record.

Catalogers should be consulted when bibliographic targets are designed to ensure that the proper forms of names and choice of entry are used. This is especially important for serials that may have undergone title changes. Catalogers should be involved in the design and wording of targets to ensure that they include all the information needed for the reproduction note in MARC field 533. (This and other MARC fields are discussed later in this chapter.) Ideally the cataloging should be brought up to standard, with authority work and subject analysis completed prior to the filming. A copy of the catalog record should be included in the BIBLIOGRAPHIC RECORD target.

Project managers and catalogers should work together to identify missing or damaged volumes or pages. Catalogers may provide guidance on how to reflect missing materials in the LIST OF IRREGULARITIES, GUIDE TO CONTENTS, and BIBLIOGRAPHIC RECORD targets, as well as in local and national versions of the online record.[17]

---

17. Nancy E. Elkington, ed., *RLG Preservation Microfilming Handbook* (Mountain View, Calif.: RLG, 1992), 20–4, 27.

Once an item has been filmed, catalogers need to know from preservation staff what data to put in the MARC 533 note field and the MARC 007 fixed field. They may need to see either the original or the film that has been made from it. It is the responsibility of the preservation administrator to provide this information if needed and to arrange for catalogers to obtain originals or films that they need to see.

Of course, bibliographic control is an element in preservation record keeping. The preservation administrator should arrange to receive reports of all preservation master negatives cataloged and should incorporate this information into statistics for the microfilming program.[18]

Tools for Cataloging Microforms

All catalogers need access to the *Anglo-American Cataloguing Rules,* second edition, revised (hereafter cited as AACR2), the *Library of Congress Rule Interpretations* (LCRI), and the *Cataloging Service Bulletin* (CSB). With few exceptions, institutions throughout the United States and Canada catalog microforms according to the LC interpretation of AACR2 and the network and/or local system guidelines that implement and enhance the rules. The LC rule interpretation of AACR2, chapter 11, requires that the item appearing on film be described as if it were still in its original hard copy form with the addition of further information describing the microform copy.[19] The National Library of Canada (NLC) does not follow the LC rule interpretation but, instead, describes the reproduction and gives details of the original in a note (field 534); other Canadian institutions generally follow the LCRI.[20] The most notable U.S. exception is for newspapers filmed under the auspices of the USNP. Those participants use a single bibliographic record to describe the original with both microform and hard copy holdings reflected in the OCLC local data records.

---

18. Some libraries have developed applications to automate information-gathering procedures for use in and sharing among the preservation and cataloging departments. For instance, a local database can be used to create information for the 007 field, from which a translation program can upload the data into the local library system and then into one of the national databases. A few examples are provided in *Automating Preservation Management in ARL Libraries,* SPEC Kit 198 (Washington, D.C.: ARL Office of Management Services, 1993). A noteworthy call for additional innovations, broad applications, and national consensus is provided in Nancy Elkington, "Preservation and Automation: Bring on the Empty Horses," *Abbey Newsletter* 15 (May 1991): 43–5.

19. See "Library of Congress Policy for Cataloging Microreproductions," *Cataloging Service Bulletin* 14 (fall 1981): 56–8, or "Library Announces Policy on Cataloging Microreproductions," *Library of Congress Information Bulletin* 40 (July 31, 1981): 245–6. For the most recent interpretation, refer to the *Library of Congress Rule Interpretations,* 2d ed. (Washington, D.C.: Cataloging Distribution Service, 1990–), chapter 11.

20. For a description of NLC practice, see John Clark and Wayne Jones, "The Cataloguing of Serial Microform Reproductions at the National Library of Canada," in *Serials Cataloging II: Modern Perspectives and International Developments,* ed. Jim E. Cole and Jim Williams (Binghamton, N.Y.: Haworth, 1992), 197–211; also published as *Serials Librarian* 22 (1992), nos. 1/2. As Clark and Jones observe, the NLC practice, which requires original cataloging of microform reproductions, is quite an expensive one.

FIGURE 34   Tools for Cataloging Microforms

Books and Serials

Association of Research Libraries' *Guidelines for Bibliographic Records for Preservation Microform Masters* (reproduced in Appendix E)

CONSER Editing Guide (CEG) and *CONSER Cataloging Manual* (CCM)

Archives and Manuscripts

Steven L. Hensen's *Archives, Personal Papers, and Manuscripts: A Cataloging Manual for Archival Repositories, Historical Societies, and Manuscript Libraries*

Diane E. Kaplan and Nancy F. Lyon's chapter 6, "Bibliographic and Archival Control," of the *RLG Archives Microfilming Manual*

Network-Specific Guides

OCLC's *Bibliographic Formats and Standards* and *OCLC Guide to Preservation Data Cataloging in RLIN II,* the *USMARC Format for Bibliographic Data,* and the *RLIN Supplement to USMARC Bibliographic Format*

SOURCE: Crystal Graham, Serials Cataloging Section Head and Microforms Cataloging Coordinator, University of California, San Diego.

Several specialized tools are essential, depending on the materials being cataloged, and they are listed in figure 34. The CONSER (Cooperative Online Serials) tools are not only essential for cataloging serials but also provide detailed instructions for cataloging and coding preservation microforms that monographic catalogers may also find valuable. Those cataloging newspapers, especially under the USNP, also use the CONSER guides. While the *USMARC Format for Bibliographic Data* is not specific to RLIN use, those cataloging on RLIN must apply it along with the *RLIN Supplement*. The OCLC materials are available from OCLC and its affiliated regional networks, and RLIN materials are available from RLG.[21] Preservation administrations should know these resources exist and might want to peruse them to get a sense of their contents but should not worry about mastering all that they contain.

Methods for Creating Microform Records

The nature of the OCLC and RLIN databases affects the options for creating microform records. RLIN functions as a union catalog, with separate records for each institution organized in "clusters" (a *cluster* is a group of records from different institutions, all describing the same title). In RLIN, libraries can alter their own records at any time, adding and subtracting data elements as needed. They

---

21. Within OCLC's *Bibliographic Formats and Standards,* pages 26 through 30 provide a summary of guidelines for cataloging reproductions and original microform publications.

can even change a record for the hard copy original into a record for the microfilm if the reproduction replaces the hard copy in the collection.

OCLC is a master record database, wherein each bibliographic item is described once in a single record used by all libraries. Institutional holdings symbols are attached to the master bibliographic records. Libraries can edit and export the records for their local use, but only libraries that are members of Enhance (for books) or CONSER (for serials) can permanently alter full-level records in the database. Minimal level records can be upgraded by any user. Local information is not included in the master record, and the master record remains in the system even if all institutional holdings symbols are deleted. Libraries may record their individual volume holdings by using OCLC's Union List Subsystem.

There are several methods for cataloging reproductions. In all of these methods, the description is based on the original hard copy publication, with details of the microform given in the 007 fixed field and 533 note. All reproductions, including reproductions of reproductions, should be treated as reproductions of the original.

Cloning

When a bibliographic record for the hard copy publication is available online, it may be cloned to produce the record for the reproduction. On OCLC this is done by using the "new" command, on RLIN with the "CREate *" command. Cloning copies the description of the hard copy record into a new record, to which are added specific fields relating to the microform (e.g., the 533 field). Templates such as those created with OCLC's constant-data feature may be used to overlay the preservation data into the new record.

Cloning is the most efficient way to catalog reproductions, but you must take care to delete from the microform record any information that relates only to the hard copy, such as the price or subscription address of the original publication. When there is no cataloging online for the hard copy, cataloging data may be taken from a catalog card and input according to the conventions for retrospective conversion, with the addition of the microform-specific fields.

Cloning and transcribing catalog cards are generally preferred over original cataloging because those techniques make efficient use of existing records as well as collocating the records for the hard copy and the microform. However, there are instances in which records created under superseded rules are unsatisfactory, incomplete, or misleading; in such cases, cataloging the reproduction originally may be more expeditious. When no record for the hard copy exists, original cataloging is required. See the section on "Full versus Minimal Level Cataloging" for considerations on that topic.

Advance Cataloging

Bibliographic control may be required at two points. The cataloging process generally begins when an item is selected for filming. As has been discussed elsewhere, it is crucial that institutions announce their intent to microfilm. This announcement should be included in the bibliographic record so that other institutions do not select the same title for filming. In addition, a bibliographic record must be created for the completed microform. OCLC and RLG have different ways for recording the information.

RLG was first to provide an online method, known as "queuing," which is often used as the generic term for the practice. Both queuing and precataloging are available for RLG members. Three options are available to OCLC users: prospective cataloging, announcing a commitment to preserve, or union listing.

Options in OCLC

Prospective Cataloging. Using prospective cataloging, you create a full-level bibliographic record for the preservation copy-to-be as if it had already been produced. This method is popular because the cataloger works from the hard copy rather than the microfilm and only has to handle the record once. Records for microforms can be created in a local system and tapeloaded into OCLC. All prospective cataloging records, whether tapeloaded or input directly, are then exchanged with RLG.

Announcing a Commitment to Preserve. The option of "Announcing a Commitment to Preserve" is similar to prospective cataloging in that a new

U.S. and international initiatives to reformat brittle materials rely on mechanisms to avoid duplication of effort. As soon as an item is selected for filming, the institution must record its decision through one of the advance cataloging options offered by national bibliographic databases such as OCLC and RLIN. *Preservation Resources.*

record is created for the microfilm. The new record includes the 007 field for the microform master and a 533 field with a note containing the anticipated filming date. The record is coded as minimal level (encoding level "K") to indicate that the filming details are not complete and to prevent the record from being "locked" on OCLC. However, the cataloger is well advised to complete the descriptive cataloging, subject analysis, and authority control while the hard copy is in hand.

After filming, details are added to the 007 and 533 fields, including the reduction ratio, number of reels, and "Filmed with" notes. This is a more complex workflow than prospective cataloging because staff must update the OCLC record after the filming is completed, but it accomplishes the dual goals of prompt notification through RLIN exchange and accuracy in the final product.

Union Listing. In its Union List Subsystem, OCLC has created two special union list groups that relate to preservation microfilming. The general Preservation Union List Group (dubbed "KPMP") is open to any institution that chooses to subscribe. A separate union list has been created for cataloging done under the USNP. In either group, an institution can record preservation actions (not limited to microfilming) in the PRES field. This field uses the same content designations as MARC field 583. Reports from the USNP are distributed in the microfiche *USNP National Union List* (available from OCLC). Users of the KPMP Preservation Union List must create a new bibliographic record for the microfilm once filming is complete, in accordance with the *ARL Guidelines.*

This method has not been popular with preservation administrators or catalogers due to the requirement for cumbersome searching and for subscription to the Union List Subsystem. The major drawbacks, though, are the facts that union list records are not exchanged with RLG and that they do not serve as a substitute for full bibliographic records. Cataloging from the film rather than the hard copy (if it was not retained after filming) can be an onerous task if the OCLC record for the original is inadequate.

RLIN Options

Queuing. The RLIN system provides a unique queuing date (QD) field. This field permits the earliest possible recording of an RLG member's intention to film a title. A queuing date field is added to the member's record for the hard copy publication, and a staff member records in it the date on which the institution decided to film the title. A preservation action note may also be added in field 583. Once the filming is completed, the QD field is removed and the 583 field is updated or deleted. The original record is modified to describe the microfilm (if the hard copy was discarded) or a new record for the microfilm is created (using the "CREate *" command).

This method offers the advantages of speed and simplicity. However, no 007 field is created for the microform, so queued records are not included in the exchange with OCLC.

Precataloging. Another option for RLG members is precataloging. When the turnaround time for filming is relatively short and the characteristics of the microfilm are known, a record for the yet-to-be-created microfilm can be entered when the filming decision is made. As in the OCLC prospective cataloging option, the chief advantages are that the cataloger does not have to revisit the record after filming and that the record is exchanged with OCLC when the filming decision is made.

Evaluating the Options

Several issues should be weighed in selecting among the advance cataloging options:

> Will queued records be accessible to those who need to know of your intent to film a title?
>
> How much time will pass between your decision to film a title and the availability of the preservation microfilm?
>
> Can you accurately predict the characteristics of the microfilm?
>
> Do you expect a high level of demand for the materials you are filming?

The primary goal of advance cataloging is to provide timely, unfettered access to the fact that a given institution has made a commitment to film a title, and the options must be weighed against that goal.

OCLC Union Listing poses a major access hurdle. Only institutions that subscribe to the OCLC Union List Subsystem can see records queued there, so that option is not recommended for bibliographic control of microform masters. Institutions that use the KPMP Preservation Union List to record local preservation actions may choose to use it as an adjunct to one of the other options.

All bibliographic control for microfilming done under the USNP uses the Union List Subsystem. For USNP participants this is the required method.

For all microfilming except that done under the USNP, one of the other options should generally be chosen instead. That decision should be made based on a combination of the decision-making factors listed previously. Figure 35 shows how an institution might approach the decision.

OCLC's prospective cataloging or RLG's precataloging yield a complete record for the yet-to-be-created microfilm as if it already existed. Thus, institutions and scholars may begin to place orders or interlibrary loan requests for the microforms. As a practical matter, then, it is best to use these options when relatively little time will pass between the decision point and the availability of the film.

When the filming process will result in longer time lags, use OCLC's "Announcing a Commitment to Preserve" or RLG's queuing option. Recognize, however, that the workflow is somewhat more complex, as it requires that the minimal record be upgraded after filming.

The other critical factor in communicating your intent to film depends on the catalog record itself. The OCLC and RLG systems "read" the database to identify master microform records to be included in the record exchange program. Only microforms identified in the 007 field as a preservation master or printing master (the "a" or "b" designation in OCLC's ǂi or the GEN subfield in RLIN) will be selected and exchanged.[22] Since no 007 field is created in RLG's queu-

---

22. The symbol "ǂ" is a conventional notation for the word "subfield," so "ǂb" means "subfield b."

FIGURE 35 Evaluating Advance Cataloging Options

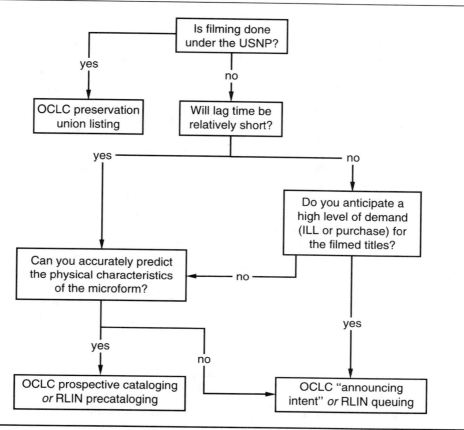

ing option, those records will not be included in the record exchange with OCLC until the filming is complete and a record is created for the microform.

Other factors will influence these general recommendations. OCLC prospective cataloging and RLG's precataloging require that you record all the data elements that describe the microfilm. You need to know in advance the characteristics of the film (that is, how many reels it will include, at what reduction ratio, on what film base and emulsion, the date of filming, and the wording of the BIBLIOGRAPHIC RECORD target) so that no updating of the master record is required after filming. This is an option only when a fixed reduction ratio is used and is usually limited to institutions that do their own preparation and reel programming.

Anticipated demand will influence the decision. If you are filming in a subject area where many others are also filming, their replacement searches are likely to yield hits on titles you have decided to film, which might be an argument for OCLC members to use the "announcing intent" option. That will reduce the risk of others placing orders for microforms that do not yet exist and will save your staff from dealing with orders that cannot yet be filled. The same issues will pertain if you are filming in a subject area that is a hotbed of scholarly activity, where researchers might begin placing interlibrary loan requests for the microforms before they have actually been created.

RLG members weighing the same factors might choose to use the QD field. However, since queued records are not included in the record exchange with OCLC, other institutions will not have ready access to them. Therefore, especially when filming in a subject area that is receiving considerable attention, precataloging may be the better choice.

The opposite argument might be made, however, when one institution or organization is filming titles so that service copies can be distributed to others that have already "subscribed" to the film product, as was the case in the ATLA projects. In such cases, prospective cataloging or precataloging would generally be the option of choice, because it guarantees that the library responsible for the filming will be the first one to create the catalog record.

Cross-correlating all these factors may sound complex when spelled out in narrative. In fact, though, the decision-making process is generally straightforward, and figure 35 suggests an approach that may be useful.

Whatever method you choose, it is critical that you record your intent in one of the national databases as soon as you make the decision to film a book or serial title. Advance cataloging is less critical for unique archival collections because there is little chance that other institutions may be screening the same items. However, even for archives, announcing your intent to film may be helpful to scholars searching for items you plan to film.

Removing Advance Cataloged Records

The preservation and cataloging units should develop mechanisms to be sure queued or prospectively cataloged records are removed if the filming decision changes. It is possible, for example, to discover that missing parts of a serial title cannot be obtained, and the resulting lacunae might be significant enough that staff will reverse the filming decision. If the records are indexed so you can search them easily, as they are with RLIN's QD field, this task is greatly simplified. These periodic checks are crucial to the national preservation effort because other institutions are making selection decisions based on your stated commitment to film a title.

Online Cataloging

This section will guide cataloging staff in appropriate application of the standards for content designation and cataloging. The preservation manager does not need to master the details but should understand the data elements and arrange to provide technical data that are needed in the catalog record. Familiarity with these guidelines will also help staff interpret records they retrieve when searching for replacements.

The discussion of data elements focuses on their use in an online environment because the majority of institutions engaged in preservation microfilming now have access to OCLC and/or RLIN.[23] Figure 36 shows how a complete record for a preservation microform might appear in OCLC and in RLIN.

MARC Field 008 and Leader

The primary fixed field code for a reproduction is for "Form of Item" (MARC field 008, byte 23; REPR in OCLC [to be called FORM after format integration is implemented], REP in RLIN), which is coded "a" for microfilm. This byte is especially important because it signals the computer that the record is for a microform, allowing users to search by that characteristic. The other bytes of the 008 field are coded for the original publication.

Before 1992 the other bytes of the 008 field were coded for the reproduction (except for the date field for serials).[24] For example, for a microfilm of a book published in Mexico filmed by the University of California, the country of publication was coded "cau" (California). Under the new coding practices, that byte is coded as "mx" (Mexico). Searchers qualifying by country or date of publication should bear in mind these changes in coding practice.

MARC Field 007: Physical Description

Field 007 carries coded data relating to the physical characteristics of the microform. Figure 37 provides a complete list of definitions for codes in MARC field 007, along with the display tags used in RLIN and OCLC. Systems differ in how they display codes in the MARC 007 field. The USMARC Format gives the codes in a single data string in the 007 field, the RLIN system uses mnemonic identifiers of each data element, and OCLC records show subfield codes using letters of the alphabet. Thus, the polarity subfield is labeled POL in RLIN and ‡d in OCLC. The RLIN display does not show the MARC 007 general material designation (which would be "h" for microform), but it is automatically supplied on output to other systems.

All elements must be coded except for the "original versus reproduction aspect" (byte 02, OR in RLIN, ‡c in OCLC), which is not currently used in describing microforms. While catalogers are allowed to use a code for "unknown" when it is difficult to determine an element from the film or record in hand, the *ARL Guidelines* urge that every effort be made to input meaningful data elements. Catalogers should seldom find themselves forced to use codes for "unknown"; the preservation staff should provide the data that are needed.

---

23. The displays and figures shown in this chapter predate format integration. Consult the following sources for the most current information about the MARC fields: *USMARC Format for Bibliographic Data: Including Guidelines for Content Designation* (Washington, D.C.: Cataloging Distribution Service, LC, 1990–), *RLIN Supplement to USMARC Bibliographic Format* (Stanford, Calif.: RLG, 1989–), *Bibliographic Formats and Standards* (Dublin, Ohio: OCLC, 1993–), and the *CONSER Editing Guide* (Washington, D.C.: Serial Record Division, LC, 1994–).

24. When the 008 field was redefined, a new subfield, ‡7 of the 533 field, was defined for recording the data relating to the reproduction that formerly was contained in the 008. In OCLC this information is recorded in the 539 field, which translates in 533 ‡7 when communicated to other systems. See the discussion of MARC field 533 for more information.

FIGURE 36 Sample OCLC and RLIN Record Displays

OCLC

```
nycg91-b67496
 OCLC:      29275663    Rec stat: n
 Entered:   19910719    Replaced: 19940928  Used: 19941102
 Type: a   Bib lvl: m  Source: d    Lang: eng
 Repr: a   Enc lvl: M  Conf pub: 0  Ctry: enk
 Indx: 0   Mod rec:    Govt pub:    Cont:
 Desc:     Int lvl:    Festschr: 0  Illus:
           F/B: 0b     Dat tp: s    Dates: 1900,
 1 010     12-34178
 2 040     ZCU ǂc ZCU
 3 007     h ǂb d ǂd a ǂe f ǂf a011 ǂg b ǂh a ǂi c ǂj a
 4 007     h ǂb d ǂd b ǂe f ǂf a011 ǂg b ǂh a ǂi a ǂj a
 5 007     h ǂb d ǂd b ǂe f ǂf a011 ǂg b ǂh a ǂi b ǂj a
 6 090     ǂb
 7 049     CUSL
 8 100 1   Hime, Henry William Lovett, ǂd 1840-
 9 245 10  Lucian, the Syrian satirist ǂh [microform], ǂc by Lieut.-Col.
           Henry W. L. Hime...
10 260     London, ǂa New York [etc.] ǂb Longmans, Green, and co., ǂc
           1900.
11 300     4 p. l., 95 p. ǂc 23 cm.
12 505 0   Life of Lucian. — Classification of Lucian's works. — The limits
           of satire. — Lucian's philosophy and religion. — Characteris-
           tics — Appendix: Lucian's knowledge of Latin.
13 533     Microfilm. ǂb New York, N.Y. : ǂc Columbia University Libraries,
           ǂd 1991. ǂe 1 microfilm reel ; 35 mm.
14 600 00  Lucian, ǂc of Samosata.
```

RLIN*

```
ID:NYCG91-B67496          RTYP:c   ST:p   FRN:   MS:n   EL:1  AD:07- 19-91
CC:9665 BLT:am     DCF:    CSC:d  MOD:    SNR:        ATC :       UD:01- 01-01
CP:enk   L:eng     INT:    GPC:   BIO:b  FIC:0   CON :
PC:s     PD:1900/          REP:a  CPI:0  FSI:0   ILC :       II:0
MMD:d   OR:b̷  POL:a    DM:f   RR: a011  COL:b    EML :a   GEN:c   BSE:a
MMD:d   OR:b̷  POL:b    DM:f   RR: a011  COL:b    EML :a   GEN:a   BSE:a
MMD:d   OR:b̷  POL:b    DM:f   RR: a011  COL:b    EML :a   GEN:b   BSE:a
010      1234178
035      (NNC) notisAGD8694
035      (CStRLIN) NYCG91-B67496
040      NNC ǂc NNC
100 1    Hime, Henry William Lovett, ǂd 1840-
245 10   Lucian, the Syrian satirist ǂh [microform], ǂc by Lieut.-Col.
         Henry W. L. Hime...
260      London, ǂa New York [etc.] ǂb Longmans, Green, and co., ǂc 1900.
300      4 p. L., 95 p. ǂc 23 cm.
505 0    Life of Lucian. — Classification of Lucian's works. — The limits
         of satire. — Lucian's philosophy and religion. — Characteristics —
         Appendix: Lucian's knowledge of Latin.
533      Microfilm. ǂb New York, N.Y. : ǂc Columbia University
         Libraries, ǂd 1991. ǂe 1 microfilm reel ; 35 mm.
583      Filmed; ǂf NEH Project (FWC) ; ǂc 1991.
590      Master negative: 91-80207-9.
590      No. 9 on a reel of 13 titles.
600 00   Lucian, ǂc of Samosata.
```

---

*For legibility, spaces were added around subfield delimiters.

FIGURE 37 MARC 007 Physical Description Fixed Field Codes Applicable to Microforms

USMARC Byte	RLIN Display	OCLC Display	Name of Field	Code	Meaning
007/00	not used	ǂa	General material designation	h	microform
007/01	MMD	ǂb	Specific material designation	a	aperture card
				b	microfilm cartridge
				c	microfilm cassette
				d	microfilm reel
				e	microfiche
				f	microfiche cassette
				g	microopaque
				z	other microform type
007/02	OR	ǂc	Original/ reproduction aspect		(not used)
007/03	POL	ǂd	Polarity	a	positive
				b	negative
				m	mixed polarity
				u	unknown
007/04	DM	ǂe	Dimensions		Microfilm:
				a	8mm
				d	16mm
				f	35mm
				g	70mm
				h	105mm
					Microfiche or microopaque:
				l	3″ × 5″ (8 × 13 cm)
				m	4″ × 5″ (11 × 15 cm, 105 × 148 mm)
				o	6″ × 9″ (16 × 23 cm)
					Aperture cards:
				p	3¼″ × 7⅜″ (9 × 19 cm)
				u	unknown
				z	other
007/05	RR	ǂf	Reduction ratio (1st byte)	a	low reduction (less than 16:1)
				b	normal reduction (16:1 to 30:1)
				c	high reduction (31:1 to 60:1)
				d	very high reduction (61:1 to 90:1)
				e	ultra high reduction (over 90:1)
				u	unknown
				v	reduction ratio varies
007/06–08			Reduction ratio (2nd–4th bytes)	- - -	(actual reduction ratio, such as 018 for 18:1)
007/09	COL	ǂg	Color	b	black & white (monochrome)
				c	color
				m	combinations of the two above
				n	unknown
				z	other

(continued)

FIGURE 37 *Continued*

USMARC Byte	RLIN Display	OCLC Display	Name of Field	Code	Meaning
007/10	EML	‡h	Emulsion	a	silver halide (i.e., silver-gelatin)
				b	diazo
				c	vesicular
				m	mixed
				n	not applicable (for microopaques only)
				u	unknown
				z	other
007/11	GEN	‡i	Generation	a	first-generation preservation master negative
				b	printing master (includes nonarchival first-generation camera negatives)
				c	service copy
				m	mixed generation
				u	unknown
007/12	BSE	‡j	Base	a	safety base, undetermined
				c	safety base, acetate undetermined
				d	safety base, diacetate
				i	nitrate base
				m	mixed base, nitrate and safety
				n	not applicable (item does not have a film base; e.g., microopaques)
				p	safety base, polyester
				r	safety based, mixed
				t	safety base, triacetate
				u	unknown
				z	other

SOURCE: Crystal Graham, Serials Cataloging Section Head and Microforms Cataloging Coordinator, University of California, San Diego.

007, Byte 11: Generation. Although all the data elements in the 007 field have value, the generation element, 007 byte 11, is critically important and should always carry meaningful data. Here the cataloger indicates which generations have been made:

"a" = the first-generation preservation master

"b" = another type of master (that is, either a printing master or a camera negative that does not meet preservation requirements)

"c" = the service copies

The 007 "generation" subfield serves two purposes: it indicates the generation and indicates adherence to preservation standards.

The 007 byte 11 is set to "a" only for first-generation preservation master negatives *that also meet national standards for film stock, processing, enclosures, and storage.* (The relevant standards are discussed in chapter 4.) If the camera negative does not meet these standards, which include strict guidelines for temperature and humidity control, it must be coded as type "b" along with printing masters. The preservation staff will typically make this determination.

OCLC and RLG use the "generation" subfield to identify records for master negatives automatically and to process them either for enhanced screen displays (such as RLIN provides, as does OCLC in its Union List Subsystem) or to create batches of records for sending in tape form to another network or to LC. Only records with the "a" or "b" code will be pulled for the OCLC/RLG record exchange. In addition, generation coding permits librarians and users to determine whether a master negative exists from which copies can be obtained either through interlibrary loan or purchase.

007, Byte 12: Base.

This code was originally defined as indicating safety base ("a") or not a safety base ("b"). The code was expanded to indicate the specific film base (for example, acetate or polyester) after research showed that safety films have different life expectancies. (See the discussions in chapter 4 regarding the 100-year LE rating for acetate and LE-500 rating for polyester bases.) Consequently, as figure 37 shows, this subfield now calls for specific information on the base type of all microform generations.

The practical benefits of careful encoding in the "base" subfield should be clear. In the future, should experience or research reveal a problem with certain film bases, the institution would be able to identify its microforms of that type and begin to screen them more carefully, change the climate-control conditions where they are stored, copy them onto other bases, or take other precautionary measures.

The international preservation effort relies in large part on the adequacy of institutional bibliographic control activities. It may often be difficult to determine which data element to use (e.g., whether a film base is nitrate, safety base acetate, safety base polyester, etc.), but staff should resist the temptation to code elements as "unknown" except when this option is unavoidable.

When an institution catalogs a title produced through a preservation microfilming program, a single record represents all three generations: the preservation master, the printing master, and the service copies (assuming all three are produced). A separate 007 field is input for each generation. If there is a service copy for use by library patrons, that 007 field is entered first, followed by the 007 for the camera master and the 007 for the printing master.[25]

> 1st 007 = service copy 007 byte 11 = c
>
> 2nd 007 = first-generation master 007 byte 11 = a
>
> 3rd 007 = printing master 007 byte 11 = b

That order is reflected in the sample records in figure 38. It shows sample values for the fixed fields describing a master negative in the OCLC, RLIN, and

---

25. The examples here follow the order prescribed for OCLC and CONSER participants: c, a, b. Others may have different practices. Variant orders make no significant difference in how the systems handle the data, but it is easier for searchers to find the desired generation if the generations are recorded in a consistent order by all institutions.

FIGURE 38 007 Sample Record Displays

OCLC

```
007 h ‡b d ‡d a ‡e f ‡f a012 ‡g b ‡h a ‡i c ‡j p
007 h ‡b d ‡d b ‡e f ‡f a012 ‡g b ‡h a ‡i a ‡j p
007 h ‡b d·‡d b ‡e f ‡f a012 ‡g b ‡h a ‡i b ‡j p
```

RLIN

```
MMD:d OR: POL:a DM:f RR:a012 COL:b EML:a GEN:c BSE:p
MMD:d OR: POL:b DM:f RR:a012 COL:b EML:a GEN:a BSE:p
MMD:d OR: POL:b DM:f RR:a012 COL:b EML:a GEN:b BSE:p
```

USMARC

```
007 hdafa012bacp
007 hdbfa012baap
007 hdbfa012babp
```

SOURCE: Crystal Graham, Serials Cataloging Section Head and Microforms Cataloging Coordinator, University of California, San Diego.

USMARC display formats. In this example, the one-character codes indicate that the microform being cataloged has the following characteristics:

All three generations are microfilm reels (‡b "d" in OCLC, "MMD:d" in RLIN).

The service copy (indicated by "c" in ‡i and GEN) is positive ("a" in ‡d and POL), while the master negative and printing master (‡i "a" and "b" or GEN "a" and "b") are negative polarity ("b" in ‡d and POL).

All three generations are on 35mm film ("f" in ‡e and DM).

The reduction ratio is in the low range, 12:1 ("a012" in ‡f and RR).

It is black-and-white ("b" in ‡g and COL).

Its emulsion is silver halide ("a" in ‡h and EML).

Three generations exist:
a service copy ("c" in ‡i and GEN);
the first generation, which also qualifies as the preservation master ("a" in ‡i and GEN);
a second-generation printing master ("b" in ‡i and GEN).

It was produced on a safety base of polyester ("p" in ‡j and BSE).

MARC Field 245: Title Statement

The general material designation "microform" is given in the catalog record in square brackets at the end of the title proper in MARC field 245, as shown in the following example:

245 10 Poems [microform] / by Emily Dickinson ; edited by two of her friends, Mabel Loomis Todd and T.W. Higginson.

MARC Field 533: Reproduction Note

The 533 field provides most of the information relating to the microform. Although the 533 is a repeatable field, only one 533 should be created for each book or serial title. (It may be repeated in records for archival materials.) It can include the information needed to describe all the generations that are produced and to cover filming done over a period of years (as may be the case when filming serials).

The 533 field may be given in AACR2 form on a cloned record that otherwise contains a pre-AACR2 description, enabling catalogers to use cataloging templates to format this field. When reproductions have been created by different agencies or in different microformats, separate bibliographic records should be created for each one rather than giving multiple 533 fields.

‡*a: Type of Reproduction.* The type of reproduction is given first, e.g., "Microfilm." The ‡a code is implied and not actually entered in the record on RLIN or OCLC.

‡*m: Dates of Publication and/or Sequential Designation of Issues Reproduced.* Subfield m is used for microfilmed serials to describe the extent of the original publication that has been reproduced. It is required in records for preservation masters of serials, even when the entire run was microfilmed. The subfield was defined in the early 1990s and does not appear on earlier records. This information is critical for communicating exactly which issues have been filmed so that other institutions will not discard other portions of the serial run in the erroneous belief that those issues have already been preserved.

The data in ‡m are given in the form specified for holdings data rather than the form prescribed for field 362. Follow guidelines in the *CONSER Editing Guide* for formatting ‡m.[26]

‡*b: Place of Reproduction.* The place given should be that of the agency responsible for the reproduction (given in ‡c), not the place of the filming if it is done by an outside contractor. If both the responsible agency and the contractor are included in the 533, ‡b should give the place of the responsible agency (as explained in the discussion of ‡c), not the place of the filmer. Thus, a microfilm produced by Research Publications for UCLA would appear as follows:

533 Microfilm. ‡b Los Angeles : ‡c University of California, Los Angeles : ‡c Research Publications, ‡d 1985. ‡e 25 microfilm reels ; 35 mm.

‡*c: Agency Responsible for Reproduction.* In the past, there was some confusion about how to interpret the "agency responsible for reproduction" data element—whether the repository arranging for the filming or the agent that

26. See additional discussion of its use in Anne Merdinger Kern and Elise Thall Calvi, "Use of USMARC Field 533 Subfield M in Bibliographic Records for Preservation Microform Masters of Serials," *Microform Review* 22 (spring 1993): 60–3.

does the filming should be recorded as publisher. The ALA/ALCTS Task Force on Bibliographic Control of Microform Master Negatives called for clarification on this point. Subsequently, a rule interpretation issued by LC clearly identifies the "agency responsible for the reproduction" as the agency "that selected the material to be filmed, arranged for filming, exercised control over production formats, has overall responsibility for quality, etc."[27]

The responsible agency should always be given in the catalog record, and the preparation staff should make every effort to include the name of the responsible agency on the BIBLIOGRAPHIC RECORD target. When the agency does not appear on the microform, the information should be provided in brackets, as shown here:

> 533 Microfilm. ‡m 3-8 (1945-1950) ‡b [La Jolla : ‡c University of California, San Diego], ‡d 1993. ‡e 2 reels ; 35 mm.

The name of the agency from which to secure copies or the agency that made the microform should be given if the agency is named on the microform (unless, in the case of a serial, it is likely to change with a new contract). When the name of the library and the filming agency both appear in a formal statement on the target, the entire statement is given in ‡c.

> 533 Microfilm. ‡m 1943-1968. ‡b Evanston, Ill. : ‡c Filmed by Research Publications for the American Theological Library Association, ‡d 1992. ‡e 1 reel ; 35 mm.

When the library and filming agent are given in separate statements, each is transcribed in a separate ‡c.

> 533 Microfilm. ‡b Washington, D.C. : ‡c Library of Congress Preservation Microfilming Program : ‡c Available from Library of Congress Photoduplication Service, ‡d 1994. ‡e 1 reel ; 35 mm.

‡d: *Date of Reproduction.*
The dates of the filming are given when available.

> 533 Microfilm. ‡m 1943-1968. ‡b Evanston, Ill. : ‡c Filmed by Research Publications for the American Theological Association, ‡d 1993-1994. ‡e 25 microfilm reels ; 35 mm.

Ongoing filming is indicated by an open date (e.g., ‡d 1994–) in ‡d.

‡e: *Physical Description of Reproduction.*
The extent of the reproduction is given in terms of the specific material designation "microfilm reel(s)." Polarity is not included in the physical description area of the 533 field. A single 533 is used to describe several generations, often of differing polarity. Polarity is specified in byte 03 of the appropriate 007 field.

---

27. *Library of Congress Rule Interpretations,* chapter 11.

‡f: Series Statement of Reproduction. In the rare case when preservation microfilms are part of a series, the series statement of the microform is given in ‡f. If the series is traced, the series is traced in field 8xx in AACR2 form. This field is important for identification of records in microform sets, such as those cataloged in the ARL Microform Project.

‡n: Note about Reproduction. Subfield n is newly defined. Prior to its definition, notes relating to the microform were tagged "500" and input following field 533. These included "Filmed with:" notes that provided the titles of other items included on the microfilm. These are now given in ‡n. Other possible notes include "Issues filmed out of order," "Missing pages," or other significant anomalies in the reproduction.

> 533 Microfilm. ‡m 1935-1939. ‡b New York : ‡c New York University, ‡d 1975. ‡e 6 microfilm reels ; 35 mm. ‡n Missing pages 50-92. ‡n Some issues filmed out of order.

It is important for the preservation administrator to report this information to the cataloger for inclusion in the bibliographic record.

‡7: Fixed-Length Data Elements of Reproduction (Field 539 on OCLC). As mentioned in the discussion of MARC field 008, ‡7 of field 533 was defined to carry the fixed field data relating to the microform. To provide subfield designations for each element, OCLC defined field 539 to carry the ‡7 information. Providing coded data relating to the microform is optional. LC and CONSER have opted not to use field 533 ‡7.

MARC Field 583: Action Note

The 583 field was created to record processing and reference actions for archives and manuscripts. In July 1987, its use was expanded to allow institutions to record local preservation action related to an item, such as notes on its condition or methods of treatment that have been or will be performed, including the decision to film. The definition of the field was expanded to give greater possibilities for automating preservation functions, but few institutions are yet exploiting its potential. Terms in the *Standard Terminology for USMARC Field 583* must be used in this field, and responsibility for that terminology rests with the Preservation and Reformatting Section of ALA/ALCTS.[28]

One drawback of the 583 field is that some preservation technologies emerge rapidly, but the process of revising and gaining approval of guidelines such as the *Standard Terminology* is often slow. For example, many institutions have begun to require application of polysulfide treatments such as the IPI SilverLock™ process (discussed in chapter 4) and would like to record those in the catalog

---

28. For the current version, see *Standard Terminology for USMARC Field 583,* prepared by the Preservation of Library Materials Section, Resources and Technical Services Division, ALA (July 1988). A revised draft is being developed as of this writing and will be available from ALA/ALCTS (see appendix B).

record for future management purposes. The 583 field seems to be the logical place to record such information, but the treatment has not yet been approved for inclusion in the *Standard Terminology.*

Institutions involved in preservation microfilming may use the 583 field to record the decision to microfilm a title and then to indicate the filming is complete. For example, the following record might appear before filming:

> 583 ‡a Will reformat ‡c 19940217 ‡k Northeast Document Conservation Center

After filming, the record would be updated as follows:

> 583 ‡a Reformatted ‡c 19940604 ‡f NEH RLG APMP ‡i microfilm ‡k Northeast Document Conservation Center

The 583 field may be used in conjunction with queuing, as shown in these examples, but it is not a substitute for the separate record for the preservation microfilm required by the *ARL Guidelines.*

The 583 field cannot be used in OCLC bibliographic records for books or serials due to the master record structure of that database. Instead, libraries have the option to use the PRES field of the local data record if they choose to participate in the KPMP Preservation Union List, described previously. In that case, the field is used to record the decision to microfilm a title and then to indicate the filming is complete. Thus, when you have decided to film the *Journal of the British Gardeners' Association,* the 583 field might appear as follows before filming:

> PRES ‡3 1-4 1907-1911; ‡a will reformat; ‡c 19940114; ‡i microfilm; ‡k Preservation Resources

After filming the record might be updated as follows:

> PRES ‡3 1-4 1907-1911; ‡a reformatted; ‡c 19940517; ‡i microfilm; ‡k Preservation Resources; ‡l original retained

Whatever the local benefits of using the field for such purposes, you are also required to create a separate bibliographic record for the preservation microfilm in accordance with the *ARL Guidelines.*

MARC Field 776: Additional Physical Form Entry

At present, different formats of a work must generally be cataloged in separate online records. If a reference work were held in paper, microform, and CD-ROM, the three versions would be found in three separate catalog records; this causes considerable frustration among users. Following the landmark Multiple Versions Forum sponsored by LC in Airlie, Virginia, in 1989, there has been increased activity on this topic, and some steps have been taken to address this issue.[29]

---

29. Perhaps the best summary of the multiple versions issue and its connection to AACR2, the *LC Rule Interpretations,* etc., is Crystal Graham, "Microform Reproductions and Multiple Versions."

The ALCTS Committee on Cataloging: Description and Access (CC:DA) issued *Guidelines for Bibliographic Description of Reproductions,* which recommends conventions for displaying records for versions of the same work in different physical formats.[30] This document also outlines some of the difficulties with communicating records with multiple tiers of information among online systems.

Numerous proposals have been made to include codes in bibliographic records to facilitate the display of related records in online systems. The first code to be implemented, the 776 field, is used to link the record for a microform reproduction to the record for the original hard copy, if one exists. Required for LC and CONSER catalogers, this field is optional for other institutions. Coding instructions are given in the *ARL Guidelines* (see appendix E) and the *CONSER Editing Guide.*

Full versus Minimal Level Cataloging

The issue of full versus minimal cataloging was resolved to a large extent by the adoption of the *ARL Guidelines.* The *Guidelines* call for the application of retrospective conversion standards to the creation of bibliographic records for preservation microfilms while specifying full coding of the preservation-specific fields (the general material designation, and fields 008/23, 007, and 533).

When AACR2 was first published, the national bibliographic networks mandated that all new cataloging conform to the new rules (as interpreted by the Library of Congress) in terms of description and in choice and form of access points. Catalogers had to create records for microforms according to the new rules, even when records for the original publications were available in the database, in their card catalogs, or in the *National Union Catalog.* To minimize the expense of full-level original cataloging, some libraries elected to create the new records at the minimal level. As a result, the catalog record for the master microform, the official record for the nation's "archival" copy, did not have subject headings, added entries, and many notes.

With the encouragement of preservation librarians, RLG modified the standards of its database. With this modification, catalogers can create bibliographic records for preservation microforms by copying the records for the originals without upgrading the bibliographic description or choice of access points to the forms prescribed by AACR2. This change was essentially an application of the standards used in retrospective conversion projects to records for microform reproductions, and the practice became the cornerstone of the *ARL Guidelines.*[31]

Occasionally, libraries need to prepare bibliographic records for preservation microfilms for which no source record is available. In that case, they may choose to apply the base-level standards set forth in the *ARL Guidelines* that are somewhere between minimal level and full level. The *Guidelines* urge cataloging institutions to consider the nature of the material—its intellectual content and its

30. *Guidelines for Bibliographic Description of Reproductions* (Chicago: ALCTS, 1995).

31. For a fuller discussion of this issue, see Crystal Graham, "Microform Reproductions and Multiple Versions," 217–19.

Several options are available to create bibliographic records for microform master negatives. Current guidelines recognize the need both to contain costs and to provide an acceptably full catalog record. *Columbia University Libraries, Preservation Division.*

bibliographic characteristics and consequent access requirements—to determine whether the level of cataloging should exceed the base level set of data elements. For purposes of access, fuller levels of cataloging are generally preferable.

When cloning records, the *ARL Guidelines* require libraries to verify name, series, and uniform title headings against the Library of Congress Name Authority File (LCNAF). If an AACR2 form of the heading is found in the LCNAF, it is used on the microform record. LC and CONSER require their catalogers to formulate an AACR2 heading if one has not already been established in the LCNAF. The *ARL Guidelines,* on the other hand, allow libraries to input headings without revision if they do not conflict with the LCNAF.

Of particular importance to preservation librarians are the preservation data elements of the MARC 007 field. As noted previously, neither the fill character nor code "u" for "unknown" should be used in MARC field 007 other than for the "original versus reproduction aspect" code. It is incumbent on preservation administrators to supply relevant data to catalogers about film base, reduction ratio, and other technical characteristics of the microfilm.

OCLC libraries set the encoding level to "K" (minimal level cataloging) when they are "Announcing a Commitment to Preserve," as described in the "Advance Cataloging" section. These records are coded as minimal level to indicate that the filming details are not complete and to prevent the record from being locked on OCLC. Other than the technical details to be added after filming, the records are already fully cataloged.

It is sometimes seen as expedient to produce minimal level records having extensive "unknown" codes and headings that do not meet AACR2 requirements. This practice saves money, but the records are less useful than they otherwise would be. This shortcut should be used judiciously, and only after extensive justification—a cataloging impact statement of sorts—has been prepared. If the record for an existing film has an aberrant heading, or if the description it gives is incomplete, a searcher may not be able to determine whether a microform found is exactly the same as the volume being searched. Also, if the MARC coding is inadequate, it may not be possible to determine if a master exists or, if it does, who holds it—information that is needed if a library is to follow procedures recommended in chapter 2. The "generation" code must be input in the 007 field so the record will be included in the OCLC/RLG record exchange.

Subject Headings

Within the statement of principles, the *ARL Guidelines* call for the provision of subject access. Libraries are urged to retain subject headings when cloning a record from the original hard copy publication and to include subject headings when creating a new record for a microform master. The *Guidelines* encourage, but do not require, verification of topical and geographic subject headings against the appropriate LC authority file. The final report of the ALA/ALCTS Task Force on Bibliographic Control of Microform Master Negatives strongly reiterates the need for subject access.

The *ARL Guidelines* also encourage funding agencies to support creation of records that—because they include subject headings—exceed the base level ARL specified. The guidelines subsequently adopted by NEH for microfilming projects allow funding for creation of one subject heading for each bibliographic record.

A solid body of research indicates the usefulness of subject headings in machine-readable records, and institutions should seek to conform to the ARL recommendations. However, as the *Guidelines* note, it is appropriate to consider the nature of the material and its consequent access requirements when formulating a cataloging policy regarding subject access.

Special Concerns in Archives and Manuscripts Control

Unlike books and serials, archival and manuscript collections are rarely cataloged item by item. Their contents are too numerous and less amenable to standardized treatment. If these difficulties were not sufficient to inhibit widespread cataloging, another would surely do so: Because each manuscript or archival record is unique, archivists are unable to distribute costs via shared cataloging on bibliographic networks, and because all cataloging would therefore be expensive original cataloging, no institution could afford the cost of doing large amounts of it. Consequently, archival collections are generally cataloged at the collection or series level rather than at the item level.

Guides and Indexes

In providing access to the contents of collections, archivists traditionally rely on guides, inventories, series descriptions, checklists, and their own knowledge of what the collections contain. When specific collections are filmed, archivists frequently prepare checklists, indexes, sales lists, or brochures that are not unlike materials produced by commercial microform publishers. NHPRC strongly encourages the preparation of guides and indexes, and its *Microform Guidelines* gives detailed instructions.[32]

As more and more archival collections are filmed, the guides and indexes that provide access to them also multiply, and it becomes increasingly difficult to determine what items are available on film. This search inefficiency constitutes a real problem. Archives and manuscripts are valuable research materials, and users need to know that microfilms exist so copies may be borrowed or purchased, thus perhaps saving an expensive research trip.

Archivists have long recognized the value of broad, general guides. In the past two decades, some useful ones have been issued. A number of large repositories, such as NARA and LC, have produced catalogs of microforms encompassing their entire collections. The *National Union Catalog of Manuscript Collections* (NUCMC), published from 1959 to 1994, contains reports from scores of American repositories.[33]

In 1994 the NUCMC program discontinued the printed product in favor of identifying and entering into RLIN records describing the collections of institutions that lack the capability to catalog their own collections on a national database.[34] The NUCMC tapes are subsequently purchased and loaded by OCLC. Descriptions and locations of the materials are then available to researchers throughout the United States and around the world via RLIN and OCLC.

A Library of Congress survey of NUCMC contributors identified many institutions in which the book and serial cataloging was done on a national database but in which there was not enough cooperation between the archives and technical services staff to ensure that archival materials would be entered into that database. Since NUCMC now limits its services to institutions without access to a national database, it is imperative that OCLC and RLG members input records for their archival collections into their respective databases.[35]

Online Cataloging of Archives and Manuscripts

Archivists have taken several significant steps to apply automated control to their collections. The RLG Archives Preservation Microfilming Project from 1990 to 1994 yielded agreement about appropriate preservation elements in records for archival collections, and the *RLG Archives Microfilming Manual* that grew out of

---

32. *Microform Guidelines*, 9–11. The NHPRC guidelines have not been revised since 1986, so they place less emphasis on online bibliographic control than do the NEH guidelines and do not address this issue of online subject headings.

33. *National Union of Manuscript Collections* (Washington, D.C.: LC, 1959–1994). Available for purchase from the Cataloging Distribution Service, LC, Washington, DC 20541.

34. For more information about this program or to submit reports, contact National Union Catalog of Manuscript Collections, Special Materials Cataloging Division, Library of Congress, Washington, DC 20540-4375; telephone (202) 707-7954; fax (202) 707-6269; Internet: nucmc@mail.loc.gov.

35. Tabb, "Collections Services Update."

the project includes a solid section on archival control, with field-by-field discussions of critical data elements in the MARC record.

The Archival and Manuscripts Control (AMC) format was designed to provide automated support not only for access but also for acquisition, accession, and management of archival materials at either the collection level (such as the papers of Daniel Webster) or for individual items (a letter from Webster to his lawyer). Format integration replaces the AMC format (and all other formats) with a single format that can be used to describe all materials. One of the key concepts of format integration is to provide data elements for archival control for all forms of material. With the advent of format integration, catalogers no longer have to decide between using the AMC or books format but, rather, can record all bibliographic data in a record for textual materials under archival control.[36]

Sometimes only selected portions of an archival collection are filmed, so the collection-level record needs to describe both paper and microfilm. To accommodate this situation, archives catalogers may create composite records with data elements describing both formats on a single record.

When an entire collection is filmed, the archives may choose to create a separate bibliographic record for the microfilm, rather than a composite record. This is particularly desirable when the microfilm is housed separately from the original to clarify for users what is available in each location. It also provides a bibliographic record other institutions can use when cataloging microfilm they have purchased from the creating repository. Such records can be created by using the cloning technique described previously for books and serials.

The bibliographic records for archives include the same coding as books and serials (fixed field "form of item" code and 007s) as well as 533 fields describing the reproductions. However, general material designators and 776 fields used for books and serials are not appropriate for composite records.

While all variable-length fields are valid for all types of materials under format integration, a few merit special mention for their value in cataloging archival materials.

MARC Field 530: Additional Physical Form Available Note.   The 530 field is used to describe which materials are available in microformat. It may include the source, cost, and order number to facilitate acquisition of microfilm copies by other institutions or individuals.

> 530 ǂa The microfilm is available (190,434 frames on 150 reels. 35 mm.) ǂb from Manuscripts and Archives, Yale University Library, ǂc at cost. ǂd Order no. HM225.

MARC Field 533: Reproduction Note.   In addition to the data elements described in the books and serials section, archives catalogers frequently make use of ǂ3 to specify what portion of the collection has been microfilmed.

---

36. *Format Integration and Its Effect on the USMARC Bibliographic Format,* prepared by the Network Development and MARC Standards Office (Washington, D.C.: Cataloging Distribution Service, LC, 1995).

533 ‡3 Correspondence files, 1900-1950. ‡a Microfilm. ‡b Smith-ville, CA : ‡c Smithville College Archives, ‡d 1992. ‡e 37 microfilm reels ; 35 mm.

The 533 field may be repeated to describe different portions of the collection.

MARC Field 540: Terms Governing Use and Reproduction Note.
The 540 field alerts users to possible restrictions on use during the filming proc-ess and informs users that the microfilm is to be consulted in lieu of the originals. The online record might appear as follows:

540 The entire collection is available on microfilm. Patrons must use film instead of the originals.

MARC Field 555: Cumulative Index/Finding Aids Note.
The 555 field provides information about the availability and location of a guide to the microfilm and may describe the degree of physical, intellectual, or bibliographic control that exists. Some examples are

555 0 ‡a Inventory available in repository ‡c Folder level control.

555 0 ‡a Microfilm guide available on Reel 1.

Whenever possible the finding aids should be filmed along with the archival materials.

MARC Field 583: Action Note.
The 583 field is used for preservation action notes. In the RLIN system, this field is also available in the Archival Control (ARC) segment. The 583 field may be used in bibliographic records on OCLC to record processing and reference actions for archives and manuscripts. Libraries should bear in mind that this field displays only at the institution where the record was created, and it should not be considered a substitute for a fully coded bibliographic record.

583 ‡a Will reformat ‡c19940217.

What to Do

Unfortunately, deciding what level of control to provide for microforms of archives and manuscripts is often difficult. Choices abound. Materials can be cat-aloged either by collection or item by item in a national database, and machine-readable descriptions may appear in local databases. Reports can be submitted to the Library of Congress for online distribution through the NUCMC program if the institution does not have access to OCLC or RLIN. Guides and indexes may be prepared either to individual collections or to the complete microform hold-ings of a repository. Access may be provided through a public card catalog. Or, as sometimes happens, nothing can be done at all—materials can be filmed and in all likelihood the existence of the films soon forgotten. For example, the landmark microfilming projects of the Historical Records Survey (1935 to 1942) are now lost.[37] Circumstances are far from ideal, yet much progress has been made in the past few years.

Controlling microforms of archives and manuscripts, either by collection or item by item, should be handled like cataloging books and serials: by staff trained in the intellectual and technical aspects of the work. The best advice on what to do is probably the least welcome: make decisions on a case-by-case basis, considering the potential usefulness of the microfilms in the scholarly community and the cost of providing access to them.

The minimum form of access to microfilmed archives and manuscripts is an archival inventory or guide produced in accordance with accepted archival practice.[38] Ordinarily, a finding aid should be created before a collection is filmed, or it may be developed as part of the editorial preparation work discussed in chapter 3. If so, it can be updated to show details about the microfilm, such as the reel and position within the reel where a given item may be found; of course, that work can be quite time-consuming. Generally speaking, few collections that are worthy of the expense of microfilming have so little value that minimal finding aids, by themselves, suffice. Prior to filming, project staff should review the accuracy and completeness of the collection description and finding aids that will be filmed with the collection.

Collections having progressively wider potential audiences should be given progressively more-detailed finding aids. Collections having the largest number of potential users warrant the fullest possible access. Examples might include the papers of J. Robert Oppenheimer, U.S. census population schedules for a state or region, papers of the Southern Tenant Farmers Union, or the LC Shaker Collection. These microfilm collections are, in effect, publications and should be treated as such. Some might be given full analytical cataloging (cataloging in which records are provided for component parts as well as the collection as a whole). Others might be cataloged as collections and provided with extensive printed guides and indexes. In all cases, collections of wide interest should be cataloged on OCLC or RLIN (either directly or through the NUCMC program).

There is no doubt that cataloging archival materials in the national databases is a boon to users and repositories nationwide and internationally. Online cataloging is a requirement in archival as well as library preservation projects funded by the NEH Division of Preservation and Access and is strongly encouraged in those supported by NHPRC. The vastly expanded access options are a positive value. In planning archives microfilming projects, however, preservation administrators and catalogers must be alert to the implications of their bibliographic control decisions. Admittedly, full bibliographic records for archives and manuscripts can be quite lengthy and arduous to produce. There is a vast array of optional fields appropriate to archival materials, and some of these (such as the 520 summary/abstract field, the 545 biographical or historical note field, and the 6xx

---

37. Clifton Dale Foster, "Microfilming Activities of the Historical Records Survey, 1935–42," *American Archivist* 48 (winter 1985): 45–55.

38. See Frederic Miller, *Arranging and Describing Archives and Manuscripts* (Chicago: SAA, 1990).

subject fields) can extend over many screens. The archives staff must determine which records warrant this level of control in the online environment, and for which a simple reference to the local finding aid will suffice.

Searching

The ability to do effective searches for microforms depends greatly on all institutions adhering to sound bibliographic control practices outlined in this chapter. The systematic exchange of preservation master microform records between OCLC and RLG (which includes international registers of microform masters) minimizes the chances that duplicate filming will occur.

The ability to do effective searches depends first on all institutions adhering to cataloging guidelines provided in this manual. The OCLC and RLG computers extract for exchange only microform records that include the "a" (for master negative) or "b" (for printing master) in byte 11 of the 007 field ($\pm$i in OCLC, GEN in RLIN).

Second, the goal of full online access remains limited by some features of the record exchange program.

Records queued for preservation action using RLIN's QD field or OCLC's Union List are not exchanged because these options do not yield an 007 field.

Records for preservation microfilm created in the USNP are visible only in the OCLC Union List Subsystem. Those without access to the system should consult the *USNP National Union List*.

The OCLC/RLG record exchange is now on a monthly basis, and it takes some additional time for the exchanged records to be processed and loaded. For some projects this frequency may not be sufficient, and other searching processes may be required. For example, in some cases an OCLC participant may need to establish a searching account on RLIN and vice versa, to avoid the delay. Very rarely, more-extensive arrangements might be warranted. For example, two institutions filming in one subject area and recording their filming decisions on different national databases might agree to search each other's local online catalogs.

OCLC and RLIN include mechanisms to identify microform records when performing searches. In OCLC, users may qualify database searches to retrieve only records for microforms. This speeds preservation searches by screening out the records for hard copy versions of a title.

The RLIN system uses asterisks to flag microform records in clusters. RLIN also lets users qualify searches by GEN code and 5xx notes, and to refine the search to retrieve only preservation microform records. There is also a simple mechanism for searching the QD fields in RLIN.

Both OCLC and RLG support sophisticated search strategies. To take best advantage of the system capabilities, it is often best for cataloging staff to do the searches or to train preservation staff to do them effectively.

Conclusion

The subject of bibliographic control of microforms is challenging for the non-specialist. Fortunately, there are many sources of expert help, whether from a professional cataloger or from outside sources such as the bibliographic networks, professional associations such as ALA and SAA, or the staffs of funding agencies such as NEH and NHPRC.

Even where duplicate effort is not a threat, ignoring the need for bibliographic control results in unconscionable waste. As one advocate of high-quality cataloging has opined, "If a book is important enough to film, it is important enough to catalog."[39] To make a preservation master negative and keep its existence a secret is to undermine the purpose of the work and misuse the medium. The time, effort, and expense of selecting and preparing items, filming them, and storing the microform properly warrant the best bibliographic control that current technology can provide.

For the first time in history, we are now capable of building a logical national bibliographic database. Through the Z39.50 protocols and the Internet we also have the facility to link electronically the individual databases that make up this logical one. The means for providing universal access to microforms are at last becoming available. At the same time, libraries have moved rapidly toward integrated local automated systems, including online public access catalogs. It is now possible for a patron to use a terminal to locate microforms of collections held anywhere in the United States. If a text was digitized in conjunction with the microfilming, it may be electronically delivered to the patron in a matter of minutes or even seconds. As we work to provide universal online public access to microforms, the worst that could happen would be to develop the capability of full access and discover that access to microforms was limited not by technology or standards or even political disputes, but merely by the failure of libraries and archives to catalog them.

At the beginning of this chapter was the prediction that sufficient bibliographic control of microforms might not be achieved until the next century. With the help of you and your colleagues to build on the achievements described here, Myrick's "long wait" is nearly over, just in advance of the year 2000.

Suggested Readings

ALCTS Task Force on Bibliographic Control of Microform Master Negatives. "Final Report and Recommendations (Jan. 2, 1992)." Adopted by ALCTS as Board Document 92.23 and published in the *ALCTS Newsletter* 3, no. 8 (1992): 102–4.

Association of Research Libraries. *Guidelines for Bibliographic Records for Preservation Microform Masters.* Prepared by Crystal Graham. Washington, D.C.: ARL, Sept. 1990. Reprinted in *Microform Review* 21 (spring 1992): 67–73 and in appendix E of this manual.

---

39. Patterson, "Hidden Treasures," 77.

Graham, Crystal. "Microform Reproductions and Multiple Versions: U.S. Cataloging Policy and Proposed Changes." In *Serials Cataloging II: Modern Perspectives and International Developments,* edited by Jim E. Cole and Jim Williams, 213–34. Binghamton, N.Y.: Haworth, 1992. Also published as *Serials Librarian* 22, nos. 1/2 (1992).

Kaplan, Diane E., and Nancy F. Lyon. "Bibliographic and Archival Control." In *RLG Archives Microfilming Manual,* edited by Nancy E. Elkington, 39–50. Mountain View, Calif.: RLG, 1994.

Cataloging Tools

Anglo-American Cataloguing Rules. 2d ed., 1988 Revision. Ottawa: Canadian Library Association; Chicago: ALA, 1988 (with Amendments 1993).

Bibliographic Formats and Standards. Dublin, Ohio: OCLC, 1993– . (loose-leaf)

Cataloging in RLIN II. 3d ed. Stanford, Calif.: RLG, 1987– . (loose-leaf)

Cataloging Service Bulletin. Washington, D.C.: LC, Processing Services, 1978– . (loose-leaf)

CONSER Cataloging Manual. Jean L. Hirons, ed. Washington, D.C.: Serial Record Division, LC, 1993– . (loose-leaf)

CONSER Editing Guide. 1994 ed. Washington, D.C.: Serial Record Division, LC, 1994– . (loose-leaf)

Hensen, Steven L. *Archives, Personal Papers, and Manuscripts: A Cataloging Manual for Archival Repositories, Historical Societies, and Manuscript Libraries.* 2d ed. Chicago: SAA, 1989.

Library of Congress Rule Interpretations. 2d ed. Washington, D.C.: LC, Cataloging Distribution Service, 1990– . (loose-leaf)

OCLC Guide to Preservation Data. Dublin, Ohio: OCLC, 1991.

RLIN Supplement to USMARC Bibliographic Format. Stanford, Calif.: RLG, 1989– . (loose-leaf)

Standard Terminology for USMARC Field 583. Prepared by the Preservation of Library Materials Section, Resources and Technical Services Division, ALA. July 1988.

USMARC Format for Bibliographic Data: Including Guidelines for Content Designation. Washington, D.C.: Cataloging Distribution Service, LC, 1994– . (loose-leaf)

6

Calculating and
Controlling Local Costs

I nto the mid-1980s, only a handful of libraries and archives in the United
States engaged in preservation microfilming, either in-house or through commercial services. However, as institutions have been faced with increasing
numbers of deteriorating materials and as the threat of brittle paper has been
documented and publicized, more institutions have started to look seriously into
the scope of their local problems and explore options for solving them. One of the
early difficulties in that process was the dearth of information about how much
it costs to develop and operate a preservation microfilming program.

That situation changed in 1986, with the publication of the RLG cost study,
conducted from 1984 to 1985.[1] Since then, more libraries and archives have
mounted preservation programs and launched microfilming projects, and greater
attention has been paid both to quantifying the cost of microfilming and to providing effective cost controls, so that now there is a reasonable body of literature
on the topic.[2] An important trend in these studies has been the move to quantify
costs beyond those of the filming operation itself—to capture not only the costs
strictly within the project, such as personnel involved in preparation and inspection, but also those that often occur outside the preservation unit, such as staff
members involved in review and selection, bibliographic control and archival
description, and catalog maintenance. These studies provide a healthy antidote to
the temptation simply to absorb or write off those sometimes hidden costs.[3]

---

1. Patricia A. McClung, "Costs Associated with Preservation Microfilming: Results of the Research
Libraries Group Study," *Library Resources & Technical Services* 30 (Oct./Dec. 1986): 363–74. McClung's
study also formed the basis for the "Cost Controls" chapter in the first edition of this book.

2. Along with McClung's RLG study, key resources are Laurie Abbott, "The APMP Cost Study," in
RLG Archives Microfilming Manual, edited by Nancy E. Elkington (Mountain View, Calif.: RLG, 1994),
171–86; and Carolyn Harris, Carol Mandel, and Robert Wolven, "A Cost Model for Preservation: The
Columbia University Libraries' Approach," *Library Resources & Technical Services* 35 (Jan. 1991): 33–54.

3. Harris, Mandel, and Wolven, "A Cost Model for Preservation," 34, point to that lack as a flaw in
previous cost studies.

This chapter has a dual purpose: to provide a framework for estimating and analyzing the costs of preservation microfilming and to suggest ways to reduce or control costs. There is a wide range of possible procedures and standards inherent in those choices, all of which have cost implications that must be weighed in balance with the goals and resources of the operation. Cost ranges used as examples in this chapter, especially those for library materials, can only be considered indicative because they are based on published library findings of the 1980s; the RLG archives cost study dates from the early 1990s. There is no substitute for careful analysis of your own local variables in the budget planning process.

Chapter 1 outlined many programmatic benefits of cooperative preservation microfilming projects. Cooperative projects also offer fiscal advantages. They provide a central resource for grant writing and financial management and may centrally handle some of the work of estimating costs. Filming agents, storage facilities, and other service providers may offer better prices to a group of institutions than to a single one. Of course, a key advantage is that such projects seem especially attractive to funding agencies.[4]

Cost Variables

Given all the possible cost variables, as well as the number of people capable of having an impact on costs, reliable documentation of the cost of preservation microfilming is hard to come by. The variables make it difficult, if not impossible, to come up with a simple and reliable formula for estimating potential costs, but a growing body of information is available to inform planning decisions. This information can be adapted and applied to your local situation to arrive at accurate estimates. In addition, institutions can collect data—both from "test runs" in advance and from cost analysis of actual operations—to gain further insight into budgetary considerations. Several cost studies outline a methodology that other institutions can employ to predict costs.[5] You should also contact institutions that have long experience with preservation microfilming, as they can provide current and practical tips on cost issues.

Libraries now tend to use a figure of $90 to $100 as the cost for filming a typical 250-page book. That figure includes all direct costs (selection, preparation, filming, inspection, and bibliographic control) associated with producing three generations of the film but excludes overhead and indirect costs.[6] Those numbers can serve well for gross estimating purposes. However, if you were to

4. See Carolyn Harris, "Cooperative Approaches to Preservation Microfilming," in *Preservation Microfilming: Planning & Production* (Chicago: ALA/ALCTS, 1989), 55–65.

5. The Columbia University Libraries cost model (see Harris, Mandel, and Wolven) is designed to be used as the basis for cost analysis in other institutions, and RLG offers to share the worksheets from its archives cost study.

6. This figure is currently accepted as a reasonable average. In addition, it reflects the average costs of the eighteen collections filmed under the RLG Great Collections Microfilming Project IV, where the average volume was 243 pages and the $90 average per volume included the filming charges and all direct institutional costs to produce three generations of 35mm film according to RLG guidelines; indirect costs

examine closely the specific details of an actual project, or even activities associated with filming a single title, you would find that the costs vary significantly from item to item, project to project, and institution to institution.

Several analyses show the variance in microfilming costs among institutions. RLG conducted a cost study from 1984 to 1985 involving seven institutions participating in its first cooperative preservation microfilming project. Total costs for all steps in the process had a median cost of $48.20, but institutional costs diverged 56 percent to 149 percent from the median.[7] As any researcher exploring microfilming costs will observe, because books vary in size, shape, contents, and physical condition, each is singular in the labor and other requirements related to filming it.

Similar or even greater variables apply to filming archival collections. RLG's Archives Preservation Microfilming Project included a cost study among fourteen institutions from 1992 to 1993. Total costs there, including all phases from selection through postfilming activities, ranged from 23¢ to 91¢ per frame, with a median of 50¢ per frame.[8] None of these studies included overhead costs such as utilities, equipment depreciation, time spent by the institutional purchasing or accounting offices, and so on.

Of course, the number of pages per title to be filmed makes a significant difference in the cost per volume. Some of the other variables may not be as obvious. Characteristics of the materials, such as their age or imprint dates, condition, completeness, organization, format, and subject, can contribute significantly to variations in the costs of selection, preparation, filming, and cataloging. Often these are not variables within your control. Additional variables, which may or may not be subject to managerial intervention, include personnel (level of staff, local labor costs, experience, skills, turnover, productivity), equipment and supplies, space and physical setup, filming agent, technical standards, and level of cataloging required. The remaining variables are necessarily subject to managerial control and include the actual procedures for the project or operation and how the project is administered. Decisions regarding planning, management, and implementation provide the greatest opportunity for controlling costs and achieving maximum results for each dollar spent.

Four major categories of costs are affected by your preservation microfilming policies and procedures regarding (1) labor, (2) supplies and equipment, (3) contract services, and (4) management and overhead. None of these exists in a vacuum. Take, for example, labor costs. If computers, software, and printing equipment are poorly maintained or ill-suited to the task at hand, labor costs may be higher than they need be because of equipment failure, operational inefficiencies, or administrative time required for troubleshooting. Similarly, labor costs may be affected by the physical arrangement of work spaces as well as the pattern (or lack thereof) of workflow through the "pipeline." Geographical location, the available labor pool, and institutional policies concerning benefits also influence

---

and administrative overhead are not reflected in that figure. Confirmed in a Dec. 20, 1994, telephone conversation between Nancy E. Elkington (RLG) and the author.

7. See McClung, "Costs Associated with Preservation Microfilming," 365.

8. Abbott, "The APMP Cost Study," 185.

labor costs. It is essential that preservation administrators—who will be most likely to recognize the expenses incurred by such limitations—make clearly articulated and well-documented reports to those in a position to provide the support or resources that can ensure maximum cost efficiency.

Labor Costs

Labor costs, the first category, are determined by the levels of staff assigned to various tasks as well as the amount of time it takes to complete each one. Too often, the availability of personnel takes precedence over a systematic pairing of people and tasks. Especially in a first filming project, managers may tend to overestimate the kind of judgment needed for a task. Take care not to overuse professional staff. The decision regarding level of staff should follow an appraisal of the required skills and expertise. It is especially useful to analyze the staff level needed for the most time-consuming tasks such as preparation because the greatest cost savings can be achieved there.[9] Despite careful planning, even the best-laid plans can be disrupted by any number of events (such as illness, family leave, vacancies, or strikes) that can wreak havoc on the budget and schedule.

Management strategies can significantly influence the effective use of the personnel budget. It may be possible to hire and retain faster, better qualified people if you pay an attractive salary. Effective managers will also use motivation techniques to keep morale and productivity high among staff members who are performing tedious and repetitive tasks. It is also useful to maintain a production orientation in which production goals are set and staff members are accountable for meeting them.

Some labor costs will be incurred outside the preservation unit, and these costs should be recognized, whether or not they are explicitly quantified. Curators, bibliographers, or selectors probably will be involved in selection decisions. Searching and cataloging will often be done in the cataloging department, and archivists may revise finding aids and offer advice on preparation decisions. Circulation staff members may retrieve and reshelve items. The acquisitions department may feel the impact if searches result in replacement orders. The tendency in most projects has been quietly to absorb those costs, but in a large filming operation the level of preservation activity will reverberate throughout the library or archives.[10]

The format and characteristics of the materials being filmed will have a significant impact on labor costs.

> Some subject areas or collections may require review for retention or withdrawal on an item-by-item basis and, sometimes, by more than one selection officer or curator.

> Very brittle or fragile materials must be handled more carefully, thereby slowing down not only the preparation work but also filming and inspection.

---

9. A useful discussion of the factors involved in this decision and their cost implications is included in Abbott, "The APMP Cost Study." Both the RLG cost studies (CPMP and APMP) and the Columbia University Libraries cost model analyze the relative involvement of staff at various levels for each activity.

10. Harris, Mandel, and Wolven, "A Cost Model for Preservation," 34.

Selection decisions may have a significant impact on costs. Scrapbooks, for example, may require extensive preparation by the institution and intentional multiple exposures at the camera, as well as increased inspection time. *Northeast Document Conservation Center. Photo by David Joyall.*

Disbinding materials before filming sometimes must be done by hand (when there are floating or irregular margins, narrow inner margins, double-page plates, etc.).

Incomplete materials require that replacement pages or incomplete issues or volumes be ordered or a duplicate edition be borrowed through interlibrary loan.

Archival and manuscript materials are frequently folded, stapled, or clipped, requiring additional preparation time.

Unusual organization of an item or series may require elaborate collation and targets.

The costs relating to steps that precede and follow filming are difficult to identify. For the most part, they are for labor. Keep in mind that often a great deal of time in the prefilming phase is expended on materials that will never be filmed because during the prefilming procedures they are removed from the "pipeline" for any number of reasons. For example, according to the Columbia University Libraries cost model for a comprehensive brittle books program, only about 42 percent of the inventoried titles will make it to the stage of searching and just 83 percent of those will be filmed.

Equipment and Supplies

Direct expenses for equipment and supplies will vary according to how much of the process is performed internally and how much is contracted to a service bureau.

A major new expense may be for automation equipment. It has been clear for several years that use of personal computers and laser printers can result in great cost efficiency for the production of targets.[11] Bar code readers linked to local circulation systems may be used for inventory control and to track items through the work stream. Work stations will be needed for bibliographic control work, searching local and distant online systems, and for automating some elements of target production, as outlined in chapter 5. Personal computers will also be needed for the record keeping functions described in chapter 3.

Equipment and supplies for quality assurance are addressed in chapter 4. You will need to determine whether it is more cost effective to purchase this equipment or to pay for the services. For example, are you doing enough filming to justify purchasing equipment such as a microscope, densitometer, and so on, or should you contract with an outside lab to perform necessary tests on film returned from the service bureau?

If filming, processing, and duplication are performed in-house, it follows that substantially more equipment, supplies, and work space will be required. In that case, you may require some construction or modification for the work space or the plumbing, electrical, HVAC, and other systems. Do not overlook the significant cost of maintenance contracts for cameras, processors, and other equipment.

Contract Services

Cost of contract services, the third cost category, can be substantial. In general, the smaller the operation, the greater the number of services you may wish to contract out. For a small, one-time project, it may not make sense to equip and staff an internal inspection unit. But the trend now, even for large research

---

11. Margaret M. Byrnes and Nancy E. Elkington, "Containing Preservation Microfilming Costs at the University of Michigan Library," *Microform Review* 16 (winter 1987): 38.

libraries with well-established in-house operations, is to use a wide variety of contract services to control costs and increase institutions' filming capacity. Some institutions contract with service bureaus, while others work through co-operative programs.

Chapter 1 addresses the cost issues and qualitative factors to weigh in choosing between in-house and contract services. It is most common for institutions to contract out various elements of the technical (filming) process, but a wide range of contract services is available:

preparing materials for filming

camera work (the actual filming)

processing the camera negative

inspecting film

chemical testing for residual thiosulfate and the effectiveness of polysulfide treatment

producing additional generations or copies of the film

bibliographic control

storing the preservation master negatives and/or printing masters

Cost controls that relate to specific services are covered later in this chapter.

Management and Overhead

To direct costs—the salaries, supplies and equipment, and services purchased from external sources—must be added the fourth cost category: management and overhead. Overhead or indirect costs are those that are often difficult to calculate in an isolated project or operation but, nevertheless, represent real costs that must be taken into account.

In a typical preservation microfilming operation, a list of indirect costs might include

hiring and training expenses

management

upgrading skills and retraining

record keeping and paperwork

The institution will also incur overhead costs including

space (not only for staff work areas and equipment, but for storage of materials in various stages of the filming queue)

utilities (water, light, heating and cooling)

building maintenance and janitorial services

equipment depreciation

postage and miscellaneous supplies

recruiting, payroll, and benefits administration costs in the personnel office purchasing and business department operations

systems office

senior administration

Though these may be difficult to estimate and quantify, they are real costs, and the administration must be aware of their impact.

Budget Planning

There are different ways to approach the institutional budget for preservation microfilming. It may be included as a line item in the collection development or technical services budget. In large research institutions, preservation departments may have separate allocations.

Grant funds are also available for developing programs and carrying out special projects. Some of the key issues related to grants are addressed in chapter 1.

Typical library or archival filming activities fall into four categories:

ongoing preservation microfilming routines

"over-the-counter" orders and mail orders from individuals and other institutions

special projects (grants, projects focusing on branch libraries, subject collections, or special or rare materials)

cooperative projects involving other institutions

Decisions that affect budget planning will be based partly on the type of activity. It is possible for an institution to have activities under way simultaneously in all four categories.

Institutions usually plan preservation budgets by calculating the general level of fiscal support for preservation activity rather than the number of items to be preserved. However, calculating unit costs can produce realistic projections of work loads and curb unrealistic expectations. There are several ways to figure the costs of an existing microfilming operation. The most realistic is to divide the time spent (or salary expenditures) by actual units of productivity, such as number of titles searched or volumes filmed, and then factor in other expenses for supplies, equipment, processing, etc., as appropriate.[12]

Each institution and type of filming activity will have its own idiosyncrasies—special procedures and internal paperwork—that will affect the cost of the filming operation. To get a handle on such variables for budget planning, divide the workflow into distinguishable steps. Then, consider the level of staff and approximate time required for each step as well as the equipment and service needs. However, before you can achieve a reasonable degree of accuracy in that exercise, you must make decisions regarding the procedures, standards, and policies to be followed. The more clearly these are articulated, documented, communi-

---

12. A good model for this approach is the Columbia University Libraries study, reported in Harris, Mandel, and Wolven, "A Cost Model for Preservation."

cated, and understood, the greater will be the efficiencies on the time side of the cost equation. Ongoing review and analysis that incorporate input from employees who actually perform the tasks will also contribute to increased efficiencies as experience is gained.

Calculating Local Costs

Until recently, most of the data on the cost of microfilming related either to the per-frame charges for the filming step alone or else to general institutional averages that were not sufficiently detailed to be compared to other situations. Figures 39 and 40 show the data that have been gathered in two published cost studies. Although the exact cost figures are now somewhat dated, they will be useful in showing where expenses may be incurred and in showing the relative time spent in various steps.

Whether for a grant proposal or for internal budget planning, it is often necessary to prepare a budget well in advance of embarking on a preservation microfilming project. Appendix F is a model worksheet you can use to calculate your own institution's microfilming costs. The worksheet provides a framework you

FIGURE 39   RLG APMP Cost Study Data

Activity*	TIME (mins.)			Average Cost ($)
	Low	High	Median	
1. Retrieval			46	$ 10.37
2. Preparation			2,280	365.08
3. Target preparation			267	58.43
4. Instructions to filmer			79	26.78
5. Transportation			64	15.39
6. Filming				783.00
7. Inspection			375	86.69
8. Preparing material for retakes			33	9.66
9. Retake inspection			66	15.30
10. Creation/revision of finding aid	4	3,600	115	35.35
11. Cataloging/AMC record control			51	16.45
12. Labeling boxes and shipment to storage			51	11.14
13. Reversing camera readiness			81	17.68
14. Withdrawals	5	60	7	2.20
15. Consultation and administration	10	1,920	257	87.48
Total			3,772	$1,541.00

*The cost study (conducted 1992–93) is for a two linear-foot group of archival materials.

SOURCE: Laurie Abbott, "The APMP Cost Study," in *RLG Archives Microfilming Manual,* edited by Nancy E. Elkington (Mountain View, Calif.: RLG, 1994), 171–86.

FIGURE 40 Columbia University Libraries Cost Model

Activity	Staff Time* (mins.)	Total This Category	% of Total Time
1. Inventory:		10.0	3.5
Shelfread and locate missing items	5.2		
Prepare worksheet	4.8		
2. Bibliographer review	3.8	3.8	1.3
3. Searching:		26.6	9.2
Columbia/RLIN searching	21.4		
Circulation charging	5.2		
4. Transport volumes to Preservation	4.6	4.6	1.6
5. Preparation:		42.0	14.5
Collation	15.1		
Target preparation and reel programming	10.6		
Queuing monographs	11.9		
Precatalog serials	1.8		
Pack/unpack	2.6		
5A. Interlibrary loan procedures[†]	102.2	102.2	35.3
6. Quality control	10.2	10.2	3.5
7. Postfilming activities		20.2	7.0
Process retakes	6.0		
Other postfilming processes	3.0		
Paperwork and packing to send master and printing master to storage	0.6		
Process service copy	10.0		
Clear circulation record	0.6		
8. Bibliographic control		30.2	10.4
Catalog monographs	27.3		
Catalog serials	0.6		
Label film	2.3		
9. Withdrawal		39.5	13.7
Bibliographic withdrawal (pull cards and delete online record)	31.9		
Item withdrawal	7.6		
Total	289.3		100

*Time estimates are given on a per-volume basis.
[†]Interlibrary loan procedures are carried out during preparation, between collation and targeting.

SOURCES: Carolyn Harris, Carol Mandel, and Robert Wolven, "A Cost Model for Preservation: The Columbia University Libraries' Approach," *Library Resources & Technical Services* 35 (Jan. 1991): 33–54; supplemented by Janet Gertz (Columbia University), electronic mail correspondence with the author, Jan. 3, 1995.

can adapt, depending on your particular circumstances. Based on ones prepared for use in the RLG cost study and subsequent projects, the model is meant to be suggestive rather than prescriptive. It does not include costs of storage. Because the basis of calculations can be so different for different media, the worksheet provides separate spaces for estimating costs of books and serials, archival materials, photographic images, drawings, and other materials such as scrapbooks or ephemera.

To aid you in planning or analyzing your own program, the remainder of this chapter provides a step-by-step discussion of some of the budgetary considerations inherent in a preservation microfilming operation. Whenever possible, available time and cost data are provided. The key steps are

prefilming
   selection
   preparation
film production
quality assurance
bibliographic control
storage

Prefilming Activities

The time required for prefilming work relates closely to the kind of materials handled in the project, especially their format and physical characteristics, but also to the efficiency of institutional practices. Some of the cost variables involved in that decision have already been addressed in this chapter.

The wide range of costs reported by the seven institutions in the 1984 RLG cost study illustrates the "variables" theme of this chapter. For the institution at the low end of the range, it took an average of 10.5 minutes to complete all of the steps per title. On the high side it took 83 minutes per title. Factors affecting the spread were the searching hit rate (less than 1 percent compared to more than 50 percent) and the amount of curatorial review required (a cursory amount was needed in a special collection of poetry, while item-by-item decisions were made on a melange of social science materials from the open stacks). Similarly, collation and target preparation took longer for social science monographs with their foldouts, charts, and maps than for the more straightforward history collections. Of course, the number of pages in the volumes also contributed to less time spent on prefilming activities.

The Columbia University cost model assumes a different kind of microfilming operation that more nearly resembles a routine brittle books program in which microfilming is but one option. This model estimates that prefilming steps require just over three hours per volume, and 54 percent of that time is spent on completing volumes through interlibrary loan. All told, prefilming operations account for 65 percent of the staff time required in the Columbia model.

RLG's APMP cost study provides solid data on the prefilming costs of archival and manuscript materials. Even more than with printed materials, the costs vary tremendously, depending on the nature of the collections and the extent to which they have been processed, organized, and used by readers in advance of the microfilming preparation. One institution's 2-foot sample required only 43 minutes for prefilming work, while another's required 265 hours. On average, prefilming activities accounted for 73 percent of the overall average time and 64 percent of the overall average costs.

Selection of Materials

For purposes of analysis, the selection steps are divided as follows: identification of materials, searching, and curatorial review.

Identification

One of the most important factors in a preservation microfilming budget is the universe from which materials will be selected for filming. Identification costs are mostly for labor associated with pulling materials, searching for those not on the shelf, getting them in call-number order, and preparing basic worksheets for use in selection and subsequent stages. As previously stated, the subject matter, format, completeness, age, and condition of the materials significantly affect the filming costs. These factors also have an impact on the degree to which searching, curatorial review, and physical preparation are necessary.

Some institutions will have a clear idea about what materials they want to film. More often the identification is among the most time-consuming and costly processes. The more clearly the category or specific collection is defined in advance of a project, the fewer the surprises, financial and otherwise, down the road. The cost of selection can be especially high if professional staff are required to review every title. As a program is fine-tuned, categorical policy decisions are possible (such as a decision to replace all heavily circulated, unique titles without further review), which will focus selectors' attention on the thorniest decisions and reduce the total amount of labor involved.

In general, the characteristics of materials to be filmed—that is, monographs and serials, archives and manuscripts, letterpress volumes, scrapbooks, and so on—drives virtually all of the other costs in the process. Time studies can be conducted for searching and processing materials; costs related to the number of volumes or pages can be calculated based on a sample of the materials. If a filming operation is focused on items screened from circulation or other service points in the institution, it still may be possible to sample this population and derive useful figures for making budget predictions.

Searching

Searching of materials, as described in chapter 2, may represent another labor-intensive aspect of the process. With so many bibliographic tools now available online (see chapter 5), the primary cost is for staff time and searching charges in OCLC and RLIN.

Keep in mind that the factors that affect searching costs today will be changing rapidly over the next decade. Converting the U.S. *National Register of Microform Masters* to machine-readable form and loading the records in OCLC and RLIN was a major boon, and online access to the Canadian, European, and

British registers of microfilm masters will affect hit rates worldwide. However, materials in non-Roman alphabet languages in the *NRMM* have not yet been converted to machine-readable form, though a proposal to do so is now pending; in the meantime, slower, manual searches of *NRMM* are still required for those. Further economies may become possible through such developments as the automated "technical services work station" concept being developed at Harvard University, LC, and elsewhere.[13]

As more records are available online or in electronic sources, the labor costs should decline in comparison to those for searching in printed sources, and the accuracy of searches should increase. However, as more and more volumes are filmed, hit rates should continue to rise, thus increasing the relative cost of searching per volume filmed. How this will affect the searching process remains to be seen. Of course, archival and manuscript materials, which by definition are unique, will not require the searching step.

When a particular subject collection or other identifiable category can be identified in advance, a sample searching analysis can be designed to collect the following information:

What is the projected hit rate in OCLC or RLIN?

What additional sources might be appropriate to search for availability of other copies, microfilms, editions, reprints, or formats to minimize duplication of effort?

Design a search strategy in which tools with the highest hit rate are searched first, as outlined in chapter 2. Tools with very low hit rates should be eliminated altogether. If the hit rate in all printed sources is low, then the cost of searching should be measured against the cost of the duplicative filming that might occur if the searching step were eliminated.

The following formula may be used to determine the break-even point between searching and filming: $C = P \times T/H$ where:

C is the cost of microfilming (including all steps, not merely camera operations)

P is the pay per hour for searchers

T is the average hours per search

H is the average number of hits per search

The formula can be further refined to reflect the real hit rate in a source—that is, the number of acceptable replacements found, not just the number of citations. For example, if 75 percent of the hits in a source qualify as replacements, the formula would be: $0.75H = P \times T/C$.[14]

---

13. The "technical services work station" is a technology that brings together online the tools for cataloging. LC has stressed development of this technology as a way to increase cataloging output and improve cost efficiency, and forthcoming Windows-compatible releases from OCLC and RLIN will support integration of these databases and off-the-shelf software.

14. The basic formula and refinements of it are offered in Robert DeCandido, "Considerations in Evaluating Searching for Microform Availability," *Microform Review* 19 (summer 1990): 116–18.

Curatorial Review

The materials to be filmed determine the extent to which curatorial review should be employed. Occasionally there are sufficient funds or justifications for filming a particular collection or group of materials "end to end" without item-by-item evaluation by a selector. Other times it is possible at the outset to establish criteria for inclusion or exclusion of materials, which can be applied by staff at lower salaries. Obviously, the most expensive option is the one in which highly paid professional bibliographers or subject specialists spend time making item-by-item judgments as to whether something warrants preservation microfilming.

Several institutions have adopted policies that illustrate these principles at work. After a cost study of its ongoing microfilming operation, the University of Michigan began automatically to film or replace any heavily circulated, brittle volume that was not part of a set and for which the library owned no other copies or editions.[15] For its Foundations of Western Civilization project, Columbia University determined that only volumes that had brittle paper *and* were structurally unsound should be considered for microfilming.[16] For the most effective use of resources, it is usually best to complete searching before curatorial review, but there will certainly be situations in which this strategy is not appropriate.

The goal of such guidelines is to require curatorial review only for the selection decisions that are most difficult. As a general principle, searching is much less expensive than making judgments.

Preparation

Preparation (described in chapter 3) requires little in the way of equipment and supplies; most of the cost is in labor. This is an area where good management, workflow planning, and standardization may yield great benefits because much of the cost effectiveness of the filming operation is determined in this step.

The Columbia University model projects 144 minutes per volume for preparation. Of that amount, 42 minutes are for preparation, target production, reel programming, and packing materials for shipment to the filming lab. The remaining 102 minutes are for interlibrary loan procedures to complete titles. Although the interlibrary loan costs are averaged across the program in the Columbia model, the bulk of the time is spent on borrowing pages and volumes to complete serials. Titles often require compiling volumes from multiple lending libraries, and multiple requests may be placed since some libraries are unwilling to lend serials. The ILL time estimates, given on line 5A of figure 40, include: searching OCLC, RLIN, and other sources to find potential lenders; filling in the manual ILL form; entering data in the project database to track ILL progress; placing the request through RLIN or other means; receiving the item and retrieving it from the library's ILL unit; updating the project database; returning the item to the ILL unit; and processing, packing, and shipping the borrowed volumes. When Columbia

15. Byrnes and Elkington, "Containing Preservation Microfilming Costs," 37–8; for background, see Janet Gertz, "The University of Michigan Brittle Book Microfilming Program: A Cost Study," *Microform Review* 16 (winter 1987): 32–6.

16. Harris, Mandel, and Wolven, "A Cost Model for Preservation," 35.

FIGURE 41   Preparation Time for Four Archives Collections

Collection	Length		Time
American Sugar Newspaper Clippings	3	feet	20 hours
Horace B. Hudson Papers	3.25	feet	122 hours
Washington & Kandiyohi Co. Naturalization Records	3	feet	23 hours
E. G. Hall Papers	2.5	feet	43 hours
	11.75	feet	208 hours
Average hours per foot			17.7 hours per foot

SOURCE: Lydia Lucas, Head of Technical Services, Division of Archives and Manuscripts, Minnesota Historical Society. Based on collections prepared in 1984.

applied its cost model in budgeting for a project to film pamphlets, the time estimate for interlibrary loan activities dropped to an average of 61 minutes per volume because fewer of the pamphlets were incomplete.[17]

In the RLG archives study, preparation work (excluding retrieval, targeting, preparation of instructions to the filmer, and transportation) accounted for 61 percent of the *time* excluding filming and 49 percent of *costs* excluding filming. The imbalance between time and cost was due to the use of nonprofessional staff for 59 percent of the preparation work.[18]

Further insight into the preparation-time question is provided by figure 41. To process four different collections ranging in length from 2.5 to 3.25 linear feet, the Minnesota Historical Society found that it took as little as 20 hours to prepare 3 linear feet of newspaper clippings from the American Crystal Sugar Company and as much as 122 hours to prepare 3.25 linear feet of the Horace P. Hudson Papers. While the American Crystal Sugar Project required a minimum amount of preparation for its newspaper clippings that were to be discarded after filming, the manuscripts and clippings in the Hudson Papers were not so straightforward. They required unfolding, cleaning, tape repair, organizing by subject and chronology, preparing technical instructions to the camera operator, transcribing some illegible text, preparing targets, writing a biographical sketch and detailed content descriptions, as well as preparing a folder list.

The complexity of most archival and manuscript collections makes it impossible to generalize with any degree of confidence about average times.[19] However, there can be little disagreement with the assertion that this type of material takes much longer to prepare than books. The Minnesota Historical Society's experience, like that of the participants in RLG's archives microfilming project,

17. This information based on electronic mail correspondence between Janet Gertz (Columbia University) and the author, Mar. 10 and June 14, 1995.

18. Abbott, 174–6.

19. Unpublished data supplied from 1985 personal correspondence between Patricia A. McClung and Lydia Lucas, Head of Technical Services, Division of Archives and Manuscripts at the Minnesota Historical Society.

points out that it is more efficient to film collections that have already been processed than to try to combine filming preparation work with arrangement and description.

Collation and Physical Preparation

The collation and physical preparation part of the process generally includes testing for brittleness, collating, removing duplicates, performing some physical treatments, preparing instruction sheets for camera operators, and completing paperwork to accompany materials to the camera operator (and after filming to accompany materials and film to the cataloging department). In the 1984 RLG CPMP cost study, this part of the process took between 5 and 45 minutes per title. The Columbia cost model estimates about 15 minutes, most of which is done by support staff.

Certain features, such as folded maps, illustrations that extend across inner margins, and missing text or pages, are likely to create difficulties farther along the line. Materials should be examined before disbinding and filming, and potential problems should be flagged. Preservation microfilming is sufficiently expensive that it is worth spending a few extra dollars to ensure that it is done correctly, particularly given that other institutions may discard their copies of an item based on the availability of your microfilm.

The extent to which other preparation steps should be undertaken (such as erasing extraneous marks and annotations, mending torn pages, etc.) is a policy matter that warrants careful thought and clear guidelines. You might consider building in a cutoff point for the staff performing the prefilming tasks so that they can bump a problem item out of the normal workflow for reevaluation before spending excessive amounts of time and effort on it.

You need to decide how much time the staff will devote to remedial activities such as mending and erasing pencil marks. For the sake of cost efficiency, only those defects that will interfere with the filmed image should be addressed during preparation. If items are to be retained, it is generally best to do repairs and conservation treatments after filming. If the originals are to be discarded, you may save money by using repair procedures that do not conform to accepted conservation guidelines.

Your decision about whether to disbind volumes will have cost implications. Filming agents' preferences and practices can differ, and some items are more easily filmed bound, while others are best filmed as single leaves. (See chapters 3 and 4.) Talk with the filming agent during the planning stage to determine what will best suit the needs of the collection and the goal of cost effectiveness. Hand disbinding of volumes will add significantly to the time requirement and, therefore, to costs.

If many items have missing pages or other parts, there may be interlibrary loan costs and terminal time. In the Columbia University model, 71 percent of the preparation time was spent on interlibrary loan work to obtain missing text for a filming project that involved many serials (as shown in figure 40). Interlibrary loan procedures can also create a backlog that will require additional storage space. Because of the delays and expense in conventional interlibrary loan, cooperative projects may include an agreement among participants to expedite loan requests.

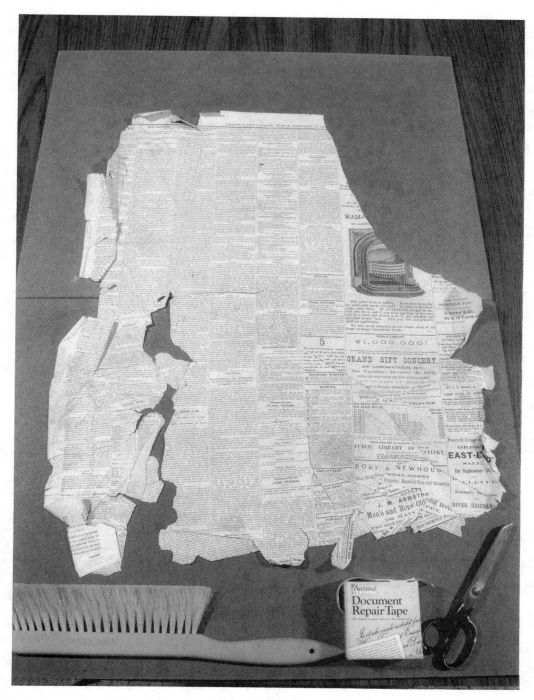

Badly damaged materials call for cost analysis. If sent to the camera in their present condition, such materials will slow production and incur a higher filming charge. Repository staff may be able to do the repairs less expensively than the filming agent, but the most cost-effective solution may be to seek a copy in better condition. *University of Kentucky Libraries Reprographics Department. Photo by Lewis Warden.*

Target Preparation and Reel Programming

As seen in earlier chapters, target preparation is closely linked with the collation step and is crucial to ensure that the film can be used successfully. In the RLG CPMP cost study, target preparation took from 5 to 27 minutes per title, depending on the materials.[20] Columbia University's current figure of 10 minutes per volume is a reasonable average. Targets can be produced by relatively inexpensive staff, which helps control costs. In the RLG archives project, target production for the two-linear-foot sample took an average of 4 hours and 27 minutes, at a cost of $58.43; another 79 minutes and $26.78 were spent to prepare instructions to the filmer.

On a moderate to large-sized project, a personal computer and laser printer will quickly pay for themselves in labor savings. Linking your software that produces targets to your online catalog or bibliographic network will also speed this operation and reduce errors that can be introduced in re-keying. Systems office personnel may be able to help you design and link databases for this application.

Before material can be sent to the filmer, you may need to organize it to indicate the order and amount of materials to be included on a particular reel. Established routines for reel programming and the use of tools designed to aid this process, cited in chapter 3, should help you control the cost.

Film Production

The institution must first choose the filming approach that will yield the highest quality in the most cost-effective way. Chapter 1 outlines factors to weigh in choosing between in-house and contracted filming, and chapter 3 provides a strategy for evaluating filmers and gathering appropriate pricing information. Chapter 4 discusses cost factors related to the selection of roll film versus microfiche.

Computing the Filming Cost

The per-frame charge from a service bureau or internal filming laboratory can be one of the most straightforward pieces of the preservation microfilming budget. However, it is imperative that the contract or agreement specify exactly what the per-frame charges include; what standards for camera work, processing, printing, and inspection will be applied; and when and at what rate special charges may be assessed.

Recent figures for the production of three generations vary widely. In the RLG Great Collections Microfilming Project (GCMP) III, from 1992 through 1993, the filming charge ranged from 23¢ to 34¢ per frame, with an average of 27.8¢ per frame. In RLG's GCMP IV (1993 to 1995), the average was 27.9¢ per frame, but costs ranged from 20¢ to 48¢ per frame.[21] Those figures do not include

---

20. McClung, "Costs Associated with Preservation Microfilming," 371.

21. GCMP III ran from January 1992 through December 1993, and GCMP IV from February 1993 through January 1995. These figures were provided by Nancy E. Elkington (RLG) in electronic mail correspondence with the author, Nov. 28, 1994.

the libraries' costs for pre- and postfilming operations, but only for the direct charges by the filming agent.

If the materials can be filmed two pages per frame (two-up), the filming costs can be determined by a simple formula: divide the number of pages by two, multiply that by the per-frame charge, and add the cost of additional frames for targets or other extra material. For routine books, assume an average of eleven targets per volume.[22] The formula can be modified for archival collections, which are typically filmed "one-up," that is, one document per frame. Targets might add 10 percent to the frame count for archival materials.[23] Add to that figure the costs for a printing master and a service copy, if you plan to produce these at the same time rather than on demand.

Filming costs may be significantly different for microfiche than for 35mm roll film. Chapter 4 provides an analysis of the differential that may apply to labor, filming, and duplication charges associated with microfiche production.

The materials you select for filming will also affect the pricing. Chapter 3 outlines a strategy for providing a sample for filming to get a reliable price estimate from the filmer. Filming costs are generally higher for some types of materials:

Newspapers usually take more time to film and proceed at the rate of one page per frame rather than two.

The disbinding decision may increase or reduce costs, depending on factors outlined in chapter 3.

Foldouts in a book might have to be filmed at reduction ratios different from the rest of the volume, and often they must be filmed in sections. In addition, they sometimes fall apart when they are unfolded and need to be mended before filming.

Oversize materials and items with foldouts must be handled carefully and may not fit in a book cradle. Bound items that are filmed on the camera bed without a book cradle are sometimes held flat with a large sheet of glass, which must be removed and replaced after each shot. This is a time-consuming procedure if implemented routinely.

Scrapbooks can rarely be filmed "as is." It may be necessary to set up each page for filming by removing materials, unfolding items, etc. Writing instructions to the filmer or preparing instructional flags may be quite complex, and multiple exposures may be required to capture all text acceptably.

If there is a wide tonal variation in paper within a volume or among archival or manuscript materials, more camera adjustments and frequent use of exposure meters are necessary.

Letterpress volumes typically present challenges in controlling exposure, which may slow production and increase costs.

22. Average established by Erich Kesse, University of Florida, and recommended by RLG in a memorandum from Nancy E. Elkington to RLG Member Representatives, June 6, 1994.

23. RLG memorandum from Gay Walker to Patti [*sic*] McClung, Oct. 6, 1988.

Collections with items of widely varying size, such as some drawings or archival collections, may require frequent changes in reduction ratios, which will slow production and increase costs.

Color and continuous-tone filming costs are higher than those for black-and-white filming.

Prices from the filming agent will generally include costs for technical and bibliographic inspections based on your specifications for quality control. Some institutional filming labs are not accustomed to the inspections required for preservation microfilm, so be sure the filming charge includes the lab's costs for inspection. In either case, you will also need to factor in the costs to conduct in-house inspections for quality assurance after the materials and film are returned from the filming agent.

Duplication

In its strictest sense, a preservation microfilming program requires a three-copy system: the *master negative* used only to create a *printing master* from which all *service copies* are made. In realistic terms, though, this may require some planning and analysis. Once you decide how many generations to produce and what film to use for each, cost calculation is straightforward.

The cost of duplication must be included in the filming budget. In a preservation microfilming project, the printing master should be a silver-gelatin copy from the camera negative. Service copies may be on whatever film stock the institution prefers. *Preservation Resources.*

Duplication charges for roll film are generally calculated by the foot rather than the frame. Creation of black-and-white silver-gelatin duplicates may run anywhere from $14 to $40 per forty-meter reel, though prices in the range of $20 to $30 are more common. A reel typically holds about five to eight average-sized monographs.

Fiche duplication costs are generally quoted on a per-sheet basis. Prices of $1 to $2 per sheet are typical, and it takes about three microfiche sheets to reproduce a typical 250-page book.

Chapter 4 ("Generations" section) stresses that a preservation microfilming program should routinely create all three generations during the initial production phase. However, there may be a few cases where it is sufficient to create the master negative and one or more service copies for your in-house use. Then, if and when you receive an order for a copy, you can proceed to generate the printing master, assuming that the request may signal potential demand. If you choose that option, be aware that the duplication cost is likely to be greater than it would have been initially because you will pay not only the duplication charges but also the storage facility's retrieval charges. If duplication is not done by the storage facility, there may be transportation charges between the storage facility and the duplication lab.

Weigh both costs and anticipated use in deciding what type of film to use for the service copies. Chapter 4 outlines factors to evaluate in choosing among silver-gelatin, diazo, and vesicular service copies.

Quality Assurance

The filmer should conduct technical and frame-by-frame inspection before returning microfilms to the client. Then staff members in the library or archives conduct inspections to assess the film's technical quality and check for bibliographic problems. A thorough, well-documented, and well-equipped quality assurance program requires that the staff members be knowledgeable about technical specifications and that they pay careful attention to whether the films meet technical standards for legibility and permanence, are bibliographically correct, and are unblemished. Chapter 4 provides guidance on quality assurance procedures.

Institutions with in-house filming facilities differ in how they divide the inspection tasks between the camera operator and the preservation office. However, most would agree that whether filming is done in-house or under contract with a service bureau, the camera operator's work must be checked carefully once the film is returned.

When planning time allocations, remember that inspection will sometimes result in the rejection of film. Then time will be required to prepare materials for return to the filmer and for inspection of the retakes.

Scrupulous attention to detail, time consuming though it may be, is the only way to ensure that quality standards are achieved. Inspection times in the SOLINET cooperative filming project average 1.5 to 2 hours per reel for complete visual, technical, and frame-by-frame bibliographic inspection of all three generations of film. With an average of eight 200- to 250-page volumes per reel in the SOLINET projects, this constitutes an average of 11 to 15 minutes per volume for complete inspection. Bibliographic inspection alone requires an average of 30 minutes per reel.[24]

In the Columbia University cost model, quality control work accounts for about 10 minutes per volume. That calculation includes an assumption that 20 percent of titles may require some retakes and reinspection. Not surprisingly, the estimate dropped significantly—to less than 2 minutes per item—when Columbia applied the model to develop a budget for a project to film pamphlets.

In the RLG archives cost study, frame-by-frame inspection for content and completeness of the 2-linear-foot sample required more than 6 hours on average, making it the second most time-consuming step in the archival filming process. Fortunately, though, since bibliographic inspection can be done by nonprofessional staff, it constituted just under 6 percent of project costs.

Formats and the condition of the materials significantly influence inspection times. Some years ago, NEDCC provided figures showing that inspection of newspapers and straightforward monographs can take less than half the time required by manuscripts, scrapbooks, and special materials such as clippings and photograph albums.[25]

As a cost control measure, many institutions have implemented spot-checking procedures in lieu of complete frame-by-frame inspection. Strictly speaking, all preservation microfilm should receive frame-by-frame inspection. However, under certain conditions and within limits discussed in chapter 4, "Managing the Quality Assurance Program" section, there are cases in which less than 100 percent inspection may be acceptable.

A quality assurance program requires that the institution have specialized equipment and supplies for technical inspection. Figure 30, chapter 4, lists the necessary materials.

Bibliographic Control

The primary factors in the cost of bibliographic control are

level and quality of existing machine-readable cataloging for the original materials. The better the existing cataloging, the less time it will take to derive and adapt the microfilm cataloging from it.

desired level of cataloging for the microfilm. Depending on the materials and institutional policies, it may be possible to realize savings by using an abbreviated cataloging standard, such as the retrospective conversion (recon) level described in chapter 5.

the decision regarding retention of the original materials. Some institutions have found that it is significantly more expensive to discard materials than to retain them because of the cataloging procedures necessitated by a withdrawal from the collection. That is especially true for libraries that maintain manual card catalogs. Other institutions have found that the

24. Christina Craig (SOLINET), electronic mail correspondence with the author, Dec. 19, 1994.

25. Personal correspondence between Patricia A. McClung and Veronica Cunningham, NEDCC, Andover, Mass., Oct. 1985.

long-term costs of continuously housing and servicing brittle materials far outweigh the costs of withdrawal. That is not to say the costs should govern the decision, but rather that they have an impact on the total bill, making generalizations about cataloging costs more difficult.

staff expertise. Cataloging time will increase if you are filming materials in languages in which the catalogers do not have fluency or if you are filming materials in formats they do not typically catalog.

Cataloging costs, like those of many other steps in the process, will depend on institutional policies, level of staff required for the work, the existence of automated linkages (for example, between your local automation system and OCLC or RLIN), and the features of the collection. In the RLG CPMP study, they accounted for 8 to 12 percent of the total costs, when minimal level (or RLG recon level) standards were applied, and up to 30 percent of the total costs if full AACR2 standards were used and records had not already been converted to AACR2. The average time per title cataloged in the 1984–1985 study ranged from approximately 10 minutes to 1 hour, with costs between $2 and $20. In the Columbia University model, cataloging required about 39 minutes per monographic volume (12 for queuing and 27 for cataloging). By contrast, when Columbia applied the model to a pamphlet-filming project—with many Slavic items that required original cataloging—the projection increased significantly.

Cataloging costs are higher for some types of materials:

For certain materials, it can be difficult to locate appropriate or adequate online records for queuing, target production, and cataloging. Some may require creation of a new machine-readable record.

Some archival and manuscript materials necessitate special organization or finding aids.

Foreign language materials, especially those in non-Roman alphabets, may pose challenges not only to cataloging personnel but also for collation and other prefilming work.

Additional cost considerations relate specifically to the particular format. All formats, including monographs, pamphlets, broadsides, letters, personal papers, archives, serials, and newspapers, have inherent bibliographic issues that affect the fiscal "bottom line." For example, if indexes or other types of finding aids are developed or massively revised in conjunction with a filming project, that work might well be the most time-consuming part of the process. While this is seldom necessary for published materials such as complicated serial runs, it is often essential for materials found in archives and manuscript collections.

Archival control may involve creation or revision of both the finding aid and the online OCLC or RLIN record. This work is subject to many variables. In the RLG archives project cost study, time required to create or update the finding aid ranged from a low of 4 minutes to a high of 60 hours, with an average of almost 2 hours for the 2-foot sample. The time requirements were not related to the quantity of materials being filmed but were most influenced by whether an adequate finding aid already existed.[26] Creation or updating of the online record

---

26. Abbott, "The APMP Cost Study," 177–8.

required 50 minutes on average and correlated closely with the time spent on preparation and finding aids.

Storage

Chapter 4 outlines the requirements for proper storage of preservation master negatives and underscores the importance of that financial commitment. Other institutions will base their retention decisions on the existence of your microfilm into perpetuity, and it will become a unique resource for scholarship and other uses. Appropriate storage for the printing master and service copy should also be taken into account when planning the budget.

The exact bill for storage will vary, depending on each institution's facilities and whether it is necessary to acquire or lease space in a vault for storing the master negative. In that case, the location and size of the vault represent additional variables that influence the costs. Storage facilities will provide detailed price lists on request. Prices will vary depending on whether film can be stored in a common vault area or whether an institution decides to lease its own vault within the storage facility. You could expect to pay an annual rental fee of $50 per drawer in common storage; each drawer holds approximately 42 reels. A 600-cubic-foot vault (minimum size at the National Underground Storage facility in Boyers, Pennsylvania) rents for $3,300 per year.[27] There may be additional charges for special equipment in private vaults, such as a hygrothermograph to monitor the environment. In addition, drawers will have to be purchased for the vault at approximately $48 each. The labor, supplies (labels, packing materials, etc.), and postage required for shipping materials to the storage facility also contribute to the total costs.

You may be able to achieve some cost reduction by sharing storage facilities. For examples, members of RLG are required to use the RLG vault at National Underground Storage for film created in RLG projects and are entitled to use that vault for storage of master negatives created in other institutional projects.

Storage costs are not included in the worksheet (appendix F) because they are not one-time or project-based costs. Once you commit to creating a preservation master, your institution bears the responsibility for providing appropriate storage into perpetuity.

Inspection of stored negatives should also be factored into your financial planning. Chapter 4 outlines the requirements for inspecting negatives every two years. No cost data are yet available for this activity because its importance has only recently been recognized by the library and archival communities.

Conclusion

When calculating and controlling the costs of preservation microfilming, as with any problem that at first seems insurmountable, it is best to proceed by breaking

---

27. Staff of National Underground Storage, Inc. (Boyers, Pa.), telephone conversation with the author, Nov. 28, 1994.

it down into manageable chunks. As more institutions begin to chip away at the corpus of deteriorating materials and as efforts continue to encourage publishers and others to use alkaline paper in the future, gradual progress is evident. It is imperative that unnecessary duplicative undertakings be avoided so that scarce resources are not wasted. In this context, sharing bibliographic information about preservation masters that have been or will be created is the single most important factor in the economics of preservation microfilming at the national and international levels. For the institution, the key factors are for you carefully to compare costs and maintain a production orientation so that you complete work as quickly as possible within the quality guidelines that govern preservation microfilming.

Suggested Readings

Abbott, Laurie. "The APMP Cost Study." In *RLG Archives Microfilming Manual,* edited by Nancy E. Elkington, 171–86. Mountain View, Calif.: RLG, 1994.

Gertz, Janet. "The University of Michigan Brittle Book Microfilming Program: A Cost Study." *Microform Review* 16 (winter 1987): 32–6.

Harris, Carolyn, Carol Mandel, and Robert Wolven. "A Cost Model for Preservation: The Columbia University Libraries' Approach." *Library Resources & Technical Services* 35 (Jan. 1991): 33–54.

Hayes, Robert. *The Magnitude, Costs and Benefits of the Preservation of Brittle Books.* Washington, D.C.: CLR, 1987.

Kantor, Paul B. *Costs of Preservation Microfilming at Research Libraries: A Study of Four Institutions.* Washington, D.C.: CLR, 1986.

McClung, Patricia A. "Costs Associated with Preservation Microfilming: Results of the Research Libraries Group Study." *Library Resources & Technical Services* 30 (Oct./Dec. 1986): 363–74.

Preservation Microfilming: Standards, Specifications, and Guidelines

The following sections contain standards of the American National Standards Institute (ANSI) along with specifications and guidelines of other organizations and institutions in the United States. Copies can be obtained from those organizations, the addresses of which are included in appendix B.

Where applicable, the citation contains both the latest edition at the time this manual was prepared and the date of the first edition of the document. ANSI rules require that standards be reviewed every five years. Sometimes that review results in a revision or withdrawal of the standard, or the standard may be deemed still valid, in which case it is reaffirmed. In the latter case, the year of adoption and reaffirmation are provided, as in "ANSI/AIIM MS11-1987 (R1993)."

National and International Standards

American National Standards must meet the following stringent requirements:

They have been created under procedures that ensure open participation of all interested parties and balanced representation of affected groups during their preparation.

They are put to vote of all interested and/or affected parties and groups.

Negative ballots must be resolved to achieve a consensus of interested/affected parties and groups.

Procedures are in place to ensure due process (a means of sorting out problems experienced by interested/affected parties and groups).

Provisions for automatic review and revision ensure that the standards are kept up to date.

The following are central to preservation microfilming:

ANSI/NAPM IT9.1-1992
American National Standard for Imaging Media (Film)—Silver-Gelatin Type—Specifications for Stability.

ANSI IT9.2-1991
American National Standard for Imaging Media—Photographic Processed Films, Plates, and Papers—Filing Enclosures and Storage Containers (first edition as PH4.20-1958; subsequently ANSI/ASC PH1.53).

ANSI IT9.5-1992
American National Standard for Imaging Media (Film)—Ammonia-Processed Diazo Films—Specifications for Stability (formerly ANSI/ASC PH1.60).

ANSI IT9.6-1991, ANSI/ISO 543-1990
American National Standard for Photography—Photographic Films—Specifications for Safety Film (first edition as Z38.3.1-1943; subsequently ANSI/ASC PH1.25).

ANSI IT9.9-1990
American National Standard for Imaging Media—Stability of Color Photographic Images—Methods for Measuring (revision of ANSI PH1.42-1969).

ANSI/NAPM IT9.11-1993
American National Standard for Imaging Media—Processed Safety Photographic Films—Storage (first edition as PH5.4-c1957; subsequently ANSI/ASC PH1.43).

ANSI IT9.12-1991, ANSI/ISO 9718-1991
American National Standard for Photography—Processed Vesicular Photographic Film—Specifications for Stability (first edition as ANSI/ASC PH1.67-1985).

ANSI/NAPM IT9.13-1992
American National Standard for Imaging Media—Photographic Films, Papers, and Plates—Glossary of Terms Pertaining to Stability.

ANSI/NAPM IT9.15-1993
American National Standard for Imaging Media (Photography)—The Effectiveness of Chemical Conversion of Silver Images Against Oxidation—Methods for Measuring.

ANSI/NAPM IT9.16-1994
American National Standard for Imaging Media—Photographic Activity Test.

ANSI/NAPM IT9.17-1993, ANSI/ISO 417-1993
American National Standard for Photography—Determination of Residual Thiosulfate and Other Related Chemicals in Processed Photographic Materials—Methods Using Iodine-Amylose, Methylene Blue and Silver Sulfide (first edition as PH 4.12-c1954; subsequently ANSI/ASC PH4.8-1985).

ANSI/AIIM MS5-1992
American National Standard for Information and Image Management—Microfiche (first edition: 1975).

ANSI/AIIM MS11-1987 (R1993)
Standard for Information and Image Management—Microfilm Jackets (first edition: 1987).

ANSI/AIIM MS14-1988
American National Standard for Information and Image Management—Specifications for 16mm and 35mm Roll Microfilm (first edition: 1947). [A revision is under way.]

ANSI/AIIM MS18-1992
American National Standard for Information and Image Management—Splices for Imaged Microfilm—Dimensions and Operational Constraints (first edition: 1987).

ANSI/AIIM MS19-1993
American National Standard for Information and Image Management—Standard Recommended Practice—Identification of Microforms (first edition: 1978).

ANSI/AIIM MS23-1991
American National Standard for Information and Image Management—Practice for Operational Procedures/Inspection and Quality Control of First-Generation, Silver Microfilm of Documents (first edition, as an industry standard: 1979). [A revision is under way.]

ANSI/AIIM MS24-1980 (R1987)
Test Target for Use in Microrecording Engineering Graphics on 35mm Microfilm (first edition: 1980). [A revision is under way.]

ANSI/AIIM MS26-1990
American National Standard for Information and Image Management—35 mm Planetary Cameras (top light)—Procedures for Determining Illumination Uniformity of Microfilming Engineering Drawings (first edition: 1984).

ANSI/AIIM MS34-1990
American National Standard Dimensions for Reels Used for 16mm and 35mm Microfilm (first edition: 1968).

ANSI/AIIM MS37-1988
American National Standard for Information and Image Management—Recommended Practice for Microphotography of Cartographic Materials (first edition: 1988). [A revision is under way.]

ANSI/AIIM MS43-1988
American National Standard for Information and Image Management—Recommended Practice for Operational Procedures/Inspection and Quality Control of Duplicate Microforms of Documents and from COM (first edition: 1988). [A revision is under way.]

ANSI/AIIM MS45-1990
American National Standard for Information and Image Management—Recommended Practice for Inspection of Stored Silver-Gelatin Microforms for Evidence of Deterioration. [A revision is under way.]

ANSI/AIIM MS48-1990
American National Standard for Information and Image Management—Recommended Practice for Microfilming Public Records on Silver-Halide Film. [A revision is under way.]

ANSI/AIIM MS51-1991, ANSI/ISO 3334-1989
American National Standard for Microcopying—ISO Test Chart No. 2—Description and Use in Photographic Documentary Reproduction.

ANSI/AIIM MS111-1994
> *American National Standard for Information and Image Management— Recommended Practice for Microfilming Printed Newspapers on 35mm Roll Microfilm* (first edition: 1977).

ANSI PH1.51-1990
> *American National Standard for Photography (Film)—Micrographic Sheet and Roll Film Dimensions* (first edition: 1979).

ANSI/NISO Z39.32-199x
> *American National Standard for Information on Microfiche Headings* (first edition: 1980; withdrawn Mar. 1991). [A revision was approved in 1995 and publication by ANSI is forthcoming.]

ANSI/NISO Z39.48-1992
> *American National Standard for Information Sciences—Permanence of Paper for Printed Publications and Documents in Libraries and Archives* (first edition: 1984).

ANSI/NISO Z39.62-1993
> *American National Standard for Eye-Legible Information on Microfilm Leaders and Trailers and on Containers of Processed Microfilm on Open Reels.*

Technical Reports

AIIM TR2-1992
> *Association for Information and Image Management Technical Report— Glossary of Imaging Technology.*

AIIM TR9-1989 (R1992)
> *Association for Information and Image Management Technical Report— Color Microforms* (first edition: 1987).

AIIM TR11-1987 (R1993)
> *Association for Information and Image Management Technical Report— Microfilm Jacket Formatting and Loading Techniques* (first edition: 1987).

AIIM TR13-1988
> *Association for Information and Image Management Technical Report— Care and Handling of Active Microform Files* (first edition: 1988). [A revision is under way.]

AIIM TR26-1993
> *Association for Information and Image Management Technical Report— Resolution as It Relates to Photographic and Electronic Imaging.*

Specifications and Guidelines

The specifications and guidelines in this section contain guidance in areas not covered in current standards, and they expand the preservation provisions of the standards in highly desirable ways. Institutions that do preservation microfilming or have work done for them under contract should, as applicable, adhere closely to the advice and recommendations presented in the following specifications and guidelines.

Association of Research Libraries. *Guidelines for Bibliographic Records for Preservation Microform Masters.* Prepared by Crystal Graham. Washington, D.C.: ARL, Sept. 1990. Reprinted in *Microform Review* 21 (spring 1992): 67–73.

Canadian Cooperative Preservation Project. *Guidelines for Preservation Microfilming in Canadian Libraries.* Ottawa: NLC, 1993.

Cybulski, Walter, ed. *United States Newspaper Program Newspaper Preservation Microfilming Manual.* Albany, N.Y.: New York State Library, forthcoming.

Elkington, Nancy E., ed. *RLG Preservation Microfilming Handbook.* Mountain View, Calif.: RLG, 1992.

Elkington, Nancy E., ed. *RLG Archives Microfilming Manual.* Mountain View, Calif.: RLG, 1994.

Reilly, James M. *IPI Storage Guide for Acetate Film.* Rochester, N.Y.: IPI, 1993.

APPENDIX ■ ■ ■ ■ ■ B

Resources for Preservation Microfilming

From the following list of organizations and institutions, you may obtain assistance in virtually any aspect of preservation microfilming. The "Information Resources" section focuses on national and regional organizations, but a number of others are available. Many state or provincial archives and libraries have preservation offices designed to provide information, referrals, and even planning assistance. Several of these serve also as conduits for state-based funding programs. Some state archival agencies maintain lists of qualified filming agents, and some function as filming agents themselves, particularly for the preservation of local public records. A growing number of colleges, universities, and other cultural organizations have preservation administrators and micrographics specialists on staff who generously provide information, training, or other assistance based on their hard-won experience.

The "Service Providers" section includes filming agents, storage facilities, and consultants along with a few institutions whose filming services, while focused on in-house work, are available to other institutions. Organizations listed in this section have performed work for clients who call for adherence not only to ANSI and ISO standards but also to the guidelines of RLG or of the Canadian Cooperative Preservation Project (see citations in appendix A). Satisfactory past performance, however, is no guarantee of equally high standards in all projects, and the recommendations offered in chapter 3 should apply to the evaluation and selection of filming agents and other service bureaus. The inclusion of certain service providers in this appendix does not indicate that the quality of their work is flawless without exception or that in coming years they will continue to meet the high standards they have in the past. Inclusion in or omission from this appendix does not constitute an endorsement or dismissal of any particular organization. An extensive directory of micrographic services, supply and equipment sources, and imaging systems is provided in the *AIIM Buying Guide: The Document Management Sourcebook* (Silver Spring, Md.: AIIM, 1995 or most recent).

The information provided for each entry here includes the organization's name and contact information (including fax number and e-mail address when available) and the name of the office or position to which you should direct preservation microfilming inquiries. A brief entry summarizes the type of information or service each source is most likely to provide.

Information Resources

American Library Association (ALA)
Association for Library Collections &
  Technical Services (ALCTS)
ATTN: Executive Director, ALCTS
50 E. Huron St.
Chicago, IL 60611
phone: (800) 545-2433 or (312) 280-5038
fax: (312) 280-3257
e-mail: alcts.office@ala.org

ALCTS includes the Preservation and Reformatting Section (PARS) within which a wide range of microfilming and other reformatting concerns are addressed. The association meets twice a year and sponsors regional institutes, preconference programs, and other national continuing-education opportunities. Publications by ALCTS include the quarterly journal, *Library Resources & Technical Services,* the bimonthly *ALCTS Newsletter,* and relevant monographs. ALCTS also administers electronic resources relevant to preservation microfilming.

**American National Standards Institute
  (ANSI)**
ATTN: Director of Sales and Customer
  Services
11 W. 42nd St.
New York, NY 10036
phone: (212) 642-4990
fax: (212) 398-0023
e-mail: info@ansi.org

The American National Standards Institute is a membership organization that develops and promulgates voluntary standards for the United States and represents U.S. interests in international standards organizations. ANSI standards relating to microforms and microfilming techniques are listed in appendix A.

**American Theological Library
  Association (ATLA)**
ATTN: Director of Preservation
820 Church St.. Ste. 300
Evanston, IL 60201-5613

phone: (708) 869-7788
fax: (708) 869-8513
e-mail: atla@atla.com

ATLA's Preservation Program in the field of religion has preserved more than 28,000 books published in the nineteenth and twentieth centuries in microfiche format (some on microfilm) as well as more than 1,400 serials from 1850 forward in 35mm microfilm format. ATLA cooperates with its member libraries in the identification and contribution of monographs and serials in need of preservation.

AMIGOS Bibliographic Council, Inc.
ATTN: Preservation Service Manager
12200 Park Central Dr., Ste. 500
Dallas, TX 75251
phone: (800) 843-8482 or (214) 851-8000
fax: (214) 991-6061
e-mail: amigos@amigos.org

AMIGOS provides workshops and technical information on preservation and supports the OCLC/AMIGOS Collection Analysis System.

**Association for Image and Information
  Management International (AIIM)**
ATTN: Librarian, Resource Center
1100 Wayne Ave., Ste. 1100
Silver Spring, MD 20910-5603
phone: (301) 587-8202
fax: (301) 587-2711
e-mail: aiim@aiim.mo.md.us

AIIM International (formerly National Micrographics Association) is a trade organization that produces books, standards, and reports. AIIM also has several annual shows and conferences on micrographics, electronic imaging, and document management. The Resource Center answers technical inquiries.

Association of Research Libraries (ARL)
ATTN: Senior Program Officer, Preservation
  and Collections Services
21 Dupont Cir., Ste. 800

Washington, DC 20036
phone: (202) 296-2296
fax: (202) 872-0884
e-mail: arlhq@cni.org

A not-for-profit membership organization comprising the libraries of North American research institutions, ARL operates as a forum for the exchange of ideas and as an agent for collective action. ARL's chief preservation objective is to meet the special needs of research libraries and of comprehensive research collections.

Canadian Institute for Historical Microreproduction
ATTN: Executive Director
P.O. Box 2428, Sta. D
Ottawa, Ontario
Canada K1P 5W5
phone: (613) 235-2628
fax: (613) 235-9752

The Institute films Canadiana within the National Library and elsewhere in Canada. It is essentially a bibliographic program with filming services provided on a contractual basis by a commercial agency.

Commission on Preservation and Access
ATTN: Program Officer
1400 16th St. NW, Ste. 740
Washington, DC 20036-2217
phone: (202) 939-3400
fax: (202) 939-3407

The primary objective of the Commission is to foster, develop, and support collaboration among libraries and allied organizations to ensure the preservation of the published and documentary record in all formats and to provide enduring access to scholarly information. It contracts for research and demonstration projects; operates task forces and committees; provides displays and materials for conferences; issues a monthly newsletter; and publishes reports on microfilming, digitization, and a wide range of other preservation topics. The Commission is supported by foundation grants and sponsored by colleges, universities, associations, libraries, publishers, and allied organizations.

Committee on Institutional Cooperation (CIC)
ATTN: Director, CIC Center for Library Initiatives
302 E. John St., Ste. 1705
Champaign, IL 61820-5698
phone: (217) 333-8475
fax: (217) 244-7127

CIC is a consortium in the upper Midwest of twelve major research universities with a comprehensive program of library resource sharing in all areas including preservation. Through three cooperative preservation microfilming projects, CIC member libraries have reformatted nearly 55,000 brittle monographs and serials and gained invaluable experience in the design and implementation of a major cooperative filming effort.

Image Permanence Institute (IPI)
ATTN: Director
Rochester Institute of Technology
70 Lomb Memorial Dr.
Rochester, NY 14623-5604
phone: (716) 475-5199
fax: (716) 475-7230

IPI is a university-based, nonprofit research laboratory devoted to image preservation. Its primary purposes are to carry on research in the stability and preservation of imaging media, educate and train preservation specialists, develop new ANSI and ISO preservation standards, perform contract testing and consultation services, and provide technical information on image stability. The Institute also sells IPI SilverLock polysulfide treatment chemicals, A-D Strips (for surveying acetate film collections for vinegar syndrome), and the *IPI Storage Guide for Acetate Film.*

National Information Standards Organization (NISO)
ATTN: Executive Director
4733 Bethesda Ave., Ste. 300

Bethesda, MD 20814
phone: (301) 654-2512
fax: (301) 654-1721
e-mail: nisohq@cni.org

NISO is a nonprofit organization that develops and promotes consensus-approved standards used in library services, publishing, and other information-related industries. NISO standards address the communication needs of these industries in areas such as information retrieval and transfer, preservation of materials, forms and records, identification systems, publication formats, and equipment and supplies. Contact the NISO headquarters to learn the status of a standard, volunteer to serve on a standard-developing committee, or suggest a new standard. To purchase a standard, contact NISO Press Fulfillment (listing follows).

**National Information Standards
Organization (NISO)**
ATTN: Press Fulfillment
P.O. Box 338
Oxon Hill, MD 20750-0338
phone: (800) 282-6476 or (301) 567-9522
fax: (301) 567-9553

Contact this office to purchase NISO standards. For other NISO business, contact the headquarters (see the previous listing).

National Library of Canada
ATTN: National and International Programs
395 Wellington St.
Ottawa, Ontario
Canada K1A 0N4
phone: (613) 943-8570
fax: (613) 947-2916

Through its Preservation Policy and Planning Officer and its Heritage Officer, the National Library of Canada serves as an information resource on a wide range of issues related to preservation microfilming and digitization technologies. The Library advises institutions on the development and application of technical guidelines as well as on the development of policy and guidelines related to microfilming and digitization. It manages the Canadian Register of Microform Masters, coordinates the Decentralized Program for Canadian Newspapers (under which newspaper microfilming projects are being mounted in the provinces), and has published *Guidelines for Preservation Microfilming in Canadian Libraries* (see appendix A).

**OCLC Online Computer Library Center,
Inc.**
6565 Frantz Rd.
Dublin, OH 43017-3395
phone: (800) 848-5878 or (614) 764-6000
fax: (614) 764-6096

To help in their preservation decisions, librarians search the OCLC Online Union Catalog (OLUC), a comprehensive international database of bibliographic information with more than 33 million records and 570 million location listings. Questions related to bibliographic control of preservation microforms should be directed to the OLUC Database Management Department, (614) 764-4360, or to the institution's OCLC-affiliated network. Direct inquiries about the Collection Analysis System to AMIGOS (see previous listing). For preservation microfilming and access services, see the entry for Preservation Resources in this appendix.

**The Research Libraries Group, Inc.
(RLG)**
ATTN: Member Support and Services
Division
1200 Villa St.
Mountain View, CA 94041-1100
phone: (415) 691-2239
fax: (415) 964-0943

Publisher of the *RLG Preservation Microfilming Handbook* and *RLG Archives Microfilming Manual,* RLG has extensive experience in preservation standards development and in planning and implementing major cooperative microfilming projects involving large research libraries. RLG operates the Research Libraries Information Network (RLIN), an international database of more than 70 million bibliographic records of which approximately 2 million are for preservation microforms. Questions related to searching and bibliographic control of preservation microforms and using the RLG Conspectus in preservation planning should be directed to the Member Support and Services Division.

Society of American Archivists (SAA)
ATTN: Education Director
600 S. Federal, Ste. 504
Chicago, IL 60605
phone: (312) 922-0140
fax: (312) 347-1452
e-mail: info@saa.mhs.compuserve.com

SAA offers publications and programs pertaining to preservation microfilming. The Preservation Section of SAA meets at the Society's annual meeting.

Southeastern Library Network, Inc. (SOLINET)
ATTN: Preservation Service Manager
1438 W. Peachtree St. NW, Ste. 200
Atlanta, GA 30309-2955
phone: (800) 999-8558 or (404) 892-0943
fax: (404) 892-7879
e-mail: solinet_information@solinet.net

SOLINET manages a grant-funded preservation microfilming program involving southeastern libraries and supports a centralized service for preparation and postfilming operations. Workshops and reference services are also available.

Service Providers

Archival Microfilm Services (formerly Micrographic Systems of Connecticut)
ATTN: President
1133 Dixwell Ave.
Hamden, CT 06514
phone: (203) 562-7943

Archival Microfilm Services focuses on preservation microfilming of bound volumes, historical records, and newspapers. It offers film production on 35mm or 16mm roll film, in-house processing, and duplication onto silver film. Production of custom targets includes creation of eye-legible targets in non-Roman alphabets. The organization has the unique capability of producing two-sided Copyflo documents on acid-free paper.

Archival Systems, Inc. (formerly Archival Survival)
ATTN: Director of Preservation Services
593 Acorn St.
Deer Park, NY 11729
phone: (516) 586-1257
fax: (516) 586-1273

The company's preservation microfilming services include filming on 35mm roll film (16mm also available), processing (including polysulfide treatment), and duplication onto silver or diazo film as well as paper copies. It can also provide scanning of film or original documents. Ancillary support services include the creation of custom targets, duplication of deteriorated cellulose acetate film, processing of 105mm film, storage of printing masters, and creation of database records for completed microfilm.

Bay Microfilm, Inc.—*see* BMI Imaging Systems.

Bell and Howell Canada Ltd.
ATTN: Preservation Microfilm Group
256 Bradwick
Concord, Ontario
Canada L4K 1K8
phone: (905) 746-1141·
fax: (905) 660-0580

Bell and Howell Canada provides preservation microfilming services and has significant experience in handling fragile materials. Its services include preparation; filming onto 35mm, 16mm, and 105mm film; processing (with polysulfide treatment available on request); and duplication onto silver, diazo, or vesicular film as well as creation of paper copy. Onsite storage of printing masters available.

BMI Imaging Systems (formerly Bay Microfilm, Inc.)
ATTN: Director of Preservation
1115 E. Arques Ave.
Sunnyvale, CA 94086
phone: (800) 359-3456 or (408) 736-7444
fax: (408) 736-4397
e-mail: bmi@ix.netcom.com

BMI provides preservation microfilming services including preparation; film production, processing, duplication, and distribution; and bibliographic control. It offers storage facilities for master negatives and printing masters as well as distribution services. The company will scan film and original documents onto various media. BMI produces a biannual catalog of microform and CD-ROM collections focusing on West Coast history. It serves as the northern California dealer for Canon micrographics and imaging equipment and offers supplies and maintenance services.

Bowling Green State University
ATTN: Micrographics Specialist, or Director
Center for Archival Collections
Jerome Library, 5th Fl.
1001 E. Wooster St.
Bowling Green, OH 43403
phone: (419) 372-2411
fax: (419) 372-0155

Since 1975 the Center for Archival Collections (CAC) has extended its records preservation program to cooperate with local political subdivisions; academic institutions; libraries; professional associations; historical, social, and cultural organizations; and the public. CAC's contractual relationship with the Genealogical Society of Utah allows for the microfilming of many northwest Ohio

public records, church records, and manuscript collections at no cost to the custodians. Both 35mm and 16mm formats are available.

CBR Consulting Services, Inc.
ATTN: Eileen F. Usovicz, Consultant
P.O. Box 22421
Kansas City, MO 64113
phone: (816) 444-8246
fax: (816) 444-8265
e-mail: leemaps1@aol.com

CBR provides workshops and technician training, third-party quality assurance, inspection of stored microfilm, evaluation of existing facilities, and project planning assistance.

Challenge Industries, Inc.
ATTN: Microfilm Manager
402 E. State St.
Ithaca, NY 14850
phone: (607) 272-8990
fax: (607) 277-7865

Challenge Industries is a nonprofit organization devoted to 35mm preservation microfilming for libraries and archives. It offers film production, processing, and duplication.

Harvard University Library
ATTN: Preservation Center
59 Plympton St.
Cambridge, MA 02138
phone: (617) 495-8596
fax: (617) 496-8344

Harvard University Library developed and makes available, free of charge, Surveyor, a Macintosh-based software package useful for surveying collection condition.

IMR Limited
ATTN: Preservation Microfilm Dept.
P.O. Box 248
Hazleton, PA 18201
phone: (800) 582-6319 or (717) 459-2213
fax: (717) 459-5443

IMR provides preservation microfilming services including preparation and target creation; filming onto 35mm film (16mm and 105mm also available); processing, with IPI SilverLock treatment on request; and duplication onto silver, diazo, or vesicular film. It also will scan film and original documents onto CD-ROM and optical disk.

Iron Mountain Records Management, Inc.

ATTN: Customer Support Representative
P.O. Box 86
Rosendale, NY 12472
phone: (914) 658-3132
fax: (914) 658-8680

Iron Mountain has provided reliable, high-security protection for vital records since 1951. The organization offers climate-controlled, limited-access underground facilities for extended-term ("archival") storage of master negatives and printing masters. Storage is available in private or shared vaults with computerized inventory control of stored microfilm and fiche. Onsite ancillary support services include diazo and silver duplication for microfilm and microfiche plus hard copy reproduction. It offers a workroom equipped for inspection of stored microfilm and microfiche. Services are available 24 hours per day, 365 days a year.

Library of Congress Photoduplication Service

ATTN: Head, Special Services Section
101 Independence Ave.
Washington, DC 20540-5236
phone: (202) 707-5661 or (202) 707-9501
fax: (202) 707-1771

LC's Photoduplication Service reference staff answers inquiries about the extent and availability of items in LC catalogs and special collections, a useful service for institutions searching for replacement copies. The Service also provides access to the Library's negative microform collection and other LC collections via reformatting methods including microfilming, photographing, photocopying, and digitizing, subject to copyright or other distribution restrictions. The nonprofit, fee-for-service Photoduplication Service also has extensive experience in preservation microfilming a wide range of archival and library materials; preparation services (e.g., collation and targeting) also are performed.

Massachusetts Institute of Technology (MIT)

ATTN: Head, Document Services
77 Massachusetts Ave., Rm. 14-0551
Cambridge, MA 02139-4307
phone: (617) 253-5667
fax: (617) 253-1690
e-mail: docs@mit.edu

MIT provides preservation microfilming, film processing and duplication, and digital scanning of paper or film for other institutions. It is also a source of technical guidance and information.

Microfilm Company of California, Inc.

ATTN: Library Reproduction Service
1977 S. Los Angeles St.
Los Angeles, CA 90011-1096
phone: (800) 255-5002 or (213) 749-2463
fax: (213) 749-8943

The company has fifty years' experience providing preservation microfilming services (filming, processing, and duplication) to universities, museums, and libraries. Its services include 35mm and 16mm microfilming, film duplication, and on-demand paper prints (Copyflo) from microfilm. The firm has special experience in handling fragile materials, Asian material, and Copyflo from uneven-quality film.

Micrographic Systems of Connecticut—

see Archival Microfilm Services.

MICROGRAPHICS, Inc.

ATTN: Jim Craig, President
1925 N.W. 2nd St., Ste. A
Gainesville, FL 32609
phone: (904) 372-6039
fax: (904) 378-6039

MICROGRAPHICS, Inc., provides preservation microfilming services on-site or at the headquarters facility. Its services include document preparation, filming, film processing, film duplication, and bibliographic control. Processing services offered include IPI SilverLock and remedial treatment for reduplication of deteriorated acetate and other films. The company also provides electronic imaging of microfilm and original documents to CD-ROM and optical disk.

Mottice Micrographics, Inc.
ATTN: Robert Mottice, President
20830 Pleasant Lake Rd.
Manchester, MI 48158
phone: (313) 428-7717
fax: (313) 761-2128

Mottice Micrographics provides training, third-party quality assurance, quality and condition audits, process control, equipment evaluation, and various other consulting services.

National Underground Storage (NUS)
ATTN: Sales Dept.
P. O. Box 6
Boyers, PA 16020
phone: (412) 794-8474
fax: (412) 794-2838

As its name implies, National Underground Storage provides secure underground facilities for extended-term ("archival") storage of master negatives and printing masters. Temperature, humidity, and air quality levels have been found to comply with ANSI/NAPM IT9.11-1993. Storage is available in private or shared vaults. Onsite ancillary support services include duplication on silver or diazo film plus hard copy reproduction through Copyflo. It offers a workroom equipped for inspection of stored microforms by client or NUS staff. Services are available 24 hours per day, 365 days a year.

Northeast Document Conservation Center (NEDCC)
ATTN: Director of Reprographic Services
100 Brickstone Sq.
Andover, MA 01810-1494
phone: (508) 470-1010
fax: (508) 475-6021
e-mail: nedccrep@world.std.com

NEDCC is a nonprofit organization committed to preservation microfilming. It specializes in hard-to-film materials including archives and continuous-tone microfilming of photographs and other materials. Its microfilming services include frame-by-frame bibliographic inspection, microfilm processing, duplication, polysulfide treatment, and offsite storage of master negatives. NEDCC also provides conservation services, photographic copying services, consultation, workshops, and a wide range of related services.

Perpetual Storage, Inc.
ATTN: Vice President of Sales
6279 E. Little Cottonwood Rd.
Sandy, UT 84092
phone: (801) 942-1950
fax: (801) 942-1952

Perpetual Storage provides climate-controlled, limited-access underground facilities for extended-term ("archival") storage of master negatives and printing masters. Storage is available in private or shared vaults. Arrangements can be made for duplication. The company offers a work space equipped for inspection of stored microforms by the client or a designated third party. Services are available 24 hours per day, 365 days a year.

Precision Micrographic Services Ltd.
ATTN: Archival Specialist
204 W. 6th Ave.
Vancouver, British Columbia
Canada V5Y 1K8
phone: (604) 873-2681
fax: (604) 873-2683

Precision Micrographic's services include preservation microfilming, with particular strength in filming newspapers as well as bound volumes. Film is produced on 35mm or 16mm roll film, and copies are available on silver or diazo film. Onsite storage of printing masters is available. Scanning of film or hard copy is also available, with output to CD-ROM and other media.

Preservation Resources (formerly
  Mid-Atlantic Preservation Service
  [MAPS])
ATTN: President
9 S. Commerce Way
Bethlehem, PA 18017-8916
phone: (800) 773-7222 or (610) 758-8700
fax: (610) 758-9700

Preservation Resources is a nonprofit organization devoted to preservation reformatting, particularly microfilming. It also provides scanning of microfilm, preparation services, bibliographic control, onsite storage of printing negatives, on-demand duplication, consultation, workshops, and a wide range of related services.

Primary Source Media—*see* Research
  Publications.

REMAC Information Corporation
ATTN: President
8445 Helgerman Ct.
Gaithersburg, MD 20877-4131
phone: (301) 948-4550
fax: (301) 948-4761

REMAC provides a wide range of preservation microfilming services for libraries and archives, focusing on brittle books and serials. Its services include film production, processing, and duplication, plus a full range of targeting and other preparation services. Special tracking software is available to provide clients with up-to-date reports on items in the filming lab.

Research Publications
ATTN: Vice President, Editorial and
  Development
12 Lunar Dr.
Woodbridge, CT 06525

phone: (800) 444-0799
fax: (203) 397-3893
e-mail: sales@rpub.com

Research Publications, an imprint of Primary Source Media, brings nearly thirty years of expertise in filming and publishing microfilm research collections to the preservation business. The company offers a wide spectrum of preservation services including project planning and control, materials preparation, target preparation, filming and storage, statistical reporting, and bibliographic access including AACR2 and full MARC cataloging.

Underground Vaults & Storage, Inc.
ATTN: Sales Dept.
P.O. Box 1723
Hutchinson, KS 67504-1723
phone: (800) 873-0906 or (316) 662-6769
fax: (316) 662-8871

As its name implies, the company provides climate-controlled, limited-access underground facilities for extended-term ("archival") storage of master negatives and printing masters. Storage is available in private or shared vaults. Arrangements can be made for duplication onto silver, diazo, or vesicular film as well as scanning. It offers a workroom equipped for inspection of stored microforms by client or company staff. Services are available 24 hours per day, 365 days a year.

University of California, Berkeley
ATTN: Library Photographic Services,
  Conservation Dept.
416 Doe Library
Berkeley, CA 94720-6000
phone: (510) 642-4946
fax: (510) 642-4664

The library's in-house program focuses on brittle books but also does a significant amount of manuscript microfilming. As the schedule permits, it will contract to microfilm for institutions outside the university.

Federal and State Funding Sources

National Endowment for the Humanities (NEH)

Div. of Preservation and Access
1100 Pennsylvania Ave. NW, Rm. 802
Washington, DC 20506
phone: (202) 606-8570
fax:　　(202) 606-8639
e-mail: preservation@neh.fed.us

NEH supports preservation microfilming projects conducted by individual libraries and archives or by institutions acting as a consortium. Sustained support is provided for national, cooperative efforts to microfilm brittle books and serials and U.S. newspapers.

National Historical Publications and Records Commission (NHPRC)

ATTN: Program Director
National Archives Bldg.
NHPRC, Rm. 607
Washington, DC 20408
phone: (202) 501-5610
fax:　　(202) 501-5601
e-mail: nhprc@arch1.nara.gov

NHPRC is a funding agency within the National Archives that supports preservation microfilming and micropublication of archival and manuscript collections relating to American history. Project reports and microform guidelines are available.

New York State Library

ATTN: New York State Program for the Conservation and Preservation of Library Research Materials
Library Development
10C47 Cultural Education Ctr.
Albany, NY 12230
phone: (518) 474-6971
fax:　　(518) 486-5254

The state's grant program provides financial support for projects that contribute to the preservation of significant research materials in libraries, archives, historical societies, and other agencies within New York. Projects may include conducting surveys, improving collection storage environments, reformatting or treating collections, or other preservation activities described in the guidelines.

Preservation Options

Option	Positive Aspects	Drawbacks
1. No action—reshelve as is	If used conscientiously and appropriately with a plan of priorities for preservation treatment, it has an effect of "benign neglect" that frees resources to preserve the more important items in the collection	Has limits in a research collection in which materials are acquired for their permanent research value Eventually results in permanent loss to the collection
2. Discard/withdraw with no replacement	Is appropriate for items found to lack value to the collection Reserves funds for items in the collection that warrant preservation attention	Has limits in research collections in which materials acquired can often be assumed to have long-term research value in some format May result in significant loss to research collections
3. Preservation in original format through controlled storage environment (placing items in conditions of controlled temperature, relative humidity, light, air quality)	Slows rate of deterioration for many types of materials Affords long-term retention of items at low unit cost	Requires major capital outlay to build, equip, and maintain such a facility Does not restore materials that have significantly deteriorated in physical strength or have damaged structures Considerably slows but does not stop deterioration If storage is in remote location, adds expense of selecting and changing catalog records of items to be moved

Option	Positive Aspects	Drawbacks
4. Repair or conserve items to retain the original format		
a. Minor repair (repair book bindings, mend tears in flat paper materials, etc.)	Retains original format Usually entails low unit cost, depending on condition	Is not suitable for materials that have sustained significant loss of paper strength and are, therefore, too fragile to benefit from simple repair Requires staff trained to perform repairs using appropriate methods and materials
b. Commercial library binding or rebinding	Is relatively inexpensive for providing primary protection of text block	Cannot be used for brittle papers Is not a long-term solution for brittle or acidic papers Generally is not suitable for rare materials Existing binding may limit future rebinding options
c. Physical conservation treatment (including cleaning, deacidification, repairs, resewing, conservation rebinding, etc.)	Preserves bibliographic/artifactual evidence Retains the original item in a stable format	Incurs high labor costs for treatments Requires skilled personnel and sophisticated resources to take on such treatment Cannot make an impact on large-scale masses of brittle materials
d. Protective enclosure (such as wrappers, phase boxes, clamshell boxes) of bound volumes	Maintains all bibliographic pieces together in original format at a relatively low cost Provides a microenvironment to buffer temperature and relative humidity fluctuations and affords protection from light and pollutants	Does not stop ongoing deterioration Is only a "phase" of preservation, a step to keep volume intact until other treatments become available or affordable

Option	Positive Aspects	Drawbacks
e. Protective enclosure of single sheets by encapsulating with polyester film (such as Mylar)	Retains original format Protects with a stable material	Should be preceded by deacidification, which is specialized and expensive Adds weight and bulk Involves significant cost and time requirements when applied on a large scale
f. Mass deacidification	Stabilizes large quantities of materials safely at low unit cost Retains material in original format	Is not yet a well-proven or widely available technology Is not suitable for all types of materials due to effects on inks, leathers, adhesives, etc. Neither restores strength to weakened papers nor repairs binding structures
5. Replace items with hard (paper) copy		
a. Replace from out-of-print market	Provides exact or near-exact duplicate of deteriorated/damaged item	Incurs high expense for some items Is not possible for rare, scarce, or unique items Is unlikely to be in better condition than your brittle copy and, therefore, is likely to require treatment in the future
b. Replace with new in-print copy	Provides near-exact duplicate of item, usually at reasonable cost	Exact edition is probably unavailable in print May not be a permanent/durable copy
c. Replace with hard copy—reprint edition	Provides exact or near-exact duplicate	May not be permanent/durable edition Sometimes incurs high cost
d. Replace with hard copy—create a photocopy in-house or purchase one and bind	Is similar in format to original Can use permanent/durable paper	Entails duplication and binding costs that can be considerable for materials in bulk Provides only one copy, so inexpensive copies are not available for wider scholarly use Requires specialized (and expensive) equipment or services to reproduce color, halftones, and illustrations

Option	Positive Aspects	Drawbacks
6. Replace item with commercially available microform	Is often the least expensive method of preserving an item Can provide paper copies for users by using reader-printers Offers significant space reduction, especially for longer serial runs	Is not appropriate for all materials Is not available for all materials Often requires the purchase of large sets rather than individual monograph texts Presents location difficulties for serials and series when part of the title is found in hard copy at one place and part in microform in another place within the repository May not have been produced in compliance with national standards (e.g., not produced on silver-gelatin film) May be technical or bibliographic problems with the film May require somewhat more extensive recataloging than other replacements Requires special equipment and facilities for reading and service
7. Create a scanned/digital image	Greatly increases access to and dissemination of the text Can be output to permanent microfilm or permanent/durable paper Provides opportunities for sophisticated and flexible methods of searching and access (provided OCR technology and extensive indexing are applied)	Does not yet yield resolution levels as high as microfilm does Incurs high costs and time commitments for indexing and OCR Often uses proprietary hardware and software that are in flux, creating problems of rapid obsolescence Requires a massive commitment to regular and expensive upgrades of hardware and software

Option	Positive Aspects	Drawbacks
		Is not yet guided by standards for scanning/digitization techniques to ensure longevity
		Cannot be considered to produce a permanent or "archival" replacement until nationally accepted standards exist for life expectancy of these media
		Storage media (CD-ROM, optical disk, tape) have low life expectancy
		Requires zealous commitment to data refreshing
		Requires more-extensive recataloging than some other replacements
		Some texts may be damaged in scanning
8. Create a permanent microform replacement	Captures and preserves intellectual content on a stable medium	Requires strict adherence to technical standards for the selection of film stock, processing procedures, and storage of master negatives
	Allows easy and inexpensive production of copies for wide dissemination	Requires more-extensive recataloging than some other replacements
	Can be scanned for digital access and generation of hard copy replacements	Some materials may be damaged in filming
	Provides significant space reduction, especially for serial publications	
	Is the only viable option for preserving content of certain materials	
	Can create hard copy (e.g., Copyflo) for appropriate items (music, dictionaries, etc.)	

APPENDIX D

Target Sequences

This appendix describes the required target series for monographs, serials, and manuscript collections. It expands on the discussion of targets in chapter 3 and augments the graphic presentations in figures 15, 16, and 17. Several of the targets are required by ANSI/AIIM standards listed in appendix A, and the staff and various working groups of RLG have defined other targets that facilitate cataloging, retrieval, and use of microforms. Some targets are required for materials in all formats, while others are required only in specific circumstances or for certain formats.

The sequences recommended here generally follow the specifications in the RLG *Preservation Microfilming Handbook* and *RLG Archives Microfilming Manual* (both cited in appendix A). The *ALA Target Packet for Use in Preservation Microfilming* (cited in the "Suggested Readings" section for chapters 3) provides further samples of targets and some camera-ready targets for use in film production. Those three resources have been heavily used in this appendix. In a number of instances—too many to indicate through footnotes—actual wording of targets or descriptions of their purpose have been adapted from the RLG handbooks and *ALA Target Packet*.

Targets may be in one of the following categories:

Required. The target must be provided at the specified frequency (for each title, each reel, each volume, etc.).

Required if necessary. If certain conditions are met, the target is required. For example, the CONTINUED ON NEXT REEL target is required when a title extends beyond one reel of film; if there are certain irregularities in the original, the LIST OF IRREGULARITIES target is mandatory.

Optional. Use of the target is at the institution's discretion.

The descriptions in this appendix explain whether each target is required, required if necessary, or optional. Each entry specifies the required frequency.

Targets may appear in one of three font sizes:

Eye-legible targets must be produced in a font large enough so that the filmed image of them can be read with the naked eye. A 60-point font generally meets this requirement if the reduction ratio is 8:1 to 14:1.

Large-type targets should be produced with a 30-point font.

Regular-type targets should have at least 10-point fonts, but larger fonts should be used when feasible.

311

The following descriptions specify the type size required for each target.

The text provides the name of each target. Names of targets that are printed on the targets appear here in SMALL CAPITAL LETTERS. At the left is a miniature sample or template of each target, some of which include (in the lower right corner) the graphic symbols suggested by ISO as discussed in chapter 3.

This appendix is divided into three sections: the target sequence for monographs (section A), serials (B), and archival and manuscript collections (C). To facilitate cross references, each target is identified by a numeral and the letter corresponding to the section. For example, the uniform density target, the second target in the monographs sequence (section A), is labeled 2A. If a target appears more than once in a sequence, it is not numbered at subsequent appearances; thus, at the second appearance of the uniform density target (at the end of the monographs sequence), you are instructed to "See item 2A," where the primary discussion of the target appears.

A. Target Sequence for Monographs

The following description explains a full range of targets that might be used when filming a monograph and the order in which they would appear if all were used. In practice, the nature of the item and institutional policies and practices will necessitate some revisions in these, and some titles will not need some of the targets addressed here. A typical target series for a monograph title is illustrated in figure 15.

At the Beginning of Each Title

1A. *START.*

Status: required
Frequency: per reel
Size: eye-legible

2A. *Uniform Density.* The filming agent generally provides this target, and it must meet the specifications of ANSI/AIIM MS26-1990. The uniform density target should be filmed immediately after the START target and immediately before the END OF REEL target on each reel, but the institution may specify that it be filmed more often (such as for each title on a reel). See the discussion of the uniform density target in chapter 3.

Status: required
Frequency: twice per reel
Size: not applicable

Reel Contents
1: <container>
2: <container>
3: <container>
4: <container>
5: <container>
6: <container>
    <ETC.>

3A. *REEL CONTENTS.* Lists the titles contained on the reel. If the institution does reel programming, this target may be produced during preparation work. Otherwise, it may be produced and spliced in after filming.

Status: optional
Frequency: per reel
Size: regular type (large type if possible)

MASTER NEGATIVE
NUMBER:
<number>

4A. *MASTER NEGATIVE NUMBER.* Provides a unique control number assigned by the institution, generally used to indicate the storage location of master negatives.

Many institutions have adopted RLG's practice, constructing the master negative number of the following elements: (a) the institution's National Union Catalog code, (b) an alphabetic designation denoting this as a master negative number (for example, "SN" for RLG cooperative projects, "MN" for many others), and (c) a numeral assigned by the institution. It is typical to give all titles on a reel the same whole number, then to indicate the position of each title on the reel by using a decimal extension. Thus, MASTER NEGATIVE NUMBER GEU MN00087.4 would be used for the fourth title on Emory University's reel #00087. (For discussion of the uses of master negative numbers and means of constructing them for RLG projects, see Nancy E. Elkington, "Master Negative Storage Numbers," in *RLG Preservation Microfilming Handbook,* edited by Nancy E. Elkington [Mountain View, Calif.: RLG, 1992], 139–42.)

Status: required
Frequency: per title
Size: eye-legible

Microfilmed <year>
<Name/City/State of Library/Institution>
as part of the
<Name of Cooperative Grant Project>
Funded in part by
<Name of Funding Agency>
Reproductions may not be made without permission
from <Name of Library/Institution>

5A. *Project Identification.* Identifies the organizations involved in the filming of a title and the year in which filming occurred. The target may also include the name and mailing address of the organization from which copies of the film may be obtained. It is customary to identify the project name, sponsor, and funding agency for grant-supported projects; for example:

Microfilmed 1991

Pitts Theology Library
EMORY UNIVERSITY
Atlanta, GA 30322

as part of the Great Collections Microfilming Project, Phase II

The Research Libraries Group, Inc.

Funded in part by the
National Endowment for the Humanities

Reproductions may not be made without permission from
the Pitts Theology Library, Emory University

You may give additional restrictions in the COPYRIGHT STATEMENT target (see item 6A).

Status: required
Frequency: per title
Size: large type

6A. *COPYRIGHT STATEMENT.* Cites the copyright law. If the institution wishes to specify additional restrictions on use or reproduction based on local policy, those may be given on the USE RESTRICTIONS target (discussed as item 7C).

Status: required
Frequency: per title
Size: large type

7A. *Eye-Legible Title.* Gives the author, title, place and date of publication, and volume number as needed. Titles may be shortened as needed for eye-legibility. When filming non-Roman alphabet language materials, a second eye-legible title target may be used after this one to display the bibliographic information in the vernacular.

Status: required
Frequency: per title
Size: eye-legible

8A. *BIBLIOGRAPHIC RECORD Target.* Provides the bibliographic record for the original item and technical information about the microfilm. (See the example shown in figure 12.) Includes the following elements:

name of the target—BIBLIOGRAPHIC RECORD target.

institution responsible for the reproduction, either the broad institutional name (for example, "Emory University") or the unit designation (for example, "Pitts Theology Library, Emory University").

name of special project, if applicable—for example, "RLG Great Collections Microfilming Project, Phase II."

master negative number, repeated here from the MASTER NEGATIVE NUMBER target (see item 4A).

bibliographic record for the original item (not the record for the microform version), which may be either a printout of the online catalog record or a photocopy of the shelflist card.

name and location of the filming agent—for example, "Preservation Resources, Bethlehem, Pa." or "University of Kentucky Libraries Reprographics Department, Lexington, Ky."

organization that owns the item (when different from the filming agent).

technical data about the microfilm: film size (for example, 35mm microfilm), image placement (for example, IIA, IB, etc.), reduction ratio, and the date filming began. It is customary to format this section so that the preparation staff or camera operator can circle or fill in the appropriate descriptors, as illustrated in figure 12. Some filming agents may wish also to include a space for the name of the camera operator so that credit can be given and retakes may be assigned to the correct operator.

Be sure to involve cataloging staff in the development of the BIBLIO-GRAPHIC RECORD target, as discussed in chapter 5, since this target is a key resource used in cataloging the microform version. Especially if you do not have a current machine-readable record, catalogers' guidance is important to ensure that the BIBLIOGRAPHIC RECORD target, as well as the eye-legible title target, contains the proper forms of names and choice of main entries.

Status: required
Frequency: per title
Size: regular type

9A.   *LIST OF IRREGULARITIES.* Lists missing pages, mutilations, errors in the original item (for example, pagination errors), and other irregularities that cannot be corrected prior to filming. If pages or volumes are borrowed from another institution, the lending institution may be named here. See the sample in figure 11.

Most institutions use a computer-generated form so that preparations staff may check off applicable irregularities and fill in other needed information.

Omit this target if there are no irregularities. If irregularities relate to specific pages, you may also use optional or in-text targets (discussed at items 10A and 13A), but beware of inserting so many as to be distracting to the user. When problems occur frequently throughout the text or extend over many pages, highlight them in the LIST OF IRREGULARITIES rather than through in-text targets.

Status: required if necessary
Frequency: per title
Size: regular type

10A.   *Optional Targets.* Provide information specific to the title being filmed. If they apply to the entire title or to large portions of its contents, they should generally be reflected in the LIST OF IRREGULARITIES but may also be placed in this position; in-text targets, filmed as full frames between text pages, should be used for defects or anomalies that are not widespread. Examples of optional targets include

SOME PAGES IN THE ORIGINAL CONTAIN FLAWS AND OTHER DEFECTS THAT APPEAR ON THE FILM—indicates that a significant portion of the original text is in poor condition because of problems such as bleed-through, poor quality printing impression, mutilations, tight binding, etc.

PAGE NUMBERING AS BOUND

Others may be developed to meet specific needs, at the institution's discretion.

Status: optional
Frequency: per title
Size: eye-legible

11A. *Technical Target.* The filming agent generally provides this target (illustrated in figure 14). It must include the five properly positioned ISO Resolution Test Charts No. 2 (as specified in ISO 3334) and meet the specifications of ANSI/AIIM MS23-1991. The technical target may also include other test elements (for example, rulers, density patches, photographic images, or gray scales) used in quality assurance operations.

The technical target must be filmed immediately preceding the text; with the possible exception of the VOLUME target (see item 12A), no text or targets should appear between the technical target and the first ten frames of text, nor may splices appear between the technical target and the first ten frames of text.

If one title requires an entire reel, the technical target is filmed again at the end of the reel. Otherwise, the technical target appears once per title, in the preliminary target sequence for each title.

Status: required
Frequency: per title
Size: not applicable

12A. *VOLUME.* When filming a multivolume monograph, use this target at the beginning of each volume—e.g., VOLUME 1.

Status: required if necessary
Frequency: per volume
Size: eye-legible

Begin Filming Text

Text may include front cover and endpapers, depending on institutional practice.

13A. *In-Text Targets.* Each in-text target is filmed as a separate frame immediately before the page or unit to which it refers. These targets may be inserted as needed when they relate to limited portions of the text. Otherwise, the anomalies should be highlighted in the LIST OF IRREGULARITIES (see item 9A). Examples of in-text targets may include

PAGE NUMBERING AS BOUND

PAGE(S) MISNUMBERED

PAGE(S) MISSING

Status: required if necessary
Frequency: per volume or unit
Size: eye-legible

At the End of Each Title

END OF TITLE

14A. *END OF TITLE.* The filming agent should have at least four inches of film between this target and the beginning of the target sequence for the next title on the reel.

Status: required
Frequency: per title
Size: eye-legible

CONTINUED ON NEXT REEL

15A. *CONTINUED ON NEXT REEL.* Use this target only when a title extends beyond one reel, as may happen with a multivolume monograph. With the exception of multivolume monographs (which may be broken between volumes), avoid reel breaks within monograph titles. (See the discussion of reel programming in chapter 3.)

Status: required if necessary
Frequency: per reel
Size: eye-legible

At the End of Each Reel

• *Uniform Density Target.* See item 2A.

END OF REEL PLEASE REWIND

16A. *END OF REEL. PLEASE REWIND.*

Status: required
Frequency: per reel
Size: eye-legible

B. Target Sequence for Serials

The following description explains a full range of targets that might be used when filming a serial title and the order in which they would appear if all were used. Consistent with RLG specifications, this sequence recommends that multiple serial titles *not* be filmed on the same reel.

The nature of the serial title and institutional policies and practices will necessitate some revisions in the recommended sequence, and some targets addressed here will not be used when filming some titles. A typical target series for a serial title is illustrated in figure 16. Additional or different targets may be useful for newspapers; consult the specialized guidelines cited in appendix A.

At the Beginning of the First Reel

1B. *START*

Status: required
Frequency: per reel
Size: eye-legible

2B. *Uniform Density.* The filming agent generally provides this target, and it must meet the specifications of ANSI/AIIM MS26-1990. The uniform density target should be filmed immediately after the START target and immediately before the END OF REEL target on each reel. See the discussion of the uniform density target in chapter 3.

Status: required
Frequency: twice per reel
Size: not applicable

3B. *MASTER NEGATIVE NUMBER.* Provides a unique control number assigned by the institution, generally used to indicate the storage location of master negatives.

MASTER NEGATIVE
NUMBER:
<number>

Many institutions have adopted RLG's practice, constructing the master negative number of the following elements: (a) the institution's NUC code, (b) an alphabetic designation denoting this as a master negative number (for example, "SN" for RLG cooperative projects, "MN" for many others), and (c) a numeral assigned by the institution. Thus, MASTER NEGATIVE NUMBER GEU MN04693 would be used for Emory University's reel #04693. (For discussion of the uses of master negative numbers and means of constructing them for RLG projects, see Nancy E. Elkington, "Master Negative Storage Numbers," in *RLG Preservation Microfilming Handbook,* edited by Nancy E. Elkington [Mountain View, Calif.: RLG, 1992], 139–42.) When multiple reels are required to film a complete serial title, each reel is given a separate master negative number, and those numbers should be in sequence. For example, a three-reel title might have master negative numbers 04693, 04694, and 04695.

Status: required
Frequency: per reel
Size: eye-legible

Microfilmed <year>
<Name/City/State of Library/Institution>
as part of the
<Name of Cooperative Grant Project>
Funded in part by
<Name of Funding Agency>
Reproductions may not be made without permission
from <Name of Library/Institution>

4B. *Project Identification.* Identifies the organizations involved in the filming of a title and the year in which filming occurred. The target may also include the name and mailing address of the organization from which copies of the film may be obtained. It is customary to identify the project name, sponsor, and funding agency for grant-supported projects; for example:

Microfilmed 1991

YALE UNIVERSITY LIBRARY
New Haven, CT 06520

as part of the
Art Serials Preservation Project

The Research Libraries Group, Inc.

Funded in part by the
National Endowment for the Humanities

Reproductions may not be made without permission from
the Yale University Library

You may give additional restrictions in the COPYRIGHT STATEMENT target.

Status: required
Frequency: per title
Size: large type

5B. *COPYRIGHT STATEMENT.* Cites the copyright law. If the institution wishes to specify additional restrictions on use or reproduction based on local policy, those may be given on the USE RESTRICTIONS target (discussed as item 7C).

Status: required
Frequency: per title
Size: large type

> <TITLE>
> <VOLUME(S)>
> <PLACE>
> <DATE(S)>

6B. *Eye-Legible Title.* Gives the title, volume(s), place and date of publication, and author as needed. Titles may be abbreviated as needed for eye-legibility. When filming non-Roman alphabet language materials, a second eye-legible title target may be used after this one to display the bibliographic information in the vernacular.

Status: required
Frequency: per title
Size: eye-legible

> BIB RECORD TARGET

7B. *BIBLIOGRAPHIC RECORD Target.* Provides the bibliographic record for the original item and technical information about the microfilm. See the example shown in figure 12. Includes the following elements:

name of the target—BIBLIOGRAPHIC RECORD target.

institution responsible for the reproduction, either the broad institutional name ("Yale University") or the unit designation ("Art and Architecture Library, Yale University").

name of special project, if applicable—for example, "RLG Art Serials Preservation Project."

master negative number, repeated here from the MASTER NEGATIVE NUMBER target (see item 3B).

bibliographic record for the original item (not the record for the microform version), which may be either a printout of the online catalog record or a photocopy of the shelflist card.

name and location of the filming agent—for example, "Preservation Resources, Bethlehem, Pa.," "University of Kentucky Libraries Reprographics Department, Lexington, Ky."

organization that owns the item (when different from the filming agent).

technical data about the microfilm: film size (for example, 35mm microfilm), image placement (for example, IIA, IB, etc.), reduction ratio, and the date filming began. It is customary to format this section so that the preparation staff or camera operator can circle or fill in the appropriate descriptors, as illustrated in figure 12. Some filming agents may wish also to include a space for the name of the camera operator so that credit can be given and retakes may be assigned to the correct operator.

Be sure to involve cataloging staff in the development of the BIBLIOGRAPHIC RECORD target, as discussed in chapter 5, since many serials have undergone significant title changes that need to be reflected in the BIBLIOGRAPHIC RECORD target, and this target is a key resource used in cataloging the microform version. Especially if you do not have a current machine-readable record, catalogers' guidance is important to ensure that the BIBLIOGRAPHIC RECORD target, as well as the eye-legible title target and others that related to the bibliographic record, contain the proper forms of names and choice of main entries.

Status: required
Frequency: per title
Size: regular type

8B. *GUIDE TO CONTENTS Target.* Details the extent of the serial title being filmed, the contents of each reel, and volumes/years/issues that are missing. (See figure 13.) Even if missing sections are recorded on the GUIDE TO CONTENTS target, in-text targets such as VOLUME(S) MISSING should be used.

Status: required on first reel of title; optional on subsequent reels
Frequency: per title
Size: regular type

9B. *Reel Contents.* Identifies reels in a series (REEL #1, REEL #2, etc.) and lists the holdings included on that reel. The first reel of a serial title is always REEL #1. Text on this target (describing the volumes, years, etc., on the reel) may be shortened to fit in the available space. If the entire title fits on one reel, omit this target.

If the institution does reel programming, this target may be produced during preparation work. Otherwise, film the entire reel, then construct the reel contents target, film the preliminary target sequence, and splice it into place. The former strategy is more straightforward and argues for the institution's doing the reel programming before filming (as recommended in chapter 3).

Status: required if necessary
Frequency: per reel
Size: eye-legible

10B. *Optional Targets.* Provide information specific to the title being filmed. If they apply to the entire title or to large portions of its contents, they should be noted in the GUIDE TO CONTENTS target but may also be placed in this position. Those that relate to a specific volume or year should appear on that unit's LIST OF IRREGULARITIES (see item 13B), and those that relate to pages or multipage sections may call for in-text targets (see item 14B). Common optional targets include

> SOME PAGES IN THE ORIGINAL CONTAIN FLAWS AND OTHER DEFECTS THAT APPEAR ON THE FILM—indicates that a significant portion of the original text is in poor condition because of problems such as bleed-through, poor quality printing impression, mutilations, tight binding, etc.
>
> FILMED AS BOUND—indicates that pages or issues may appear out of sequence throughout the film because the original was bound out of order.
>
> STATEMENT ON DUPLICATE IMAGES—often used when filming illustrated materials that may require multiple exposures throughout the film (see the sample in Elkington, *RLG Preservation Microfilming Handbook,* 144). If only a few items require multiple exposures, these should be identified in in-text targets (see item 14B).

Others may be developed to meet specific needs, at the institution's discretion, and some are provided in the *ALA Target Packet.*

Status: optional
Frequency: per title
Size: eye-legible

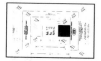

11B. *Technical Target.* The filming agent generally provides this target (illustrated in figure 14). It must include the five properly positioned ISO Resolution Test Charts No. 2 (as specified in ISO 3334) and meet the specifications of ANSI/AIIM MS23-1991. The technical target may also include other test elements (for example, rulers, density patches, photographic images, or gray scales) used in quality assurance operations.

No splices should appear between the technical target and the first ten pages of text. The technical target is filmed again before the END OF REEL target.

Status: required
Frequency: twice per reel
Size: not applicable

12B. *VOLUME.* Identifies units (generally volume and year) within a serial title—for example:

VOLUME 18
1955

(or)

MAY 1947

Individual issues need not be targeted, but separate cumulative indexes, supplements, etc., should be identified with targets and should be filmed preceding the volumes to which they relate.

If a serial title consists of only one volume or unit, the VOLUME target should nonetheless be filmed.

Status: required if necessary
Frequency: per volume (or other major unit)
Size: eye-legible

13B. *LIST OF IRREGULARITIES.* Lists volume- or unit-specific irregularities (such as missing issues/months/pages, mutilations, pagination errors in the original item, and other errors and irregularities) that cannot be corrected prior to filming. See the sample in figure 11. If issues or volumes are borrowed from another institution, the lending institution may be named here.

Most institutions use a computer-generated form so that preparations staff may check off applicable irregularities and fill in other needed information.

Omit this target if there are no irregularities or if they are adequately documented in the GUIDE TO CONTENTS target. If irregularities relate to specific pages, you may also use in-text targets (discussed at item 14B), but beware of inserting so many as to be distracting to the user.

Status: required if necessary
Frequency: per volume
Size: regular type

Begin Filming Text

14B. *In-Text Targets.* Each in-text target is filmed as a full frame immediately before the page or unit to which it refers. These targets may be inserted as needed when they relate to limited portions of the text. Otherwise, they should be noted in the GUIDE TO CONTENTS (see item 8B) if they apply to the entire title or in the unit LIST OF IRREGULARITIES (see item 13B) if they apply to a volume, year, or other unit. Examples of in-text targets may include

VOLUME(S) MISSING

NUMBER(S) MISSING

ISSUE(S) MISSING

MONTH(S) MISSING

YEAR(S) MISSING

PAGE(S) MISSING

TITLE CHANGE (with the new title given on the target) (As noted in item 7B, be sure bibliographic targets such as this one reflect cataloging decisions regarding access points and forms of names.)

Status: required if necessary
Frequency: per page or unit
Size: eye-legible

At the End of Each Reel

If the material covered by the BIBLIOGRAPHIC RECORD target extends over more than one reel, the following should appear at the end of each reel (except the last reel):

15B. *CONTINUED ON NEXT REEL.* Use this target when a serial title extends beyond one reel.

Status: required if necessary
Frequency: per reel
Size: eye-legible

• *Technical Target.* See item 11B.

• *Uniform Density Target.* See item 2B.

16B. *END OF REEL. PLEASE REWIND.*

Status: required
Frequency: per reel
Size: eye-legible

At the Beginning of the Second and Subsequent Reels

If the material covered by the BIBLIOGRAPHIC RECORD target extends over more than one reel, the following targets shall be filmed at the beginning of additional reels:

- *START.* See item 1B.

- *Uniform Density Target.* See item 2B.

- *MASTER NEGATIVE NUMBER.* See item 3B.

- *COPYRIGHT STATEMENT.* See item 5B.

- *Eye-Legible Title.* See item 6B—optional on second and subsequent reels.

- *BIBLIOGRAPHIC RECORD Target.* See item 7B—optional on second and subsequent reels.

- *GUIDE TO CONTENTS Target.* See item 8B—optional on second and subsequent reels.

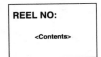

- *Reel Contents.* See item 9B.

- *Technical Target.* See item 11B.

<VOLUME OR UNIT>

• *VOLUME.* See item 12B.

Resume filming text, as described at items 13B–16B.

At the End of the Last Reel

END OF TITLE

17B. *END OF TITLE*

Status: required
Frequency: per title
Size: eye-legible

• *Technical Target.* See item 11B.

• *Uniform Density.* See item 2B.

END OF REEL PLEASE REWIND

• *END OF REEL. PLEASE REWIND.* See item 16B.

C. Target Sequence for Archives and Manuscripts

The following description explains a full range of targets that might be used when filming an archival or manuscript collection and the order in which they would appear if all were used. In practice, the nature of the collection and institutional policies and practices will necessitate some revisions in these, and some collections will not need some of the targets addressed here. A typical target series for a manuscript collection is illustrated in figure 17.

At the Beginning of the First Reel

START

1C. *START*

Status: required
Frequency: per reel
Size: eye-legible

2C. *Uniform Density.* The filming agent generally provides this target, and it must meet the specifications of ANSI/AIIM MS26-1990. The uniform density target should be filmed in the preliminary target sequence and again at the end of each reel of archival materials. See the discussion of the uniform density target in chapter 3.

Status: required
Frequency: twice per reel
Size: not applicable

MASTER NEGATIVE NUMBER:
<number>

3C. *MASTER NEGATIVE NUMBER.* Provides a unique control number assigned by the institution, generally used to indicate the storage location of master negatives.

Each reel must have a unique master negative number. Many institutions have adopted RLG's practice, constructing the master negative number of the following elements: (a) the institution's NUC code, (b) an alphabetic designation denoting this as a master negative number (for example, "SN" for RLG cooperative projects or perhaps "MN" or some other combination for others), and (c) a numeral assigned by the institution. (For discussion of the uses of master negative numbers and means of constructing them for RLG projects, see Nancy E. Elkington, "Master Negative Storage Numbers," in *RLG Preservation Microfilming Handbook,* ed. Nancy E. Elkington [Mountain View, Calif.: RLG, 1992], 139–42.) When multiple reels are required to film a collection, each reel is given a separate master negative number, and those numbers should be in sequence. For example, a three-reel collection filmed by Cornell University in an RLG cooperative project might have master negative numbers NIC SN00401, NIC SN00402, and NIC SN00403.

Status: required
Frequency: per reel
Size: eye-legible

Microfilmed <year>
<Name/City/State of Library/Institution>
as part of the
<Name of Cooperative Grant Project>
Funded in part by
<Name of Funding Agency>
Reproductions may not be made without permission
from <Name of Library/Institution>

4C. *Project Identification.* Identifies the organizations involved in the filming of a collection and the year in which filming occurred. The target may also include the name and mailing address of the organization from which copies of the film may be obtained. It is customary to identify the project name, sponsor, and funding agency for grant-supported projects; for example:

Microfilmed 1993

Department of Manuscripts and University Archives
CORNELL UNIVERSITY LIBRARY
Ithaca, NY 14853

as part of the Archives Preservation Microfilming Project

The Research Libraries Group, Inc.

Funded in part by the
National Endowment for the Humanities

Reproductions may not be made without permission from the
Department of Manuscripts and University Archives
Cornell University Library

You may give additional restrictions in the COPYRIGHT STATEMENT (see item 6C) or USE RESTRICTIONS target (see item 7C).

Status: required on first reel; optional on subsequent reels
Frequency: per collection
Size: large type

<COLLECTION NAME>

<Dates>

<Size of Collection>

5C. *Collection.* Gives summary information about the entire collection (even if only a portion is being filmed). Includes the name of the collection, date span, and volume of material (for example, number of cubic/linear feet). (Analogous to eye-legible title in the monograph and serials sequences.) Elements of the target may be shortened as necessary for eye-legibility. When filming non-Roman alphabet language materials, a second collection target may be used after this one to display the bibliographic information in the vernacular.

Status: required on first reel; optional on subsequent reels
Frequency: per collection
Size: eye-legible

COPYRIGHT STATEMENT

The copyright law of the United States - Title 17, United States Code - concerns the making of photocopies or other reproductions of copyrighted material.

This institution reserves the right to refuse to accept a copy order if, in its judgment, fulfillment of the order would involve violation of the copyright law.

6C. *COPYRIGHT STATEMENT.* Cites the copyright law. Further restrictions may be given in the USE RESTRICTIONS target.

Status: required on first reel; optional on subsequent reels
Frequency: per collection
Size: regular type (large type if possible)

USE RESTRICTIONS/
DONOR IDENTIFICATION

<Insert statement specific to collection being filmed>

7C. *USE RESTRICTIONS.* The institution may specify additional restrictions on use or reproduction based on local policy and donor requirements. May also include information about closed series and restrictions on access to original documents, researcher-use forms, citation form, and information described in the donor identification target (item 8C).

Status: optional
Frequency: per collection
Size: regular type (large type if possible)

This collection was donated to <institution> by <donor> in <month> <year>.

8C. *Donor Identification.* May be a statement (as illustrated at left), deed of gift, copy of contract, letter of transmittal, etc. Optional targets inserted after this one might include letters from the donor, descriptive information about the circumstances surrounding the donation, the relationship of the donor to the creator of the collection, etc.

Status: optional
Frequency: per collection
Size: regular type (large type if possible)

9C. *Optional Targets.* Provide information specific to the collection being filmed. They may expand on the donor identification target (as described at item 8C), give locations of related collections, refer users to separate indexes or supplementary bibliographic data, or explain features of the documents. Examples of the latter include

SOME PAGES IN THE ORIGINAL CONTAIN FLAWS AND OTHER DEFECTS THAT APPEAR ON THE FILM—used to indicate a significant portion of the original text is in poor condition because of problems such as bleed-through, poor quality printing impression, mutilations, tight binding, etc.

STATEMENT ON DUPLICATE IMAGES—often used when filming scrapbooks, letterpress copies, and other materials that may require multiple exposures throughout the film. (See the sample in Elkington, *RLG Preservation Microfilming Handbook,* 144.) If only a few items require multiple exposures, they should be identified in intext targets (see item 21C).

FILMED AS BOUND—indicates pages may appear out of sequence throughout the film because the original was bound out of order.

Others may be developed to meet specific needs, at the institution's discretion.

Optional targets that apply to the entire collection or to large portions of its contents should be placed in this position. Those that relate to a specific series, folder, or item should generally appear as in-text targets (see items 20C and 21C).

Status: optional
Frequency: per collection
Size: eye-legible

10C. *PORTION FILMED.* Identifies the portions that are included on microfilm if the entire collection is not filmed.

Status: required if necessary
Frequency: per collection
Size: large type

11C. *BRIEF RECORD Target.* Provides the bibliographic record for the collection and technical information about the microfilm, analogous to the BIBLIOGRAPHIC RECORD target for monographs and serials. Includes the following elements:

name of the target—BRIEF RECORD target.

institution responsible for the reproduction, either the broad institutional name ("Cornell University") or the unit designation ("Department of Manuscripts and University Archives, Cornell University Library").

name of special project, if applicable—for example, "RLG Archives Preservation Microfilming Project."

master negative number, repeated here from the MASTER NEGATIVE NUMBER target (see item 3C).

bibliographic record for the original item (not the record for the microform version), which may be either a printout of the online catalog record or photocopy of a catalog card. To fit the record into the available space, RLG members use the RLIN AMC "PARtial" (brief form) display of the bibliographic record, with the RLIN AMC "LONg" record on the full record target (see item 12C).

name and location of the filming agent—for example, "Preservation Resources, Bethlehem, Pa.," or "Cornell Photo Services, Ithaca, N.Y."

organization that owns the item (when different from the filming agent).

technical data about the microfilm: film size (for example, 35mm microfilm), image placement (for example, IIA, IB, etc.), reduction ratio, and the date filming began. It is customary to format this section so that the preparation staff or camera operator can circle or fill in the appropriate descriptors, as illustrated in figure 12. Some filming agents may wish also to include a space for the name of the camera operator so that credit can be given and retakes may be assigned to the correct operator.

Be sure to involve cataloging staff in the development of the BRIEF RECORD target, as discussed in chapter 5, since this target is a key resource used in cataloging the microform version.

Status: required on first reel; optional on subsequent reels
Frequency: per collection
Size: regular type

 12C. *Full Record.* Since catalog records for manuscript materials may be too long to fit in the space available on the BRIEF RECORD target, a printout of the full bibliographic record should be filmed. It may run to several pages.

Status: required
Frequency: per collection
Size: regular type

13C. *Finding Aid.* The finding aid for the collection should be filmed in its entirety. It may be several pages in length, or it could be a published guide that is hundreds of pages long.

Status: required on first reel; optional on subsequent reels
Frequency: per collection
Size: regular type

14C. *GUIDE TO CONTENTS Target.* Details the contents of the collection being filmed and the contents of each reel.

Status: required on first reel; optional on subsequent reels
Frequency: per collection
Size: regular type

15C. *Reel Contents.* Identifies reels in a series (REEL #1, REEL #2, etc.) and records the holdings included on each reel. For example:

CONTENTS FOR REEL #1
Series II: Explorations in Southeast Asia, Box 1
Series III: Work on natural history in France, Box 2

The first reel of a collection is always REEL #1. Text on this target may be shortened to fit in the available space. If the entire collection fits on one reel, omit this target because the PORTION FILMED target (see item 10C) will serve the purpose.

If the institution does reel programming, this target may be produced during preparation work. Otherwise, film the entire reel, then construct the reel contents target, film the preliminary target sequence, and splice it into place. The former strategy is more straightforward and argues for the institution's doing the reel programming before filming (as recommended in chapter 3).

Status: required if necessary
Frequency: per reel
Size: large type

16C. *Technical Target.* The filming agent generally provides this target (illustrated in figure 14). It must include the five properly positioned ISO Resolution Test Charts No. 2 (as specified in ISO 3334) and meet the specifications of ANSI/AIIM MS23-1991. The technical target may also include other test elements (for example, rulers, density patches, photographic images, or gray scales) used in quality assurance operations.

No splices should appear between the technical target and the first ten frames of the collection. The technical target is filmed again before the END OF REEL target or LAST REEL target.

Status: required
Frequency: twice per reel
Size: not applicable

17C. *SERIES/CONTAINER.* Identifies the series and containers (boxes and folders) that appear on the frames of film after this target—for example:

Explorations in Southeast Asia
Box 1
Folders 12–42

Status: required
Frequency: per container
Size: eye-legible

FOLDER <No.>
<Title>

18C. *FOLDER.* This target appears before the contents of each folder. At a minimum, it provides the folder number or name. It may also include a brief description of the physical contents and dates of materials included in the folder; for example:

Folder 12
Notebook and four 3″ × 4″ cards with notes,
1866

If a bound volume of manuscripts (such as a diary, journal, account book, or scrapbook) is inside a container but not in a folder, prepare an item target (described at item 19C).

Status: required
Frequency: per folder
Size: large type

<Volume Title>

19C. *Item.* Most often used for bound materials (such as diaries, journals, account books, or scrapbooks) filmed within a collection, especially when they lack title pages or other descriptive information. For example:

Journal, 1881–1882
Bangkok

(or)

Diary of
James R. Osgood,
1882–1883

Status: required if necessary
Frequency: per item
Size: large type

Begin filming documents immediately after the FOLDER and/or item target.

BLANK PAGES
NOT FILMED

20C. *BLANK PAGES NOT FILMED.* Used when two or more leaves in a bound volume are blank, in which case this target is filmed in lieu of the blank pages.

Status: required if necessary
Frequency: per item
Size: eye-legible

21C. *In-Text Targets.* Each in-text target is filmed immediately before the page or unit to which it refers. These targets may be inserted as needed when they relate to narrow portions of the document. Examples of in-text targets may include

PAGE(S) MISSING

BREAK IN TEXT

Beware of inserting so many in-text targets as to be distracting to the user. When problems occur frequently throughout the text or extend over many pages, highlight them in optional targets (see item 9C) in the preliminary sequence rather than through in-text targets.

Status: optional
Frequency: per item
Size: large type (preferably eye-legible)

At the End of Each Reel

If the collection covered by the BRIEF RECORD target extends over more than one reel, the following should appear at the end of each reel (except the last reel):

<table>
<tr><td>

CONTINUED
ON
NEXT REEL

</td><td>

22C. *CONTINUED ON NEXT REEL.* Use this target when a collection extends beyond one reel.

Status: required if necessary
Frequency: per reel
Size: eye-legible

</td></tr>
</table>

- *Technical Target.* See item 16C.

- *Uniform Density Target.* See item 2C.

<table>
<tr><td>

END OF REEL
PLEASE
REWIND

</td><td>

23C. *END OF REEL. PLEASE REWIND.* Used on every reel except the last reel of a collection; see item 24C.

Status: required if necessary
Frequency: per reel
Size: eye-legible

</td></tr>
</table>

At the Beginning of the Second and Subsequent Reels

If the material covered by the BRIEF RECORD target extends over more than one reel, the following targets shall be filmed at the beginning of additional reels:

• *START.* See item 1C.

• *Uniform Density Target.* See item 2C.

• *MASTER NEGATIVE NUMBER.* See item 3C.

• *Collection.* See item 5C—optional on second and subsequent reels.

• *COPYRIGHT STATEMENT.* See item 6C—optional on second and subsequent reels.

• *BRIEF RECORD Target.* See item 11C—optional on second and subsequent reels.

• *GUIDE TO CONTENTS.* See item 14C—optional on second and subsequent reels.

• *Reel Contents.* See item 15C.

• *Technical Target.* See item 16C.

Resume filming text, as described at items 17C–21C.

At the End of the Last Reel

- *Technical Target.* See item 16C.

- *Uniform Density Target.* See item 2C.

LAST REEL OF COLLECTION Please Rewind

24C. *LAST REEL OF COLLECTION. PLEASE REWIND.*

Status: required
Frequency: per collection
Size: eye-legible

APPENDIX E

Association of Research Libraries Guidelines for Bibliographic Records for Preservation Microform Masters

Prepared by Crystal Graham, ARL Visiting Program Officer, under the auspices of the Association of Research Libraries Committee on Bibliographic Control, Dorothy Gregor, Chair

As the national preservation efforts gain momentum, as the national funding for preservation microfilming increases, and as plans for large-scale microfilming move forward, an essential requirement is the establishment of a national preservation database through cooperative efforts of participating libraries via bibliographic utilities and the Library of Congress.

The essential characteristics of such a comprehensive bibliographic system are the availability in each major utility of machine-readable records for preservation microform masters, the adherence to agreed-upon guidelines for bibliographic description, the ability to identify and locate existing preservation microform masters, and the capacity to use bibliographic records online or to hold them in local databases.

Under ideal conditions records for microform masters would be included in a national database, such as the CONSER database for serials, and they would conform to the standards for national full-level bibliographic records. The current reality that research libraries face is inconsistent application of cataloging policies, considerable variation in levels of cataloging, and the existence of several separate bibliographic utilities. Yet there is an urgent need for agreement on guidelines for bibliographic control. The use of agreed-upon bibliographic standards for preservation microform masters will foster and support cooperative preservation efforts, improve access to reformatted scholarly resources, and promote effective sharing of bibliographic information. Given the challenge of building the bibliographic infrastructure to support large-scale, coordinated preservation microfilming, the ARL Committee on Bibliographic Control has developed these guidelines for preservation microform masters. The guidelines are intended for use in cataloging preservation microform masters of books and printed serials.

Originally published in September 1990 by the Association for Research Libraries and reprinted here with its permission, "the guidelines are intended for use in cataloging preservation microform masters of books and printed serials. They establish a minimum set of data elements aimed to achieve the standardization that is the preeminent requirement for preservation microform records." They have been endorsed by the Association for Library Collections & Technical Services (ALCTS) of the American Library Association.

No attempt has been made to include data elements relating to other types of materials such as music, maps, or manuscripts. The guidelines are not intended to be used for newspapers cataloged under the auspices of the United States Newspaper Program, which has its own guidelines.

The guidelines are intended to provide mutually acceptable standards for record fullness and consistency. Recognizing that the long-term needs for effective access to preservation microform masters must be balanced with the need to achieve a high level of record usefulness at a practical cost, the guidelines do not prescribe a full-level cataloging record; rather, they define the base level below which a preservation microform master record should not go. The proposed base level sets of data elements aim to achieve the standardization that is the preeminent requirement for a comprehensive system of bibliographic control for national preservation efforts.

The ARL Committee on Bibliographic Control enthusiastically supports the recommendation of the recent LC-sponsored Multiple Versions Forum to use the *USMARC Format for Holdings Data* for communication of data describing microform reproductions. Until consolidation of this information into the holdings format is implemented the inclusion of preservation data in bibliographic format is mandated. This process can be expedited by applying the standards used in retrospective conversion to the creation of new records for microform masters when usable source records are available in network databases or local card catalogs.

Organization

The guidelines consist of a general introduction and separate guidelines for books and serials.

1. Definition
2. Principles Underlying Bibliographic Control of Preservation Microform Masters
3. Guidelines for Bibliographic Records for Preservation Microform Masters of Books
   A. Description of Data Elements for Books
   B. Procedure for Verifying Name and Subject Headings
   C. Encoding Requirements
   D. Relationship to Network Requirements
4. Guidelines for Bibliographic Records for Preservation Microform Masters of Serials
   A. Description of Data Elements for Serials
   B. Guidelines for Input of Successive or Latest Entry Records
   C. Procedure for Verifying Name and Subject Headings
   D. Encoding Requirements
   E. Relationship to Network Requirements

1. Definition

Preservation microform masters, or master negatives, are first-generation micro-reproductions of library materials that meet archival standards for film stock, processing, enclosures, and storage. Adherence to preservation standards for film stock (ANSI IT9.1-1988), production (ANSI AIIM MS23), enclosures (ANSI IT9.2-1989) and storage (ANSI PH1.43-1983) is implicit.*

2. Principles Underlying Bibliographic Control of Preservation Microform Masters

Preservation microform masters are a primary medium for insuring the availability to posterity of our intellectual heritage. Those who own and control them have a responsibility to treat them as valuable public property. The bibliographic records that provide access to them are no less valuable and warrant processing that assures their quality, usefulness, longevity, and universal availability. Hence the following principles:

a. Adherence to standards for bibliographic records is an essential element in a preservation microfilming program.

b. The bibliographic record for the preservation microform master should contain a standard base level set of data elements.

c. When a bibliographic record for the microform or the original hard copy publication is readily available in either manual or machine-readable form, that source record may be used as the basis of the new bibliographic record for the preservation microform master. When the source record includes data elements in addition to those prescribed in the standard for the national base level preservation record, all appropriate data elements should be retained in the record for the preservation microform master.

d. The cataloging institution should consider the nature of the material, that is, its intellectual content and its bibliographic characteristics and consequent access requirements, to determine whether the level of cataloging should exceed the base level set of data elements.

e. The Committee encourages the provision of subject access even though subject access is not a requirement of these guidelines. Online catalog use studies indicate the desirability and usefulness of subject headings in machine-readable records. Libraries should retain subject headings when adapting a record for the hard copy publication. They are encouraged to include subject headings when creating a new record for a preservation microform master. ARL encourages funding agencies to support generation of records that exceed the base level.

f. Bibliographic utilities should exchange all records for preservation microform masters in a timely manner and should not place restrictions on distribution or use of these records.

---

* Current versions of those standards are listed in appendix A. *Ed.*

3. Guidelines for Bibliographic Records for Preservation Microform Masters of Books

A. Description of Data Elements for Books

The bibliographic record for the preservation microform master should describe the original hard copy publication, in conformity with the Library of Congress rule interpretation of Chapter 11 of the *Anglo-American Cataloguing Rules, Second Edition* (AACR2). Information about the microform should be given in the 245 ǂh subfield, 533 note field, 007 physical description field and appropriate 008 fixed field data elements. A separate record should be prepared for each preservation microform master, but multiple generations resulting from a single filming operation may be represented in one record. The record must contain all of the national base level preservation record data elements shown in the following chart. Every attempt should be made to supply meaningful data in these fields. When the required information is not available, the field should include the appropriate designation. (For example, when the specific reduction ratio is unknown, code the 007 fixed field bytes 06–08 as "– – –").

When a bibliographic record for the microform or the original hard copy publication is readily available in either manual or machine-readable form, it may be cloned as the basis for the new bibliographic record for the microform master. (The terminology for cloning a machine-readable record varies from system to system, e.g., "cre*" in RLIN, "new" in OCLC, and "new .nolink" in Utlas). Description and choice of access points should be verified as described in Part 3B. It is permissible to add a general material designation (GMD) and a 533 field with ISBD punctuation to records which otherwise contain pre-AACR2 description.

In anticipation of the ability to restructure the display of records for multiple versions, the Library of Congress plans to include a 776 linking entry field containing the record number of the bibliographic record for the original hard copy publication, when one exists. Other libraries have the option of including this field in their records. (See addendum for LC's procedure for using the 776 field.)

When no source record is available to form the basis of the microform record, a new cataloging record should be created according to the *Anglo-American Cataloguing Rules, Second Edition, 1988 revision* (and updates), as interpreted by the Library of Congress.

The following table specifies the minimal data elements that must be present in a national preservation record. Only those fields and their subfields that are mandatory are listed with the exception that system-generated fields are not included. While local needs may require a fuller record than that presented here, this national preservation record meets the requirements for books as given in the *USMARC Format for Bibliographic Data*. In addition to the elements listed here, the provision of subject headings and the inclusion of at least one name access point, where appropriate, are considered especially desirable.

National Base Level Preservation Record Data Elements for Books

M = Mandatory
MA = Mandatory if applicable and available

MARC Field

Leader 05 — Record status	M
06 — Type of record	M
07 — Bibliographic level	M
17 — Encoding level	M
18 — Descriptive cataloging form	M
007 — Physical description fixed field	M
00 — Category of material	M
01 — Specific material designation	M
03 — Positive/negative aspect	M
04 — Dimensions	M
05 — Reduction ratio range	M
06 to 08 — Reduction ratio	M
09 — Color	M
10 — Emulsion on film	M
11 — Generation	M
12 — Base of film	M
008 — Fixed-length data elements	
06 — Type of date/publication status	M
07 to 10 — Date 1	M
11 to 14 — Date 2	M
15 to 17 — Place of publication	M
23 — Form of item	M
35 to 37 — Language	M
39 — Cataloging source	M
040 — Cataloging source	M
1XX — Main entry	MA
245 — Title statement	M
ǂa — Title proper	M
ǂb — Remainder of title	MA
ǂc — Remainder of title page transcription/ statement of responsibility	MA
ǂh — Medium	M
ǂn — Number of part/section of a work	MA
ǂp — Name of part/section of a work	MA
250 — Edition statement of the original	MA
ǂa — Edition statement	M
260 — Imprint statement of the original	M
ǂa — Place of publication, distribution, etc.	MA
ǂb — Name of publisher, distribution, etc.	MA
ǂc — Date of publication, distribution, etc.	M

300 — Physical description of the original	M
‡a — Extent	M
4XX — Series statement of the original	MA
533 — Reproduction note	M
‡a — Type of reproduction	M
‡b — Place of reproduction	M
‡c — Agency responsible for reproduction	M
‡d — Date of reproduction	M
‡e — Physical description of reproduction	M
‡f — Series statement of microform	MA

B. Procedure for Verifying Name and Subject Headings

Name, series, and uniform title access points on bibliographic records for preservation microform masters must be verified against the Library of Congress Name Authority File (LCNAF). This includes all name, series, and title headings used as main or added entries (MARC tags 1xx, 240, 400, 410, 411, 440, 600, 610, 611, 630, 7xx [except 740], and 8xx fields). No verification is required for untraced series.

Where it can be determined that access points in a source record have already been verified against the LCNAF, the headings may be accepted and need not be verified again. All other name and title access points should be verified against the latest version of the LCNAF. The AACR2 forms of headings found in the LCNAF should be used on the final record contributed to the national preservation database. If AACR2 forms of headings are not found in the LCNAF, the headings may be used as found on the source record. Alternatively, headings may be established according to the *Anglo-American Cataloguing Rules, Second Edition, 1988 revision* (and updates) as interpreted by the Library of Congress.

Libraries are encouraged, but not required, to verify topical and geographic subject headings against the appropriate LC authority file. Modernization of subject subdivisions and spelling out of abbreviations is also considered desirable.

C. Encoding Requirements

These guidelines require full content designation of all fields that are present, including tags, indicators, and subfield codes.

D. Relationship to Network Requirements

All records input must conform to network requirements.

4. Guidelines for Bibliographic Records for Preservation Microform Masters of Serials

A. Description of Data Elements for Serials

The bibliographic record for the preservation microform master should describe the original hard copy publication, in conformity with the Library of Congress rule interpretation of Chapter 11 of the *Anglo-American Cataloguing Rules, Sec-*

ond Edition (AACR2). Information about the microform should be given in the 245 ╪h subfield, 533 note field, 007 physical description field and appropriate 008 fixed field data elements. A separate record should be prepared for each preservation microform master, but multiple generations resulting from a single filming operation may be represented on one record. The record must contain all of the national base level preservation record data elements shown in the following chart. Every attempt should be made to supply meaningful data in these fields. When the required information is not available, the field should include the appropriate designation. (For example, when the specific reduction ratio is unknown, code the 007 fixed field bytes 06–08 as "– – –").

When a bibliographic record for the microform or the original hard copy publication is readily available in either manual or machine-readable form, it may be cloned as the basis for the new bibliographic record for the microform master. (The terminology for cloning a machine-readable record varies from system to system, e.g., "cre*" in RLIN, "new" in OCLC, and "new .nolink" in Utlas.) Description and choice of access points may be accepted as found on the source record. When more than one source record is available, the library should select one in conformity with the successive/latest entry guidelines given in Part 4B. Form of access points should be verified as described in Part 4C. It is permissible to add a general material designation (GMD) and a 533 field with ISBD punctuation to records which otherwise contain pre-AACR2 description.

In anticipation of the ability to restructure the display of records for multiple versions, the Library of Congress and other CONSER participants will include a 776 linking entry field containing the record number of the bibliographic record for the original hard copy publication, when one exists. Other libraries have the option of including this field in their records. (See addendum for LC's procedure for using the 776 field.)

The intention of these guidelines is to encourage the use of existing cataloging copy as a basis for the new record for the preservation microform master. Nonetheless some recataloging will inevitably be required, such as the adjustment of linking entry fields in order to put serials records in a logical sequence. Current rules for choice of entry and the definition of a title change occasionally make it possible to subsume into a single record a succession of records created under AACR1. The guidelines cannot possibly anticipate all the circumstances under which records created under superseded rules are unsatisfactory, incomplete, or misleading. Catalogers will need to exercise judgment on a case-by-case basis in accordance with the policies of their institutions.

When no source record is available to form the basis of the preservation microform master record, a new cataloging record must be created according to the *Anglo-American Cataloguing Rules, Second Edition, 1988 revision* (and updates), as interpreted by the Library of Congress.

The following table specifies the minimum data elements that should be present in a national preservation record. Only those fields and their subfields that are mandatory are listed with the exception that system-generated fields are not included. While local needs may require a fuller record than that presented here, this national preservation record meets the national level requirements for serials as given in the *USMARC Format for Bibliographic Data*. In addition to the elements listed here, the provision of subject headings and the inclusion of at least one name access point, where appropriate, are considered especially desirable.

National Base Level Preservation Record Data Elements for Serials

M = Mandatory
MA = Mandatory if applicable and available

MARC Field

Leader 05 — Record status	M
06 — Type of record	M
07 — Bibliographic level	M
17 — Encoding level	M
18 — Descriptive cataloging form	M
007 — Physical description fixed field	M
00 — Category of material	M
01 — Specific material designation	M
03 — Positive/negative aspect	M
04 — Dimensions	M
05 — Reduction ratio range	M
06 to 08 — Reduction ratio	M
09 — Color	M
10 — Emulsion on film	M
11 — Generation	M
12 — Base of film	M
008 — Fixed length data elements	M
07 to 10 — Beginning date	M
11 to 14 — Ending date of publication	M
15 to 17 — Country of publication	M
23 — Form of item	M
34 — Successive/Latest entry indicator	M
35 to 37 — Language	M
39 — Cataloging source	M
022 — ISSN	MA
040 — Cataloging source	M
1XX — Main entry	MA
240 — Uniform title	MA
245 — Title statement	M
╪a — Title proper	M
╪c — Remainder of title page transcription/ statement of responsibility	MA
╪h — Medium	M
╪n — Number of part/section of a work	MA
╪p — Name of part/section of a work	MA
246 — Varying form of title	MA
247 — Former title or title variations	MA

250 — Edition statement	MA
260 — Imprint statement	M
‡a — Place of publication, distribution, etc.	MA
‡b — Name of publisher, distribution, etc.	MA
	(M if AACR2)
‡c — Date of publication, distributor, etc.	MA
300 — Physical description	M
‡a — Extent	M
362 — Material specific details	MA
4XX — Series statement	MA
533 — Reproduction note	M
‡a — Type of reproduction	M
‡m — Enumeration/chronology	M
‡b — Place of reproduction	M
‡c — Agency responsible for reproduction	M
‡d — Date of reproduction	MA
‡e — Physical description of reproduction	M
‡f — Series statement of microform	MA
780 — Preceding entry	MA
785 — Succeeding entry	MA

B. Guidelines for Input of Successive or Latest Entry Records

Although successive entry cataloging is considered preferable, existing latest entry records may be cloned as the basis for the new records when no successive entry cataloging is available. Catalogers always have the option of creating successive entry records but are not required to do so when latest entry records already exist.

a. When successive entry records for the original publication or the microform are available either online or in the cataloging institution's catalog, the record(s) for the microform must be successive entry.

b. When the only existing cataloging record for the original publication or the microform is latest entry, the cataloging institution is encouraged but not required to create successive entry records.

c. When a latest entry record exists and successive entry records are available for only some of the titles in the serial run, the cataloging institution is encouraged but not required to create successive entry records for the other titles microformed.

d. When no existing cataloging records for the original publication or the microform are available, the cataloging institution must input successive entry records for the microform.

Latest/Successive Entry Guidelines		
Local Record	**Online Record**	**Action**
Successive	None	Input successive entry record
	Successive	Clone successive entry record
	Latest entry	Input successive entry record
Latest entry	None	May input latest entry record but encouraged to input successive entry records
	Successive for all titles	Clone successive entry records
	Successive for some titles	May input latest entry record but encouraged to clone and input successive entry records
	Latest entry	May clone latest entry record
None	None	Input successive entry records
	Successive for all titles	Clone successive entry records
	Successive for some titles & no latest entry	Clone and input successive entry records
	Latest entry & successive for some titles	May clone latest entry record but encouraged to clone and input successive entry records
	Latest entry	May clone latest entry record

C. Procedure for Verifying Name and Subject Headings

Name and series access points on bibliographic records for preservation micro-form masters must be verified against the Library of Congress Name Authority File (LCNAF). This includes all name and series headings used as main or added entries (MARC tags 1xx, 400, 410, 411, 440, 600, 610, 611, 700, 710, 711, and 8xx). No verification is required for untraced series.

Where it can be determined that access points in a source record have already been verified against the LCNAF, the headings may be accepted and need not be verified again. All other name and series headings should be verified against the latest version of the LCNAF. The AACR2 forms of headings found in the LCNAF should be used on the final record contributed to the national preservation database. If AACR2 forms of headings are not found in the LCNAF, the headings may be used as found on the source record. Alternatively, headings may be established according to the *Anglo-American Cataloguing Rules, Second Edition, 1988 revision* (and updates) as interpreted by the Library of Congress.

Libraries are encouraged, but not required, to verify topical and geographic subject headings against the appropriate LC authority file. Modernization of subject subdivisions and spelling out of abbreviations is also considered desirable.

D. Encoding Requirements

These guidelines require full content designation of all fields that are present, including tags, indicators, and subfield codes.

E. Relationship to Network Requirements

All records input must conform to network requirements.

ADDENDUM

Library of Congress procedures for using the 776 field to link original and microform records

Field 776

Apply the following conventions to the 776 field that links the record for the microform to the record for the original:

1. Add the field to the record for the microform according to the order determined appropriate to the input/update system being used.
2. Use in the first indicator position the value 1 (do not display note). The second indicator position is not defined for use (ƀ).
3. Give in the ‡c subfield the designation "Original"; do not end with a period.
4. Give in the ‡w subfield the LCCN of the record for the original preceded by LC's NUC symbol (DLC) enclosed within parentheses. Include any prefix with blank fill (ƀ), followed by the two digits of the year series, followed by the six digits of the serial number with zero fill, for example: ppƀyy000ddd

    where

    p = letter of a prefix

    ƀ = blank if no letter of a prefix

    y = digits for year series

    d = digits for serial portion of number

    0 = zero fill for serial numbers of less than 6 digits

    In the absence of an LCCN, give the system ID of the record for the original, prefixed by the system's NUC code in parentheses.

Examples:

Record # for Original	776 Field
LC: sf77–170	776 1ƀ ‡c Original ‡w (DLC)sfƀ77000170
LC: med47–1541	776 1ƀ ‡c Original ‡w (DLC)med47001541
LC: 24–20326	776 1ƀ ‡c Original ‡w (DLC)ƀƀƀ24020326
OCLC: 2250071	776 1ƀ ‡c Original ‡w (OCoLC)2250071
RLIN: ILCO86-B2461	776 1ƀ ‡c Original ‡w (CStRLIN)ILCO86-B2461

APPENDIX F
■■■■■

Worksheet for Estimating Project Costs

This worksheet, adapted from RLG models, has been designed for use in calculating costs for a wide range of library and archival collections. It is based on unit costs. For traditional library materials, this will be a volume count. To plan the budget for filming other formats, you will need to determine what unit you will base your figures on. It may be linear feet or boxes for archival collections, file folders or individual visual materials, or individual scrapbooks. It is less important what you define as the unit basis for your calculations than that you apply the basis consistently. Throughout this worksheet, the following groupings apply:

For item **2**, unpublished documents include archives, and manuscripts.

For item **5**, other units might include scrapbooks, albums, and ephemera.

A. Size of Target Population

Define and calculate the size of the entire target population before the searching and curatorial review steps occur. For item **1**, if filming serials or multivolume sets, you will need an accurate knowledge of the number of volumes per title.

1. Published Volumes	2. Unpublished Documents	3. Drawings	4. Photographic Images	5. Other Units

B. Percentage of Eliminated Materials

Estimate the percentage of materials expected to be eliminated by curatorial review. This step may require a sample study.

1. Published Volumes	2. Unpublished Documents	3. Drawings	4. Photographic Images	5. Other Units
%	%	%	%	%

C. Hit Rate

Anticipate the searching "hit rate," that is, the percentage of titles expected to be available on film, fiche, or other format. It will probably be necessary to conduct a pilot search project to arrive at this percentage. Depending on the project, it may be advisable to reverse the order of curatorial review and searching. Some curators will prefer to review materials that have been searched, while others will be able to screen materials before the searching step.

1. Published Volumes	2. Unpublished Documents	3. Drawings	4. Photographic Images	5. Other Units
%	%	%	%	%

D. Population to Film

Identify the actual population to be filmed. Reduce the numbers in **A,** first by the percentage in **B,** then by the percentage in **C.**

1. Published Volumes	2. Unpublished Documents	3. Drawings	4. Photographic Images	5. Other Units

E. Average Number of Volumes per Title

Calculate the average number of volumes per title.

	1. Published Volumes
a. Number of published volumes to be filmed (from **D.1**)	
b. Number of titles to be filmed	
c. *Volumes per title* (a ÷ b)	

F. Local Prefilming Unit Cost

Estimate the local costs per unit (volume, item, etc.) for prefilming activities by estimating times for each step, then estimating costs based on the level of staff performing each step.

Prefilming Activity	1. Published Volumes		2. Unpublished Documents		3. Drawings		4. Photographic Images		5. Other Units	
	Time	Cost	Time	Cost	Time	Cost	Time	Cost	Time	Cost
Identification										
Retrieval										
Update circulation records										
Search										
Curatorial review										
Preparation										
Mend/ photocopy										
Prepare targets										
Reel programming										
Prepare instructions to filmer										
Prefilming cost (sum of costs above)										

G. Bibliographic Control Cost

Estimate the time needed for bibliographic control (including queuing, prospective cataloging, or updating records) for each unit. Provide costs based on the cataloging of logical units—title basis for published documents (from **E.1.b**), collection or series level for archives and manuscript collections, etc. Consider whether the item already has been cataloged, whether an online record already exists, whether the original needs to be withdrawn from the collection, the standard of cataloging applied, the level of staff to be assigned to the task, etc. Do not include costs covered in section **N**.

1. Published Volumes	2. Unpublished Documents	3. Drawings	4. Photographic Images	5. Other Units

H. Average Number of Pages

Calculate the average number of pages per volume, item, or other unit among those in the to-be-filmed category. A sample study is recommended for this calculation.

1. Published Volumes	2. Unpublished Documents	3. Drawings	4. Photographic Images	5. Other Units

I. Average Number of Frames

Calculate the average number of microfilm frames per volume or unit. Generally assume two pages per frame for published or bound materials unless filming oversized volumes or ones that will require multiple exposures. Generally assume one item per microfilm frame for drawings, documents, and photographs. If filming cannot be accomplished in a single frame, factor in the frames needed for sectionalized filming. Be sure to estimate the number of targets that may be needed for each title or item.

Average	1. Published Volumes	2. Unpublished Documents	3. Drawings	4. Photographic Images	5. Other Units
a. Number of frames					
b. Number of targets					
c. *Total frames*					

J. Filmer's Per-Frame Charge

Get an estimate from the filmer (whether in-house or external) for the per-frame cost of producing the master negative, printing master, and service copy (as many generations as are applicable). This should include all charges from the filmer (such as inspection, supplies, insurance, transportation, special handling, etc.).

1. Published Volumes	2. Unpublished Documents	3. Drawings	4. Photographic Images	5. Other Units

K. Per-Unit Cost

Calculate the per-unit or per-volume cost for creating the microfilm by multiplying the answer from item **I.c** by the corresponding answer from **J.**

1. Published Volumes	2. Unpublished Documents	3. Drawings	4. Photographic Images	5. Other Units

L. Local Inspection Cost

Calculate local inspection costs. (The filmer's inspection costs should be included under **J.**) Remember to factor in a percentage for inspection of retakes.

1. Published Volumes		2. Unpublished Documents		3. Drawings		4. Photographic Images		5. Other Units	
Time	Cost	Time	Cost	Time	Cost	Time	Cost	Time	Cost

M. Local Postfilming Cost

Calculate the cost of other postfilming activities.

Postfilming Activity	1. Published Volumes		2. Unpublished Documents		3. Drawings		4. Photographic Images		5. Other Units	
	Time	Cost	Time	Cost	Time	Cost	Time	Cost	Time	Cost
Reshelve or withdraw originals										
Label microfilm boxes										
Clear circulation record										
Send masters to storage										
Local postfilming cost (sum of costs above)										

N. Other Local Costs

Estimate other local costs. Among administrative costs, include hiring and training staff, contract negotiations, supervision, etc.

Other Local Costs	1. Published Volumes	2. Unpublished Documents	3. Drawings	4. Photographic Images	5. Other Units
Administrative costs					
Telecommuni- cations					
Online OCLC/ RLIN charges					
Supplies/ equipment					
Curatorial involvement					
Other local costs					
a. Sum of costs above					
b. Number of volumes (from **D**)					
c. Unit cost (a ÷ b)					

BUDGET SUMMARY

O. Local Cost

Determine the local costs budget subtotal.

Local Costs	1. Published Volumes	2. Unpublished Documents	3. Drawings	4. Photographic Images	5. Other Units
Prefilming cost (from **F**)					
Bibliographic control cost (from **G**)					
Inspection cost (from **L**)					
Postfilming cost (from **M**)					
Other (from **N.c**)					
a. Sum of above					
b. Population (from **D**)					
c. *Local cost* (a × b)					

P. Filming Cost

Determine the filming cost budget subtotal.

	1. Published Volumes	2. Unpublished Documents	3. Drawings	4. Photographic Images	5. Other Units
a. Per-unit filming cost (from **K**)					
b. Population (from **D**)					
c. *Filming cost* (a × b)					

Q. Total Project Cost

Calculate the total project cost.

	1. Published Volumes	2. Unpublished Documents	3. Drawings	4. Photographic Images	5. Other Units
a. Local cost (from **O**)					
b. Filming cost (from **P**)					
c. Project subtotal (a × b)					

Total project cost (sum of all answers to **c**)   = _____

Glossary

This glossary provides definitions for the technical terms used in this manual as well as for some that librarians and archivists are likely to encounter in communications with filming agents and other specialists. It is not intended to substitute for more extensive sources or other related dictionaries. Most of the terms in this glossary have been adapted from other sources, which are listed below, or from the first edition of this manual.

Association for Information and Image Management Technical Report—Glossary of Imaging Technology. AIIM TR2-1992. Silver Spring, Md.: AIIM, 1992.

Elkington, Nancy E., ed. *RLG Preservation Microfilming Handbook.* Mountain View, Calif.: RLG, 1992.

Lynn, M. Stuart. *Preservation and Access Technology—The Relationship Between Digital and Other Media Conversion Processes: A Structured Glossary of Technical Terms.* Washington, D.C.: Commission on Preservation and Access, Aug. 1990.

accelerated aging   laboratory method of speeding the deterioration of a product to estimate its long-time storage and use characteristics.

acetate film (acetate base)   safety film with a base composed principally of cellulose acetate or triacetate. See also *cellulose triacetate.*

acid-free   imprecise term denoting a substance having a pH of 7.0 or greater.

advance cataloging   methods of recording data about a microform master negative in a national bibliographic database (e.g., OCLC or RLIN) before the film is created. See also *precataloging, prospective cataloging,* and *queuing.*

aging   changes in characteristics of materials related to time.

ambient light   (1) surrounding light. (2) general room illumination or light level.

AMC format   see *Archival and Manuscript Control format.*

ammonium thiosulfate   salt used in some fixing solutions to dissolve and remove the silver halides remaining in film after development. Because it acts more quickly than sodium thiosulfate, fixing baths made with ammonium thiosulfate are often called "rapid fixers."

antihalation undercoat   separate layer of light-absorbing dye located between the film emulsion and the base to suppress light reflection. During processing of the film, the dye layer becomes transparent.

aperture   narrow rectangular opening in the optical system of a camera through which light passes to expose the film.

aperture card   paper card with one or more rectangular openings specifically designed for the mounting or insertion of microfilm of a specified size.

Archival and Manuscript Control (AMC) format   set of MARC codes used from 1983 to 1996 to encode bibliographic records for archives and manuscripts. Format integration extends the concept of archival control to all types of materials (books, visual materials, music, etc.), so the separate AMC format is retired.

archival medium   recording material that can be expected to retain information permanently so that such information can be retrieved without significant loss when properly stored (however, there is no such material, and it is not a term to be used in ANSI-based specifications). See also *LE designation* and *life expectancy.*

archival quality   imprecise term pertaining to the ability of an item permanently to retain its original characteristics; the ability to resist deterioration. Use of this term is now discouraged, and others with more specific, quantitative meanings should be used instead. See also *archival medium, LE designation,* and *life expectancy.*

archival storage conditions   see *extended-term storage conditions.*

archives   (1) the documents created or received and accumulated by a person or organization in the course of the conduct of affairs and preserved because of their continuing value. Historically, the term referred more narrowly to the noncurrent records of an organization or institution. (2) the building or part of a building where archival materials are located. (3) the agency or program responsible for the selection, acquisition, preservation, and provision of access to archival materials.

artifactual value   term applied to permanently valuable records that have aesthetic, historical, or physical qualities and characteristics that require preservation of the original format. Although all records possess qualities and characteristics beyond their intellectual content, those with artifactual value have them to such a significant degree that the originals generally must be retained. See also *historical value* and *intrinsic value.*

automatic exposure control   camera component that senses the brightness of a document and adjusts shutter time or light intensity during filming. Use of such devices is not common in preservation microfilming.

background   portion of a document, drawing, microform, or other item that does not include the lines, lettering, illustration, or other information.

background density   see under *density.*

base   see *film base.*

base-plus-fog density   see under *density.*

bibliographic inspection   verification of the microfilm to ensure that all targets are correct and that all targets and text have been filmed in their proper order and in their entirety. Cf. *technical inspection.*

bleed-through   undesired appearance of information from the back of a document when its front is photographed or otherwise copied. It may be a result of ink, paint, or another medium migrating from the surface of one side of a sheet of paper to the surface of the verso or an effect associated with translucent paper wherein the text from an underlying sheet (or the verso of the same sheet) can be seen through the sheet. The latter is more precisely termed "show-through."

blemish   see *redox blemish.*

book cradle   device that supports bound volumes for microfilming in a position so that pages are open flat and approximately parallel to the focal plane of the camera.

brittleness   property of a material that causes it to break or crack when deformed by folding or flexing. In the practical test, if a corner of a leaf of paper cannot withstand two double folds without breaking off, it is deemed brittle.

butt splice   splice in which two pieces of film are butted together without any overlap and adhered by taping, heat welding, or ultrasonic welding; butt weld.

camera bed   the camera base or bottom support of some planetary cameras to which the column and light arms, or other camera support, are attached. Documents are generally placed on the bed or in a book cradle atop the bed for filming.

camera master   see *camera negative.*

camera negative   film used in the camera for exposure; first-generation film. It is possible to produce a camera negative that does not qualify as a master negative under RLG specifications or for purposes of bibliographic control. See also *master negative.*

cellulose acetate   see *cellulose triacetate.*

cellulose ester   broad class of polymers used as film supports. Usually compounded of cellulose and one or more organic acids (except in cellulose nitrate, compounded of cellulose and nitric acid, which is inorganic). Cellulose esters include cellulose diacetate, cellulose triacetate, and cellulose nitrate.

cellulose nitrate   transparent plastic that was used from about 1890 as a film base but, because of its flammability, has not been manufactured since 1951. See also *cellulose ester.*

cellulose triacetate   transparent plastic used widely as a film base because of its transparency and relative nonflammability. It is acceptable under ANSI standards but is not allowed under RLG specifications. See also *cellulose ester.*

chain lines   in handmade paper, parallel watermark lines (often about one inch apart) that correspond to the chain wires on a paper mold. Chain lines are visible when paper is held up to transmitted light and generally run parallel with the grain direction of the paper. They are often simulated on machine-made paper.

cine mode   (1) arrangement of images on roll microfilm in which the lines of print or writing are perpendicular to the length of the film for horizontal script and parallel for vertical script. (2) arrangement of images on a microfiche in which the first microimage is in the top left-hand corner of the grid pattern and succeeding microimages appear in sequence from top to bottom and in columns from left to right. Synonymous with *orientation A, portrait orientation,* and *vertical mode.* Cf. *comic mode.*

clamshell box   custom-fitted protective enclosure used especially for bound volumes. Traditionally made of two "trays," attached to a case, which interlock securely when closed. Also known as a "double-tray box." See also *protective enclosure.*

collate   to review an item (usually by examination of signatures, leaves, and illustrations) to ascertain whether it is complete and in the correct order, to note any irregularities, and to identify any problems that may require additional preparation.

color microfilm   microfilm that provides a record of and displays with reasonable accuracy the colors (in addition to black and white) in the original document. See also *silver dye bleach film.*

COM   see *computer-output microfilm.*

comic mode   (1) arrangement of images on roll microfilm in which the lines of print or writing are parallel to the length of the film for horizontal script and perpendicular for vertical script. (2) arrangement of images on a microfiche in which the first microimage is in the top left-hand corner of the grid pattern and succeeding microimages appear in sequence from left to right and in rows from top to bottom. Synonymous with *horizontal mode, landscape orientation,* and *orientation B.* Cf. *cine mode.*

computer-output microfilm (COM)   microforms containing data produced by a recorder from computer-generated electrical signals.

computer workstation   microcomputer device capable of supporting the creation, storage, access, distribution, or presentation of data files including digital electronic documents.

CONSER (Cooperative ONline SERials)   cooperative program for online serials cataloging whose members include the national libraries of the United States and Canada, selected university and United States federal libraries, and participants in the United States Newspaper Program.

conservation   the programmatic component of preservation that uses chemical and physical techniques to maintain, as much as possible or feasible, the physical integrity of materials in their original format. Conservation treatment (usually an item-by-item approach) may be carried out to return deteriorated or damaged items to stable and usable condition or to render materials capable of being safely duplicated. Treatment also may be performed to reverse previous treatment that over time has proven to be unsuitable or that has placed an item in jeopardy because of unstable components. Cf. *preservation.*

Conspectus   tool developed by RLG and widely adopted for assessing the relative strengths of library collections to aid in coordinating collecting and resource-sharing activities. Arranged by subject and LC classification, it contains standardized codes for collecting levels and languages, presenting a composite picture of historic collecting patterns and strengths as well as current collecting policies. The RLG Conspectus can be searched online and incorporates scope notes describing completed preservation projects among RLG members.

container   generic term for boxes, cans, cartridges, cassettes, and other structures for enclosing microforms.

continuous-tone image   monochromatic (black and white), nontextual images that contain a varying gradation of gray densities between black and white; e.g., photograph or lithograph.

continuous-tone microfilming   photographic process in which an image with varying shades of gray is produced, generally using low-contrast film.

contrast   expression of the relationship between the high and low brightness (reflectivity) of a subject or between the high and low density of a photographic image. A photographic image is said to have high contrast if the difference between the maximum and minimum density is great; it has low contrast if the difference is slight.

copyboard   resting surface, frame, platform, or other device for holding and supporting material as it is photographed.

cradle   see *book cradle*.

deacidification   chemical treatment by which acidity in paper (a major factor in its deterioration) is neutralized so that the pH is raised to at least 7.0. In most cases, an alkaline buffer (reserve) is added to counteract acids that may be introduced in the future, especially from airborne pollutants. May be applied to individual items (documents, leaves, etc.) or through mass deacidification, in which a large number are treated simultaneously.

defect   imperfection in original source materials or the resulting microform.

dense   relatively opaque; term generally applied to images or areas of a film negative that are darker than normal.

densitometer   instrument used to determine the density of an image or film base by measuring the amount of light reflected or transmitted under standardized geometrical and spectral conditions. Transmission densitometers are generally used in quality assurance operations for preservation microfilming; reflectance densitometers are sometimes used during filming as an aid in exposure control.

densitometric method   see *silver densitometric method*.

density   opacity of film; light-absorbing quality of a processed photographic image. Key density measures on a master negative are the maximum density and the minimum density.

> **background density** is the opacity of the noninformation area of a microform.
>
> **base-plus-fog density** is a measure of the density of a film that has not been exposed but that has been developed and fixed. The inherent density of the film base plus the inherent chemical fog of the developed emulsion. Synonymous with *minimum density* or *Dmin*.
>
> **maximum density (Dmax)** is the highest obtainable density for a particular photosensitive material as measured in the dark part of the camera negative image.
>
> **minimum density (Dmin)** is the lowest density obtainable in a processed film as measured in the clear part of the camera negative on which there is no image. Synonymous with *base-plus-fog density*.

uniform density is a measure of consistent opacity across a microfilm frame, generally obtained by uneven illumination of the filming surface. RLG specifications define the maximum permissible density range for preservation microfilming. See also *uniform density target.*

diazo film film type that contains one or more photosensitive layers composed of diazonium salts in a polymeric (plastic) material that, after exposure to light and development, react with couplers (compounds) to form an azo dye image after film processing. Although the color of the image is determined by the composition of the diazonium compound and the couplers used in the process, it generally appears blue or near-black. Diazo film gives polarity identical to that of the original; i.e., a positive image will produce a positive image, and a negative image will produce a negative image. In preservation microfilming, diazo film is suitable only for making service copies.

digital image scanner device for scanning the pages of a document and transforming the scanned image into digital electronic signals corresponding to the physical state at each part of the search area. One small element of the document (known as a pixel) is encoded quantitatively by a digital number that contains sufficient information to represent the image content of the pixel. A fax machine is a type of digital image scanner.

digitization process by which a document is captured through scanning and is converted to an electronic form (normally as a sequence of *0*s and *1*s known as bits). The scanned image is stored electronically, usually on magnetic or optical storage media. During the scanning or through subsequent action (generally optical character recognition, internal character recognition, or intelligent character recognition software), the document may in whole or in part be stored as an image, unformatted text, formatted text, or in compound form. See also *imaging.*

direct-duplicating film direct-image film; film that will retain the same polarity as the previous generation or, when used as camera film, as the original material: tone for tone, black for black, white for white, negative for negative, or positive for positive. Cf. *image-reversing film.*

disbind to remove a text block from its case and remove the spine (often using a guillotine). Employed for tightly bound volumes and for those with brittle paper when a volume cannot be opened fully enough for successful filming. The term also is used for other less-radical treatments that require rebinding, e.g., removing the case and separating the volume into sections, cutting some sewing threads, etc.

distribution copy see *service copy.*

Dmax see under *density.*

Dmin see under *density.*

dry-process silver film nongelatin silver film that is developed by the application of heat. This type of film is not used in preservation microfilming.

duplicate (1) copy of a microform made by contact printing or by optical means. (2) to make multiple copies of a document or microfilm, usually with the aid of a master or intermediate copy.

durability degree to which a material retains its original physical or mechanical properties (for example, strength, folding endurance, tear resistance) during sustained use.

emulsion   single or multilayered coating consisting of light-sensitive materials in a medium that is carried as a thin layer on a film base. For example, silver halide crystals suspended in gelatin form a silver-gelatin emulsion. An *emulsion layer* is the image layer of photographic films, papers, and plates. The *emulsion side* is the side of a photographic film, plate, or paper on which the light-sensitive materials are coated. In silver film it is typically the dull side. The converse of the base side (which is shiny).

encapsulation   process whereby a flat document of paper or other fibrous writing material (such as papyrus) is held between two sheets of transparent polyester film by sealing around the edges, thus providing physical support and protection from handling and storage hazards. It is a quick, simple, and completely reversible process.

expose in sections   see *sectionalized filming.*

exposure   (1) act of subjecting a sensitive material to light. (2) time during which a sensitized material is subjected to light. (3) product of light intensity and the time during which it acts on the photosensitive material.

exposure counter   mechanical device on some cameras, film holders, etc., that indicates the number of frames or sheets of film or other sensitized material that have been exposed or that remain to be exposed.

exposure meter   instrument for measuring either illuminance on the subject (incident light) or light reflected from the subject. May be used to select shutter times, lens settings, or lamp settings. See also *light meter.*

exposure setting   time used to control the quantity of light received by photosensitive material.

extended-term storage conditions   environmental controls, housing, and containers suitable for the preservation of recorded information having permanent value. Under ANSI standards, a set of specifications that enables film to achieve its maximum life expectancy. Previously known as "archival storage conditions." See also *life expectancy.*

eye-legible   capable of being read by humans without magnification.

eye-legible type   on a target, font size that is legible without magnification after filming. Under ANSI/AIIM standards, the resulting font on the processed film must be 2mm (approximately 0.08″) high, and a 60-point font generally satisfies that requirement.

fading   loss of density in photographic images.

fast film   photographic material having high sensitivity to light.

fiche   see *microfiche.*

field   (1) area covered or "seen" by the optical system of a camera. (2) unit of data within a bibliographic record.

file   (1) collection of records; an organized collection of information directed toward some purpose. (2) data stored for later processing by a computer or computer-output microfilmer.

film   combination of a flexible transparent base and one or more photosensitive layers in roll or sheet form. See also *diazo film, dry-process silver film, silver dye bleach film, silver film, silver-gelatin film, silver-halide film,* and *vesicular film.*

film base   plastic support, typically of polyester or cellulose triacetate, onto which the emulsion and backing layers are coated.

film generation   see *generation*.

film size   film width, generally expressed in millimeters, e.g., 35mm.

filming agent   organization or unit that provides microfilm production services (particularly photography, processing, and duplication) to clients within or outside the organization. Cf. *service bureau*.

fixer   mixture of chemicals used in fixing.

fixing   processing step that converts the residual light-sensitive crystals into water-soluble salts that can be washed from the film or photographic paper to stabilize the developed image and prevent further reaction with light.

flag   thin sheet or strip of paper inserted in (not adhered to) a volume or a set of documents, generally to alert the camera operator to anomalies or problems or to instruct the camera operator to take a specified action.

flats   two pieces of matched optical glass polished to a high degree of smoothness and evenness used to hold film flat during projection or viewing, as in a microfilm reader. Often removable for ease in cleaning.

fog   nonimage photographic density. A defect in film that can be caused by the action of stray light during exposure or processing, improperly compounded processing solutions, improperly stored or outdated photographic materials, or improper handling. See also *base-plus-fog density* under *density*.

foldout   an insert, larger than the trim size of a volume, that must be folded before insertion.

format integration   a change to the USMARC Format for Bibliographic Data involving the validation of a uniform set of codes (i.e., tags, indicators, and subfield codes) in the catalog records for all types of materials (e.g., books, visual materials, music, etc.)

foxing   small, usually reddish-brown spots that discolor paper, thought to be caused by the presence of a trace metal (such as iron) in paper, fungal growth, or a combination of these factors.

frame   that area of microfilm on which light can fall in a camera during a single exposure.

gauffered edges   edges of a book that have been decorated by impressing heated finishing tools or rolls that indent small repeating patterns. Usually, but not always, done after gilding.

gelatin   colloidal protein used as a medium to hold silver halide crystals in suspension in photographic emulsions, as a protective layer over emulsions, as a carrier for dyes in filters, etc.

generation   one of the successive stages of photographic reproduction of an original or a master film. The first generation is the camera film. Copies made from this first generation are second-generation, etc. Preservation microfilming generally encompasses a first generation (camera negative or master negative), second generation (printing master), and third generation (service copy) made from the printing master.

glass flats   see *flats*.

gray scale   array of adjacent neutral-density areas varying by a predetermined rate or step from black to white. See *step tablet*.

guideline recommended practice or procedure to be followed so that a uniformly high quality product may be achieved; generally, such recommendations are open to local interpretation where sensible and defensible. Cf. *specification* and *standard*. See also *preservation guidelines*.

gutter combined marginal space formed by adjacent margins of any two pages of an open volume.

halftone technique of producing the illusion of continuous tones in conventional printing processes by photographing the image through an etched screen. The finer the screen (measured in lines per inch), the higher the quality of the resulting negative.

halide compound of chlorine, iodine, bromine, or fluorine with another element. The compounds are called halogens. The silver salts of these halogens are the light-sensitive materials used in silver-halide emulsions.

hard copy volume, document, or other material produced on paper.

heading inscription, readable without magnification, placed at the top of a microfiche sheet or microfilm jacket to identify its contents; header.

high contrast relationship of image tones in which the light and dark areas are represented by extreme differences in density.

hinge in a bound volume, the internal juncture of the board paper (pastedown) and flyleaf. Cf. *joint*.

historical value inherent worth of a book or binding that transcends the information transmitted by its printed words due to its original production details and accidents of time such as association with a historical event. See also *artifactual value* and *intrinsic value*.

hit in bibliographic searching, a citation for a reproduction of the exact title and edition being sought. For preservation purposes, a hit is often defined as either a reprint published on permanent/durable paper or a microform that can be expected to meet preservation guidelines.

holdings maintenance a variety of basic preservation procedures designed to prolong the useful life of archival records and defer the need for conservation treatment. Includes dusting shelves and boxes, unfolding or unrolling documents for flat storage, replacing poor-quality enclosures, removing damaging fasteners, placing weak or damaged documents in protective enclosures (e.g., polyester sleeves), and reproducing unstable documents (e.g., newsprint or telefacsimile copies) on permanent/durable media.

horizontal mode see *comic mode*.

housing see *storage housing*.

hypo shortened form of "sodium hyposulfite" and, therefore, an incorrect term for fixing baths that now consist of sodium thiosulfate or ammonium thiosulfate.

image area (1) the part of a recording area reserved for the images. (2) the area of a jacket containing film channels for the storage of strips of microfilm images.

image arrangement placement of frames on a microform. See also *one-up*, *simplex*, and *two-up*.

image orientation placement of images with respect to the edges of the film. See also *cine mode* and *comic mode*.

image-reversing film   film that, when conventionally processed, reverses the polarity and tonal scale of the previous generation or, when used as camera film, of the original material: white for black, black for white, negative for positive, and positive for negative. Cf. *direct-duplicating film.*

imaging   digitization process in which the document is electronically captured (usually with the aid of a digital image scanner) or created as "electronic pictures," without the interpretation of the actual content, and stored as a sequence of *1*s and *0*s (bits). The electronic pictures are composed of dots, and no distinction is made between text and other information (such as pictures, graphs, etc.). Thus, the letter *b* is not stored as a character per se, but as a "picture" of the letter *b*. Image representations may be converted into text representations by applying various character recognition techniques.

informational content   see *intellectual content.*

inspection station   area where technical film inspection is done; likely to include a light box, a densitometer, a loupe, a microscope, rewinds, a film reader, etc.

instructional flag   see *flag.*

intellectual content   the ideas, thoughts, information, etc. expressed within a document as distinct from the mode of their presentation.

interleaving   insertion of unprinted (white, black, or tinted) sheets of paper to minimize the effects of bleed-through or to aid in the drying process after humidification, etc.

intermediate   duplicate microform specifically prepared for producing further copies. See also *printing master.*

Internet   a network of networks; the largest packet-switching network in the world, designed to provide a communications infrastructure to support a wide range of computer-based services such as electronic mail, information retrieval, and teleconferencing.

intrinsic value   inherent worth of a document based on factors such as age, uniqueness or value of informational content, physical format, artistic or aesthetic qualities, scarcity, circumstances of creation, signature, or attached seals. Materials having intrinsic value generally warrant preservation in their original form (though a microform or other copy may be created as a surrogate to satisfy most research needs), while those lacking intrinsic value often can be copied to preserve informational content. See also *artifactual value* and *historical value.*

jacket   flat, transparent plastic carrier with one or more film channels made to hold one or more pieces of microfilm. Most often used with 16mm microfilm. Synonymous with *microfilm jacket.*

joint   exterior juncture of the spine and covers of a bound volume. Cf. *hinge.*

LAN   see *local area network.*

landscape orientation   mode of rendering an image in which the vertical dimension of the presentation is less than the horizontal dimension. Cf. *portrait orientation.* See also *comic mode.*

latent image   invisible image produced by action of light on a photosensitive material and made visible by development.

latent image fade   change in the effects of light on a photosensitive surface that occurs during the time between exposure and development. The amount and rate of change depends on time, temperature, humidity, storage conditions, and type of emulsion.

LE (life expectancy) designation   a rating for the life expectancy of recording materials and systems. The numeral following the letters *LE* is a prediction of the minimum life expectancy in years for which information can be retrieved without significant loss when properly stored; e.g., an LE-500 designation indicates that information can be retrieved after at least 500 years of storage. See also *life expectancy*. Cf. *archival quality*.

leader   a length of nonimage-bearing photographic film at the beginning of a roll of microfilm, used for protection and for threading into micrographics equipment. Cf. *trailer*.

letter book   used in archives to describe three types of material: a book in which correspondence was copied by writing the original letter with copying ink, placing it against a dampened sheet of thin paper (leaves of which made up the book) and applying pressure; a book of blank or lined pages on which are written letters, either drafts written by the author or fair copies made by the author or by a clerk; a book comprising copies of loose letters that have been bound together, or one into which such copies are pasted onto guards or pages.

letterpress copies   documents, generally on tissue-like translucent paper, produced by transferring ink through direct contact with the original by using moisture and pressure in a copy press.

life expectancy (LE)   length of time that information is retrievable. See also *LE designation*.

light box   device for inspecting film. It provides diffused illumination that is evenly dispersed over the viewing area by employing a translucent surface illuminated from below or behind.

light meter   instrument used to measure the intensity of incident, reflected, or transmitted light. Often used to balance the lights on a microfilm camera. See also *exposure meter*.

line pair   in a resolution test chart, an adjacent black line and white line. See also *line pairs per millimeter* and *system resolution*.

line pairs per millimeter   a measure of system resolution, referring to the number of line pairs that are discernible in a microimage. The numeral beside the smallest test pattern that is resolved is multiplied by the reduction to arrive at the line pairs per millimeter. See also *system resolution*.

listserv   electronic mailing list that distributes postings to all subscribers simultaneously via the Internet.

local area network (LAN)   communications network that transports data between and among computers and computer workstations that are geographically close, usually within the same building. Multiple LANs may be connected in a geographically compact area such as a university campus.

loupe   small hand-held magnifier, usually set in an eyepiece, used in quality assurance inspections.

low contrast   relationship of image tones in which the light and dark areas are represented by small differences in density.

MARC   see *MAchine-Readable Cataloging.*

MAchine-Readable Cataloging (MARC)   set of standards defined for encoding cataloging records to facilitate their exchange between different computer systems.

mask   opaque material or device in a microfilming camera that protects specific areas of photosensitive material from exposure.

mask size   measurement of the adjustable mask in a microfilming camera that determines the height and width of each frame. May be used in calculations for reel programming.

mass deacidification   see *deacidification.*

master negative   in preservation microfilming, a first-generation silver-gelatin, safety-base camera negative that is manufactured, processed, and stored in accordance with nationally accepted standards, specifications, and guidelines to achieve a life expectancy of at least 500 years. Although the terms "camera negative" and "master negative" are often used interchangeably, it is possible to produce a camera negative that does not meet the RLG specifications for a master negative, and—for purposes of bibliographic control—only camera negatives that meet ANSI standards for film stock, processing, enclosures, and storage can be coded as master negatives in MARC field 007. Cf. *camera negative.*

maximum density   see under *density.*

measles effect   see *redox blemish.*

medium contrast   relationship of image tones in which the light and dark areas are represented by moderate differences in density.

medium-term storage conditions   circumstances suitable for the preservation of recorded information for a minimum of 10 years. Cf. *extended-term storage conditions.*

methylene blue   chemical dye formed during the testing of processed microimages using the methylene-blue test method.

methylene blue test   preferred method of measuring residual thiosulfate in preservation microfilm. See also *residual thiosulfate ion.*

microcard   see *micro-opaque.*

microfiche   microform in the shape of a rectangular sheet having one or more microimages usually arranged in a grid pattern with a heading area across the top. In the United States, microfiche sheets are typically 105mm × 148mm (approximately 4″ × 6″).

microfilm   (1) high-resolution photographic film in the shape of a strip or roll, used to record images reduced in size from the original. (2) to record microphotographs on film.

microfilm jacket   see *jacket.*

microform   generic term for any form (including microfilm and microfiche) that contains photographically created images too small to be read by humans without magnification.

micrographics   techniques associated with the production, handling, and use of microforms; generally considered a subfield of reprography.

micro-opaque   very small image on a reflective (as opposed to transparent) base, usually of paper, viewed by reflection rather than projection.

microscopic blemish   see *redox blemish.*

minimum density   see under *density*.

multiple exposures   successive exposures of the same subject. May be intentional (e.g., two photographs at different exposure settings to capture an original having both text and continuous-tone images) or an accidental defect.

negative   image in which the polarity is opposite that of the original. Cf. *positive*.

negative-appearing image   image in which the lines and characters appear light against a dark background.

nitrate film   see *cellulose nitrate*.

OCR scanner   see *optical character recognition scanner*.

one-up   simplex arrangement in which each frame of microfilm includes one document, leaf, or page. Cf. *two-up*.

optical character recognition (OCR) scanner   digital image scanner that interprets the textual portion of a document and converts it to digital codes representing text. See also *digitization*.

optical disk   digital storage medium made of a metal alloy recording surface sandwiched between a rigid substrate and a protective coating, usually of plastic. Information is stored as submicrometer-sized holes in the disk and is recorded and read by laser beams focused on the disk. Includes the 5¼″-diameter CD-ROM format as well as 12″ and other sizes.

orientation A   see *cine mode*.

orientation B   see *comic mode*.

original   source document that is reproduced.

oversewing   in binding, a method of sewing by hand or machine thin sections of leaves to one another near the back edge to create a text block. Used extensively in library binding from the 1920s, declining in the 1980s and later.

oversize   volume that is too large to be shelved in normal sequence in normal shelving area. In the United States, volumes more than 30cm (11.81″) are generally included in this category. In microfilming, materials that, when fully extended, are larger than the available image area when a camera is set at reduction ratios of 8:1 to 14:1.

permanence   degree to which a material retains its original chemical properties over time and resists deterioration from acids and impurities introduced either during the manufacturing/production process or from the external environment. Permanence of microform products is specified in various ANSI and ISO standards.

permanent record   record determined by the appropriate public records authority to have sufficient value to warrant its continued retention and preservation. See also *archives*.

pH scale   measure of the hydrogen ion concentration in a solution, which indicates the extent to which the solution is acidic or alkaline. The pH scale ranges from 0 to 14, with 7.0 being the point of neutrality. Numbers below 7.0 signify increasing acidity, while numbers ranging above 7.0 signify increasing alkalinity. The scale is logarithmic; thus, each whole number increase or decrease represents a tenfold change.

phase box custom-fitted protective enclosure used primarily for bound volumes. Traditionally made of two pieces of heavy-weight paper board that are cut and creased to produce a base board, four walls, and four flaps. The flaps fold over and enwrap the volume, and the box is held closed by button-and-string ties, Velcro dots, or similar means. Derives its name from the concept that such boxing may be used as one phase of preservation until the item can be reformatted, repaired, rebound, or otherwise conserved. See also *protective enclosure.*

photographic film material that can yield a visible image and that consists of one or more photosensitive layers coated on transparent plastic. See also *diazo film, dry-process silver film, silver dye bleach film, silver film, silver-gelatin film, silver-halide film,* and *vesicular film.*

pixel smallest graphic element that can be displayed on a computer screen or by a printer. May be a single dot or a particular arrangement of dots, the purpose of which is to represent color, value, and hue at a specific point in the image.

planetary camera type of microfilm camera in which the film and the documents being photographed remain stationary during exposure. The page(s) or document(s) is on a plane surface while being filmed. Also known as a flat-bed camera. See also *rotary camera* and *step-and-repeat camera.*

polarity change or retention of the dark-to-light relationship of an image, i.e., a first-generation negative to a second-generation positive indicates a polarity change, while a first-generation negative to a second-generation negative indicates the polarity is retained. See also *sign-maintaining* and *sign-reversing.*

polyester flexible, transparent plastic film made from polyethylene terephthalate and used as a film base because of its dimensional stability, strength, resistance to tearing, and relative nonflammability.

polyethylene terephthalate see *polyester.*

polysulfide treatment process in which sulfur compounds are used to convert the silver in silver-gelatin film to silver sulfide, which can better resist oxidation caused by high temperature, high humidity, and atmospheric pollutants. May be applied during film processing or as a postprocessing step.

portrait orientation mode of rendering an image in which the vertical dimension of the presentation is greater than the horizontal dimension. Cf. *landscape orientation.* See also *cine mode.*

positive image in which the polarity is the same as that of the original. Cf. *negative.*

positive-appearing image image in which the lines and characters appear dark against a light background.

precataloging method used in the RLIN system to create a MARC record for a microform master negative before the film is created. See also *advance cataloging, prospective cataloging,* and *queuing.*

preservation the totality of processes and operations associated with the protection, maintenance, and stabilization of documents against damage or deterioration and with the treatment of damaged or deteriorated documents. May include the transfer of information to another medium, such as microfilm, whereby the intellectual content of the original is largely preserved. Cf. *conservation.*

preservation guidelines requirements that must be met by a given type of recording material or process for it to meet specified characteristics of permanence and/or durability.

preservation microfilm microfilm manufactured, processed, and stored in accordance with nationally accepted standards, specifications, and guidelines to achieve a life expectancy of at least 500 years.

preservation microfilming the activities of selection, preparation, film production, quality assurance, bibliographic control, and storage associated with the production of microforms that may be undertaken to preserve the intellectual content of deteriorated, unstable, or damaged materials, to provide a security copy of highly valuable records, and/or to provide a use copy to minimize handling of original materials. Entails the use of materials and methods that have maximum longevity and creates a master negative film product that is housed under controlled storage conditions and used only to make a printing master. Cf. *source document microfilming.*

preservation photocopy plain paper copy created by the xerographic process, intended to preserve the intellectual content of an unstable or damaged original document. To meet preservation requirements, specifications regarding paper quality, toner type, and the fusion of toner to paper must be met.

pressure sensitive characteristic of a material in which an adhesive bond is caused by physical contact.

printing master in preservation microfilming, a silver-gelatin, safety-base duplicate negative created directly from the camera negative and processed and stored in accordance with nationally accepted standards, specifications, and guidelines. The second generation of preservation microfilm and the source from which all subsequent service copies are made. Duplicate negative; printing negative.

processed film film that has been exposed to light and has been treated to produce a fixed or stabilized visible image.

processing series of steps involved in the treatment of exposed photographic material by chemical or physical means to make the latent image visible and ultimately usable. For silver-gelatin film, includes developing, fixing, washing, and drying.

processor machine that performs the various operations necessary to process photographic material.

programming see *reel programming.*

prospective cataloging method used on the OCLC system to create a MARC record for a microform master negative before the film is created. See also *advance cataloging, precataloging,* and *queuing.*

protective enclosure container (box, envelope) made of durable, chemically stable materials and designed to provide physical support and a barrier against environmental factors such as light, pollutants, etc. Protective enclosures for bound volumes range from lightweight paper wrappers to sturdier, custom-made phase boxes and clamshell boxes. See also *clamshell box* and *phase box.*

quality assurance procedures undertaken by or at the request of the institution/organization that initiates, manages, and pays for microfilming services to assess the product's compliance with standards and guidelines, generally performed independent of the film-producing organization.

quality control (1) planned systematic activities necessary to ensure that a medium, module, or system component conforms to established technical requirements. (2) all actions that are taken to ensure that a department or organization delivers products that meet performance requirements and that adhere to standards and specifications. (3) policies, procedures, and systematic actions established for the purpose of providing and maintaining a certain degree of confidence in the longevity of the product and performed by the film-producing organization, service bureau, or other organization.

Quality Index (QI) subjective relationship between legibility of printed text and the resolution pattern resolved in a microimage. Used to predetermine legibility in the third-generation (service copy) microfilm. Entails measuring the lowercase "e" and evaluating the resolution test chart. Governed by ANSI/AIIM MS23 and further refined by RLG specifications. Cf. *system resolution.*

queuing series of steps taken to update an RLIN record including the date on which a decision was made to preserve a title or group of documents. After filming is complete, a record for the microform master negative is created and the queuing date is removed from the queued record. See also *advance cataloging, precataloging,* and *prospective cataloging.*

raw stock unexposed, unprocessed photographic film, paper, or other recording material.

record group body of organizationally related records established on the basis of provenance by an archives for control purposes. A record group constitutes the archives (or that portion in the custody of an archival institution) of an autonomous record-keeping corporate body.

record series see *series.*

red spot see *redox blemish.*

redox blemish film defect that may appear on silver-gelatin film as microscopic spots, usually reddish or yellowish in color, caused by exposure to high temperature, high humidity, and atmospheric pollutants (including peroxides emitted from inappropriate storage containers). Shortened from the "reduction-oxidation" chemical process through which such blemishes are formed. Synonymous with *measles effect, microscopic blemish,* and *red spots.*

reduction factor by which an original is made smaller in the microimage; e.g., a reduction of 12×.

reduction ratio relationship (ratio) between the dimensions of the original document and the corresponding dimensions of the microimage; e.g., a reduction ratio of 12:1.

reel break point in the filming of a series of documents, volumes, etc. at which the camera operator ends one reel and begins another. See also *reel programming.*

reel programming the prefilming task of determining which volumes, documents, etc. will be filmed together on the same reel of microfilm. Reel programming is a combination of calculating the maximum number of exposures per reel (based on the reduction, frame position, and mask size) and, using this figure, deciding where an appropriate bibliographic or chronological break can be made to end the reel.

reformat   to reproduce a document in a different physical form or medium; e.g., through microfilming, photocopying, digitization, etc.

refresh   to repeat or recopy data or information at regular intervals.

reprography   the science, technology, and practice of reproducing documents. Encompasses virtually all processes for copying or reproduction using light, heat, or electrical radiation, including microreproduction.

residual hypo   see *hypo* and *residual thiosulfate ion.*

residual thiosulfate ion   ammonium or sodium thiosulfate remaining in film or paper after washing. Sometimes incorrectly termed residual hypo. Its presence is measured by the methylene blue test or silver densitometric method.

resolution   the ability of a photographic system to record fine detail. Measured on microfilm by using a microscope to view the photographed resolution test charts (generally, as part of the technical target). See also *Quality Index* and *system resolution.*

resolution test chart   chart containing a graded series of blocks of lines and spaces (line pairs) used for determining the optical performance of microfilm equipment and the resolution characteristics of materials used in microfilming. The ISO Resolution Test Chart No. 2 (governed by ISO 3334) is generally used in microfilming, and five of the test charts must be properly positioned on the technical target as specified by ANSI/AIIM MS23. See also *technical target.*

retake   to refilm documents or portions of documents.

rewind   (1) support and a device consisting of a spindle (shaft) geared to a crank, used in pairs to transport film from one reel to another. (2) act of transferring film from one reel to another.

RLG Conspectus   see *Conspectus.*

roll microfilm   microfilm that is or can be put on a reel, spool, or core.

rotary camera   type of microfilm camera, not used in preservation microfilming, that photographs documents while they are being moved by some form of transport mechanism. The document transport mechanism is connected to a film-transport mechanism, and the film also moves during exposure. See also *planetary camera* and *step-and-repeat camera.*

safety film   comparatively nonflammable film support (base) that meets ANSI and ISO requirements for such film. May include safety cellulose-ester (acetate) base and safety polyethylene terephthalate (polyester) base.

scanner   see *digital image scanner* and *optical character recognition scanner.*

scanning   technique for converting human-readable images (e.g., from paper or microform) into digital form. See also *digital image scanner* and *optical character recognition scanner.*

second-generation microfilm   microfilm copy made from the camera negative. See also *printing master.*

sectionalized filming   process in which more than one photograph (exposure) is taken to capture sections of the whole document at the original reduction ratio if the document is larger than the maximum area of a camera's coverage at that reduction ratio.

series   record series. In archives, file units or documents arranged in accordance with a filing system or maintained as a unit because they result from the same accumulation or filing process, function, or activity; have a particular form; or have some other relationship arising out of their creation, receipt, or use.

service bureau   organization that provides filming, duplication, storage, or other micrographic-related services to other organizations. Cf. *filming agent.*

service copy   distribution copy; use copy. Microform copy (generally, but not always, a film positive) distributed for end use.

sharpness   (1) degree of line/edge clarity. (2) subjective visual sensation of the slope of the boundary between a light and a dark area.

sheet film   precut rectangle (not in roll form) of flexible, transparent base material coated with a photosensitive emulsion.

sign-maintaining   term used to describe film in which the polarity of the original film is retained in the duplicate; e.g., diazo is a sign-maintaining film.

sign-reversing   term used to describe film in which the polarity of the original film is reversed in the duplicate; e.g., vesicular film is generally sign-reversing.

signature   two or more sheets of paper, stacked and folded as a group, generally to form a text block.

silver densitometric method   test that detects and measures thiosulfate or other potentially harmful residual chemicals in processed film. Produces a yellow stain for density measurement. See also *residual thiosulfate ion.*

silver dye bleach film   color film based on a process in which a positive color image is made directly from the original. Cyan, magenta, and yellow dyes are incorporated in the emulsion at the time of manufacture and are selectively bleached during the chemical process.

silver film   photographic film of which the photosensitive layer is composed of silver halides suspended in a suitable binder. When developed, the image is formed by metallic silver in black-and-white film. Includes silver-gelatin film, which is the only type capable of an LE-500 rating.

silver-gelatin film   film composed of silver-halide crystals in a gelatin emulsion. See also *silver film* and *gelatin.*

silver halide   compound of silver and one of the following elements known as halogens: chlorine, bromine, iodine, or fluorine.

silver-halide film   any film (including silver-gelatin film) that uses silver halide as the light-sensitive material. See also *silver film* and *silver halide.*

simplex   method of recording images one by one in which a single frame (whether consisting of one or two document pages) appears within the usable width of the microfilm. The simplex format is generally used in preservation microfilming. See also *one-up* and *two-up.*

skew   condition in which edges or angles on a document are not aligned exactly parallel with or perpendicular to the edges of the film. RLG specifications define limits on skew, but, at present, it is not addressed in ANSI/AIIM MS23 or other key ANSI standards.

slow film   photographic material having moderate or relatively low sensitivity to light.

sodium thiosulfate salt used in many fixing solutions that dissolves and removes the silver halides remaining in film after development. Sometimes incorrectly termed *hypo.*

source document microfilming conversion of documents to microimages. Cf. *preservation microfilming.*

specification document that describes the essential and technical requirements for items, materials, and services, including procedures for determining that the requirements have been met. Cf. *guideline* and *standard.*

splice joint made by attaching two pieces of film together so they will function as a single piece when passing through a camera, processor, viewer, or other apparatus. While ANSI standards allow splicing via cementing, taping, and ultrasonic or heat welding, preservation microfilming guidelines require use of only ultrasonic splices for polyester film bases, allow splices only in the camera negative, and limit the number of splices allowed on a reel. See also *butt splice* and *ultrasonic splice.*

splicer device for joining strips of photographic film or paper.

stability degree to which negatives or prints resist change by the action of light, heat, or atmospheric gases.

standard published document approved by ANSI, ISO, or other national and international standards-making organizations that establishes engineering and technical limitations and applications for items, materials, processes, methods, designs, and engineering practices. Cf. *guideline* and *specification.*

static mark black spot, streak, or treelike mark produced on sensitive materials by discharges of static electricity during handling or winding and made visible by developing.

step-and-repeat camera type of microfilm camera that can record a series of separate images on microfiche according to a predetermined format to form an orderly grid pattern of rows and columns. See also *planetary camera* and *rotary camera.*

step tablet (1) length of film containing gradations of density, which may or may not be calibrated. A calibrated step wedge is used as a standard in the calibration of a densitometer. (2) gray scale, series of tones in steps of regularly increasing known densities from white to black on a film base or glass plate. Used for processing and printing control.

step test graded series of exposures made to determine the optimum exposures for films or other media.

storage housing physical structure supporting photographic materials and their enclosures.

strip-up microfiche production technique, not acceptable under preservation guidelines, in which short lengths of roll film are attached in rows to a transparent support, which is then used as a master.

system resolution measure of a photographic system's ability to record fine detail; the product of the line pairs per millimeter clearly discernable on the resolution test chart and the reduction used to film it, as outlined in ANSI/AIIM MS23. Preservation microfilming specifications often require system resolution of at least 120 line pairs per millimeter, but some cameras may achieve significantly higher resolution. For printed texts, both system resolution and the Quality Index method may be used as part of technical inspection, but only the system resolution measure is applicable to documents in which there is no lowercase "e."

target   (1) any graphic or textual document or chart containing identification information, coding, test charts, or information that helps patrons use and interpret the microform. (2) an aid to technical or bibliographic control that is photographed on the film along with items, titles, collections, reels, etc.

technical inspection   assessment of technical film characteristics to ensure that all generations meet the institution's guidelines for density, resolution, image stability, and life expectancy. Cf. *bibliographic inspection.*

technical target   aid to technical control that facilitates the testing of system resolution and application of the Quality Index method for each reel, title, or collection. Must include the resolution test charts and may include other test elements (e.g., rulers, density patches, gray scales, etc.). See also *target.*

test chart   see *resolution test chart.*

test target   see *technical target.*

text block   the leaves of a volume after they have been bound together.

thiosulfate   see *ammonium thiosulfate* and *sodium thiosulfate.*

tonal range   relative ability of a light-sensitive material to reproduce accurately the varying tones between black and white.

trailer   length of nonimage-bearing photographic film following the last frame on a roll of microfilm. Cf. *leader.*

two-up   simplex arrangement in which two pages or leaves are photographed at the same time in the same frame. Cf. *one-up.*

ultrasonic splice   butt splice formed by internal friction when vibration (created by high-speed sound waves) and pressure are applied.

uniform density   see under *density.*

uniform density target   clean white sheet of paper or board (of a size, reflectance, and composition specified by ANSI/AIIM MS26-1990) that fills the frame area and is filmed on each reel. During technical inspection, density readings are taken on the filmed image of the uniform density target to ensure that the background density is consistent across the frame.

use copy   see *service copy.*

USMARC   United States version of the MARC formats. See also *MAchine-Readable Cataloging.*

vertical mode   see *cine mode.*

vesicular film   polyester photographic film in which the light-sensitive component is suspended in a thermoplastic layer. On exposure, the component creates nitrogen vesicles (microbubbles) that form the latent image. The latent image becomes visible in the form of vesicles when heat is applied and the plastic layer is allowed to cool. Vesicular film generally reverses the polarity of the original and may be beige, gray, or light blue in color.

vinegar syndrome   slow chemical decomposition of acetate plastics that results in the formation of acetic acid. The main symptoms are a vinegar-like odor and buckling, shrinking, and embrittlement of the film.

watermark   image or symbol (sometimes including letters and numerals) formed in a sheet of paper and visible when the paper is held up to transmitted light. In handmade papers, the watermark forms as fewer fibers settle over a raised area woven into the mold, resulting in greater translucency of the sheet in that area. Watermarks are simulated in machine-made paper by a device that impresses a design in the wet mat of fibers. Variations in design over time and place may allow the watermark to be used in dating and localizing paper production.

workstation   see *computer workstation.*

wrapper   see *protective enclosure.*

Index

Page numbers in *italics* indicate material found in figures and photograph captions. Page numbers followed by the letter "n" indicate material found in footnotes.